DAOISM IN HISTORY

Essays in honour of Liu Ts'un-yan

Edited by Benjamin Penny

 Routledge
Taylor & Francis Group

LONDON AND NEW YORK

First published 2006
by Routledge
2 Park Square, Milton Park, Abingdon, Oxon OX14 4RN

Simultaneously published in the USA and Canada
by Routledge
270 Madison Ave, New York, NY 10016

Routledge is an imprint of the Taylor & Francis Group, an informa business

Transferred to Digital Printing 2010

© 2006 Selection and editorial matter Benjamin Penny;
individual chapters, the contributors

Typeset in Times New Roman by
Graphicraft Limited, Hong Kong

British Library Cataloguing in Publication Data
A catalogue record for this book is available from
the British Library

Library of Congress Cataloging-in-Publication Data
Daoism in history: essays in honour of Liu Ts'un-yan /
Edited by Benjamin Penny.
p. cm. – (Routledge studies in Taoism)
Includes bibliographical references and index.
1. Taoism–History.   I. Liu, Ts'un-yan. II. Penny, Benjamin, 1959–
III. Series.

BL1910.D3955 2005
299.5'14'09–dc22
2004030619

ISBN10: 0–415–34852–8 (hbk)
ISBN10: 0–415–59929–6 (pbk)
ISBN10: 0–203–54921–X (ebk)

ISBN13: 978–0–415–34852–2 (hbk)
ISBN13: 978–0–415–59929–0 (pbk)
ISBN13: 978–0–203–54921–6 (ebk)

DAOISM IN HISTORY

THE UNIVERSITY OF
WINCHESTER

The study c
China, Japa
are rewritir
'China's inc
(some publi
leading schc
and the US.

These ess
what Daois
These inclu

- Daoism
- Daoism
- the dev
- Daoist
- Daoist

Daoism in F
Professor Li
Zhang a H
the pivotal
glossary as

The field
areas of rese
tion is a ma

Benjamin P
History, Re
National Ur
Tibet (Rout

the Falun Gong and the discovery of Chinese religions by the west.

ROUTLEDGE STUDIES IN TAOISM

Series Editors: T. H. Barrett, School of Oriental and African Studies, University of London; Russell Kirkland, University of Georgia; Benjamin Penny, Australian National University; and Monica Esposito, Kyoto University.

The *Routledge Studies in Taoism* series publishes books of high scholarly standards. The series includes monographic studies, surveys and annotated translations of primary sources and technical reference works with a wide scope. Occasionally, translations of books first published in other languages might also be considered for inclusion in the series.

DAOISM IN HISTORY
Essays in honour of Liu Ts'un-yan
Edited by Benjamin Penny

FOR EMERITUS PROFESSOR LIU TS'UN-YAN

Emeritus Professor Liu Ts'un-yan on his retirement from The Australian National University, 1983. Courtesy, ANU Photography.

CONTENTS

CONTENTS

ILLUSTRATIONS

CONTRIBUTORS

T. H. Barrett was born in Britain and after graduating from the University of Cambridge studied at Yale and in Japan before returning to Cambridge to teach. Since 1986 he has been Professor of East Asian History at the School of Oriental and African Studies, London, where he is currently a member of the Department of the Study of Religions. His main interests lie in the history of East Asian religion; this has recently involved him in research into religion and the emergence of printing.

Stephen R. Bokenkamp, Associate Professor of Classical Chinese at Indiana University, specializes in the study of early medieval Daoism and literature. He is co-editor of the *Journal of Chinese Religions*. His recent works include *Early Daoist Scriptures* (University of California Press, 1997) and 'Lu Xiujing, Buddhism, and the First Daoist Canon', in Scott Pearce, Audrey Spiro and Patricia Ebrey (eds), *Culture and Power in the Reconstitution of the Chinese Realm, 200–600* (Cambridge: Harvard University Press, 2001).

Liu Ts'un-yan is Emeritus Professor of Chinese Studies at the Australian National University. Arriving at the ANU in 1962, he became head of the department of Chinese in 1966, retiring in 1982. He was honoured as an Officer in the Order of Australia in 1992 and was a founding fellow of the Australian Academy of the Humanities. He has had numerous visiting appointments in Europe, America and East Asia and holds two honorary doctorates. Since his retirement, he has continued his research in Chinese literature, philosophy and religion.

Maeda Shigeki (1956–2005) graduated from Waseda University, where he also took his Masters degree. He taught at the Tōyō bunka kenkyūjo at Tokyo University, Nagoya University, and at Kogakukan and Mie universities. His publications include *Shoki Dōkyō kyōten no keisei* (*The Formation of Early Daoist Scriptures*, Tokyo: Kyūko shoin, 2004). He was co-editor of *Dōkyō to Chūgoku shisō* (*Daoism and Chinese Thought*, Tokyo: Yūzankaku shuppan, 2000), and collaborated on Ishida Hidemi and Shirasugi Etsuo (eds), *Kōtei daikei reisū* (An annotated translation of *Huangdi neijing lingshu*, Tokyo: Tōyō gakujutsu shuppansha, 1999–2000). He also contributed to

Dōkyō bunka kenkyūkai (eds), *Dōkyō bunka e no tenbō* (*Perspectives on Daoist Culture*, Tokyo: Hirakawa shuppansha, 1994) and Maruyama Hiroshi and Masuo Shinichirō (eds), *Dōkyō no Kyōten o Yomu* (*Reading Daoist Scriptures*, Tokyo: Taishūkan shoten, 2001).

Christine Mollier is researcher at the Centre national de la recherche scientifique (CNRS), Paris, France, where she has been a member of the Dunhuang manuscript project. A specialist on early medieval Daoist eschatology, she is the author of *Une apocalypse taoïste du Ve siècle, Le Livre des incantations divines des grottes abyssales* (1990), 'La Méthode de l'empereur du Nord du mont Fengdu' (1997) and 'De l'inconvénient d'être mortel chez les taoïstes de la haute Pureté' (2001), and collaborated on the fifth volume of the *Catalogue des manuscrits chinois du fonds Pelliot de Dunhuang* (1995). Recently she has been involved in Buddho-Daoist studies, and her articles in this area include 'Les Cuisines de Laozi et du Buddha' (2000) and 'Les talismans de Dunhuang' (2004). She is currently working on a book project on Buddho-Daoist scriptural and iconographical exchanges.

Peter Nickerson is Associate Professor of Religion at Duke University. He is the author of *Taoism, Bureaucracy, and Popular Religion in Early Medieval China* (Harvard University Asia Center, forthcoming) and other pieces concerning the history of the early Daoist religion. Currently, he is doing fieldwork on vernacular Daoism and related popular practices in contemporary Taiwan, especially in the contexts of social/cultural and ritual theory. He lives with his wife, son, hound, and cats in Person County, North Carolina.

Benjamin Penny is Research Fellow in the Division of Pacific and Asian History, Research School of Pacific and Asian Studies at the Australian National University. He is editor of *Religion and Biography in China and Tibet* (2002) and is currently working on projects about Falun Gong, the biographies of Zhang Daoling and the discovery and description of Chinese religions by nineteenth-century Protestant missionaries.

Fabrizio Pregadio is Acting Associate Professor at the Department of Religious Studies, Stanford University. He is interested in Daoist doctrine and its different formulations throughout history. His recent publications include 'The Notion of "Form" and the Ways of Liberation in Daoism', *Cahiers d'Extrême-Asie*, 14 (2004). He is the author of *Great Clarity: Daoism and Alchemy in Medieval China* (Stanford University Press, 2005) and is the editor of *The Encyclopedia of Taoism* (Routledge, 2005). He is currently working on the textual and exegetical tradition of the *Zhouyi cantong qi*, the scripture that forms the basis of a large part of Chinese alchemy.

Franciscus Verellen is Director of the Ecole Française d'Extrême-Orient, where he also holds the chair in History of Daoism. His current research is on the ritual and communal organization of the early Heavenly Master movement. Among his recent publications are 'The Twenty-four Dioceses and Zhang Daoling' in *Pilgrims, Patrons, and Place*, edited by Phyllis Granoff and Koichi Shinohara (University of British Columbia Press, 2003) and 'The Heavenly Master Liturgical Agenda According to Chisong zi's Petition Almanac' in *Cahiers d'Extrême-Asie* 14 (2004). With Kristofer Schipper he is editor of *The Taoist Canon* (University of Chicago Press, 2004).

ACKNOWLEDGEMENTS

The origins of this collection of essays lie in a conference held in honour of Emeritus Professor Liu Ts'un-yan at the Humanities Research Centre (HRC) of the Australian National University in 1999. Without the generous support of the HRC – recognizing Professor Liu as one of the most notable scholars in the humanities to have worked at this university – the conference would not have taken place and this volume would not have appeared. I would also like to acknowledge the Embassy of France, Canberra, and the Goethe Institut, Sydney, for their help in providing airfares for two of the participants. Some of the papers presented at that conference are published here; some of those who attended it chose to submit different papers for this collection; and some who were unable to attend have been kind enough to allow their work to appear in this volume. To all these people I owe a debt of gratitude, not least for their patience and understanding.

While working on this volume I have received support from the Centre for Cross-Cultural Research of the Australian National University and from the Australian Research Council. I have also benefited directly from others in producing this book. I would like to thank Stephen R. Bokenkamp, a visiting fellow at the HRC during the period of the conference, for his unfailing support; Stephanie Anderson, Jamie Greenbaum and Meredith McKinney for their translation work; David Free and Wong Fung-hsien for their editorial assistance; Darrell Dorrington, Toshio Takagi and especially Renata Osborne from the Menzies Library, ANU. I would also like to acknowledge my mother Glen Rose for her estimable proofreading; the two readers for Routledge for their valuable comments; and the two editors with whom I have worked, Jonathan Price and Dorothea Schaefter. This collection of essays is the first volume in the Routledge Studies in Taoism – for this honour I thank my series co-editors T. H. Barrett, Russell Kirkland and Monica Esposito.

Throughout this project, I have burdened my partner Gillian Russell with seemingly endless discussions, concerns, trivialities, panics and obscurities. She has been the very soul of patience, always encouraging, and I thank her deeply, as I do our son Tom who has also lived through the project.

My final thanks go to Professor Liu himself, scholar, teacher and sage, a deep well of knowledge, and an inspiration.

PART ONE

1

ON DREAMING OF BEING LEFT-HANDED

Liu Ts'un-yan and Daoist Studies

Benjamin Penny

In 1980, Liu Ts'un-yan gave a talk to the Asia Society of Canberra, where he has been living since joining the Australian National University in 1962. The occasion was to celebrate the International Year of the Child and in the talk he evocatively described his early life and education, his parents and the Beijing in which he grew up until the family moved to Shanghai when he was twelve. This memoir reveals a childhood lived on the cusp of modernity. Liu was born in 1917. His father had gained the first degree in the imperial exam system in 1898, but later learned German and studied medicine before shifting to the Customs College, eventually working with the Office of Revenue and Customs in Beijing, where Liu was born. The marriage of Liu's mother and father was arranged. She had never been to school but was, in Liu's words, 'not illiterate, and she was capable of reading and writing family letters, and was quite familiar with some of the story books written in verse, or in prose, but intermingled with verses'.[1] Liu tells us that his father took two concubines while Liu himself was a child.

This juxtaposition of the ancient and modern can also be seen in Liu's education, which he began at home, with his father tutoring him in reading characters. The first books he read were the traditional three beginners' texts, the *Sanzi jing* or *Three Character Classic*, the *Baijiaxing* or the *One Hundred Family Names* and the *Qianzi wen* or *Text of a Thousand Words*. These books he learned off by heart in a similar way to those of the traditional syllabus that he studied later: the Five Classics and the Four Books of the Confucian Canon. But into a scene that could have come from hundreds of years before, Western modernity asserted itself: Liu tells us that one Sunday afternoon as he was memorizing part of the *Shujing*, the *Classic of History*, his father suggested they go to the cinema. (They went to see D. W. Griffith's *Way Down East* (1920), starring Lillian Gish.) He later attended a primary school attached to the Ministry of Foreign Affairs, which not only offered English tuition but was also co-educational.

Two years after Liu was born, Édouard Chavannes's 'Le jet des dragons' (a translation of the *Taishang lingbao yugui mingzhen dazhai yangong yi*) was published in Paris.[2] T. H. Barrett has described this 'superbly documented study of a Taoist ritual' as 'the first translation directly from the *Tao-tsang* into a European language'.[3] In several ways, Chavannes's publication marked the beginning of a new era for Daoist Studies. First, it elevated the study of Daoism and its textual tradition to a status comparable with that of other Asian and European religious traditions. Second, it brought the apparatus of rigorous philology to bear on Daoist canonical texts. Third, it marked the emigration of Daoist studies from the homeland of the tradition. The trajectory that Daoist studies has followed since Chavannes's time finds a parallel in Liu's life and scholarly career. In pointing out the previously ignored deep layers of reference to Daoism in Chinese culture in general and in fiction in particular, his work has demonstrated what can be accomplished when the Daoist tradition is taken seriously. With his Olympian range of reference in the Chinese literary, philosophical, religious and historical archives, a scholarly practice that draws on both Qing and Western philological practice, and an energetic and adventurous cast of mind, his writings stand as a monument to a triumphant sinology. And finally, of course, like the study of Daoism, Liu too has emigrated, living and working in a country and an institution – when he arrived in it at least – that looked to Europe and America for its exemplars despite its location on the southern edge of Asia.

Scholars of Daoism in the West who have come to the study for its own sake are all, in some sense, Chavannes's intellectual descendants. For Liu, as for Chen Guofu, two years his senior, and other Chinese scholars of Daoism of their generation, a scholarly interest in Daoism often grew out of initial interests in other fields. For Chen, it was his interests in the history of Chinese alchemy that led (inevitably, we would say with the benefit of hindsight) to his magisterial studies of the Daoist canon. For Liu, on the other hand, it was his interests in Chinese popular fiction that led to in-depth studies of the religion. Beginning in 1935, with his *Zhongguo wenxue shi fafan, An Introduction to the History of Chinese Literature*,[4] he proceeded to write no fewer than four more books on literary themes before the first that explicitly mentions Daoism in its title: his 1962 *Buddhist and Taoist Influences on Chinese Novels*, subtitled *The Authorship of The Feng Shen Yen I*.[5] This work, which served as his doctoral thesis for the University of London, not only determined the actual author of the novel (disproving the traditional ascription) and traced its literary antecedents, but, equally importantly from the perspective of more than four decades later, presented a brilliant exposition of the integration of Daoist and Buddhist lore into the text. Indeed, Liu's discussions of gods and numinous places represented the introduction of these topics to an English-speaking audience more used to thinking of the Daoist religious tradition (if they thought of it at all) as the degraded, superstitious, irrational remnant of a once great philosophy. Moreover, Liu demonstrated the reliance of the author on both Daoist and

Buddhist sources in this work, as well as the interpenetration of both religions, and Confucian thought, in the author's own religious outlook. Liu wrote that, 'though [he was] a devoted Taoist priest and at the same time a Tantric Buddhist, [he was] in his blood a Chinese scholar whose basic characteristic was Confucianist'.[6] Scholarship on Daoism that sees the religion as less than hermetically sealed, as a tradition that has interacted productively with other religious and philosophical traditions, and especially that has focused on the mutually constitutive relations between Buddhism and Daoism, has proved to be among the most invigorating in the field. Liu's contributions in this area can be seen as formative.

Liu's abiding interest in Chinese popular literature is evident from his subsequent publications in the field, which include single-author studies, surveys of manuscripts and printed works, edited volumes, translations and, indeed, creative works of his own. However, it is specifically with his works on Daoism that we are concerned here. But as his work in literary studies is always firmly grounded in the historical, so in his work on Daoist religion and Daoist texts he is acutely aware of the particular social and historical contexts of Daoist beliefs, ideas, writings and institutions: for Liu the study of Daoism has always been 'in history'.

At the most general level, Liu has written on both the nature of Daoism as a whole and the history of the Daoist canon in particular. In the latter case his 1973 essay 'The Compilation and Historical Value of the *Tao-tsang*', a masterwork of clarity and brevity, has often been the first of Liu's writings that students in Western countries have encountered.[7] In the former, his 1982 lecture to the Australian Association for the Study of Religions, 'The Essence of Taoism: Its Philosophical, Historical and Religious Aspects', manages to conduct a survey of the philosophy and the religion that was accessible to his audience of scholars largely unfamiliar with Chinese religions and, in its observations concerning the progression of Daoism over 2500 years, makes observations that remain provocative and stimulating even after more than two decades of significant developments in Daoist Studies.[8]

Liu's work on particular topics in the history of Daoism has often addressed fundamental questions for the tradition, such as the foundational significance of the *Daode jing*, the *Classic of the Way and its Power* to give its usual English title, and the circumstances of the founding of the religion. Liu's four essays on the tradition of the *Daode jing* discuss, in turn, Gu Huan's fifth-century commentary, important both in its own right and as part of the development of the Chongxuan (double mystery) school of interpretation that culminated in the Tang,[9] the commentaries by the three emperors Xuanzong of the Tang dynasty, Huizong of the Song and Taizu of the Ming, and the famous *Xiang'er*. The two essays on the emperors' commentaries, the first a book-length study in itself, are of considerable importance given both the extensive discussions of the place of the ruler in the text itself and the pivotal position of Daoism in the courts of these three dynasties.[10] Liu's 1991 essay on the *Xiang'er* is a characteristically

5

detailed study, daunting in its fearsome range of reference, yet concise and illuminating in the directions it points to for further investigation into the commentary.[11]

Liu has also addressed at some length and originality the formative question for Daoism: the status of its supposed founder Zhang Ling, or Zhang Daoling. Translated in this book, the recent essay 'Was Celestial Master Zhang a Historical Figure?' represents the culmination of many years of painstaking research. It is typical of Liu's publications on the history of Daoism that in this essay he uncovers new evidence to address a question for which useful historical sources are famously scarce.[12] A smaller, but no less intriguing, essay on a related question is his study of the women associated with the first three Celestial Masters Zhang.[13]

However, the particular period of Daoist history that Liu has perhaps contributed to most profoundly is the Ming. In a series of essays beginning with his 1966 study of the sixteenth-century author of the *Fengshen yanyi*, Lu Xixing, Liu has provided the guiding points for any further study of Ming Daoism, uncovering important figures who had been unjustly forgotten over the years, revealing the Daoist predilections of famous personages not thought to be interested in Daoism and, in general, demonstrating the profoundly Daoist nature of that dynasty.[14]

In addition to studies on questions specifically concerning the history of Daoism, Liu has demonstrated the use to which Daoist texts can be put to address questions beyond the religion. In his 1973 essay 'The Compilation and Historical Value of the *Tao-tsang*', referred to above, Liu points to cases of scholars who have used the Canon in research whose primary interest is not Daoism. 'Detailed studies of this kind', he notes, 'could help to stir up interest among scholars whose main field of research is not religious, but historical.'[15] Among his own studies, Liu has shown the way in using material from the *Daozang* to illuminate non-Daoist subjects. One example of this is his 1976 essay 'Traces of Zoroastrian and Manichaean Activities in Pre-T'ang China'. In this work, through judicious and insightful reading of the *Yuanshi wuliang duren shangpin miaojing* (i.e. the *Duren jing*), Liu argued that both Zoroastrianism and Manichaeism were introduced – and actively practised – in China long before the previously accepted dates.[16] Again, in his 1972 essay 'The Taoists' Knowledge of Tuberculosis in the Twelfth Century' he demonstrates that at least by 1158 aspects of tuberculosis were known in Daoist circles, including the progression of the disease, the contagious nature of clothes and utensils used by the sufferer and the fact that it was caused by a pathogen.[17]

This brief appreciation of Liu's contributions to the study of Daoism is, of course, inadequate in indicating the effect of his work on the field and, by necessity, limits its remarks to a few selected works. Most of the examples of Liu's work highlighted here have been articles and books he wrote in English in recognition of the probable readership of this book, but the bulk of his writings consists of a full seven volumes of essays in Chinese, a large proportion of which are concerned with Daoism.[18] A brief perusal of this body of work will indicate the immense depth of knowledge that Liu has developed over a long scholarly career. Despite his extraordinary erudition, Liu has never neglected his duty – as he has seen it – to pass on his knowledge in a spirit of scholarly generosity, as several generations of students and colleagues at the Australian National University and elsewhere will attest, and to play his part in the development of Chinese studies, especially in Australia, where many of today's leaders in the field sat at his feet in their student days. More than thirty years ago Paul Demiéville described Liu as 'this hard worker, this open-minded and kindly man, one of the best sinologues of our times', and it is a judgement with which many who know Liu as a scholar and a friend will concur.[19]

Some of the essays in this collection were first given at a conference in Professor Liu's honour at the Humanities Research Centre of the Australian National University. Representing contemporary Daoist studies as they do, it is significant that the authors of these essays, all a generation or two younger than Liu, come from as far afield as Japan, France, Italy, the USA, the UK and Australia. When they came to the study of Daoism it had become an accepted part – though initially a small one – of Chinese studies in the West, as well as in East Asia. For a promising student Daoism has been, and perhaps still is, an idiosyncratic choice of specialisation, but it is now accepted as part of the scholarly landscape. When Liu took it up, it was far from having this status. Indeed, the areas of his two great contributions – Daoism and popular literature – were both fields that did not appear among the authorised areas of study of the traditional Chinese scholar. For Liu, therefore, with his thoroughly traditional grounding in the Confucian tradition, a concentration in these areas was, to say the least, unusual. This cast of mind, awake to the possibilities of things proscribed by dogmatic conservatism, is hinted at in the anecdote that concludes his talk referred to at the beginning of this chapter:

> I have been living in this country for seventeen years, and in those seventeen years, I have met more than a dozen friends and students who are left-handed. For the whole country we may have several tens of thousands of left-handed people. This does not seem to have worried you. However, in China, at least in my childhood, a child by the age of five or six had already been trained in the proper way of using chopsticks, and left-handedness was certainly one of the things to be nipped in the bud. Hence you seldom find a left-handed Chinese. But this does not necessarily mean that sometimes I do not dream of being left-handed.[20]

The study of Daoism is, perhaps, as left-handed as it is possible to get in Chinese studies, and was all the more so when Liu began his studies in the field. In a scholarly sense at least, Liu's dream of being left-handed has come into being in true wakefulness.

Notes

1 Liu Ts'un-yan, 'My Childhood and My Dreams', in *New Excursions from the Hall of Harmonious Wind* (Leiden: E. J. Brill, 1984), 357–77, p. 359. For a more detailed account of the Beijing of Liu's childhood, see his novel *Dadu* (Tianjin: Baihua wenyi chubanshe, 1996), a revision of *Qingchun* (Hong Kong: Xingdao ribao, 1968).

2 Édouard Chavannes, 'Le jet des dragons', *Mémoires concernant l'Asie Orientale*, 3 (1919), 53–220. This publication was posthumous – Chavannes had died in 1918.

3 T. H. Barrett, 'Introduction' to Henri Maspero (trans. Frank A. Kierman Jr), *Taoism and Chinese Religion* (Amherst: University of Massachusetts Press: 1981), vii–xxiii, p. xii.

4 Liu Ts'un-yan, *Zhongguo wenxue shi fafan* (Suzhou: Wenyi shuju, 1935).

5 Liu Ts'un-yan, *Buddhist and Taoist Influences on Chinese Novels* (Wiesbaden: Kommissionsverlag Otto Harrassowitz, 1962). For an incomplete list of Liu's works in both English and Chinese, see the appendix to Lee Cheuk Yin and Chan Man Sing (eds), *Daoyuan binfen lu* (English title: *A Daoist Florilegium*, Hong Kong: Shangwu yinshu guan, 2002). For a complete bibliography of his works in English, see Wang Gungwu, Rafe de Crespigny and Igor de Rachewiltz (eds), *Sino-Asiatica* (Canberra: Faculty of Asian Studies, Australian National University, 2002).

6 Liu, *Buddhist and Taoist Influences*, p. 192.

7 Liu Ts'un-yan, 'The Compilation and Historical Value of the *Tao-tsang*', in Donald Leslie, Colin Mackerras and Wang Gungwu (eds), *Essays on the Sources for Chinese History* (Canberra: Australian National University Press, 1973), 104–19. On a related subject, see his 'Daozang keben zhi si ge riqi', in Sakai Tadao sensei koki shukuga kinen no kai (ed.), *Rekishi ni okeru minshū to bunka. Sakai Tadao sensei koki shukuga kinen ronshū* (Tokyo: Kokusho Kankōkai, 1982), reprinted in his *Hefeng tang wenji* (Shanghai: Shanghai guji chubanshe, 1991), vol. 2, 942–73.

8 Liu Ts'un-yan, 'The Essence of Taoism: Its Philosophical, Historical and Religious Aspects', reprinted in his *New Excursions*, 117–44. Examples in Chinese of Liu's surveys of Daoist history are 'Daojiao she shenma?', *Hefeng tang xinwenji* (Taipei: Xinwenfeng chuban gongsi, 1997), vol. 1, 231–40, and 'Yiqian babainianlai de daojiao', in *Hefeng tang wenji*, vol. 2, 649–71.

9 Liu Ts'un-yan, 'Lun Daozangben Gu Huan zhu Laozi zhi xingzhi', in *Hefeng tang wenji*, vol. 1, 204–22.

10 Liu Ts'un-yan, 'Daozangben sansheng zhu Daode jing huijian', and 'Daozangben sansheng zhu Daode jing zhi deshi', in *Hefeng tang wenji*, vol. 1, 223–471 and 472–94. For a short summary in English see his 'On the Art of Ruling a Big Country: Views of Three Chinese Emperors', the 34th George Ernest Morrison Lecture in Ethnology, 1974, most conveniently consulted in *East Asian History*, 11 (June 1996), 75–90.

11 Liu Ts'un-yan, '*Xiang'er zhu* yu Daojiao', in *Hefeng tang xinwenji*, vol. 1, 281–337.

12 The essay was originally published in Chinese as 'Han Zhang tianshi shi bushi lishi renwu?', in *Daojiaoshi tanyuan* (Beijing: Beijing daxue chubanshe, 2000), 67–136.

13 Liu Ts'un-yan, 'Zhang tianshi de qinümen', in *Hefeng tang wenji*, vol. 2, 672–6.

14 See, for studies in English, collected in *Selected Papers from the Hall of Harmonious Wind* (Leiden: E. J. Brill, 1976), 'The Penetration of Taoism into the Ming Neo-Confucian Elite', 76–148, 'Lin Chao-en: the Master of the Three

Teachings', 149–74, 'Lu Hsi-hsing: A Confucian Scholar, Taoist Priest and Buddhist Devotee of the Sixteenth Century', 175–202, 'Lu Hsi-Hsing and his Commentaries on the Ts'an T'ung Ch'i', 203–31 and 'Yüan Huang and his Four Admonitions', 232–56; in *New Excursions* see 'Wang Yang-ming and Taoism', 147–67, 'Shao Yüan-chieh and T'ao Chung-wen', 168–83, and 'Wu Shou-yang: The Return to the Pure Essence', 184–208.

15 Liu Ts'un-yan, 'The Compilation', p. 118.
16 Liu Ts'un-yan, 'Traces of Zoroastrian and Manichaean Activities in Pre-T'ang China', in *Selected Papers*, 3–55.
17 Liu Ts'un-yan, 'The Taoists' Knowledge of Tuberculosis in the Twelfth Century', in *Selected Papers*, 59–75.
18 See his *Hefeng tang wenji*, *Hefeng tang xinwenji*, *Daojia yu daoshu* (Shanghai: Shanghai guji chubanshe, 1999), *Daojiaoshi tanyuan*.
19 P. Demiéville, 'Preface' to Liu, *Selected Papers from the Hall of Harmonious Wind*, vii–viii, p. viii.
20 Liu Ts'un-yan, 'My Childhood and My Dreams,' p. 377. In cricket, strangely, the delivery known as a 'Chinaman' is one bowled by a left-handed spin bowler. The name is said to derive from a West Indian bowler of Chinese extraction of the 1930s, E. E. Achong.

2

'LET LIVING AND DEAD TAKE SEPARATE PATHS'

Bureaucratisation and textualisation in
early Chinese mortuary ritual

Peter Nickerson

On December 24 of the year 147 CE, not far from the Former Han capital of Chang'an (now Sanlicun in the north-east of Chang'an County), a burial was conducted for a woman of the Jia family, who had died at the age of twenty-four. We know nothing of who she was, or why she died so young. We know a great deal, comparatively speaking, of how her death was understood. In 1957 six earthenware jars were excavated from her grave, and on each of the jars there was written, in vermilion ink, the following text:

> In the first year of *jianhe*, in the eleventh month, whose first day was *dingwei*, on the fourteenth, the Envoy of the Celestial Monarch respectfully on behalf of the Jia's household separates and releases them from the subterrestrial (spirits). When the recently deceased woman Jia died, she was just twenty-four. [Re-]calculate [the life-spans] in your name-records! Perhaps it is an overlapping due to the year and month [of birth] being the same [as someone else due to die]. Collate the dates of death! Perhaps it is an overlapping due to the day and time being the same. Collate the dates of death![1]
>
> [The Envoy of the Celestial Monarch] announces to the Directorate of Destiny above and the Directorate of Emoluments below the [dates] which pertain to the descendants and orders the Envoys of the Augustus of the Tomb to transmit his announcements.
>
> Therefore [the deceased] substitutes for herself lead men. The lead men are devoted[2] and can husk grain and cook. They can get in a cart and drive it; they can grasp a brush and write. [The Envoy] announces to the Lofty Chief of the Centre and to the Patroller on the Paths:[3] for a thousand autumns, for ten thousand years, never let fall [any of] these [offerings] . . . [Here the text breaks off.][4]

This document, known as a 'grave-securing writ' (*zhenmu wen*), portrays death above all as a bureaucratic affair. Ms Jia's early death is attributed to a mistake to which all bureaucratic systems are liable: a mix-up of the files. She could not really have been fated to have died so young, the survivors claim. It must be that her records had been confused with those of someone else born in the same year and month – probably someone who was due to die (since the cyclical year designations repeat every sixty years) at the age of eighty-four – or perhaps the afterworld administration should have summoned another person who was born on the same day and in the same hour.

The commands of the writ are issued in the name of a subordinate, an 'Envoy' (*shizhe*) of an otherworldly emperor, the Celestial Monarch (Tiandi). The Envoy insists that Ms Jia's records be checked in order to ensure that she was genuinely destined to die when she did,[5] and he further informs the Directorates of Destiny and Emoluments of the vital statistics pertaining to Ms Jia's living kin, so that the error will not be compounded, leading others in the family to share her untimely fate. Finally, the extant text, not disdaining to deal with the consequences should it turn out that the death was unavoidable, raises one more issue before it lapses into illegibility: the inclusion in the burial of lead figurines as surrogates. Like the empire of the living, the subjects of the underworld regime were expected to provide not only taxes but labour, and thoughtful kin would make sure that the deceased herself or himself would be spared such duties. The afterlife regime addressed by the grave-securing writs, with its extensive system of record keeping, offices and directorates, and taxation and corvée, all presided over by a celestial monarch and his servants, was in many ways an accurate copy of the administration of this world.

What, though, is meant by the Envoy 'separating and releasing' (*biejie*) the household from 'the subterrestrial' (*dixia*)? As we will discover, *jie* – 'releasing', 'gaining release from' or 'dispersing' – is a central concept both in law and in magico-religious practice. It may refer to releasing a culprit from punishment, but it also may denote the exorcism, or 'dispersing', of malign spirits, such as demons of the subterrestrial realm that might be offended by the intrusion into their territory represented by the digging of the grave and the burial of the corpse.[6] In other grave-securing writs and similar mortuary documents from the late Han, the exorcistic, incantory elements stand out even more noticeably. A writ might face its apotropaic task in general terms – 'Let living and dead take separate paths, a myriad *li* apart from one another' – or it might attempt to remove more specific hazards relating to spectral attack or the pollution of death, such as 'noxious demons and corpse infusions'. Beneath their manifest reliance on procedures that were textually based and bureaucratic, these documents were firmly grounded in archaic religious practices that were oral, exorcistic and even ecstatic.

The interplay between bureaucratic, hierarchised and literate forms of religious and ritual expression, on the one hand, and their exorcistic, mantic and oral counterparts in popular religion, on the other, is a central issue in the study of Daoism. The present chapter seeks to further the understanding of this problem by examining some of its earliest historical roots. The highly bureaucratised religion of the grave-securing writs, which Anna Seidel has astutely termed a kind of 'proto-Taoism', will be viewed against the background of older forms of mortuary belief and practice. From one perspective, the writs may be seen as the apogee, prior to Daoism, of a tradition of bureaucratised mortuary exorcism that developed during the Warring States period. However, the writs are also deeply rooted in practices that were not bureaucratised, including the exorcism of corpses and tombs and of spirits of pollution and disease, as well as the recalling of the souls of the dead. There existed too a long-lived tradition of mortuary practice in which masked shaman-exorcists, such as the so-called *fangxiang*, danced and chanted in order to exorcise malevolent demons, to prevent the soul of the departed from wandering and to protect the survivors.

Thus, though overlain by concerns that are articulated in terms of law and morality, the primary motivations behind the writs remained the need to dispel the pollution of death and malevolent spirits of the earth, and to keep the dead apart from the living. The proto-Daoist conception of death embodied by the grave-securing writs had so much in common with archaic mortuary ritual that the effect of the bureaucratisation that characterised the writs must have been confined to a relatively limited sphere. Bureaucratisation, in religion and perhaps even in political administration, built upon, rather than replaced, magico-religious practices that dealt with the exorcism of malign forces.

If this is so, then the revisions to the history of Daoism that made possible the emergence of a vital field of study over the past three or four decades must be further revised. The appearance in the second century of an organized Daoist religion could finally be perceived as a seminal event – even a 'religious revolution', in Michel Strickmann's words[7] – when the bureaucratised way of the Celestial Master was counterpoised to the non-bureaucratic, ecstatic religion of popular god-cults. The Celestial Masters communicated with their gods by dispatching documents; the profane communicated with theirs through spirit-mediums and propitiated them with bloody sacrificial offerings. This contrast has been made less stark by Seidel's work on grave-securing writs: a highly bureaucratised religion had existed prior to Daoism, one that differed little from Daoism except for the soteriological implications of the latter's eschatology. But Seidel's formulation lessens the 'revolutionary' implications of the Way of the Celestial Master only by attributing some of the achievements of that revolution to Daoism's forerunners, the 'village elders, exorcists and specialists in funerary rites' who created the grave-securing writs.[8] It does not question whether the creation of medieval, bureaucratised religion (and the 'ethical polarisation' that went along with it)[9] was of necessity revolutionary. Comparison of the religion of the grave-securing writs with elements of archaic mortuary practice will show that it was not.

The beginnings of bureaucratised, tomb-centred mortuary practice

Two of the principal features of the grave-securing writs of the Han and associated practices – the employment of ritual forms that mirrored the operations of the centralised, bureaucratic regimes that emerged during the Warring States period (i.e. from around the fifth century BCE), and the focus of mortuary concerns on the tomb rather than on the ancestral temple – appeared in some contexts centuries earlier. This section briefly traces these early developments.

Little is known about the earliest beliefs and cults relating to the underworld. The 'Yellow Springs' are often pointed to as the realm of the dead, and the story of Duke Zhuang of Zheng, which the *Zuozhuan* records under the year 722 BCE, is often cited. Duke Zhuang's mother had betrayed him, and in anger he had sworn to her: 'I will not see you again until I have reached the Yellow Springs.' After her death he regretted his oath and, in order to see her, dug 'into the earth until he reached the springs' (from where he was even able to retrieve her, alive once more).[10] However, in the received literature, the Yellow Springs remained, as Joseph Needham has put it, 'a concept much more poetical than philosophical or scientific',[11] and early notions of the underworld must be extrapolated from archaeological or very sparse textual evidence. Based on the depth to which Shang royal tombs were dug – in some cases up to 12.8 metres – David Keightley has suggested that the seepage of ground water into the tombs dug out of the yellow earth might have created very palpable 'yellow springs'. Sarah Allan has speculated that, in Shang myth, the Yellow Springs were ruled by the Yellow Monarch (Huangdi), 'the Lord of the Underworld, the counterpart of Shangdi, the Lord on High'. The Monarch's earthen yellow is, in ancient colour symbolism, the opposite of *xuan*, the colour of the dark heavens of the Lord on High. The Yellow Monarch is also linked with the dragon, an inhabitant, along with fish, of the watery realm of the Yellow Springs.[12]

There is likewise not much one can say about very early rituals intended to influence the fate of the soul in the underworld. Invoking the dual soul conception, Allan attributes this to the fact that neither the *po*-soul nor the 'Lord Below' – that is, the Yellow Monarch – had a cult until the Warring States period. Instead, rites for ancestors were oriented towards the *hun*-soul. Wu Hung has remarked similarly with respect to a connected topic – the emphasis in the Shang and early Zhou on the temple and the sacrifices made there, as opposed to offerings made at the grave-site: 'The temple system was the religious form that matched the lineage-oriented Shang-Zhou society: the tomb sacrifice for individuals could only be secondary.'[13] The paucity of documentation for beliefs about the underworld should therefore not be surprising.

From a slightly different perspective, in a highly suggestive article Lothar von Falkenhausen has discussed how, prior to the Warring States period, the Zhou noble's tomb was integrated into (and in effect, one might add, subordinated to) the rites of the ancestral temple:

In a tomb, a male aristocrat was buried with the paraphernalia enabling him to perform what, according to the *Zuo Zhuan*, were the state's two chief duties: warfare and sacrifice. The former activity . . . is symbolised by chariots and weapons, the latter by ritual vessels . . . This liminal reduction of a human person, just as he was about to be ritually transformed into an ancestor, to the basic ritual dimensions of his social existence, may have served to mark the tomb as a locus specifically linked to the ritual sphere in the world above ground.

. . . How exactly the temple–tomb connection was conceptualised we do not know – perhaps in terms of a mystical relationship between the periodically replenished contents of the vessels on the ancestral altar with their counterparts sealed away in the tomb. In any case, everything about the Western Zhou tombs, just like the overall sacrificial process, emphasised the compatibility, solidarity, and interconnectedness of the living and the dead.

Falkenhausen further casts doubt on the prevalence of *hun/po* dualism in the Western Zhou and proposes instead that the tomb itself functioned within the cult to the soul centred in the ancestral temple. Hence the lack of interest in the tomb and the underworld: the focus remained on the ancestors who 'came from "their high positions above"' to partake of offerings in the temple; the tomb, in a sense, merely provided a way of ensuring the continued connection between living and dead, perhaps through the sacrificial vessels buried there.[14]

All this was to change, as so many things changed in Chinese society, during the Warring States transition. Wu Hung has remarked on the shift in emphasis 'from temple to tomb'. He has attributed this change to a (relatively ephemeral) need for a 'new social elite' to express new 'political messages' using tombs and their rites: the shift had started when newly risen individuals and families, whose power was gained through dominance in economic and military spheres, not through ancestry (symbolised by the temple), began to challenge the old Zhou nobility.[15]

Falkenhausen has placed these changes in an even broader context, and one that is of special significance for our study because of the important role played therein by both bureaucratisation, and, although he does not use the term, exorcism. Falkenhausen refers to Seidel's work on the grave-securing writs and tries to trace the writs' continual emphasis on the separation of living and dead back to certain aspects of mortuary practice and thought that first appeared around the middle of the Eastern Zhou. (I use the term exorcism here because of the effort to get the dead away, and keep them away, from the living.) According to Falkenhausen, 'by mid-Eastern Zhou times, the temple sacrifices to the ancestors had become, as it were, uncoupled from the concern with their tombs'. Instead of facilitating continued contact in the temple between ancestors and descendants, the tomb became instead a structure whose purpose was to separate the two parties.

Both tomb architecture and the type of grave goods used reflect this trend. Since the tomb was to become the permanent abode of the deceased, he or she had to be provided with a satisfactory (and secure) domicile. Thus, as opposed to the shaft burials of earlier times, catacomb tombs were created, with the area containing the corpse partitioned off from the vertical portion of the excavation. A catacomb tomb not only separated the body more completely from the living than did a shaft-style tomb; it also resembled more closely dwellings built for the living. Elite burials in particular came to be constructed as models of the daylight world, equipped with all the comforts of home. Grave goods proliferated in variety (in contrast to the early Zhou graves that contained only the implements of sacrifice and war) at the same time as they declined markedly in quality. Real items were seldom used – the *mingqi* or 'spirit-vessels' prescribed in the *Liji* and other texts of the Warring States and Han (such as the *Xunzi*) were unusable imitations of real objects. The *mingqi* were justified, according to these texts, precisely because they allowed for the proper treatment of the dead: treating them not 'as if they were entirely dead', yet neither 'as if they were entirely alive'.[16] In other words, *mingqi* were another means of affirming that the dead should be separate from the living – items for the dead and items for the living had to be different – but at the same time *mingqi* provided for the welfare of the deceased in the tomb, making it less likely that he or she would return and impose upon surviving kin, demanding sustenance. The summoning of the soul prior to the mortuary rites was, suggests Falkenhausen, similarly intended to prevent the dead from revisiting the living.[17]

The above changes show how late Zhou mortuary practice turned towards 'exorcism' in the treatment of the dead. They indicate as well a profound reorientation in comparison to the early Zhou, when the mortuary and sacrificial regime centred on the joyous communion of the living and the ancestral spirits. The creation in the late Zhou of subterranean domiciles for the dead that imitated in every way the dwellings of the living occurred concurrently with a bureaucratisation of the underworld, parallel with the contemporaneous bureaucratisation of social and political arrangements among the living. Falkenhausen writes that, while the notion of 'venerating the spirits but keeping one's distance from them' may have been attributed to Confucius and his school,

> this idea seems to have been 'in the air' in middle Eastern Zhou times; and the associated phenomena – from the use of *mingqi* to the soul-recalling ritual – seem to prefigure funerary practices that in later times have been associated with religious Taoism. Lurking from behind the idea of constructing tombs that were world models is the important 'proto-Taoist' idea that the afterworld of the dead, though hermetically separate from ours, was nevertheless a mirror-image of the world of the living, with a hierarchy of ghosts corresponding to the administration system of the secular state.[18]

A scrap of early textual evidence, interpreted most creatively by Donald Harper, is of great relevance to this history of mortuary bureaucratisation. Harper recounts what he terms a case of 'resurrection', which took place in the year 297 BCE in the state of Qin. His discussion is based on a document written on bamboo slips excavated from a tomb in Fangmatan, Gansu, in 1986 and a transcription of the same made by Li Xueqin.[19] The document is in the form of a report by a local official to the Jin Royal Scribe. It details the story of one Dan, originally from the state of Wei, who had stabbed a man and subsequently killed himself. Dan's patron, Xi Wu, a general of Wei, believing that Dan 'was not yet fated to die', 'made a declaration' to that effect to 'the Scribe of the Directorate of Destiny (*Siming shi*), Gongsun Qiang'. The Directorate apparently having agreed with Xi Wu, Dan was allowed to return from the dead and depart from his tomb, after which he arrived in the territory of the aforesaid local official. Dan at that time also took it upon himself to offer several items of information about the proper way of making offerings to the dead at their graves, which are included in the report as well.

Harper's main interest in this laconic but fascinating document centres on the issue of the resurrection of Dan as a precursor of later Daoist notions of 'release from the corpse' (or 'by means of a corpse', *shijie*).[20] However, it is the bureaucratic handling of death evinced by the Fangmatan document that is of greatest significance for the present study. Dan's release is effected by a declaration – perhaps in the form of a document placed in the tomb – made to the Scribe of the Directorate of Destiny, a clerical subordinate of the astral deity who oversees lifespans. Moreover, the Scribe is a former human being: Gongsun Qiang's rise to power in Cao was credited with the downfall of that state in 488 BCE, and he was said to have been captured and killed by the invading state of Song.[21] Thus, this third-century BCE text already anticipates 'the hierarchy of ghosts corresponding to the administration system of the secular state', as Falkenhausen has put it.

Furthermore, by linking the document to a number of other texts excavated from tombs, Harper is able to make a strong claim for a pattern of Warring States and Han bureaucratic practice in which documents created by living officials were despatched to their counterparts in the underworld. In some cases documents were prepared in duplicate, with one placed in the tomb and the other filed in the archives of the living. This was the case with the map of the graveyard of King Cuo of Zhongshan in Hebei, who died in the late fourth century BCE. Other documents from the Former Han which closely resemble the Fangmatan text have led Harper to suggest that it may not have been uncommon for officials to insert into graves 'memoranda . . . to the underworld authorities to inform them of the arrival of the newly deceased'.[22]

As the archaeological record becomes more fully revealed, the extent to which religious developments in the Latter Han – such as the creation of grave-securing writs and the emergence of the Daoist Way of the Celestial Master itself – were anticipated as early as the Warring States period

16

becomes strikingly apparent. The change in the focus of concern for the dead from the ancestral temple to the tomb was accompanied by the emergence of practices and beliefs that would provide formative influences for much of later Chinese religion. The shift from temple to tomb meant, first of all, a change in the emphasis of the prevailing ritual paradigm: from sacrifice to exorcism. The classical Zhou ancestral rites were above all devoted to maintaining, through shared sacrificial meals in the temple, a close communion between living and dead. The cult of the tomb, on the other hand, as it developed during the Warring States period was instead aimed at separating the living and the dead: providing the deceased with a dwelling in the underworld that was inescapable and from which, since it was appointed with all the things that would be needed in the underworld (or at least *mingqi* imitations thereof), the deceased would not desire to leave. The new focus on underworld and tomb was also accompanied by the bureaucratisation of the cosmology of the afterworld and of mortuary practice. As tombs came to resemble the houses of the living, so the afterworld domain in which the tomb was situated came similarly to be conceived along the lines of the newly emerging centralised bureaucratic state. Since the underworld had begun to be understood as overseen by a cadre of officials, it was therefore most appropriately communicated with through documents in bureaucratic format despatched by their this-worldly colleagues.[23]

Death pollution and exorcism in ancient times

The above developments can be traced on the basis of datable archaeological evidence, and they tell us much about the history of both the bureaucratic and the exorcistic elements of the Han grave-securing writs like the one that introduced this chapter. However, there are some kinds of questions about historical experience that are difficult to answer solely on the basis of buried (non-textual) artefacts: Falkenhausen's conclusions about the role of the tomb in separating living and dead are themselves based on the application to earlier centuries of Seidel's understanding of the Han grave-securing writs. In other words, when it comes to thought and motivation, it is best, when possible, to take into account the evidence of texts. In order, for instance, to truly understand mortuary exorcism in ancient China, and hence the beliefs and practices from which the proto-Daoist grave-securing writs developed, it is necessary to understand the anxieties people felt concerning death; in order to do that, one must consult the ritual canons and other written works.

Fears surrounding death and burial in ancient China were above all connected with the pollution of death and closely related matters. The ancestral cult itself – in particular as interpreted by scholarly exegetes in Eastern Zhou and Han times and set out in classical texts such as the *Zhouli*, the *Yili* and the *Liji* – seems to have been 'optimistic' in its theology and emotional tone, showing little evidence of distress over the possible negative consequences of death, for either the deceased or the survivors.

Instead it assumed that the rites properly carried out would ensure the felicity of the ancestral soul and hence the ancestor's beneficent treatment of descendants.[24] That same literary record, however, also preserves traces of very different attitudes. The treatment of corpses and the conduct of mortuary ritual as set out in the classical ritual texts included ritual actions that clearly addressed issues of death pollution. Exorcistic action was taken to protect the corpse from the depredations of demons of putrefaction. Corpses themselves were exorcised by shamans, and the coffins, shrouds and other trappings of the mortuary rite were interpreted as insulating the survivors from the corpse. By Han times, texts recounting more popular practices indicate a further, yet connected, element: the propitiation and subsequent dispelling of the spirits of the earth and soil disturbed by the burial. Proto-Daoist and Daoist mortuary practices emerged out of this milieu; the counterparts of the optimistic attitudes that prevailed around the ancestral temple were the fears and anxieties that were focused on the tomb.

As I have discussed elsewhere in some detail this archaic complex of mortuary practices and ideologies,[25] I will keep the discussion here relatively brief. Certainly chief among the predecessors of the ritualists who used the grave-securing writs must be figures like the *fangxiang* exorcist – the best known, as his services were used at the Han dynastic court. At the end of the old year, during the Nuo or 'Great Exorcism', he would, assisted by dancers in animal masks and costumes, process through the palace rooms, armed and chanting exorcistic incantations in order to drive off demons of pestilence. More germane to our purposes, it was also his function during royal funerals to leap into the grave-pit and strike each of its four sides with his halberd in order to exorcise the malefic spirits of putrefaction that would otherwise devour the corpse. It is more than likely that it was the fear of the corrupting corpse itself – of death pollution – that was filially displaced from the body of the deceased to distinct demonic beings.

Hence it is not surprising that, along with this apprehension felt by the living on behalf of the dead, there existed also the survivors' fear *of* the dead. Evidence for such anxieties – often using the term 'loathing' (*wu*) – is more than ample in early texts. Ziyou is reported in the *Liji* to have provided the following justification for certain mortuary practices:

> When a person dies, there arises a feeling of loathing [of the corpse]. Its inertness makes us [want to] reject it. On this account there is the wrapping it in the shroud, and there are the curtains, plumes (and other ornaments of the coffin), to preserve people from that feeling of loathing.[26]

The early Tang commentator Kong Yingda (574–648) makes clear that this explanation for the accoutrements of the funeral rite is intrinsically linked to death pollution: 'when a human body is dead, its form and substance rot and become corrupt'.[27] And of course the funeral rite as a whole was explained in similar terms – through the well known equation of 'burying [in funerals]' (*zang*) with 'hiding away' (*cang*). Finally, one might note the practice of rulers approaching corpses during mourning rites only when accompanied by 'a shaman (*wu*) with a peach-wand, an invocator (*zhu*) with his reed[-brush] and a lance-bearer – loathing [the presence of death]'.[28] And Kong Yingda explains this employment of ritualists bearing exorcistic implements similarly: 'the reason why [the shaman, invocator and lance-bearer are employed] is that one loathes [the deceased's] evil and perverse vapour (*xiongxie zhiqi*)'.[29]

Finally, there is one more kind of danger associated with burial and death pollution that must be considered in our account of early mortuary practice: the act of digging deep into the earth, as required for the construction of dwellings (*zhai*), was thought to disturb the spirits of the earth and bring their anger down upon the living. Wang Chong (27–91), recording the customs of the Jiangnan region of his own day, described in great detail the rites for 'dispersing [the spirits of] the soil' (*jietu*).[30] This ritual similarly required the services of a shaman, who employed 'a human figurine to represent a demonic being' (an image of the soil spirits themselves?); the shaman would then make both an invocation and an offering to the offended spirits.[31] Once again, the dangerous consequences of death and burial were dealt with through exorcisms assisted by shamans.

The summoning of the soul

The role of shamans in funeral rites was not restricted to defending the corpse from hungry demons and neutralising the corpse's noxious influences; nor were the dangers of death for the survivors limited to those posed by corrupting flesh. The more subtle elements of the personality – what we might loosely call the 'soul' – were also both threatened and threatening, and these problems too were often addressed through rites carried out by shamans. The best known literary evidence for such rites is of course that provided by the *Chuci*, which contains two poems, the 'Summons of the (Hun-)Soul' ('Zhaohun') and the 'Great Summons' ('Dazhao'), for the calling back of the soul of the sick, the dying or the dead. And, whatever be the specific purpose of the 'Zhaohun' poem, there are a number of indications that the ritual of soul-recalling more generally was in fact employed for the benefit of the dead.[32]

Not surprisingly, the potential of the soul to wander imperilled not only the deceased but also the living. As we have seen in the case of the fears that were directed towards the corpse, incipient corruption and the demons that were conceived to cause it threatened both the dead body itself and the survivors who might be exposed to the pollution of death. In the same way, a wandering soul was a problem for the living because of their concern for the welfare of the dead and the comfort of the soul, but also and especially because of their concern for their own welfare. If not provided with a safe post-mortem home and thus left prey to the depredations of the non-human world (which were so eloquently depicted by the *Chuci*), the spirit of the deceased might lash out at living kin. A soul deprived of the sustenance of sacrificial offerings could of course behave similarly. Finally, and perhaps most importantly, failure to attach the deceased to a permanent home in the next world might also allow the soul to return to exact vengeance for any scores that had remained unsettled at the time of death.

One of the earliest recorded speculations on the nature of the soul is presented as an attempt to account for the ability of the dead to wreak revenge upon the living. While the question of the exact natures of the *hun* and *po* souls need not concern us here, the statement made in connection with the same *Zuozhuan* episode speaks for itself: 'When a ghost (*gui*) has a place to return (*gui*), it does not become a baneful demon (*li*)'.[33] Exorcistic rites that were aimed at the corpse and its pollution thus had as their counterparts rites of summoning and emplacement (themselves, as will be shown, in effect exorcisms), which were directed towards the soul. (That such a 'place of return' might also – depending on historical period and social class – mean the ancestral temple has already been discussed.) In this way, funeral procedures that exorcised the tomb (and sometimes the corpse), then summoned the soul and placed it together with the body in the grave, could protect – and could protect the living from – both corpse and soul.

Beyond the classical rites for the dead and the cult of ancestors as they are described in late Zhou and Han ritual texts – and as they are evinced by excavated tombs, ritual bronzes and other material remains (likewise mostly coming from the highest social strata) – it is difficult to say with any certainty what may have constituted mortuary practice and belief in ancient China. The religion of the people simply produced very little in the way of textual or other material traces that can be interpreted in significant ways.

Nevertheless, fragments of evidence from the texts of the literati allow one to piece together a portrait of a type of shaman-exorcist much like the *fangxiang*. Ying Shao in the *Fengsu tongyi* refers to a 'griffon head [mask]' (*qitou*, or 'spirit-mask') whose function was to preserve (*cun*) the *hun*-soul of the deceased and prevent it from floating about. The mask (or the ritualist who wore it) was also called 'striking-the-pit' (*chukuang*).[34] These apparent resemblances between the *qitou* and the *fangxiang* (here not only the protection of the deceased but also the 'striking [of] the [grave-]pit') are made explicitly in the *Youyang zazu* of Duan Chengshi (*c.*800–863). Duan refers to a specialist who performed 'funeral music' (*yuesang*) and used the griffon head to secure the *hun*-soul of the deceased. 'If he has four eyes he is called a *fangxiang*; if he has two eyes he is called a dervish (*qi*).'[35] From the above I believe that we may infer with some confidence not only what constituted the fears about death that were dealt with in archaic mortuary ritual, but also something about the type of ritualist who combated them: especially on the popular level, a masked dancer, probably in some sense of the word a shaman, whose gyrations were accompanied, as Granet suggests, by drumming and 'cris provoquaient des états d'extase et de possession'.[36]

Tomb ordinances and the bureaucratisation
of exorcism

Now that we know something of the ritual specialists who were the pre-decessors (and quite likely later the competitors) of those who wrote the grave-securing writs of the Latter Han, let us turn again to those documents, and from the ecstatic again to the bureaucratic.[37] As noted above, Anna Seidel has shown that these mortuary documents indicate the existence of a kind of 'proto-Taoist' religion, which 'became Taoism' when its practices were subsumed under the revelation of the Most High Lord Lao to the first Celestial Master, Zhang Daoling.[38] Thus the grave-securing writs are essential sources for understanding the emergence of the Daoist religion out of pre-existing local traditions.

The oldest grave-securing writ listed by Ikeda On is dated 133 CE,[39] and, while it already shows indications of a religious mentality vastly different from that of the shamanic and exorcistic rites recounted in sections above, it is also evident that the notion of death it implies is still deeply rooted in earlier conceptions of mortuary exorcism.

> In the second year of *yangjia*, the eighth month, whose first day was *yisi*, on the sixth day, which is *jiaxu*,[40] the Envoy of the Celestial Monarch, respectfully on behalf of the household of Cao Bolu moves disaster away and eliminates odium, putting them a thousand *li* away. Odium [flees? is removed by?] the great peach, and demons that arrive [ ][ ] may not remain. That from which they are relieved (?) . . . [ ][ ]. Let the living attain nine, the dead attain five. Let living and dead take separate paths, a myriad *li* apart from one another. From now on, let the descendants always be protected, their longevity like metal and stone, without inauspiciousness until the end. With what is a pledge-offering made? – [this bottle] is filled with divine medicine, and sealed with the seal of the Yellow God's Emblem of Transcendence.[41] [Observe this] in accordance with the statutes and ordinances.

There are in this document some signs of the bureaucratising process – at the outset, the essential fact of the ritual employment of a written text, rather than merely a spell, chant, or ritual gesture. Furthermore, the grave is secured by a servant of a divine ruler, the Envoy of the Celestial Monarch, and the closing formula, 'in accordance with the statutes and ordinances' (*ru lüling*), is a standard phrase in Han official communications that indicates that the matter under discussion is subject to the provisions of the legal code and should be dealt with as prescribed therein. This may imply that some kind of actual written formulary served as the basis for the religion of the grave-securing writs;[42] it is in any event a clear indication of the assimilation of ritual practice to state bureaucratic practice.

Be that as it may, the bulk of the writ composed for Cao Bolu continues to speak the old language of exorcism, of 'dispersing and eliminating' (*jiechu*).

Apotropaic objects abound: we have already seen that peach-wood figured significantly in the exorcisms of corpses by shamans, and the seal of the Yellow God's Emblem of Transcendence is named in Ge Hong's *Baopuzi* as a means of repelling tigers and wolves that have descended upon one's residence.[43] The 'divine medicine' (*shenyao*) itself may have been intended to inhibit the decomposition of the corpse.[44] The events commanded by the writ are similarly exorcistic in intent: disaster, odium (referring especially to the 'odium of the soil' – see the analysis of the next writ) and demons are to go far away, thus leaving only good fortune and longevity for surviving descendants. Moreover, one additional exorcistic element – one that has already been highlighted as characteristic of the evolution of mortuary practice in Warring States and later times – emerges with great clarity in this and most other grave-securing ordinances: the theme of the separation of the living and the dead ('let living and dead take separate paths'), which in effect meant driving the dead away from the living. The numerology invoked by the writ can be similarly explained: nine, the number of the living and of longevity, refers to various series of nine vertically ascending stages, such as the nine layers of Mount Kunlun that ascend to the Gate of Heaven (cf. the next writ translated, which states 'the living construct high daises'); five, the number of the dead, pertains to China's five sacred mountains or Marchmounts, the horizontally deployed five directions and other quintuplets that figure importantly in mortuary belief. Thus, for the living to attain nine and the dead five is for each to get what is appropriate to it, and hence to be kept apart from the other.[45] The medium might have differed from the corpse and tomb exorcisms carried out by the *fangxiang* and the *qitou*, but the message remained in many ways the same.

A somewhat different impression is yielded by a grave-securing writ of just forty years later:

> In the second year of *xiping*, in the twelfth month [early 174], whose first day is *yisi*, on the sixteenth day, which is *gengshen*, the Envoy of the Celestial Monarch declares to – the rulers of the left, the right and the centre of the Zhang family's three mounds and five tombs, the Assistant of the Sepulchre, the Director of the Sepulchre, the Director of the Office that Rules Sepulchres, the Hostel Chief of the Gate of the *Hun*-soul, the Attack Patrol of the Sepulchre[46] and the others, [and also] dares to announce to the Assistant of the Mound, the Sire of the Tomb,[47] the Subterrestrial Two Thousand Bushel Officials, the Marksman of the East of the Sepulchre, the Sire of the West of the Sepulchre, the Special Minister for Subterrestrial Attacks,[48] the Squad Chiefs[49] of Haoli and the others:

> Today is auspicious and good, and for no other reason [is this announcement being made], but only because the deceased, Zhang Shujing, had a barren fate and died young, and is due to return below and [enter] the mound and tomb.

The Yellow God gave birth to the Five Marchmounts,[50] and he rules over the registers of the living.[51] He summons the *hun-* and *po-*souls, and rules over the records of the dead.[52] The living construct high daises; the dead return and bury themselves deep. Their eyebrows and beards having fallen off (?), they descend and become soil and ashes.

For this reason are offered: medicine for exemption from forced labour, with the desire that there will be no dead among those of later generations; nine roots of Shangdang ginseng,[53] with the desire that they be taken in replacement of the living; lead men, to be taken in replacement of the dead; and yellow beans and melon seeds, for the dead to take to pay the subterrestrial levies. Let the regulations be made watertight.[54] Let the odium of the soil be driven off, with the desire that evil be kept from propagating.

Once these orders have been transmitted, the civil servants of the earth shall be bound, and are not to trouble the Zhang household again. Quickly, quickly, in accordance with the statutes and ordinances.[55]

The available evidence is too limited to allow any conclusions as to whether either the space of forty years or the distance between Shaanxi, from whose soil the older, Cao Bolu writ was excavated, and Shanxi, where this writ for Zhang Shujing was found, could account for the great differences between the two texts. In some respects, of course, they are very similar. Both have roughly the same format, with the Celestial Envoy as the chief figure and the 'in accordance with the statutes and ordinances' closing. The Zhang Shujing ordinance shares the same goals as the earlier one, and, with its identification of the 'odium' (*jiu*) concerned as the 'odium of the soil' (*tujiu*), it further clarifies those goals: the odium of the soil refers principally to the offence caused to the earth by the construction of the grave and the interment of the polluting corpse.[56] In the case of the grave-securing writs, though, the culprits are not demons, but the deceased and his family themselves, since they are the miscreants who have violated (*fan*) the earth. Both writs also insist that the dead be kept apart from the living, with the more recent writ, in the same manner as the earlier one, enforcing the separation by exemplifying it in parallel prose that proclaims the ascent of the living and the descent of the dead into the earth.

The Zhang Shujing writ of 174 also provides a great deal more detail about the spirits of the earth that might be disturbed by the burial, and it is at this point that it begins to depart significantly from the Cao Bolu writ of 133. The pantheon of the later writ, though it contains some titles appropriate either to gods or to feudal lords – e.g. *hou* (marksman) and *bo* (sire) – is otherwise redolent of bureaucracy, mixing titles actually used in the Han state – Hostel Chief (*tingzhang*), Director (*ling*), Two Thousand Bushels (*erqian shi*) – with those that appear to be fictional, e.g. the Special Minister for Subterrestrial Attacks (*dixia ji teqing*). More strikingly, the underworld is conceived as operating in the same manner as the state administration. The Yellow God keeps registers on both the living and the dead, and death brings no relief from taxes.

The Zhang Shujing writ employs different means of 'dispersing [the spirits of] the soil' than does the older document; the divergence is evinced by the change in the offerings presented. The pledge-offering of the older writ is apotropaic, while here the ginseng roots and lead men are clearly meant as surrogates, and the tax provisions are intended to mollify the offended spirits and prevent the 'civil servants of the earth' (*dili*) from troubling the living. Labour was expected of the dead in the underworld, as suggested not only by the provision of human substitutes here, but also by the inclusion in the grave of 'medicine for exemption from forced labour' (*fuchu zhi yao*). A further writ makes reference to netherworld versions of corvée registers, or registers for mutual responsibility groups of five households (*wuzhi ji*).[57] The concept of an underworld (ideally) 'hermetically separate' from this world – with living and dead taking separate paths – but closely mirroring this-worldly socio-political structures, which first appeared around the beginning of the Warring States period, was close to complete by the time of this grave-securing writ.

The idea that registers were kept on the dead provided an additional way of articulating the fear that the dead might refuse to sever, or be prevented from severing, relations with the living: the registers of those due to die could become confused with those of people who were fated to live much longer. Prior to the offering of the lead men, the woman Jia writ of 147 first tries to see if the death had not been a mistake in the first place, as the Envoy exhorts the otherworldly scribes to '[Re-]calculate [the lifespans] in your name-records!' and 'Collate the dates of death!' in order to make sure that the deceased Ms Jia had not been mistaken for someone else born in the same year and month, or on the same day at the same hour.

An additional possibility was that a recently deceased family member's fate could become entangled with that of another member of the household. In a writ dated 156, the Envoy announces to the Assistant of the Mound, the Sire of the Tomb and the Subterrestrial Two Thousand Bushel Official:

> The one in the household of Cheng who died is styled Taochui. His date and time of death have become overlapped with the fated span of another; his registers have become stuck to those of another living member of his household. Restore this person's fated span, and erase the overlapping writing. Erase the records binding him to a group of five [see above], so that the dead and the living have different files.[58]

In this case, one suspects, not long after the death of Cheng Taochui, another member of the household became ill. This was attributed to the files of the latter having become attached to those of Taochui; thus, unwittingly, the living kinsman's name had been transferred from the registers of the living to those of the dead.

From earliest times one of the most popular offshoots of the bureaucrat-isation of the other world was this new way of explaining untimely death. Attributing death to clerical error provided new hopes for the resuscitation of the dead (once the error could be found and rectified) and, most notably, new narrative devices for the authoritative description of the afterlife. From the third-century BCE resurrection of Dan down to recent days, Chinese literature is full of tales of those who, owing to some miscalculation, died before their fated time, and, the mistake having been discovered, were sent back to the land of the living to recount their adventures in the land of the shades.

Consistent with the development of an afterworld clerical bureaucracy is the emergence of a new, highly legalistic, connotation for the word *jie*, to 'disperse', 'release' or 'gain release from'. *Jie* has already appeared above in Wang Chong's phrase for propitiatory exorcisms – 'to disperse and elim-inate' (*jiechu*) – but in the grave-securing writs *jie* also came to mean to 'absolve' or 'gain absolution from', as it did in Han law. This special con-notation of *jie* can be further elucidated when Wu Rongzeng's convincing argument – that the phase *jieshi* should be read *jiezhe*, to release from [liab-ility for] punishment – is taken into consideration.[59] 'Release from punish-ment' is one of the principal goals of the grave-securing writs. A writ composed in 173 for one Chen Shujing states its purpose: 'to eliminate harm on behalf of the living and to release the dead from punishment' (*wei sheng ren chu yang wei si ren jie shilzhe*).[60] The term 'earth prison', or hell (*diyu*), had yet to enter the Chinese religious lexicon, but one late Han tomb ord-inance does mention 'prison scribes who rule the tomb' (*zhumu yushi*), and Seidel is no doubt correct in claiming that the makers of the late Han grave-securing jars believed the afterlife to be a place of judgement where the newly deceased could be thrown into prison for their misdeeds.[61]

The grave-securing writs of the Latter Han thus exemplify the trend towards bureaucratisation in the highest degree. They use administrative jargon ('in accordance with the statutes and ordinances') and purport to represent the commands of a celestial monarch, which are transmitted through a subordinate to the pantheon of the spirit-functionaries of the tomb and the soil. The netherworld not only has its officialdom; it also has prisons, levies taxes and keeps files on its subjects, whom it organises into mutual responsibility groups of five households in order to facilitate their assign-ment to corvée labour duties. On one level of analysis, at least, one cannot avoid concluding that the makers of the writs had, *à la* Durkheim, created the afterworld in the image of the early imperial Chinese regime.

From another perspective, we have seen that many of the motivations of the grave-securing writs had little (at least directly) to do with government administrative practice, being based instead on the oral rites of exorcists and shamans. Using or invoking the powers of apotropaic objects and sub-stances (peach-wood, exorcistic talismans, 'divine medicine'), the writs sought the same ends as had the *fangxiang* who exorcised the tomb, the shaman who 'dispersed [the spirits of] the soil' and the masked, 'griffon-headed' *qitou* who danced to recall souls. Like the *fangxiang*, the writs secured the grave by dispelling potentially hostile spirits of the tomb, though these spirits had become 'civil servants' of the earth more susceptible to documentary orders than to exorcistic chants. Like the shaman described by Wang Chong, the writs attempted to remove the 'odium of the soil', the offence to the spirits of the earth provoked by the digging of the grave and the intrusion of the corpse. Like the *qitou* (and, it has been suggested, like the ritualist whose performances served as the model for the 'Summons of the Soul', above), the overriding goal of the grave-securing writs was to effect the separation of living and dead by irrevocably lodging the potentially malevolent, wandering spirit in the tomb.

How bureaucratisation did (and did not) affect pre-existing traditions of mortuary practice is now somewhat clearer, but one issue remains to be treated. It was noted that the grave-securing writs implied an afterworld that included prisons for the incarceration of miscreant souls. But what, precisely, were the misdeeds for which the dead could be held accountable? A resolution of that question would say much about the degree to which moral behaviour had begun to be a concern in the assessment of afterworld fates, and hence the degree to which the writs represented the beginning of the religious revolution that (ostensibly) would be consummated by the Daoists.

The continued importance of the offence to the earth inherent in the construction of the tomb and the burial of the corpse has already been mentioned, but there are signs that other factors may have been in operation as well. The Chen Shujing writ of 173 quoted above ends – after the 'in accordance with the statutes and ordinances' closing formula – with a cryptic postscript: 'the good, the Chens will enjoy auspicious prosperity; the evil, the five essences will suffer the harm themselves' (*shanzhe Chenshi ji chang ezhe wu jing zi shou qi yang*).[62] Building on a reading that was based on a transcription in which *jing* (essences) had been left as a lacuna, in turn filled in by another translator as 'generations' (presumably *dai* or *shi*), Seidel has understood these sentences as referring to the behaviour of the deceased *while alive*, and to be conditional: if the departed was good in life, his descendants will enjoy prosperity; if he was evil, his descendants will suffer harm. Thus the whole mechanism of recompense and retribution in the other world, with its implications for living descendants, would appear already to have been in place in the proto-Daoism of the second century. However, since there is very little in the writs that is not directly explainable by the idea that the odium was incurred by the digging of the grave and the interment, one would have to hesitate before placing too much interpretive weight on this one, vague, passage.[63]

Instead (and this is precisely the reason why this question is so difficult to resolve) one should take note of the way in which the legalistic language of the writs is itself ambiguous. The judicial metaphor mediates, one might say, between archaic anxieties over pollution and emerging medieval worries about sin. The vocabulary of crime, imprisonment, and release could be applied to afterworld judicature, but also to pollution and other taboos –

'offences to the earth' from which one must seek release (*jie*) – and to moral failings from which one must seek absolution (*jie*). The basic otherworldly administrative structure – the registration of mortals; the keeping of files that recorded births, good and bad behaviour and fated times of death; and the judgement of souls in accordance with the contents of those files – could accommodate a spectrum of religious concerns and ways of conceptualising death. In a sense, the question of the degree to which the grave-securing writs reflected the trend towards 'ethical polarisation' is not a crucial one. As moral behaviour became increasingly decisive in the determination of afterworld destinies, it could easily be given more weight by the underworld magistrates without any significant revision of the 'statutes and ordinances' upon which their decisions were based.

On the other hand, though the writs might take cognizance of sin, the basic worries about the pollution of the corpse and the hostility of the soul were not thereby supplanted. One lacunary tomb ordinance, which has been dated to the second century,[64] can only be translated provisionally, but it provides some suggestive evidence regarding the way in which ancient beliefs about death pollution and the return of the malevolent dead persisted within the framework of the tomb ordinances and their bureaucratic ideology. This ordinance is classified by Ikeda as a tomb contract (*muquan*), rather than a grave-securing jar, apparently because it is made of lead and thus has a physical form similar to that of other engraved 'contracts'. But the text has nothing to do with the purchase of a grave-plot, as is the case with most of the 'land purchase contracts' found in tombs. Instead, it reads like a grave-securing writ, since it communicates the orders of the Celestial Monarch, announces the arrival of the deceased in the afterworld and seeks to enforce the separation of living and dead:

> in the [ ] [month] whose first day was *yihai*, on the twenty-second day, which is a *bingshen* day, grasping the orders sent down by the Celestial Monarch, we announce that Liu Boping, formerly of Dongdi Village, Luodong Township, had a meagre fate and [died] young . . . Medicines could not cure him. Let the punishment [that resulted from] the overlapping of years and months[65] and the noxious demons and corpse infusions of the same time all return to the grave-mound.[66] The Lord of Mount Tai summons . . .
>
> [In happiness, let there be no] pining for the other, in suffering let there be no thought for the other. The living belong to Chang'an,[67] the dead to Mount Tai. Let dead and living be in separate places, and not interfere with one another. The water of the (Yellow) River must be clear.[68] Mount Tai . . . the Six Ding.[69] There is the Teaching of the Celestial Monarch; let all be in accordance with its statutes and ordinances.

The notion of Mount Tai as a destination for the souls of the dead is expressed in a number of late Han ordinance texts. At this point, though,

what needs to be stressed is the connection the Liu Boping ordinance makes
between burial and the removal of 'noxious demons and corpse infusions'
(*zhigui shizhu*). This *zhi* is a rare character, but Han and Six Dynasties
glosses connect it closely to demons of tombs, ghosts of the malevolent dead
and the spirits exorcised by the *fangxiang* during the Nuo. *Zhi* is explained
in the *Shuowen* as 'a baneful demon' (*ligui*); that is, as a vengeful or otherwise harmful ghost. The prototypical vengeful ghost of the *Zuozhuan* was
called a *li* (above). The *Shuowen* also quotes Zheng Xuan's explication of *li*:
Zheng identifies *li* with 'the vapour of corpses that accumulates in great
tumuli' (*da ling ji shi zhi qi*) and in turn with the malign influences dispelled
by the *fangxiang* in the Nuo. Finally, Guo Pu (276–324) in his commentary
on the *Shanhai jing* makes an even more explicit identification, equating the
zhi with the *chimei*, one of the malign beings attacked by the *fangxiang*
and his assistants as they performed the Nuo.[70] One of the objects of this
second-century tomb ordinance was thus to send *zhigui*, noxious demons,
back to the grave together with the deceased, and these demons have been
shown to be creatures similar to or identical with the demonic beings exorcised during the Nuo. Additionally, the *zhigui* emanated from tombs and
were understood as a condensed form of the pollution of death, the 'vapour
of corpses'.

The 'corpse infusions' (*shizhu*) of the Liu Boping ordinance have similar
sources. These too are demons of disease; five distinct types are named in
the *Zhouhou beiji fang*, which has been attributed to Ge Hong.[71] In Daoist
conceptions of demonic agents of disease, *zhu* became the principal term
for the 'infusion' or 'pouring' of spectral pathogens into the body of the
afflicted. Thus, in the Liu Boping tomb ordinance, the greater goal of the
separation of living and dead is achieved as much through a pandaemonic
'great exorcism' as through the bureaucratic transfer of the deceased (from
the administration of the living – Chang'an – to the administration of the
dead: Mount Tai). Liu Boping is to answer the summons of Mount Tai's
lord, but so are all manner of other spirits associated with the hazards posed
by death.

This ordinance demonstrates how the dangers surrounding death that
pertained in archaic religion continued to be addressed in proto-Daoist tomb
ordinances. Earlier sections pointed to three principal sources for such
dangers: the corpse and its pollution; the vengeful, wandering soul; and
spirits of the earth offended by the burial. While in a number of the late
Han grave-securing writs heretofore examined the emphasis was placed on
the last issue – the dissolution of the 'odium of the soil' – the Liu Boping
ordinance focuses instead on the first two matters. In so doing, it employs a
type of displacement made already familiar by the example of the *fangxiang*.
Just as anxiety over the corruption of the corpse was expressed indirectly
when the *fangxiang* drove off the demons of decay that might devour the
body, so in the above ordinance the deceased is sent off *together with* vengeful ghosts and demons of pollution and disease. The fear of the dead Liu
Boping himself has been attached instead to demons 'of the same time'.[72]

In these late Han grave-securing writs and related ordinances, then, despite the fact that they were written in the form of imperial commands or other legally binding communications, and despite the bureaucratic nature of the deities involved and the cosmology implied, the religious conceptions of the shamans and exorcists who were the professional predecessors of the creators of the ordinances were not abandoned. Standing in the same tradition of mortuary exorcism as the *fangxiang*, the users of grave-securing writs sought to neutralise potentially hostile spirits of the tomb, though they had become 'civil servants of the earth' that were best controlled through written documents, rather than elemental demons that needed to be despatched by means of oral spells and violent, exorcistic action (such as the *fangxiang's* striking of the sides of the grave-pit). Like the ancient royal shamans, the makers of the writs protected the survivors from the contagion of the death pollution through the employment of apotropaic objects. In transferring the deceased to the charge of the underworld authorities, the grave-securing writs accomplished the same goals as had the masked, dancing soul-summoners like griffon-headed *qitou*: both the writs and the *qitou* kept the soul from aimlessly 'floating about', lodging it instead in its 'quiet and reposeful home', which was the tomb, from whence it would not desire to (and indeed could not) depart to trouble the living.

The bureaucratisation of death and burial represented by the late Han tomb ordinances did not bring about a complete reconception of the consequences of death. Bureaucratic and exorcistic death ritual had been developing hand-in-hand since the Warring States period. Whatever 'ethical polarisation' may have been occurring in the late Han was reflected in grave-securing ordinances in a way that built upon, rather than supplanted, pre-existing structures of thought. Indeed, it may even be possible that the ritualists who used the grave-securing writs during burials themselves impersonated the Celestial Monarch's envoy:[73] a form of shamanism/possession/theatre that brings the religious world of the writs even closer to that of the archaic shaman-exorcists.

Bureaucracy, exorcism and the textualisation of religion

In tracing the development of certain strands of mortuary ritual up to the time of the proto-Daoist grave-securing writs of the late Han, we have found a great degree of continuity between the writs and their oral, shamanic predecessors. At the same time, we have observed at many points the highly bureaucratic nature of the language, theology and cosmology of the writs: their use of phrases drawn from state administrative documents; the prevalence of official titles in their pantheons; their image of an afterlife patterned after the worldly empire, including even the levying of taxes and the registration of the underworld population in mutual responsibility groups of five. Can one really claim to have found, then, an unbroken chain of transmission of thought and practice from the archaic shaman-exorcists to those who made the grave-securing writs? The fact that these documents would have to have been produced by ritualists who were relatively literate begins to point away from the ecstatic performances of the *fangxiang*. Since the documents possessed in themselves some ritual efficacy – they were based on a written code – the ritual practitioner assumed a different role: he became a scribe for the god rather than his medium (at least to some degree; see the speculation just above). In addition to the type of personnel involved, conceptually speaking one's interpretation must somehow allow for substantial change: when the prevailing notion of mortuary exorcism became centred on the idea of *jie* – not solely in the magico-religious sense of 'dispersing' or 'gaining release from' (demonic harassment), but also in the judicial sense of 'release' from legally imposed punishment – the powerful model of state legal administration appears as if it could have severed the writs' links with ecstatic oral performance.

How one handles this question hinges on how one assesses the relationship between the oral and the ecstatic on the one hand, and the written and the bureaucratic on the other. As for the oral versus the written, writing of course has an enormous impact, not only on culture in general, but also more specifically on social structure and patterns of authority.[74] In religion, for instance, if ritual requires the use of documents, then only the literate may be priests, and only those with access to the services of the literate may benefit from their ministrations. The channels of spiritual power will become both narrowed and increasingly steeply pitched and hierarchised.

Moreover, the Warring States religious and mortuary trends highlighted above – bureaucratisation and the development of exorcistically based mortuary practice, which in some respects reached their pre-Daoist peak in the textualised religion of the grave-securing writs – coincided with sociopolitical developments that were also expressed in hierarchisation, bureaucratisation and textualisation. In the Warring States period, political systems become more steeply hierarchical, as a collegial nobility was replaced by a paramount ruler, and bureaucratic, as the feudal subordinates of the ruler became the officials of a centralised, rationalised regime. Moreover, as Mark Edward Lewis has argued, the emerging Warring States polity was also characterised by greater dependence upon the written word: agreements made by means of sacrificial blood covenants (*meng*) gave way to bonds (*yue*) based on the written texts of oaths; success in warfare was now a matter not of individual heroism and martial skill, but of mastery of the literature of the art of war; and the myths of shamanic deities were reinterpreted as stories of the origins of warfare, law and other civilised institutions, institutions that could only be fully understood and perfected by the newly emerging class of literate civil servants.[75] The textualisation of religion was paralleled by the textualisation of government and social organisation, and both were accompanied by increasing hierarchisation.

Thus again the focus on bureaucratisation and literacy has led to an emphasis on discontinuity, between early Zhou and Warring States society, and between archaic religion and the new religious trends embodied in

Warring States mortuary practice and the grave-securing writs of the Han. But the distinction between writing and speech may be overdrawn. Jacques Derrida, for example, argues that it is not the distinction between written and oral culture that is fundamental; instead, the essential matter is that of the creation of 'classificatory difference' itself, which is common to all cultures.

> If writing is no longer understood in the narrow sense of linear and phonetic notation, it should be possible to say that all societies capable of producing ... their proper names, and of bringing classificatory difference into play, practice writing in general. No reality or concept would therefore correspond to the expression 'society without writing'.[76]

If one follows Derrida on this point, one is led away from an emphasis on the distinction between oral mortuary ritual and rites employing written documents, and instead is encouraged to undertake the examination of the 'writing' of culture in the broader sense: the creation of categories and their oppositions, which, whether expressed orally or in written form, define the cultural arena in which ritual action takes place.

For that matter, while, insofar as the grave-securing writs are concerned, I have relied largely on the transcriptions provided by Ikeda, examination of the entire inscriptions on the grave-securing bottles further blurs this distinction between the oral and the written. As alluded to above, many of the texts are accompanied by talismanic diagrams (*fu*), such as the Yellow God's Emblem of Transcendence (*Huangshen yuezhang*).[77] In another context – that of contemporary Daoist and popular practice – K. M. Schipper has already noted how the written yet illegible *fu* mediate between oral and written religious cultures.[78]

From such a perspective, the continuities between archaic oral and medieval textually based Chinese mortuary rites do indeed stand out to a marked degree. Archaic exorcistic ritual employed the fundamental 'classificatory difference' of life over and against death, of pure yang against polluting yin. The same use of exorcistic ritual to separate living and dead then simply became *textually* realized in the grave-securing writs, whose parallel prose exemplified in literary form that same separation:

Let the living attain nine,	the dead attain five.
The living construct high daises;	the dead return and bury themselves deep.
Heaven above is deep azure,	Earth below is vast and vague.
The dead return to yin,	the living return to yang.
The living have their villages,	the dead have their townships.
The living belong to Chang'an in the west;	the dead belong to Mount Tai in the east.[79]

Spiritual power, even when placed within a bureaucratic setting, still meant the power to exorcise impurities. One might say the same, even, for political power. Mark Edward Lewis has emphasised the subversion of popular religion and myth by the Warring States literati, who reinterpreted the myths of the people in order to meet the ends of emerging centralised authority.[80] However, it might also be claimed that the nature of religio-political power was not thereby completely reformulated. When the literati appropriated the myths of the tutelary deities of exorcists, they also attributed to their autocratic rulers (and in a sense to themselves, see n. 82 below) power that remained on a certain level exorcistic. Mencius gave this account of the cycles of disorder (caused by water and animals) and regeneration (brought about by the actions of Sages) that had moulded Chinese history:

> The world has existed for a long time, now in peace, now in disorder. In the time of Yao, the water reversed its natural course, flooding the central regions, and the reptiles made their homes there, depriving the people of a settled life. In low-lying regions, people lived in nests; in high regions, they lived in caves . . . Yu was entrusted with the task of controlling [the Flood]. He led the flood water into the seas by cutting channels for it in the ground, and drove the reptiles into grassy marshes. The water, flowing through the channels, formed the Yangtze, the Huai, the Yellow River and the Han. Obstacles receded and the birds and beasts harmful to men were annihilated. Only then were the people able to level the ground and live on it.[81]

The dissolution of human society – the reduction of humans to beasts (living in nests and caves) – is represented as the result of the incursion of the forces of the yin world: water and animals, especially aquatic reptiles. Yu (who himself remained a tutelary deity of exorcists) restored order through what in effect was an act of exorcism, drawing off the flood waters into the sea (separating wet and dry, yin and yang) and killing off harmful animals (separating the human and the non-human).[82]

Thus it should not be entirely surprising that aspects of both the political ideology and the mortuary traditions that developed during the Warring States period and matured in early imperial times should have embodied elements of exorcism; both were founded on the same cosmology, the same way of constructing 'classificatory difference' and deploying it in symbolic and practical action to create a human order. The restoration of political order shares much with the restoration of cosmic order that is brought about through death ritual; funerals similarly must counteract the intrusion of too much yin, in the highly palpable form of death, into the yang world of the living.[83]

Lest it be thought that *all* religious handling of death must be similarly exorcistic, and thus that the continuities between the archaic rites of the *fangxiang* and the bureaucratic procedures of the grave-securing writs were entirely unavoidable – and thus unremarkable – comparison of our data with early Christianity is illuminating. Robin Lane Fox has observed that the Christian veneration for the remains of martyrs reflected ideas about death that had existed neither in paganism nor in Judaism. He writes:

> How new were these beliefs in the power of martyrs' remains? There was nothing comparable in pagan cult . . .
>
> . . . Mosaic law had declared a grave to be unclean for the living. In Christianity, however, the dead were a primary focus of hope and interest from the beginning . . . There was no uncleanness about tombs or corpses . . . The new Christian attitude towards the dead and their relics marked a break in previous religious life. Before long, church leaders were digging up corpses and breaking them into fragments, a type of grave robbery which pagans had never countenanced. The Christians' concern for bits of the dead continued to disgust non-Christian cultures: in 1601, when the first Jesuit missionary tried to make contact with the Emperor of China, the Emperor's minister of ceremonies warned against the bones that would be brought into the palace, 'inauspicious pieces of refuse'.[84]

Of course, it would not do to draw this contrast too starkly: relic worship was not without its adherents in China. Han Yu (768–824) had raised the same arguments about the polluting nature of relics centuries before the arrival of the Jesuits in order to try to suppress the enthusiastic worship of the putative remains of the Buddha.[85] Still, the Christian evidence shows that new religious ideas might very well be reflected in mortuary practice and the conception of death. Life and death might be juxtaposed in novel ways, making the bones of the dead sources of purifying spiritual power rather than frightening contagion. The perpetuation of the exorcistic paradigm of mortuary ritual by the makers of the grave-securing writs is by no means insignificant for an understanding of religious change in medieval China. The impact of bureaucratisation – and the concomitant textualisation – may have been more in the arena of the restriction of access to channels of supernatural power, and may have had less to do with the kind of power that was exercised.

Notes

1 The portion of the writ that relates to the name-records of the deceased and the possibility of overlapping dates is discussed by Anna Seidel ('Traces of Han Religion in Funeral Texts Found in Tombs', in Akizuki Kan'ei (ed.), *Dōkyō to shūkyō bunka* (Tokyo: Hirakawa shuppansha, 1987), pp. 21–57, pp. 32–3). I follow several of her suggestions for emendation and interpretation, e.g. reading *chou*, to calculate, for *deng*; reading *ji*, records, for *jie*; and taking *ming* as *jiming*, cockcrow, hence *shi*, time. However, I punctuate differently; rather than following Ikeda's *chou ru ming ji, huo tong sui yue, chong fu gou jiao ri si* (Seidel: 'Compute your registers of names, whether year and month concord [with the actual hour of death (Seidel's interpolation)], check, compare and recheck [*ch'ung fu*] the day of death!'), I prefer to punctuate *chou ru ming ji, huo tong sui yue*

PETER NICKERSON

chong fu, gou jiao ri si, which allows one consistently to interpret the phrase *chong fu* as denoting the 'overlapping' of registers, in this and other Han tomb ordinances (e.g. Ikeda On, 'Chūgoku rekidai boken ryakkō', *Tōyō bunka kenkyūjo kiyō*, 86 (1981), 193–278, pp. 223–4, contract no. 21; p. 271, jar no. 3). For other interpretations of some of these terms, see Liu Zhaorui, '*Taiping jing* yu kaogu faxian de Han zhenmuwen', *Shijie zongjiao yanjiu*, 4 (1992), 111–19.

2 *Chi chi*. Cf. *Dai kanwa jiten* (henceforth 'M') 17141, where *chi* is defined as 'to dispense, give in charity, benefit' – hence 'to give of oneself', 'devoted'?

3 Concerning various guardian spirits of roads and paths and their role in proto-Daoist and Daoist tomb documents, see my 'Opening the Way: Exorcism, Travel, and Soteriology in Early Daoist Mortuary Practice and Its Antecedents', in Livia Kohn and Harold D. Roth (eds), *Daoist Identity: History, Lineage, and Ritual* (Honolulu: University of Hawaii Press, 2002).

4 Ikeda, 'Chūgoku rekidai boken ryakkō', pp. 270–1, no. 2.

5 Prevailing notions of death allowed for the revival of the 'dead' even after much time had passed following the initial loss of consciousness – hence the many 'return from death' narratives of medieval literature (see below), and hence also the nagging fear that even an encoffined or an interred corpse might yet return to life. See, for example, the story of Yan Ji recorded in *Jinshu* (Beijing: Zhonghua shuju, 1974), 88:2285–6.

6 In addition to the writs proper, on the same grave-securing bottles are also inscribed diagrams of the Northern Dipper and texts claiming control over the odium of demons of those who died early or violent deaths (Monika Drexler, 'On Talismans of the Later Han Dynasty', Paper presented at the Second International Academic Conference on Daoist Culture, Huanglong gong, Lefu Mountains, Guangdong, China, 27–31 December 1998, p. 8).

7 'On the Alchemy of T'ao Hung-ching', in Holmes Welch and Anna Seidel (eds), *Facets of Taoism: Essays in Chinese Religion* (New Haven, CT: Yale University Press, 1979), pp. 123–92, pp. 165–6.

8 Anna Seidel, 'Chronicle of Taoist Studies in the West, 1950–1990', *Cahiers d'Extrême-Asie*, 5 (1989–90), 223–347, p. 237.

9 See Joseph Needham's discussion of the 'ethical polarisation': the determination that good and evil people should have different destinations in the afterlife (*Science and Civilisation in China. Vol. 5, Chemistry and Chemical Technology. Part 2, Spagyrical Discovery and Invention: Magisteries of Gold and Immortality* (Cambridge: Cambridge University Press, 1974), pp. 77–113). This notion, Needham holds, was introduced to China only along with Buddhism, a position with which Strickmann, believing that Daoism developed similar attitudes independently, has taken exception ('Alchemy of T'ao Hung-ching', pp. 178–85).

10 *Zuozhuan* (Shisan jing zhushu edn, Taipei, 1985), vol. 2, 2:15b–20b (6:35A–37B), Yin 1; cf. James Legge (trans.), *The Ch'un Ts'ew, with the Tso Chuen*, Chinese Classics vol. 5 (reprint, Hong Kong: Hong Kong University Press, 1960), pp. 5–6, (hereafter cited as Legge, *Tso chuan*).

11 Needham, *Science and Civilisation in China*, vol. 5, part 2, p. 88.

12 David Keightley, 'Dead but not Gone: The Role of Mortuary Practices in the Formation of Neolithic and Early Bronze Age Chinese Culture, *c.*8000 to 1000 BC', Paper prepared for the Conference on Ritual and the Social Significance of Death in Chinese Society, Oracle, Arizona, 2–7 January 1985, pp. 12–14; Sarah Allan, *The Shape of the Turtle: Myth, Art, and Cosmos in Early China* (Albany: State University of New York Press, 1991), pp. 64–7, 162.

13 Wu Hung, 'From Temple to Tomb: Ancient Chinese Art and Religion in Transition', *Early China*, 13 (1988), 78–115, pp. 88–90.

34

14 Lothar von Falkenhausen, 'Sources of Taoism: Reflections on Archaeological Indicators of Religious Change in Eastern Zhou China', *Taoist Resources*, 5, 2 (Dec. 1994), 1–12, p. 4.

15 Wu Hung, 'From Temple to Tomb', p. 90.

16 See Burton Watson (trans.), *Hsün-tzu: Basic Writings* (New York: Columbia University Press, 1963), p. 104; *Liji* (Shisan jing zhushu edn), vol. 5, 8:5b7ff, 5:144A, 'Tangong shang'; James Legge (trans.), *Li Chi: Book of Rites* (reprint, New Hyde Park, NY: University Books, 1967), vol. 1, p. 148.

17 von Falkenhausen, 'Sources of Taoism', esp. pp. 4–7. On the summoning of the soul, see below.

18 von Falkenhausen, 'Sources of Taoism', pp. 8–9.

19 Donald Harper, 'Resurrection in Warring States Popular Religion', *Taoist Resources*, 5, 2 (1994), 13–28; Li Xueqin, 'Fangmatan jianzhong de zhiguai gushi', *Wenwu*, 4 (1990), 43–7.

20 Regarding *shijie*, see Ursula-Angelika Cedzich, 'Corpse Deliverance, Substitute Bodies, Name Change, and Feigned Death: Aspects of Metamorphosis and Immortality in Early Medieval China', *Journal of Chinese Religions*, 29 (2001), 1–68; Isabelle Robinet, 'Metamorphosis and Deliverance from the Corpse in Taoism', *History of Religions*, 19 (1979), 37–70; Strickmann, 'Alchemy of T'ao Hung-ching', pp. 182–4, esp. n. 172; Seidel, 'Traces of Han Religion'; Seidel, 'Post-mortem Immortality, or: The Taoist Resurrection of the Body', in S. Shaked, D. Shulman and G. G. Stroumsa (eds), *Gilgul: Essays on Transformation, Revolution and Permanence in the History of Religions dedicated to R. J. Zwi Werblowsky* (Leiden: E. J. Brill, 1987), pp. 223–7.

21 On the Siming, see *Shiji* (Beijing: Zhonghua shuju, 1959), 27:1293–4 and n.; *Fengsu tongyi jiaozhu* (Wang Liqi edn, Beijing: Zhonghua shuju, 1981), 8:65; Eduard Erkes, 'The God of Death in Ancient China', *T'oung Pao*, 35 (1940), 185–210; David Hawkes, *The Songs of the South* (Harmondsworth: Penguin, 1985), pp. 109–12. On Kongsun Qiang, see *Zuozhuan*, 58:11a–12a (6:1011a–b), Ai 7–8; Legge, *Tso chuan*, pp. 814, 816. It should also be pointed out the Kongsun Qiang died prematurely and by violence, a biographical feature common to many officials in the Daoist bureaucracies of the dead that appear later.

22 Harper, 'Resurrection', esp. pp. 16–20.

23 Strong arguments have been made that Chinese religion was in some senses 'bureaucratic' as early as the late Shang (David N. Keightley, 'The Religious Commitment: Shang Theology and the Genesis of Chinese Political Culture', *History of Religions*, 17, 3/4 (1978), 211–25); and the claim has also been made that Shang administration was at least 'proto-bureaucratic' (Herrlee G. Creel, *The Origins of Statecraft in China* (Chicago: University of Chicago Press, 1970), vol. 1, p. 34). Nonetheless, in the same way as one can speak of Chinese governance becoming markedly more bureaucratised under the centralised, 'de-feudalised' Warring States, Qin and Han regimes, one may say the same for the religious practices that employed many of the same new forms and techniques in the spiritual realm.

24 Cf. David N. Keightley, 'Early Civilization in China: Reflections on How It Became Chinese', in Paul S. Ropp (ed.), *The Heritage of China* (Berkeley: University of California Press, 1990), pp. 15–54.

25 See my 'Taoism, Death, and Bureaucracy', PhD dissertation, Dept of History, University of California, Berkeley, 1996, pp. 105–33; also 'Great Petition for Sepulchral Plaints', in Stephen R. Bokenkamp, with a contribution by Peter Nickerson, *Early Daoist Scriptures* (Berkeley: University of California Press, 1997), pp. 239–43; and 'Opening the Way'.

PETER NICKERSON

26 Legge, *Liji*, vol. 1, p. 177; *Liji*, 9:26a6–9 (5:175B), 'Tangong xia'. Throughout the present study, James Legge's translations of the Classics, when cited, have been adapted, especially in order to preserve consistency of terminology.
27 *Liji*, 9:27b4 (5:176A), 'Tangong xia'.
28 Legge, *Liji*, vol. 1, p. 172; *Liji*, 9:18b4–5 (5:171B), 'Tangong xia'.
29 *Liji*, 9:18b8 (5:171B), 'Tangong xia'.
30 *Jie* – to 'untie', 'undo', 'release', 'gain release from', or 'disperse' – is an exceedingly difficult word to translate in a way that will reflect its full semantic range. *Jie* is, for example, the exact antonym of 'binding' (*jie*), which term was used as the title of a third-century BCE demonology – 'Spellbinding'. While in the Zhou *jie* (binding) had meant 'to obligate oneself to the spirits by means of a written document', by Han times it had come to refer to the interrogation of criminal suspects. *Jie* (binding) is also cognate with *jie*, a 'knot which cannot be untied' (Donald Harper, 'A Chinese Demonography of the Third Century BC', *Harvard Journal of Asiatic Studies*, 45, 2 (1985), 459–98, pp. 471–5, quoting Shirakawa Shizuka and *Shuowen*, respectively). Thus *jie*, to untie, unbind – and, in Han law, to pardon or excuse from punishment (see *Hanshu* (Beijing: Zhonghua shuju, 1962), 51:3355 and 3356 n. 4, where it is glossed as *mian*; also cf. Seidel, 'Traces of Han Religion', p. 45) – is semantically opposed to *jie*, to bind, in both legal and magico-religious practice. *Jie* (to unbind) therefore might often be understood in ritual contexts as 'to undo the spell of', and thereby 'to disperse'.
31 *Lunheng jiaoshi* (Beijing: Zhonghua shuju, 1990), 25:1044, '*Jie chu*'. This passage appears to make no specific mention of tombs. The term "dwelling" (*zhai*), though, had always been applied to both the houses of the living and those of the dead.
32 See 'Taoism, Death, and Bureaucracy', p. 122 and app. 3.
33 *Zuozhuan*, 40:7a–8b (6:682A–B), Xiang, 30; 44:11b10–14b4 (6:763A–64B), Zhao 7.
34 *Fengsu tongyi, yiwen*, 1:88; *Taiping yulan* (Shanghai: Zhonghua shuju, 1960), 552:10a3–4 (3:2501).
35 *Youyang zazu* (Taipei: Taiwan xuesheng shuju, 1975), 13:69–70. *Qi* means to dance drunkenly or wildly (M1101). Cf. the translation of this passage in Jiang Shaoyuan (Kiang Chao-yuan), Fan Ren (trans.), *Le voyage dans la Chine ancienne, considéré principalement sous son aspect magique et religieux* (Shanghai: Commission mixte des oeuvres franco-chinoises, Office de publication, 1937), pp. 92–3.
36 Marcel Granet, *Danses et légendes de la Chine ancienne* (Paris: F. Aloan, 1926), p. 333.
37 The religious and other aspects of the Han grave-securing writs have been relatively extensively studied – most notably by Anna Seidel ('Tokens of Immortality'; 'Geleitbrief an die Unterwelt: Jenseitsvorstellungen in den Graburkunden der Späteren Han Zeit', in Gert Naundorf, Karl-Heinz Pohl and Hans-Hermann Schmidt (eds), *Religion und Philosophie in Ostasien: Festschrift für Hans Steininger zum 65. Geburtstag* (Würzburg: Königshausen + Neumann, 1985), pp. 161–84; 'Traces of Han Religion'; '*Post-mortem* Immortality'), and also by Harada Masami ('Minzoku shiryō to shite no boken', *Philosophia*, 45 (1963), 1–26; 'Bokenbun ni mirareru meikai no kami to sono saishi', *Tōhō shūkyō*, 29 (1967), 17–35); Wu Rongzeng ('Zhenmuwen zhong suo jiandao de Donghan daowu guanxi', *Wenwu*, 3 (1981), 56–63); Terry F. Kleeman ('Land Contracts and Related Documents', in *Makio Ryōkai Hakase shōju kinen ronshū, Chūgoku no shūkyō: shisō to kagaku* (Tokyo: Kokusho kankōkai, 1984), pp. 1–34); Wang Yucheng ('Donghan Dao fu shili', *Kaogu xuebao*, 1 (1991), 45–56; 'Luoyang yangguang nian zhushu taoguan kaoshi', *Zhongyuan wenwu*, 1 (1993), 71–6, 81; 'Nanliwang taoshu yu xiangguan zongjiao wenti yanjiu', *Kaogu yu wenwu*, 2 (1996), 61–9); Ursula-Angelika Cedzich ('Ghosts and Demons, Law and Order: Grave Quelling Texts and Early Taoist

36

Liturgy', *Taoist Resources*, 4, 2 (Dec. 1993), 23–35); and Monika Drexler, 'On Talismans'. Here the intent is only to treat those aspects of the topic that bear most directly on our own subject.

38 Seidel, 'Chronicle', p. 237.
39 Ikeda, 'Chūgoku rekidai boken ryakkō', p. 270, no. 1.
40 The next character in the transcription is *xu*. Could this mean 'all' (cf. M10110.5), as in 'all of the above calendrical designations apply together'?
41 On the *Huangshen yuezhang*, see Drexler, 'On Talismans', p. 3; Donald Harper, 'The *Wu Shih Erh Ping Fang*: Translation and Prolegomena', PhD dissertation, Dept of Oriental Languages, University of California, Berkeley, 1982, pp. 473–6; Michel Strickmann, *Chinese Magical Medicine* (ed. Bernard Faure) (Stanford, CA: Stanford University Press, 2002), pp. 141–2 and n.
42 See Seidel, 'Traces of Han Religion', pp. 39–41.
43 Ge Hong, *Baopuzi neipian jiaoshi* (ed. Wang Ming), revised and enlarged edn (Beijing: Zhonghua shuju, 1985), 17:313. The later *Xiaodao lun* also claims that the same was used by Daoists (the 'Sect of the Three Zhang') to kill demons (Drexler, 'On Talismans', p. 3).
44 Seidel ('Traces of Han Religion', p. 53 n. 91) cites Harada ('Meikai no kami', p. 21) on this point, although the relationship between the medicine and the decomposition of the corpse is not completely clear in Harada's account. Other ordinance texts similarly mention the inclusion (either physically or merely textually) of apotropaic and/or preservative substances such as realgar, arsenic and laminar malachite (Drexler, 'On Talismans', p. 6).
45 See Seidel, 'Traces of Han Religion', p. 31 and n. 37. See also Drexler's ('On Talismans', p. 7) suggestive interpretation, in which the nine and the five have astral connotations, referring to the nine stars of the constellation Wei, which pertain to matters of birth, and the five stars of the constellation Gui, which relate to ancestor worship and the dead.
46 *Zhongzhong yuji*; cf. Charles O. Hucker, *A Dictionary of Official Titles in Imperial China* (Stanford, CA: Stanford University Press, 1985), p. 584 (nos 8036–7), which lists the related *Yuji jiangjun* as a prestige title used in Tang and Sung times.
47 Accepting Ikeda's emendation.
48 Reading *zhi* as *te*, following M20057.
49 Cf. Hucker, *A Dictionary of Official Titles*, p. 568 (no. 7732).
50 Seidel amends *sheng*, 'to give birth to', to *zhu*, 'to rule' ('Traces of Han Religion', p. 30). The former reading may still be acceptable, however, in light of the sources that name the Yellow Monarch as the grandfather of the Lord of Mount Tai. See *Bowu zhi*, ch. 6, by Zhang Hua (232–300), which says that Mount Tai is called the Celestial Grandson (*tiansun*), which means the grandson of the Celestial Monarch (quoted in *Soushen ji* (Beijing: Zhonghua shuju, 1979), 4:46 n. 3; cf. Édouard Chavannes, *Le T'ai Chan: essai de monographie d'un culte chinois*, Annales du Musée Guimet, vol. 21 (Paris: Ernest Leroux, 1910), p. 26; Hayashi Minao, *Kandai no kamigami* (Kyoto: Rinsen shoten, 1989), pp. 203–4, n. 14).
51 Reading *lu*, 'registers', following Guo Moruo ('You Wang Xie muzhi de chutu lundao "Lanting xü" de zhenwei', *Wenwu*, 6 (1965), 22) and Seidel ('Traces of Han Religion', p. 30), rather than Ikeda's *lu*, 'emoluments'.
52 Cf. Sarah Allan's speculations (referred to above) regarding the dominion of the Yellow Monarch (Huangdi) over the underworld and the dead.
53 On Shangdang ginseng, or *dangshen*, see G. A. Stuart, *Chinese Materia Medica: vegetable kingdom* (Taipei: Southern Materials Center, 1976 reprint of the 1911 edn printed at the American Presbyterian Mission Press, Shanghai), pp. 16–17.
54 *Lizhi muli* (?). Cf. *muli*, oyster (M19933.37), hence 'shut tightly' or an 'open and shut' case? Also cf. Harada ('Meikai no kami', p. 21), who seems to interpret

PETER NICKERSON

muli simply as a spell (perhaps along the lines of 'abracadabra' and other magical nonsense syllables, or, closer to China, the pseudo-Sanskrit spells used by Daoists and Chinese Buddhists). Or could *muli* be referring to the complete, oyster-like containment of the deceased by the tomb?

55 Ikeda, 'Chūgoku rekidai boken ryakkō', p. 273, no. 6.
56 Harper explains *jiu* as spiritual odium that falls on evildoers. The term is often used in exorcistic contexts, for instance in the phrase *gaojiu*, a 'declaration to helpful spirits to bring their vengeance upon demonic miscreants' (Harper, 'Demonography', pp. 460–1 n. 4, pp. 480–1).
57 Ikeda, 'Chūgoku rekidai boken ryakkō', p. 271, no. 3; see below and Seidel, 'Traces of Han Religion', p. 33 and n. 44. Also cf. the Squad Chief of Haoli in the writ translated above; the groups of five may in some contexts indicate military units of five soldiers.
58 Ikeda, 'Chūgoku rekidai boken ryakkō', p. 271, no. 3.
59 Wu cites a convincing array of contemporaneous and commentary literature supporting the reading of *shi* as *zhe*. The *Shuowen* glosses *zhe* as *fa*, 'to punish' (Wu Rongzeng, p. 57). Cf. the variant for *zhe* used in the Lingbao scriptures, as in the phrase 'criminal *hun*-souls with culpability from past lives' (*suzhe zuihun*; DZ 369, 2b1).
60 Ikeda, 'Chūgoku rekidai boken ryakkō', p. 272, no. 5.
61 Ikeda, 'Chūgoku rekidai boken ryakkō', p. 215–16, no. 7; Seidel, 'Traces of Han Religion', pp. 42–6; cf. Laurence G. Thompson, 'On the Prehistory of Hell in China', *Journal of Chinese Religions*, 17 (1989), 27–41.
62 Ikeda, 'Chūgoku rekidai boken ryakkō',p. 272, no. 5. Cf. the passage from a writ of 166 translated by Drexler ('On Talismans', p. 6): 'the Four Seasons and the Five Phases can . . . remove (noxious influences) [and] may (the descendants get) happiness, wealth, and honours without end' (second interpolation mine).
63 In this writ, both philological problems and possibilities for alternative interpretations abound. For a discussion, see 'Taoism, Death, and Bureaucracy', pp. 156–8 and n. 100.
64 Harada, 'Meikai no kami', p. 8, following Luo Zhenyu; Ikeda, 'Chūgoku rekidai boken ryakkō', pp. 223–4, contract no. 21.
65 *Suiyue chongfu shi* [=*zhe*] – perhaps these are the baneful forces resulting from the alignment of the sexagesimal signs of Liu's fated time of death with the actual date and time. Regarding 'overlapping', cf. n. 1 above.
66 Reading *mufu* as *muqiu*, as suggested by Ikeda.
67 This statement is found in numerous ordinances with Latter Han dates, and thus the reference is figurative rather than actual.
68 *Xu Heshui qing* – perhaps 'this separation will remain in force until the water of the Yellow River runs clear', a Chinese equivalent of hell freezing over? If so, perhaps the next phrase refers to Mount Tai crumbling.
69 The *liuding* refer to the six stem-branch binoms in the sexagesimal cycle whose first component is *ding* (the fourth celestial stem). In occult literature, the Six Ding are personified by goddesses who may be summoned by the adept. See, for example, *Hou Hanshu* (Beijing: Zhonghua shuju, 1982), 50:1676 and n.; *Baopuzi* 15:272–3 and passim.
70 See Xu Shen, *Shuowen jiezi duanzhu*, annotated by Duan Yucai (Chengdu: Chengdu guji shudian, 1981), 9A.461A2–5; *Shanhai jing jianshu* (Chengdu: Bashu shushe, 1985), 2:32b10–33a3; *Liji* 15:15b6–7 (5:305A), 17:21a9 (5:347A), 'Yueling'; Derk Bodde, *Festivals in Classical China* (Princeton, NJ: Princeton University Press, 1975), pp. 84, 102; and Rémi Mathieu, *Étude sur la mythologie et l'ethnologie de la Chine ancienne: traduction annotée du 'Shanhai jing'* (Paris: Collège de France, Institut des hautes études chinoises, 1983), vol. 1, p. 124, n. 2.

71 See Strickmann, *Chinese Magical Medicine*, pp. 76–7. Strickmann apparently accepts the attribution, as does Unschuld, but Bokenkamp considers it 'doubtful'. The supplement to the text written by Tao Hongjing in any case provides a *terminus ad quem* of *c*.500. See Paul U. Unschuld, *Medicine in China: A History of Pharmaceutics* (Berkeley: University of California Press, 1986), p. 149; Stephen R. Bokenkamp, 'Ko Hung', in William H. Nienhauser Jr (ed. and comp.), *The Indiana Companion to Traditional Chinese Literature* (Bloomington: Indiana University Press, 1986), p. 482. For another example of the use of inscriptions in Latter Han mortuary texts to exorcise the demons of corpses, see Drexler, 'On Talismans', p. 5.

72 I further suspect that the ordinance's reference to contemporaneous (*tongshi*) demons is a dim reflection of hemerological and calendarological concerns that are much more clearly articulated elsewhere, particularly in later Daoist demonology. That is, it was often the case that specific demons of disease and death were associated with specific days or times and their cyclical signs, as in the Liu Boping ordinance where the tomb and corpse demons appear to be linked to the day of death of the departed. If this is so, it may explain an inscription on a wooden tablet found in a tomb that has been dated to the late Eastern Han. It reads: 'If there is a death on an *yisi* day, the [responsible] demon's name is Celestial Radiance (Tianguang)' (Zhu Jiang, 'Jiangsu Gaoyu Shaojiaguo Handai yizhi de qingli', *Kaogu*, 10 (1960), pp. 20–1). Cf. Seidel's and Cedzich's interpretations of this text (Seidel, 'Geleitbrief an die Unterwelt', p. 176; Ursula-Angelika Cedzich, 'Das Ritual der Himmelsmeister im Spiegel früherer Quellen: Übersetzung und Untersuchung des liturgischen Materials im dritten *chüan* des *Teng-chen yin-chüeh*', PhD dissertation, Julius-Maximilians-Universität, Würzburg, 1987, pp. 55–6). See also the lists of demons of days in the *Nuqing guilü*, DZ 790, 1:4a–7b.

73 I am much indebted to Dr Monika Drexler, who, following Wu Rongzeng, has made this suggestion to me.

74 Cf. the comments of Claude Lévi-Strauss: 'The only phenomenon with which writing has always been concomitant is the creation of cities and empires, that is the integration of large numbers of individuals into a political system, and their grading into castes or classes. Such, at any rate, is the typical pattern of development to be observed from Egypt to China, at the time when writing first emerged: it seems to have favoured the exploitation of human beings rather than their enlightenment' (*Tristes Tropiques* (New York: Penguin Books, 1984), pp. 298–9).

75 Mark Edward Lewis, *Sanctioned Violence in Early China* (Albany: State University of New York Press, 1990), pp. 67–80, 98–103, 185–205.

76 Jacques Derrida, *Of Grammatology* (Baltimore: Johns Hopkins University Press, 1976), pp. 101–40, esp. p. 109.

77 For other examples, see Drexler, 'On Talismans,' pp. 4–5.

78 K. M. Schipper, 'Vernacular and Classical Ritual in Taoism', *Journal of Asian Studies*, 45, 1 (1985), 21–57.

79 Ikeda, 'Chūgoku rekidai boken ryakkō', p. 270, no. 1; p. 273, nos 6–7.

80 Lewis, *Sanctioned Violence*, chapter 5.

81 *Mencius*, IIIB.9; D. C. Lau (trans.), *Mencius* (Harmondsworth: Penguin Books, 1970), pp. 113–14.

82 Mencius casts the remainder of Chinese history down to his own time from the same mould. When 'the way of the Sages declined' and 'tyrants arose one after another', those tyrants turned houses and fields into hunting parks and ponds, again allowing the incursion of the animalian into the human realm, and again order was restored when the Duke of Zhou 'drove tigers, leopards and rhinoceroses to the distant wilds'. The efforts of the Confucian literati on behalf of orthodoxy were simply the continuation of the struggle on a different plane. Mencius's own

diatribes against Yang Zhu and Mozi were also aimed at separating people from animals, for to deny one's ruler, like Yang Zhu, or one's father, like Mozi, 'is to be no different from the beasts' (*Mencius*, IIIB.9; Lau, pp. 113–14).

83 Cf. Richard Huntington and Peter Metcalf, *Celebrations of Death: The Anthropology of Mortuary Ritual* (Cambridge: Cambridge University Press, 1979), p. 117.
84 Robin Lane Fox, *Pagans and Christians* (New York: Knopf, 1987), pp. 447–8.
85 Kenneth K. S. Ch'en, *Buddhism in China: A Historical Survey* (Princeton, NJ: Princeton University Press, 1964), pp. 225–6.

3

PRELIMINARY CONSIDERATIONS IN THE SEARCH FOR A DAOIST *DHAMMAPADA*

T. H. Barrett

In this age of decline, in which nothing less than the instant gratification of religious appetites is likely to make any headway in an increasingly crowded market place, little books of wisdom are virtually the only sort we have left. Yet within the Buddhist tradition, so compassionately aware of the puny capacity of mankind for spiritual improvement, one little book of wisdom has for centuries offered as an expedient bait just those bite-sized morsels of moral pabulum which are all that a mass market will tolerate. The *Dhammapada*, to use the title under which this anthology of Buddhist verses is best known in the West, was an international success long before the rise of modern publishing, as we may readily see from its four Chinese translations. Indeed, these multiple Chinese versions were themselves discussed and in one case translated by Samuel Beal more than one hundred years ago, resulting in 1902 in a mass market reprint as bijou in its Edwardian way as anything in any New Age bookstore today.[1]

Such bookstores are, of course, repositories of precisely that level of universal wisdom that transcends not only all linguistic, but also all religious barriers. The *Dhammapada* is no exception – and that not simply because some of its verses have been suspected of deriving from pre-Buddhist origins.[2] No doubt the reason for its success throughout Asian and now Western history has had much to do with its ability to address all sorts and conditions of people, from very different cultural and religious backgrounds. It is, indeed, as my title and the context implies, the relations between this little work and Daoism that form the focus of the following remarks. Even so, it is not my purpose at this point to offer any conclusive insights into this possible relationship; instead, the actual topic covered goes no further than the preliminary problems that need to be investigated if we wish to explore that question.

That may sound a rather restricted aim, but more positively, I hope that these remarks may be seen as constituting a case study, an illustration demonstrating the need to take seriously questions of textual transmission if we are to solve some of the outstanding problems in the early history of Daoism, and in particular the need to take seriously questions concerning the transmission not only of Daoist materials themselves, but also of those early materials in the Chinese Buddhist canon that bear upon the history of the relationship between the two religions. As a case study, the focus is admittedly narrow, homing in on the implications of no more than one sentence – and just one further word in particular. This may seem at first sight a classic example of what John Fairbank once denounced as the tradition of 'micro-sinology', establishing facts for facts' sake.[3] Or again, to be positive, it may be taken as an example of Paul Thompson's call to address the dangerously neglected task of rectifying our texts.[4] In fact, all I wish to do is to find some answer to a perfectly quotidian question that every historian must ask of any source: who wrote these words, and when?

Obviously, at one level to speak of a Daoist *Dhammapada* could be understood as a comment on the sinification of the original text by the very process of translation itself, the sort of topic that has worried historians since the time of Arthur Wright, to say nothing of his Japanese predecessors. Such an approach would seem to be required, perhaps, by the very specimen of Chinese selected from the earliest version for reproduction in Beal's introduction in order to show its affinity with the Pāli.[5] For on the opening page of this we are confronted by a term that has already generated a considerable amount of discussion concerning Daoist influence on Buddhism, or perhaps vice versa.[6] That is the term *shouyi*, or 'preserving the one,' although as far as I am aware discussion hitherto has not paid particular attention to this specific source. But I do not propose to linger long over so celebrated a question, despite its interest in view of what I shall go on to argue later. For as it happens the earliest clear occurrence of the term *shouyi* by modern standards of dating is actually in a text that is now very much in the limelight, thanks to its identification as an early classic of Chinese spiritual self-cultivation, namely the *Neiye*.[7] This essay is currently to be found (as it was indeed also at the time of this translation of the *Dhammapada*, which goes back to the middle of the third century CE) preserved as a section in the work known as the *Guanzi*, where one recent translator has rendered the phrase in question 'focus your power of awareness'.[8] In the third century CE, then, the term was already such an old one for mental self-discipline, and so non-sectarian in any way (the *Guanzi*, though earlier listed as a Daoist text, is so self-evidently eclectic that its classification was later changed), that any translator using it would have seen it as simply a term in general use in the Chinese language to refer to mental discipline. Whatever he would have understood by 'Daoist' (which is, of course, another question) it was at this point not – for all the earlier discussion of scholars to which I have already alluded – a Daoist term. Much the same could probably be said of the other translation terms used; it is not, then, in the translation process that I would look for a Daoist *Dhammapada*.

Instead, I propose to consider the much more intriguing question raised by the preface to this first translation as to whether an entire text of the *Dhammapada* was at one time taken over and, perhaps after some refashioning, propagated by a native Chinese religious movement that modern scholars have long associated with the emergence of Daoism as currently understood. This would not itself be an unprecedented discovery. It has been known for some time, for example, that the *Sūtra in Forty-two Sections*, which in the view of the great Chinese Indologist Ji Xianlin is in fact an anthology very like the *Dhammapada*, was taken into the late fourth-century CE Daoist textual tradition known to us as the Shangqing revelations.[9] But the preface to which I allude was written over one hundred years earlier than that, since it is by common agreement more or less contemporary with the earliest surviving translation of the *Dhammapada* itself, having clearly been written by an associate of the original translators.

By 'common agreement' I refer to a veritable host of scholars – for example, just among Europeans, Sylvain Lévi, Erik Zürcher, Charles Willemen and, most recently, Antonino Forte – all of whom, following the lead of Tang Yongtong, have taken the preface to be a genuine and valuable witness to the early history of Chinese Buddhism, probably from the brush of the pioneer translator Zhi Qian.[10] For that matter, Willemen has translated the entire document into English, so it is hardly an obscure source either.[11] If its apparently sensational significance for Daoist studies has been almost completely missed hitherto, however, this may be because previous renderings of the key passage, produced in the context of Buddhist studies, have not paid sufficient attention to its precise overtones for historians of Daoism. The result has been that although it was taken up among scholars of Daoism some time ago by Stephen Bokenkamp, who ingeniously pointed out a number of significant links between the circle of translators whence the text emanated and the Lingbao scriptures over one and a half centuries later, he was obliged to report that 'it would strain credulity to try to reconstruct the full story from these bits of evidence'.[12]

Our contention is that credulity need not be strained. Once the key sentence is correctly understood in the light of one other important contextual clue, the information gathered by Professor Bokenkamp (and earlier, but much less profitably, by Fukui Kōjun), concerning references to Buddhist translators from within Daoist works, makes perfect sense. Rather than repeat this information, however, the object of the present exercise is to show how sources external to the Daoist tradition may be brought to bear to confirm the workings of that tradition itself, a method of research that has in the past been outstandingly pioneered by Professor Liu Ts'un-yan.

Here, however, we seek to apply the method in miniature, concentrating our attention, as I have said, on a single sentence, and eventually adducing also, in order to maximise its value, one single additional word. The passage in question occurs in the midst of the document's opening discussion of the meaning of *Dhammapada*, Chinese *faju*, explaining the latter element as equivalent to gāthās (i.e. verses) – and evidently prompting the thought that numbers of verses could be used as a criterion to distinguish different recensions. Willemen, for example, translates it as 'in recent times, Mr Ko has transmitted 700 gāthās', which is in itself a perfectly legitimate rendering.[13] But the context has naturally made scholars of Buddhism think of an individual translator, a 'Master Ko' in Zürcher's rendering, whereas the original phrase, in pinyin transcription *Geshi*, simply means 'a member, or members, of the Ge family', and the transmission involved, though implying in general terms some form of interpersonal transaction over space or time, need not be tied to translation at all.

Since the writing of the translation and the preface are located unambiguously in South China, the mention of a Ge family, and especially a Ge family involved in religion, can surely, as Professor Bokenkamp has already recognised, point to one particular line only: that most famously represented in the fourth century CE by Ge Hong (283–343), author of the great compendium of Daoist (and other southern) lore, the *Baopuzi*, but earlier by his great-uncle Ge Xuan, and later (among others) by a contemporary and alleged emulator of the Shangqing revelations, Ge Chaofu.[14] We know that Ge Hong was aware of Buddhism as a religious practice, since he mentions it, and some have suspected that he was to a certain extent familiar with its literature.[15] But could it be that Ge Xuan or, as Bokenkamp suggests, some other forebear of Hong's at this much earlier point already possessed and indeed circulated a *Dhammapada*?

The possibility cannot be entirely ruled out, but there are some indications to the contrary that, however slight, need to be taken seriously. First, the phrase translated as 'recent times' (*jinshi*, 'in a recent generation') by Willemen seems quite out of context for a sentence simply following on the introduction of the 'verse' as a unit of measurement. It may be that the entire sentence is out of place, and should be moved later to follow the writer's discussion of an earlier attempt at translation in the late second century CE, now lost. Even so, and though between the late second century and the mid-third dramatic changes had taken place (such as the disappearance of the Han dynasty), to speak as if the two were separate ages seems slightly overblown. The suspicion begins to form that this sentence is in fact a later editorial gloss that has crept into the text.

This suspicion is further strengthened by a comparison of the two surviving versions of the preface, for the version translated by Willemen, curiously sandwiched between different parts of the text rather than prefixed to the front, may also be compared with one preserved by the great sixth-century Buddhist bibliographer Sengyou in his invaluable compilation of c.518, the *Chu sanzang jiji*.[16] Once the purely textual errors in our printed editions have been accounted for, the two versions, though both including the sentence in question in identical form, do not emerge as absolutely 100 per cent the same, as we shall see, suggesting possible different editorial recensions. This would not be surprising: we know that Sengyou, though a southerner, based a great deal of his work on earlier researches by the pioneering northern Buddhist leader Daoan (312–385), and it may be, for example, that the version of the preface preserved with the main text represents one that had already undergone editorial intervention prior to the work done by Sengyou in compiling the *Chu sanzang jiji*. Or such indeed is one among the possibilities to which we shall in due course return.

Before we consider the evidence for this in greater detail, however, it is worth asking what overtones our gloss would have if it actually derived from a much later Buddhist hand, of the late fourth century or perhaps of some time in the fifth. For particularly in the latter case the situation would have been entirely different from that confronting Zhi Qian in the mid-third century. Daoism in the intervening period had grown doctrinally and organisationally, so that it could be portrayed as an alternative to the dharma of the Buddha; indeed, by the middle of the fifth century it could inspire in North China a persecution of Buddhism in an attempt at supplanting the foreign religion altogether.[17]

Reference to the 'Ge family' would then carry nuances of hostility, characterising a rival as no more than representative of some special interest, and reducing 'issues' to 'personalities,' just as our own politicians are wont to do today. Indeed, this is a ploy that Chinese Buddhist writers have evidently not forgotten. I notice, for example, that the movement known to us as the Taiping Rebellion (or, if we wish, 'Revolutionary Movement') is described by one of our Chinese Buddhist contemporaries as 'the troubles of Hong and Yang', thus fixing the spotlight firmly on the main leaders at the expense of any larger social or religious issues.[18] But talk of the Ge family as a whole may prompt thoughts of another basically Buddhist-dominated field of historiography outside China. Those familiar with Japanese writing on Daoism may at this point recall having seen the phrase 'Way of the Ge Family' (*Geshi dao*) in that literature, and the term is in a sense germane to the point I am making, though it demands a further word of explanation in itself.

The expression 'Way of the Ge Family' would at first sight appear to be analogous to other similar appelations found in our Six Dynasties sources, such as the 'Way of the Li Family' (*Lijia dao*), which certainly is mentioned in the *Baopuzi*.[19] But, as both the originator of the phrase in Japan, Fukui Kōjun, and its latest proponent, Kobayashi Masayoshi, make explicitly clear, it is simply a contemporary coinage they have introduced for the sake of convenience – in the former case, in order to discuss the transmission of the *Shenxian zhuan*, and in the latter, in order to distinguish the work of Ge Chaofu from the creation of the bulk of what we now call the Lingbao revelations.[20] But Fukui, though he misses the particular gloss we are considering, does adduce pejorative Buddhist references to the Ges as religious leaders, which he feels justifies the coinage, though most of them are even later than the time of Sengyou.[21] There is, however, at least one case in the fifth century where Daoists are lumped together as 'followers of the Zhangs and the Ges', the Zhangs in this case being presumably the three generations of the Celestial Masters. The dates of the author of this gibe, Ming Sengshao, are not fully known, but he died in 483.[22]

Unfortunately the only clue we have to the date of our gloss is to be found in the editorial discrepancy that I have already mentioned, and that raises a problematic point in more ways than one. For, as Zürcher already pointed out, the text independent of Sengyou 'shows traces of fourth or fifth century redaction', since it writes at one point of the translator 'turning Sanskrit (*fan*) into [the language of] Qin', whereas Sengyou's text preserves or restores what must have been the original reading 'turning the foreign (*hu*) into [the language of] Han', a usage that in its terminology for Chinese at least seems consistent with the rest of the text, in both versions.[23]

Now this raises the whole question of using dynastic names as extended to cover the denizens of China and their language for the dating of texts. The issue is not a simple one, and I am uncomfortably aware that in touching on it in the past I have deliberately followed the expedient path of oversimplification rather than engage in a full discussion of the possibilities raised by such usages, mainly for fear of introducing an extended digression into a narrative directed towards other matters. Here, however, eliciting the greatest possible amount of information out of the most minimal clues is essential to any search for the lost Daoist *Dhammapada*, so it is more appropriate to reconsider the matter with regard both to this text and to other Daoist sources that have proved problematic in terms of dating.

Specifically, after having written in the past that 'there is no possible explanation' for the Daoist text known as the *Commands and Admonitions for the Families of the Great Dao* using the term 'people of Qin' for the Chinese at the date of its alleged composition, I should expand this flat statement.[24] There is a possible explanation (other than that it is a historical reference, which does not seem to me to be the case) and a possible context perhaps appreciably more likely for a Daoist source than for a Buddhist text. But (if I may be permitted to introduce the matter at this point by simply stating my conclusions) in the final analysis this alternative explanation does not verify the date claimed, and though it does not strictly speaking falsify it either, it points once again in my own view to the relative plausibility of a later, alternative time of composition. Since, however, in terms of the dating of our gloss on the *Dhammapada* of the Ge family these considerations concern only a minor possibility, I defer discussion of them until after an assessment of the normal and more general usage to be found in Chinese Buddhist texts.

Phrases signifying 'the Chinese language' may, of course, be found scattered throughout glosses all through the translated literature of Buddhism, and a full survey would take account of the totality of these materials. The reliability of the resulting findings, furthermore, would inevitably depend on a sound grasp of the editorial processes that all those texts had undergone prior to being fixed in print, or perhaps in standard manuscript editions at a slightly earlier stage. One attempt at a full survey of all detectable early glosses, spread over a four-part article, has in fact already been carried out by a Japanese researcher named Suzuki Hiromi. This, however, confines itself only to all surviving 'half-size' interlineated notes, while admitting from the start that other glosses, perhaps equally numerous, also exist that have been 'written into' the text as a result of not having been kept separate by means of differentiation by size.[25]

Even so, the results are worth describing briefly. When a corpus of reliably dated translations is used, the vast majority of such interlineated notes turn out to antedate the change in translation style that took place in the first decade of the fifth century due to the activities of the great translator Kumārajīva; the terminology of the glosses (surveyed in the second article) confirms this dating. This raises the possibility that all such early glosses were added at one time, since, as already mentioned, we know that Daoan was involved in drawing up a definitive Buddhist canon at least by means of a definitive catalogue in the preceding generation; Suzuki duly raises the hypothesis that this material all derives from him in the first article.

The third article, however, presents a union list, spanning a larger database than used in the first two, combining all mentions of the language 'Chinese' in dynastic terms within such interlineated glosses. There are nineteen mentions of the Jin, six of the Han and seven of the Qin; the rest (seven cases in all) name various later dynasties. Most are consistent with the known dates of translations. Two anomalous cases are dealt with in the final article, in one instance by adducing evidence that a text containing a gloss mentioning the Han may well be of that date, rather than a product of the Jin translator to whom it is ascribed; similar doubts (not so well documented) are also raised with regard to a reverse case, where a supposedly Han text mentions the Jin in a gloss. But it will be obvious that since the way in which material has been identified is only partial, the results obtained in this survey are not entirely secure, even if the hypotheses raised are worth bearing in mind.

For present purposes, then, since it is precisely traces of editorial intervention that we are trying to track down, it would seem safest to confine a preliminary survey to a more narrowly defined corpus of evidence that has so far been found quite reliable by scholars, and that probably represents as good a collection of early Buddhist materials as we are likely to get, namely the very collection by Sengyou that we have made reference to already. One of the prime attractions of this compilation, moreover, is that the documentary section of the work possesses the particular advantage of having been thoroughly concordanced, thus making it possible to make definitive statements at least within the limits of the materials represented.[26]

The results are most intriguing. First, it must be said that 'Chinese' for Buddhist translators at this point is usually contrasted with 'Hu', which I have translated above as 'foreign', since it is a rather vague term, despite its strong association with Central Asians. But there would seem to be an undeniable tendency in Chinese printings of the canon to replace this term in the text with 'Sanskrit' (*fan*), something more redolent of genuine Indian origins. This is one problem in the systematic editing of the whole canon that has clearly affected Sengyou's compilation in its printed transmission, and since the process of substitution may have begun before the era of printing, it is therefore not safe to attempt any definitive statement as to what may have constituted, at any one point in the early evolution of Buddhist terminology, the opposite of 'Chinese'.[27] I am therefore obliged within the confines of this study to leave the matter aside entirely, save to say that accusations of systematic later editing have been laid against both the Daoist canon and the original (i.e. South Asian) Buddhist canon, and that while we yet lack the means to cope with accusations of such enormity, it would be a mistake to suppose that they are merely the province of conspiracy theorists.[28] But the terms equivalent to 'Chinese', by contrast, show such a range of variation (with no textual emendations in printed copies) as to reassure us that they were not tampered with; instead, they seem to represent the very stuff of contemporary terminology.

Within Sengyou's materials, only three basic terms are used in compounds with words for speech, writing and so forth: Han, Jin and Qin. No lesser dynasties – in these materials, not even Wu – appear to lend their names to the language spoken within their borders. Of these three 'Han' seems to be chronologically the most widely used term, since it occurs both in the preface we have been studying and in the writings of Sengyou himself.[29] In the fourth and fifth centuries it is used in the South by Daoci (albeit with reference to translators in Luoyang) and in the North, under the Later Qin dynasty, by Zhu Fonian.[30] It is used by the bibliographer Daoan, but in a more scholarly fashion with reference only to translations carried out under the Han dynasty, though at one point he does slip up and use the term 'Jin' in relation to this period; this of course could explain the anomaly noticed in Suzuki's survey.[31] Otherwise he uses 'Jin' scrupulously when on Jin territory and 'Qin' when on (Former) Qin territory during the course of his eventful career.[32] His fellow-monks seem always to abide by this principle, if they are not using the looser term 'Han'. Even as far away as Dunhuang, Chinese is indicated by reference to the Jin while they are the ruling power; when that changes, the term changes.[33]

There is, however, one interesting exception. In 421, under the non-Chinese Juqu rulers of the state of Northern Liang, the monk Daolang uses the term 'Qin' with reference to the Chinese language.[34] Some vestigial remnants of the Former Qin empire under which Daoan had spent his later days still existed and claimed the name at this point, but it seems unlikely that Daolang was making any sort of political point about residual loyalties in his terminology. Instead, if he is not just using an earlier term out of habit, it might be best here to see 'Qin' as a particular term of the north-west, describing China and the Chinese people and language especially from the viewpoint of the frontier's non-Chinese inhabitants. Long ago Paul Pelliot identified this usage among the Xiongnu of the first century BCE, and we should recall that the Juqu were of Xiongnu stock.[35] Recently, I have been urged in conversation by Terry Kleeman of the University of Colorado to consider this the most likely explanation of the reference to 'people of Qin' in the *Commands and Admonitions for the Families of the Great Dao*. This does indeed seem a possibility, provided that we are prepared to place the composition of the text in an ethnically mixed north-western environment.

This does not do much to delimit the date in that case or any other, since, as we have suggested, it seems that this usage was quite a durable one. And in order to place it potentially in the fifth century, we are not dependent on Daolang alone, but may also refer to materials of Daoist origin. Dunhuang manuscripts of the *Laozi huahu jing* – the *Scripture on Laozi's Conversion of the Barbarians* – show that the tenth fascicle (recovered as P2004) at one time consisted of a small corpus of poetry, entitled *Laozi huahu jing: xuan ge*.[36] These 'Mysterious Songs', then, to improvise a translation of the chapter title, at one time formed part of a celebrated polemical work that was traditionally, like the *Commands and Admonitions*, ascribed to the mid-third century. Modern scholarship has, however, fixed this poetic section at any rate firmly in the middle of the fifth, since, for example, they unambiguously put a major persecution of Buddhism in the recent past.[37] They are of interest for a number of reasons. For example, their early reference to the incarnated lives of Laozi as *bian* encourages me in the belief that the same term used with regard to the Dunhuang literature that we now call *bianwen* originally meant 'a birth story' or *jātaka*, before coming to mean just 'a story'.[38] They confirm too what outside observers of Northern Wei Daoism of the fifth century also hint: that despite his domination of our court-centred sources, the reformist hierarch Kou Qianzhi was not the beginning and the end of the northern Daoism of that era.[39] Most conveniently, moreover, the 'Mysterious Songs' are all completely concordanced by Matsūra Takeshi as part of his series covering the entire corpus of poetry before the Sui, as recompiled by Lu Qinli.[40] And though these verses would seem in some regards to envisage a Daoism more developed than that of the *Commands and Admonitions* (explicable as the result of the intervening efforts towards innovation of Kou Qianzhi), a number of echoes of that work would seem to be present.[41]

In particular, the songs speak several times of China as 'Qin', or 'Qin of the East', *dong Qin* (perhaps thus in contradistinction to the recently perished Western Qin state, last claimant of the name?), and never as the Central Kingdom, though there are one or two references also to 'Han' people.[42] Once again, the terms are embedded in a historical narrative, but once again seem to my eye anachronistic, unconnected with the historical Qin dynasty. The sense of separation from the Hu peoples is also particularly strong, as one would expect in a work on the polemical theme of Laozi's journey west to India to convert the barbarians through the inferior medium of Buddhism. This brings us back, however, to one of the most vexing puzzles in the *Commands and Admonitions*, namely its earlier version of the same story. That the roots of the tale are very ancient is quite clear, and Ōfuchi Ninji has most ingeniously shown early traces of it well before the supposed date of the *Commands and Admonitions*.[43] But such ancient versions seem to have been entirely eirenic, not depicting the mass subordination of the Buddhists, 'knocking their heads millions of times', to quote the text of the *Commands and Admonitions* in Stephen Bokenkamp's excellent translation.[44] While Gustav Haloun showed some time ago that interethnic tensions in the area were no novelty of the fourth century and its dramatic fall in Chinese fortunes in the area, the sensibilities on display here would seem to point to an era of very clear division between Hu and Qin peoples, such as was created by the deliberately conservative cultural policies of the early Northern Wei.[45] The Celestial Masters of the mid-third century, after all, were by contrast renowned for their multi-ethnic appeal.[46] Admittedly, there is some counter-evidence in the shape of sources indicating that the first anti-Buddhist propaganda on the theme of the 'Conversion of the Barbarians' was composed by a priest of the Celestial Masters in Chang'an soon after 300 CE, according to Zürcher's dating, but even this is half a century after the supposed date of the *Commands and Admonitions*, and our sources represent it as due to personal pique on the part of the priest, Wang Fou, rather than ethnic hatred.[47]

Although it would be possible to prolong discussion of the links between the *Commands and Admonitions* and the 'Mysterious Songs', such as their shared concepts of *zhongmin*, or 'seed people' of the new millennial world, which seems fourth century rather than third century in origin, we should return to the main point at issue.[48] Here it is after all only possible to give incidental comments on other texts, but as far as concerns the 700 verse *Dhammapada* transmitted by the Ge family, we have effectively covered all the non-Daoist evidence that appears to be to hand, and it is time to draw together our findings.

The gloss informing us of this possible Daoist *Dhammapada* could have been written anywhere, but at least we can be sure that it was written by someone aware of religion in south China, and so most probably someone located (albeit not necessarily permanently) in the South. The glossator, to judge from his or her reference to 'recent times', can only have lived considerably later than the late second century CE, say about the start of the fourth century CE, at the earliest. We can be quite sure, too, that the gloss was written before the time of Sengyou – since he does not mark off the sentence as his own – and also at or before the time of someone capable of accidentally referring to Chinese as 'Qin'. If that someone lived in the north-west, thought in ethnic terms and added the gloss himself or herself, then it could be as late as the late fifth century, about the time we find the Ge family the object of Buddhist slurs anyhow.[49] But if the gloss and scribal error reflect, as is more probable, the work of a cleric living under a dynasty named Qin (Former, Later, Western or whatever), that brings the latest possible date back to the start of the fifth century. This, then, in sum makes it probable that the Ge family transmitted (most likely from senior to junior, though this we do not know) a version of the *Dhammapada* during the fourth century CE.

It remains to be explained how it happened that Sengyou later came into possession of the version of the preface containing this gloss. There is, on reflection, one hypothesis that accounts for all the evidence we have discussed, and that does not, I am inclined to think, 'strain credulity'. First, the *Dhammapada* and its preface are collected by Daoan while he is making his ground-breaking bibliography of Buddhist texts in the South (Jin); he adds the gloss at some point before its completion in 374.[50] Next, he copies it out as part of continued bibliographic and translation enterprises in the North (Former Qin), accidentally slipping in an anachronism – as we now know he was capable of doing. When the *Dhammapada* is later incorporated into early manuscript versions of the translated canon in North China, which are probably ancestral to the printed editions, they include the preface on the basis of his copy.[51] Sengyou either works from a copy of Daoan's bibliographical materials left in the South, or (less probably) takes over his scholarly *nachlass* in a later form, but silently corrects his mistake.

On this hypothesis, then, we can place the use by the Ge family of a *Dhammapada* very precisely in the years immediately prior to 374. But there is, of course, one rather basic objection to all of the foregoing, from start to finish, namely that so far no one working on the Lingbao legacy has come across any trace of echoes, fragments or quotations of any Daoist *Dhammapada* at all. One elegant solution to such doubts would be to take up the hint offered by Ji Xianlin, and to regard the *Sūtra in Forty-two Sections* as the Daoist *Dhammapada*. This would have the added benefit of answering the difficult question raised by Wang Weicheng over sixty years ago as to why Daoan never mentions this famous sutra, despite having clearly had ample opportunity to find and catalogue it: he knew it, but he saw it as a non-Buddhist confection.[52] I believe that such a slicing of this notorious Gordian knot of early Chinese Buddhist studies could indeed account for the recurrence of names such as Zhu Falan in different texts examined by Bokenkamp and by Wang, but not for the specific count in our problem sentence of 700 gāthās. The *Sūtra in Forty-two Sections* is not a verse text, and it would seem unnatural to measure it in such terms – even if Buddhist texts are sometimes counted in notional 'lines' – and to rate it at such a length, when it is already divided into enumerated sections. Though such a bold solution has its attractions, I cannot bring myself to put my faith in it.[53]

The only other counter-argument that I can offer is that if by contrast the Ge family work is indeed still present in whole or in part in the Lingbao corpus, it may not be possible to detect verbal parallels of the sort that leap to the eye from the page or, for the less erudite among us like myself, leap from the concordance or index. The search can only be conducted at the level of ideas, thus requiring the prior absorption into the memory of the contents of the *Dhammapada*. But, as I pointed out at the start, that should require no extraordinary effort, and may even confer some karmic merit. Finding a Daoist *Dhammapada* may prove difficult; as a preliminary consideration finding a handy translation of the *Dhammapada* should be easy. As for the little matter of establishing the complete textual histories of the entire Daoist and Buddhist canons, the actual covert aim of the foregoing remarks, my brief study of one sentence and one word has persuaded me that this is a topic that we would do well to be aware of, even if it may be some time before we see significant research results in this field.[54]

Notes

1 Samuel Beal, *Texts from the Buddhist Canon, Commonly Known as the Dhammapada, with Accompanying Narratives* (London: Trübner and Co., 1902). The first edition, which was a more respectable octavo size, was put out by the same publishers in 1878.
2 See p. 193 of K. R. Norman, 'Dhammapada 97: a misunderstood paradox', in K. R. Norman, *Collected Papers* (Oxford: The Pali Text Society, 1991), vol. 2, pp. 187–93; originally in *Indologica Taurinensia*, 7 (1979), 325–31.
3 John K. Fairbank, *China Perceived* (New York: Vintage Books, 1974), p. 213.
4 P. M. Thompson, *The Shen Tzu Fragments* (Oxford: Oxford University Press, 1979), p. xvii.
5 Beal, *Dhammapada* (1902), pp. 17–20, which is followed by the same section as translated from Pāli by Max Müller.
6 The fullest study of the term in question in English is by Bernard Faure, and occupies pp. 112–14 of his essay 'The Concept of One-Practice Samādhi in Early Ch'an', in Peter N. Gregory (ed.), *Traditions of Meditation in Chinese Buddhism* (Honolulu: University of Hawaii Press, 1986), 99–128. Among the earlier studies drawn on by Faure, the most detailed is Yoshioka Yoshitoyo, *Dōkyō to Bukkyō* (Tokyo: Kokusho kankōkai, 1976), vol. 3, pp. 285–351.
7 The significance of this work is perhaps best brought out on pp. 240–3 of William H. Baxter, 'Situating the Date of the Lao-tzu: The Probable Date of the *Tao-te-ching*', in Livia Kohn and Michael LaFargue (eds), *Lao-tzu and the Tao-te-ching* (Albany: State University of New York Press, 1998), pp. 231–53.
8 W. Allen Rickett, *Guanzi: Political, Economic and Philosophical Essays from Early China* (Princeton, NJ: Princeton University Press, 1998), vol. 2, p. 54. Note also Harold D. Roth, *Original Tao* (New York: Columbia University Press, 1999), p. 92, and also pp. 115–16, 146–50.
9 The most detailed study of this text in relation to Daoism is once again in Yoshioka, *Dōkyō to Bukkyō*, vol. 3, pp. 3–38, though once again I would not endorse his conclusions unreservedly. Ji Xianlin, on pp. 25–6 of 'Zai tan futu yu fo', *Zhonghua foxue xuebao*, 5 (1992), 19–30, argues that the text was a *Dhammapada* equivalent put together in the Kushan empire. I am grateful to Professor Aramaki Noritoshi of Kyoto University for bringing to my attention the yet more radical possibility (which I am inclined to accept) that the text is a cento of early Chinese Buddhist translations put together in southern occultist (i.e. 'Daoist') circles.
10 Sylvain Lévi, 'L'Apramāda-varga. Etude sur les recensions des Dharmapadas', *Journal Asiatique*, 20 (Sept.–Oct. 1912), 203–94 (this I have not had occasion to consult); Erik Zürcher, *The Buddhist Conquest of China* (Leiden: E. J. Brill, 1959), pp. 47–8 and notes; Antonino Forte, *The Hostage An Shigao and His Offspring* (Kyoto: ISEAS, 1995), p. 78, n. 38; and see next note.
11 Charles Willemen, 'The Prefaces to the Chinese Dharmapadas *Fa-chü ching* and *Ch'u-yao ching*', *T'oung pao*, 59 (1973), 203–19.
12 See pp. 466–7 of Stephen R. Bokenkamp, 'Sources of the Ling-pao Scriptures', in M. Strickmann (ed.), *Tantric and Taoist Studies in Honour of R. A Stein* (Mélanges Chinois et Bouddhiques, XXI; Brussels: Institut Belge des Hautes Études Chinoises, 1983), pp. 434–86.
13 Willemen, 'Prefaces', p. 211, and n. 37. His translation is based on the text in the *Faju jing* (that is, the earliest *Dhammapada*) itself, T. no. 210, p. 566 in Taishō Canon, vol. 4.
14 Bokenkamp, 'Sources', provides *passim* plenty of information on various members of the family, incorporating the very useful genealogical information in the

Zhen'gao. Others have generally tended to focus only on Ge Hong himself: cf. Jay Sailey, *The Master who Embraces Simplicity* (San Francisco: Chinese Materials Center, 1978), pp. 242–72 (autobiography), 277–304 (biography).

15 Sailey, *The Master who Embraces Simplicity*, p. 143; Honda Wataru, *Hōbokushi* (*Chūgoku koten bungaku taikei*, vol. 8, Tokyo: Heibonsha, 1969), p. 71, n. 10; p. 243.

16 T.2145. The value of this source is amply demonstrated by Zürcher's work, among others.

17 Richard Mather, 'K'ou Ch'ien-chih and the Taoist Theocracy at the Northern Wei Court, 425–45', in Holmes Welch and Anna Seidel (eds), *Facets of Taoism* (New Haven, CT: Yale University Press, 1979), pp. 103–22.

18 Shi Dongchu, *Zhongguo fojiao jindaishi* (Taibei: Zhongguo Fojiao wenhua guan, 1974), p. 64.

19 And which has attracted the most attention from Japanese scholarship itself: see the entry in Noguchi Tetsurō, Sakade Yoshinobu, Fukui Fumimasa and Yamada Toshiaki (eds), *Dōkyō jiten* (Tokyo: Hirakawa shuppansha, 1994), p. 590, for references.

20 Fukui Kōjun, 'Kashidō no kenkyū', *Tōyō shisō kenkyū*, 5 (1953), 45–86, and 'Kashidō to Bukkyō', *Indogaku Bukkyōgaku kenkyū*, 4 (1953), 51–3; Kobayashi Masayoshi, *Rikuchō Dōkyōshi no kenkyū* (Tokyo: Sōbunsha, 1990), p. 13.

21 Fukui, 'Kashidō no kenkyū', p. 45; 'Kashidō to Bukkyō', p. 51.

22 Ming Sengshao, 'Zheng Erjiao lun', in Sengyou (comp.), *Hongming ji*, 6, p. 38a (antepenultimate column), in edition of Taishō Canon, vol. 52. Biographies in *Nan Qi shu*, 54, and *Nan Shi*, 51.

23 Zürcher, *Buddhist Conquest*, p. 334, n. 119.

24 On p. 93 of T. H. Barrett, 'The Emergence of the Taoist Papacy in the T'ang Dynasty', *Asia Major* (third series), 7, 1 (1994), 89–106. I adopt the translation for the title of this text from Stephen R. Bokenkamp, with a contribution by Peter Nickerson, *Early Daoist Scriptures* (Berkeley: University of California Press, 1997). Bokenkamp provides on pp. 149–85 an excellent translation and study, notwithstanding my reservations concerning the date adopted by him.

25 Suzuki Hiromi, 'Koyaku, kyūyaku seiten no warichū ni tsuite', *Indogaku Bukkyōgaku kenkyū*, 78 (March 1991), 90–2; 79 (Dec. 1991), 43–5; 82 (March 1993), 17–19; 84 (Dec. 1993), 39–41; title changed in the last article to 'Kanyaku seiten . . .'

26 Nakajima Ryūzō (ed.), *Shutsu sanzō ki shū jokan sakuin* (Kyoto: Hōyū shoten, 1991). In fact Suzuki Hiromi's third article does attempt to incorporate this material as it appears in interlineated notes (chart two); the considerable amount that is overlooked, however, only goes to underline the provisional nature of the larger survey. Chart two also incorporates information from several other biographical and bibliographical texts, and unearths one or two new snippets of information, such as a reference to 'Chinese' as 'Wu', from the third-century southern dynasty of that name.

27 Cf. textual notes 9 on p. 60 and 1 on p. 61 of the Taishō Canon edition of his work (hereinafter *CSZJJ*), just for example.

28 For Daoism, see Bokenkamp, 'Sources', pp. 467–8; for early Buddhism, Gregory Schopen, *Bones, Stones, and Buddhist Monks: Collected Papers on the Archaeology, Epigraphy, and Texts of Monastic Buddhism in India* (Honolulu: University of Hawaii Press, 1997), p. 91: 'the total absence of rules regarding stūpas in the Pāli Vinaya would seem to make sense only if they had been systematically removed'. It is only fair to say that not all Indologists share this opinion.

29 *CSZJJ*, 9, p. 67c14.

30 *CSZJJ*, 9, p. 64a1; 7, p. 51c12.

31 *CSZJJ*, 7, p. 47b16; 10, p. 69.b.21; cf. 6, p. 45a, antepenultimate column.
32 E.g. *CSZJJ*, 6, p. 44c20 (Jin); 10, p. 73c18 (Qin).
33 *CSZJJ*, 7, p. 50b4, 8; 9, p. 62b, affords examples from Dunhuang under the Jin; cf. from the north-west in later times 9, p. 64c4.
34 *CSZJJ*, 8, p. 59c23. For Daolang's situation, see Susan Juhl, 'Cultural Exchange in Northern Liang', in S. Clausen, R. Storrs, A. Wedell-Wedellsborg (eds), *Cultural Encounters: China, Japan and the West* (Aarhus: Aarhus University Press, 1995), pp. 55–82; Daolang himself appears on p. 67.
35 Pelliot's remarks may be found on pp. 736 and 738 of his 'L'origine du nom de "Chine"', *T'oung pao*, 13 (1912), 727–42.
36 Cf. Ōfuchi Ninji, *Tonkō Dōkyō: Mokuroku hen* (Tokyo: Fukutake shoten, 1978), p. 323.
37 Wang Zhongmin, *Dunhuang guji xulu* (Beijing: Zhonghua, 1979), pp. 260–4 (including end paragraph of introduction).
38 T. H. Barrett, 'The origin of the term *pien-wen*: an alternative hypothesis', *Journal of the Royal Asiatic Society* (third series), 2, 2 (July 1992), 241–6. This hypothesis seems also to have occurred independently to Zhan Shizhuang, *Daojiao wenxue shi* (Shanghai: Shanghai wenyi, 1992), pp. 116–24.
39 *Dongxian zhuan*, 1, p. 31, as reconstructed in Yan Pingyi (ed.), *Daojiao yanjiu ziliao*, vol. 1 (Taipei: Yiwen yinshuguan, 1974), wherein Kou is remembered by northerners ('many' of whom still practise his Way) as a magus who distributed particularly effective talismans, not as a government-backed religious supremo at all; cf. Li Fengmao, 'Dongxian zhuan zhi zhucheng ji neirong', *Zhongguo gudian xiaoshuo yanjiu zhuanji*, 1 (1979), 77–98, which places this text in sixth-century south China.
40 Matsūra Takeshi, *Hokugi shi sakuin* (Fukuoka: Tōka shoten, 1986), reprinting the original text of the songs from Lu Qinli, *Xian Qin, Han, Wei, Jin, Nanbeichao shi* (Beijing: Zhonghua shuju, 1983), pp. 2247–55; Lu was actually the first person to publish on these poems, as Wang (n. 37 above) points out.
41 Mather, 'K'ou Ch'ien-chih', details the reforms; the source cited in n. 39 above suggests that they did not have the radical sort of impact of changes enforced by a modern totalitarian state, but no doubt the dynasty did have some influence on Daoism thanks to his work.
42 Matsūra, *Hokugi shi sakuin*, pp. 49, 71, 105.
43 Ōfuchi Ninji, *Shoki no Dōkyō* (Tokyo: Sōbunsha, 1991), pp. 469–84.
44 Bokenkamp, *Early Daoist Scriptures*, p. 170.
45 Gustav Haloun, 'The Liang-chou rebellion, 184–221 AD', *Asia Major*, second series, 1, 1 (1949), 119–32, though even this can be interpreted as a split between a culturally mixed area, including its own Chinese element, and the rest of China: cf. Denis Twitchett and Michael Loewe (eds), *Cambridge History of China* (Cambridge: Cambridge University Press, 1986), vol. 1, pp. 432–5 (by Yü Ying-shih). By contrast Lu Yaodong, *Cong Pingcheng dao Luoyang* (Taibei: Lianjing chuban shiye gongsi, 1979), pp. 28–73, documents the early Northern Wei sense of a completely separate tribal identity: as far as they were concerned, all Chinese were 'men of Jin' (p. 52).
46 Terry F. Kleeman, *Great Perfection: Religion and Ethnicity in a Chinese Millennial Kingdom* (Honolulu: University of Hawaii Press, 1998), pp. 77, 120.
47 Zürcher, *Buddhist Conquest*, pp. 293–307; the final page does include some references suggesting fear of foreigners, but not among the local, already only semi-Chinese, inhabitants of the north-west.
48 Kobayashi, *Rikuchō Dōkyōshi no kenkyū*, pp. 336–41. Naturally, there is much more that could be said on both sides about the *Commands and Admonitions*, as indeed about related texts, such as the *Xiang'er* commentary on Laozi.

49 I do not know when 'Qin' ceased to be used as a term for 'Chinese'; presumably it could have continued until linguistic reunification of the country at the end of the sixth century. It re-emerges in prefaces of the early ninth century as a term for the standard, northern-based dialect: see E. G. Pulleyblank, *Middle Chinese: A Study in Historical Phonology* (Vancouver: UBC Press, 1983), p. 61.
50 Zürcher, *Buddhist Conquest*, p. 195.
51 The earliest manuscript from an organised comprehensive canon that survives is actually Northern Wei (479), but though like canons no doubt existed in the South also, I am assuming that as with many aspects of government, the Tang took over its Buddhist canon via the Northern Zhou and Sui from the Northern Wei, and that its superbly organised and officially produced manuscript canon formed the basis of Song and later printed versions. See Jao Tsongyi, 'Fong Hi, des Wei du Nord, et les manuscrites bouddhiques trouvés à Touen-houang', in Michel Soymié, (ed.), *Contributions aux Études sur Touen-houang* (Genève-Paris: Librarie Droz, 1979), pp. 87–9, and Fang Guangchang, *Fojiao dazangjing shi* (Beijing: Zhongguo shehui kexue chubanshe, 1991).
52 Wang Weicheng, '*Sishizhangjing*: Daoan jinglu quezai yuanyin', reprinted in Zhang Mantao (ed.), *Xiandai fojiao xueshu congkan* (Taibei: Dasheng wenhua chubanshe, 1978), vol. 11, pp. 35–41, from *Yanjing xuebao* 18, Feb. 1935.
53 One way towards such a solution would be to suppose that the present '42 sections' actually derive from a larger anthology of Buddhist texts. But Yoshioka's textual researches on the Shangqing borrowings (see n. 9 above) appear to show that in the second half of the fourth century the text was about the same size as now.
54 I understand that the differences between the Dunhuang manuscripts and canonical Daoist literature have attracted the interest of other scholars besides Bokenkamp (see n. 28 above), notably Maeda Shigeki. Doubts concerning the systematic editing of the early Chinese Buddhist canon have already been raised by Tan Shibao, *Han-Tang foshi tanzhen* (Guangzhou: Zhongshan daxue chubanshe, 1991), pp. 249–63; I hope myself to be able to enlarge upon one of his points in due course.

4

THE *VIŚVANTARA-JĀTAKA* IN BUDDHIST AND DAOIST TRANSLATION

Stephen R. Bokenkamp

Modern scholars wield a surprisingly short supply of conceptual tools when they come to study the relationships between early medieval Daoism and Buddhism. So far, the task has primarily been conceived to be the uncovering of 'Buddhist borrowings' or 'Buddhist influence' in Daoist scriptures. For such work, little more than a sharp spade is needed. I have elsewhere criticised our lack of interpretive imagination, suggesting that the term 'influence' itself can be held responsible for narrowing our view of what is in fact a rich and fascinating period of religious ferment and cross-fertilisation.[1] I will not repeat any of that argument here. Instead, inspired by the scholarly courage Professor Liu Ts'un-yan has shown over his long scholarly career, I would like to offer for consideration a few additional tools, drawn promiscuously from the disciplines of anthropology and literary studies.

Just as an anthropologist in the field will 'look for the way a raconteur adapts an inherited theme to his audience, so that the specificity of time and place shows through the universality of the topos', so I want to look at the way one Daoist and three Buddhist translators in China adapted a popular Buddhist tale to their time and place.[2] Another way of putting this is that I wish to see what can be learned by applying the concept of 'implied audience' to this shared tale.

I focus here on one of the most popular of the Buddhist jātaka or 'birth stories', through which the Buddha recounts the details of his former lives. The tale of Prince Viśvantara (Pali: Vessantara), known as Sudāna (Skt 'he of good gifts') in Chinese recensions, tells of the penultimate life of the Buddha. This popular story has been retold in every language of Buddhism and appears frequently in early Buddhist art.[3] The earliest attested version of the tale in any language figures prominently in Kang Senghui's (*fl.* 250 CE) *Liudu jijing*: the *Collection of Scriptures on the Six Pāramitās*.[4] Two more early Chinese translations will also be treated here, one attributed to Zhi Qian (*fl.* 220–250) and another completed *c.*400 by Shengjian.[5] This latter version has been translated by Édouard Chavannes. The former, which has not to my knowledge been studied, was most probably translated in the fifth or sixth century.[6] We shall refer to its unknown translator as the 'pseudo-Zhi Qian'.

As Erik Zürcher first noticed, there is a Daoist version of this tale as well, found in the Lingbao scriptures.[7] The Lingbao 'translation' of the Sudāna tale appears in the *Zhihui dingzhi tongwei jing*, the *Scripture of Wisdom for Fixing Aspirations and Apprehending the Subtle*.[8] This text was a proselytising morality tract, popular in its time and very similar in organisation and emphasis to what would in later religious history be known as *shan shu*.[9] Like the works of the Buddhist translators, this scripture was crafted for a wide audience, for it extols the 'essential [doctrines] in simplified writing' to be transmitted orally, rather than through complex scriptures.[10]

In the section of the *Dingzhi tongwei jing* that concerns us here, the Celestial Worthy tells of the former lives of two deities, one of whom was once his son. The son is now the Perfected of the Left Mystery (Zuoxuan zhenren) and his wife in that former existence is now the Perfected of the Right Mystery (Youxuan zhenren), a Buddhist deity. The Celestial Worthy goes on to explain that, while he has created 'two paths that return to the One', the Perfected of the Right and his fellow practitioners can have the scriptures for free, while the Perfected of the Left and company will have to pay an offering of good faith. When the latter objects, the Celestial Worthy responds that since Buddhists adopt poverty and request alms to spread merit, they should receive the scripture free of charge.[11]

That the Lingbao account of these deities' former existence draws on a Buddhist *jātaka* is incontestable. Put into the Celestial Worthy's mouth at the end of the tale we find the most popular *jātaka* plot outlines conveniently listed:

> The two Perfected said: 'It was bitter to have sold our child in order to support the [Daoist] dharma.' The Celestial Worthy said: 'There is no limit to those who were able to do likewise. One sold his body to support the dharma; one threw his body to a hungry tiger; one sliced off his own flesh to feed a bird; one killed himself to give [his flesh] to beasts; one placed his wife and children into bondage; one gave his head to another. I could relate examples of such people to the end of the kalpa cycle and I still would not have told of them all. Why is this? All such as these were Perfected who achieved the Dao and performed such signs to convert the ignorant.'[12]

Each one of these acts is recorded in the opening pages of Kang Senghui's collection.[13] Further debts to Kang Senghui's *jātaka* collection can be seen in the Lingbao scriptures' own collection of *jātaka* stories, the *Benxing jing* or *Scripture of the Original Acts*.[14]

Let me first give a summary of the Buddhist story, one general enough to fit all three of the Chinese Buddhist recensions we will treat:

Sudāna, son of the king of Śibi, had, since he reached the age of cognition, devoted himself to charity. Everyone who comes to him is granted their request, no matter how extreme. Eventually, Sudāna gives away to Brahmins sent by an enemy kingdom the prize possession of his father's kingdom – a white elephant equal in war to sixty elephants. At this, the ministers of the kingdom convince the king that his son must be banished to the mountains for a period of ten years, so that he might come to regret his deeds. After distributing all of his wealth, the prince agrees to go. Despite Sudāna's objection that she is unsuited for the challenge, having been brought up with the luxuries of the palace, Sudāna's wife Mādrī insists on accompanying him, bringing along their two children, a son and a daughter.

True to his nature, Sudāna gives away their horses, their carriage and all of their rich adornments before they reach the mountains where they entrust themselves to the tutelage of a Master by the name of Accuta.

Meanwhile, in a distant land lives the old and exceedingly ugly Brahmin, with his young, attractive wife. After being teased by young men at the well where she draws water, the Brahmin's wife desires slaves so that she will no longer have to fetch water. She sends the old Brahmin off to beg the children of the well-known Sudāna. Seeing the old crank coming up the mountain, the two children know well enough what is about to happen, and so they hide. Sudāna finds them, helps the Brahmin to bind their hands and sends them off, screeching that they will be eaten by this old demon, who looks nothing like the Brahmins they have seen. Mādrī, who has been gathering fruits and nuts in the forest, returns to find her children gone. Sudāna eventually tells her, 'Honey, I donated the kids.'

Observing from his heavenly perch this extreme devotion to the Buddhist Way, Śakra himself transforms into a Brahmin and tests Sudāna by asking for his wife. When Sudāna grants this wish, Śakra gives her back.

Of course all of this ends well for all concerned. Not only is Sudāna restored to his family and kingdom to live happily ever after, he proves, in fact, the penultimate earthly existence of the historical Buddha himself. Such is the noble rebirth to which one who practises charity can aspire! His wife, children and all the other characters in the story are also reborn as notable Buddhist figures.

This is, and was meant to be, a horrifying tale. It is even more disturbing than stories relating how Bodhisattvas cut off their own flesh to feed birds or plucked out their eyes to satisfy undeserving Brahmins, for Sudāna gives what we regard as not his to give. Far from appearing a religious hero, Sudāna seems a selfish cad. He betrays his father, tries repeatedly to abandon his family and seems concerned only with his own pursuit of the brutal requirements of the bodhisattva path and the first of the 'Six Perfections' to which he has dedicated himself.

Reiko Ohnuma, in her study of tales of self-mutilation or voluntary death (Skt *dehadāna*, 'the gift of the body') in Indian Buddhist narrative literature, confronts this issue forthrightly. Her observations are useful here as well. Ohnuma observes that such tales of religious giving are meant both as examples of 'model gifts' and as 'models of giving':

> As a model gift, or exemplary gift, *dehadāna* suggests the bodhisattva's 'otherness', but as a model or example of giving in general, *dehadāna* suggests the bodhisattva's 'imitability'. The first demands our admiration and cultic devotion toward the glorious feat of the bodhisattva, while the second demands that we imitate the bodhisattva and engage in *dāna* ourselves.[15]

According to Ohnuma, both of these features derive from the fact that the gift of the body is depicted as 'maximally difficult, maximally costful, maximally personal, and wholly pure in intention'. In portraying the full perfection of the Buddhist path, these tales concurrently exemplify the self-sacrifice, absence of attachment and purity of intention required in any offering of even the most trivial gift.[16] Such extreme examples of giving, then, are *meant* to explore the abandonment of normal social obligations. They are *meant* to shock the listener. Exemplary beings have given all, and this stands as warrant for the lesser sacrifices – donations from the laity and renunciation on the part of monks – required by Buddhist practice.

Nonetheless, Ohnuma confesses that she finds 'an inherent tension between the "selflessness" that *dāna* is supposed to help cultivate, and the extreme "assertion of self" that the gift of the body necessarily involves, especially when the donor is a king who has abundant obligations to others'.[17] As I have suggested above, this tension is even more pronounced in the case of Sudāna. His gift does not involve *his* body at all. In that he eliminates from his life those to whom he has clear and intimate obligations, while leaving himself hearty and hale, his gifts seem simply selfish. What could be more selfish than the betrayal of others in pursuit of one's own religious goals? We shall return to this point below.

Before leaving Ohnuma's helpful observations, however, we need to take note of her literary analysis of *dehadāna* tales. Ohnuma discusses eight conventional character-types found in the tales she has studied: (a) the donor; (b) the recipient; (c) Śakra as recipient; (d) the opposer; (e) the false donor; (f) the envoy; (g) the reluctant helper; and (h) the bystanders, grievers or commentators. Four of these are important to our discussion. The donor in our tale is, of course, Sudāna. The recipients of his various gifts are all duplicitous Brahmins, whose unworthiness serves to highlight the pure nature of his sacrifices. Śakra appears as recipient only once, demanding Sudāna's wife as a test of his commitment. Just as in the tales Ohnuma studied, the appearance of this god seems to provide divine verification of the donor's worth, directing the audience's understanding of the deeds they have witnessed. 'Opposers' in our story include Sudāna's father, the ministers who denounce him, his wife and his children, who hide away in the brushpile at the approach of the old Brahmin. As Ohnuma notes, 'opposers' stand for social obligations. The social obligations represented in the Sudāna tale seem relatively clear-cut. The father and ministers stand for political duties; the children for the ties of familial obligation; and the wife for love, to include sexual love.

How well do these observations apply to the Daoist retelling of this tale, unfettered as it was from the pretence of normal translation? The Lingbao tale might be summarised as follows:

Many kalpas ago there was a rich man by the name of Yao Jingxin ('delights in pure faithfulness'). Concerned to repay heaven for his blessings, but aware that the Dao needs nothing, Jingxin asks his wife what he should do. She suggests that the best way to repay heaven would be to support their local Daoist, who lives on a nearby mountain. This they do.

When Jingxin and his wife die, they enjoin their son, Fajie ('dharma precepts'), to continue the support. He undertakes his father's task with redoubled zeal, giving not only to the Daoist but to all the needy who come to his attention, until his fortune is nearly depleted. All that remain are his house and outbuildings, too extensive for anyone but a prince and, at any rate, unsalable because they seem ill-omened. Still desiring to support the Daoist's services for his parents, Fajie hits upon the idea of selling his second son, the eight-year-old Ciyin ('second heir'), nicknamed Anu, for 100,000 cash to his wife's eldest sister, who has no male heir. After discussing the matter with his wife, telling her that he will redeem the child once the house has sold, she sets out with the child. The aunt, pleased with the child, fills three carts with 500,000 cash. Ciyin, not wanting to upset his aunt, does not cry out when his mother is about to depart. Instead, he begs another 10,000 on his own account to give to his father. His aunt, adding another 90,000 on her own behalf, increases this additional gift to 100,000. Ciyin, in presenting the additional money to his mother, specifies that 60,000 are to be used for his parents' daily needs, 20,000 for his brother and 20,000, on his behalf, for the Daoist.

Fajie takes the money to support the Daoist's rituals. When the Daoist, who had originally asked Fajie to bring nothing, learns the source of this new-found wealth, he does not speak but goes on with the rites. Returning home afterwards, Fajie finds all of his storehouses magically full once more. Uneasy at this sudden and unexplained largesse, Fajie returns to report it to the Daoist, who relates a dream he had in which a spirit presented him with a *ruyi* sceptre. In the dream, Fajie accepted the present. Fajie further announces his fortune to the king, who confirms it as heaven-granted. Finally, Fajie accepts the wealth.

In this case, too, we are told who each of these characters is in later life. Fajie is the now Perfected of the Left and his wife Perfected of the Right, respectively Daoist and Buddhist deities. Their children then ride up on celestial conveyances with large retinues and Fajie's mother is revealed to be the Grand Lady of the Central Watch. Not surprisingly, given the Buddhist model, Yao Jingxin proves to be the Celestial Worthy himself.

When we attempt to apply Ohnuma's character-types to this tale, none but the role of 'donor' seems to fit. In fact, all of the characters, with the possible exception of the Daoist, are specifically portrayed as donors. Since Yao Jingxin is not a king, there are no advisors to oppose his donations. The family members, who often play the role of 'opposer' in Buddhist tales, are here fully complicit in the acts of extreme charity. Yao Jingxin first suggests the idea of repaying the Dao, but it is his wife who provides the means by which this might be done. Fajie follows his father's wishes, but both he and his wife act in concert in the matter of selling their youngest son. Both the aunt and the youngest son find ways to add their own contributions to the Daoist. Even the eldest son, who does not specifically give anything, is shown to have the same pure intentions. In parting from his brother, he consoles him with the words 'It will not be long before [I too participate] with an act of fortune-causing virtue!' – expressing his own willingness to be sold in his turn.

Opposers in Buddhist tales serve to make explicit the very real quotidian demands that must be ignored in pursuit of religious charity. Such concerns are voiced in our Daoist tale, but by the family members themselves, as they weigh the alternatives and consequences of their actions. Take, for example, the paramount gift, that of the youngest son, Ciyin:

> [Fajie] asked his wife: 'I remember hearing once that your elder sister would be happy to have one of our sons. Are you willing now to grant this?' His wife, not knowing why he asked, immediately responded: 'I would rather we both die! Why would we let a son such as ours disappear from before our eyes? Selling a child to preserve one's own life only increases the anguish. I would rather die.' Her husband responded: 'I do not intend to sell a son to fill my belly, nor to provide for myself.' His wife said: 'Why then?' 'We have run out of provisions to support that Daoist in the mountains. I wish to uphold the posthumous wishes of my father. How could I forget them?' His wife immediately wiped away her tears, knelt and said: 'Now, though we are destitute, this has in fact been on my mind as well. If it is a matter of fortune-bearing merit like this, and moreover the last wishes of your father, how could we not do it?'[18]

61

Here, the wife's initial, unconsidered objections function as do the words of the 'opposers' in Buddhist tales, prompting Fajie to utter the formula 'it is not for . . . or for . . . but for . . .' that typically expresses the pure intentions of the bodhisattva. Yet, as her subsequent words and actions demonstrate, she does not oppose the gift. Similar expressions of the extreme nature of this donation are found in the negotiations and parting words of the family members. On each occurrence these observations end, as does the above passage, with the reaffirmation of the importance of giving to support the Dao.

As donors, none of the family members approaches anything like the pre-eminent status given to Sudāna in the Buddhist tales. Instead, we find not only complicity, but family negotiation with regard to the transaction. This extends to what might be called 'emotional calibration',[19] as each of the family members strives to insure that the others are fully cognizant of the importance and meaning of the act. The best example of this is the gift of money from the youngest son, Ciyin. As his mother is about to depart, and despite his resolve not to upset his aunt, he joins the two women in copious tears. Then:

> Ciyin knelt before his aunt and said: 'Today I am my aunt's child, no different from if she had given birth to me. It is just that when we humans part, we are still grief-stricken. I hope my aunt will forgive me. Now I wish to beg 10,000 in cash to give to my father and send back in my mother's cart.' The aunt was moved to pity by the young child's intentions, commiserating with and respecting him all the more, so she counted out 100,000 in cash, saying: 'I give this to you so that you might give as you wish.' Ciyin again knelt and said: 'You have granted too much money!' Then he said to his mother: 'I give 60,000 to my dear father and mother as a token of my resolve to support my parents. It shall be a slight token for your daily needs. I wish to give it to you for your own support, and not for other uses. I give 20,000 to my elder brother, with the hope that as he supports you, he will remember me. I give the remaining 20,000 to the mountain-dwelling Daoist, with the wish that my father and mother, us brothers, and my aunt might meet with good fortune.'

If that were not clear enough, the narrator adds: 'The reason he did not say "all meet with good fortune" but mentioned his aunt meeting with fortune as well was that he feared offending his aunt.'

The major apparent difference between the Buddhist tale and that of the Lingbao scriptures is the greater care taken in the latter that all members of the family participate, if not equally at least conspicuously, in the economy of the gift. Indeed, all members of the family seem to work together to ensure that this will happen, as, for instance, does Ciyin through giving money to his older brother to be used in the support of their parents. As they perform these acts, they show extreme consideration of one another's feelings, adding emotional dimensions to the already complex web of giving. The merit-producing flow of capital depicted in this story thus fully justifies the glorious future incarnations of each of the participants in a way that is not as apparent in the source text.

It is easy to see from these modifications that Chinese society was not unaccustomed to the notion that giving involves spiritual capital.[20] In China, it seems, somewhat surprisingly perhaps, even supreme sacrifices such as the sale of children to support religious institutions could be contemplated, as long as social expectations were properly met. What was finally vital was that the gift represent the entire family as a cohesive social unit and that each member be made to feel a part of the transaction.

Such observations lead us to wonder whether we might find traces of similar concerns in Chinese translations of the Sudāna tale. Is there, in other words, evidence that Chinese translators might have tailored their productions to the expectations of their audience through including elements of participation, complicity or emotional calibration between Sudāna and the members of his family?

In searching for traces of such adjustments, we need to be cautious. First of all, we need to avoid stark, and ultimately falsifying, distinctions between 'Indian' and 'Chinese' sensibilities. As Gregory Schopen has demonstrated, Indian Buddhism was indeed a religion possessed of filial piety.[21] It is wrong-headed to portray Buddhism as incompatible with 'family-centred' Chinese values in any simple way. The matter is a good deal more complex than filial piety on the one hand and renunciation on the other.

Further, we need to acknowledge the limitations of our resources. We have no access to the texts from which Chinese translators of the *Viśvantara-jātaka* worked. It might be possible to gain some notion of what early texts of the *jātaka* might have looked like through text-critical comparisons of surviving versions, but the sheer number of such versions, as well as the number of languages involved, has so far discouraged scholars from undertaking the task.[22] Comparisons of variant versions of the *jātaka* done to date indicate that there are four main textual versions of the story.[23] These textual witnesses that might attest to the written versions brought to China actually show a greater degree of variation than do the three Chinese versions dealt with here.[24] We are thus far from even a cogent hypothesis as to the nature of our translator's sources. Indeed, translators might even have worked from oral versions as memorised by informants rather than from texts. Given the popularity of the tale in all corners of the Buddhist world, this method of transmitting certain versions of the tale to China is distinctly possible. Even textual versions were most probably meant more for monks who would recite the tale as part of their proselytising activities, rather than for interested elite readers.

Such obstacles might seem to render any comparison of Chinese Buddhist translations of the *Viśvantara-jātaka* with its Daoist retelling futile. Can we say more than 'here is another instance of Buddhist influence'? I would argue that we can. Whether working from written or oral 'texts', Chinese translators made the same choices all translators make in their work. We do not need to hypothesise that since these translators were writing for Chinese audiences they made certain adjustments – whether in choosing which version to translate or in matters of elision, interpolation and word choice – to emphasise aspects of the tale they thought might appeal to that audience. This is obvious to the point of tautology. All translators write for an intended audience. Given our limitations, we might not be able to identify the source text or even state with assurance whether or not any single element in a translation was added out of consideration of the imagined audience, but we can mark distinctions between versions, notice trends and form hypotheses as to how this tale needed to be told in China. In this regard, our Daoist version is an invaluable witness. In that the Daoist author was free to reshape the tale as he wished, the changes he incorporated give us clues as to where we might begin to look.

We will search, then, not for shifts in the basic plot, for there are none that we can confidently say did not appear in the source text(s), but for possible interpolations – bits of conversation, gestures or narrative explanations – that seem to introduce elements of family complicity into the story. Further, and this is most important to keep in mind, our final hypothesis will be based not on any one of these, but on the weight of all currently available evidence.

We will find it useful as well to begin our search through an examination of Sudāna's dealings with his wife, Mādrī. This is because elite women in early medieval China occupied somewhat special positions *vis-à-vis* their husbands. Marriages were arrangements between families rather than individuals and wives retained their family names. Because of this, they commonly enjoyed a greater measure of prestige and influence over family affairs through their ties with their natal clans than in later periods.[25] As it was during this period in Chinese history that both Buddhism and Daoism strove for acceptance among the elite, we do indeed find in other contexts increasing attention to the perceived needs of women. This social background helps to explain why, in the Daoist tale, negotiations concerning the gifts begin in each case with the husband consulting his wife, whose name is never given. Thus, as a way of focusing our search, we will pay particular attention to Mādrī's level of involvement in Sudāna's sacrifice.

In Kang Senghui's translation of the *Viśvantara-jātaka*, there is very little that could be interpreted as emotional calibration. The only instance in which it does occur is, however, striking.[26] When Sudāna goes to his wife to tell her of his banishment, Mādrī, after her initial shock, responds that she wishes the kingdom to prosper and its inhabitants to gain eternal wealth and blessing, so Sudāna should go into the wilderness to fulfil his oath of giving. She reminds him that she has been 'of the same mind' (*wu zhe tongyuan*) throughout and will accompany him willingly, both because of her ties to him and 'how much more so for the way of humaneness' (*qi rendao zai*). Her only worry is that, with nothing further to give, his oath will be unfulfillable. Sudāna responds that if someone comes to ask for his wife and children he will not refuse. At this, Mādrī proclaims that she will not dare oppose him in this, since his mission is that of a Buddha. When later Mādrī returns to find the children gone, wondering 'to whom have you given them? You should have told me earlier!' Sudāna reminds her that the words of her earlier promise were 'very clear'.[27] Whether by interpolation or translation choice, Kang Senghui thus portrays Mādrī as having previously assented to the gift of herself and her children, a feature that we do not find in the extant Pali or Sanskrit *Viśvantara-jātaka*, nor in the Tang-period translation of Yijing (635–713).[28]

The translation of Shengjian contains this prior negotiation between Sudāna and Mādrī in almost the same words, indicating that no matter what text he had in front of him, he had probably also seen Kang Senghui's translation. When Mādrī returns to find the children missing, however, Shengjian's version portrays Sudāna as reminding Mādrī not of this promise, but of an even earlier one made in a previous lifetime. 'Do you remember', he says, 'my request made during the time of Dīpamkara Buddha? At that time I was named Biduowei and the son of a Brahmin. You were Xutuoluo, the daughter of a Brahmin.[29] You had seven flowers and I had [only] five hundred in silver with which I bought the flowers from you to scatter before the Buddha. But you gave the remaining two flowers for me to present to the Buddha with the wish that you be reborn as my wife, never to leave me in good or bad times. At that time, I made a demand of you that if you were my wife, you should always follow my wishes. I said that in gifts of charity I would never disappoint anyone, except only that I would not give my own father and mother. I asked that in giving you always follow my wishes and at that time you promised that you would do so.'[30]

This tale of the Buddha's previous life is taken from another *jātaka* that recounts the Buddha's existence as the young Brahmin lad, Māṇava. The connection between the two stories was probably suggested by the fact that both the flower-girl and Mādrī are former existences of Gautama's wife. But who made the addition? A reference to this *jātaka* that includes the names Biduowei and Xutuoluo occurs in the *Asheshi wangnü Ashuda pusa jing*, attributed to Dharmarakṣa (*fl.* 265–310), but probably translated earlier.[31] Kang Senghui also translates a version of the tale. Both mention only five flowers, rather than seven, and contain no reference to the flower-seller's promise to be a submissive wife in future lives, much less Māṇava's important conditions.[32] The earliest Chinese version of this *jātaka* I have yet found that contains the flower-seller's promise not to object should her future husband practise extreme giving is Buddhayaśas' *Sifen lü*, translated *c.*415.[33] But none of these translations or references to the Māṇava tale contain overt reference to the *Viśvantara-jātaka*. Nor, to my knowledge, was the Māṇava story inserted into any of the other Chinese versions of the *Viśvantara-jātaka*. In fact, such intertextual references between *jātakas* are rare.[34] This leads us to suspect that such 'cross-references', whereby the flower-girl is made to promise that she will not object to extreme giving on the part of her future husband, found in translations of the Māṇava tale made *after* Shengjian's translation, have been inserted with full knowledge of the connections he drew between the two stories.

If it looks unlikely that anyone made a connection between the two stories before Shengjian, it is still possible that Shengjian came into possession of and chose to translate a version of the *Viśvantara-jātaka* that already contained this fragment of the Māṇava tale. But there is further indication that Shengjian himself may have been ultimately responsible. Whoever first added it, the Māṇava fragment fits poorly with the rest of the story. First, as mentioned above, this promise from a previous life is not mentioned when Mādrī first allows that she would be content that she and her children be given away. Nor is the promise she made in this life alluded to again when the past-life promise is recalled. Second, though she 'awakens to her karmic destiny' when reminded of her past-life promise, she seems to forget it immediately and objects again, only a few lines later in the story, when Sudāna wants to give her to the disguised Śakra. It thus seems to me most likely that the Māṇava tale was added by Shengjian to reiterate and emphasise the point, unimportant to redactors outside China, that Mādrī had previously agreed to the gift of her children. Less important than this hypothesis, however, is our recognition that this is the story that Shengjian felt he needed to relate.

Whether added by Shengjian or by another, the result of this interpolation is that Mādrī, like Fajie's wife in the Daoist retelling, is now shown to have made a prior commitment that entails the loss of children. In Kang Senghui's translation, she makes one promise; but in Shengjian's she makes two. This latter version, we have reason to suspect, would have appealed more fully to a Chinese audience accustomed to familial negotiations.[35]

If Shengjian's Mādrī cannot seem to remember promises for even a few days, the pseudo-Zhi Qian's Mādrī proves a most attentive learner. The moment of negotiation in this story comes when Sudāna is about to grant Mādrī to the disguised Śakra: 'The Bodhisattva reported to his wife: "This Brahmin begs that I give you to him. How do you feel about it?" She immediately responded: "As you wish. I belong to you. How could I follow my own inclinations?" '[36]

This is a learned response on Mādrī's part, for the pseudo-Zhi Qian mentions neither of her promises found in Shengjian's translation. Instead, after he gives the children away, Sudāna says to her: 'Do you not know of *my* original oath? I will give everything I have to others.'[37] After hearing her accusatory plaint on the subject of his apparent 'heartlessness', delivered in five-character gāthā, Sudāna delivers a long disquisition, part of it in eight-character gāthā, on the subject of impermanence, concluding that she too should be joyous at the future peace they will earn. Hearing this, Mādrī falls silent and offers no further complaint.

When we compare this with the translations of Kang Senghui and Shengjian, or even later translations, such lengthy discourses on impermanence, stressing over and over again the context in which Sudāna's actions make sense, stand out as the most distinctive feature of the pseudo-Zhi Qian's version of the tale. At times, these speeches are constructed in such a way that they even contradict the action of the story. For instance, when Sudāna is about to give the children to the old Brahmin, he describes them as 'young, lacking in wisdom, and still unable to understand speech'. Despite this description, the children immediately grasp their father's garments and act the part of the 'opposer', protesting that their father's actions performed in the name of the dharma do not in fact seem to accord with the dharma. The children's lengthy and well crafted speech serves as occasion for yet another remark on the impermanence of human relations from Sudāna.

It is not that Sudāna is portrayed as lacking in human emotions, but rather that he is able to see beyond the event to a greater good. As he explains later, his children are truly 'lacking in wisdom', in that they cannot understand the reasons for his actions. Thus, seeing his children bound, he commits himself to the achievement of *Anuttara-samyaksambodhi*, so as to 'remove everything that fetters all sentient beings'.[38] All of this reassures us, if not the children, concerning Sudāna's motives – until we remember that these eloquent children were described as not understanding speech.

In this case, then, our suspicion that these expositions on standard Buddhist doctrine might have been added rests on the fact that they seem so poorly integrated into the narrative. Again, whether taken from some source text or introduced by the translator, these elements seem directed to the particular needs of a Chinese audience. Significantly, by the time this tale appeared, the needs of this intended audience had shifted somewhat. They no longer need to see negotiation between characters in the tale. Now, emotional calibration is directed outwards. Characters within the story still voice familial concerns, but the calming explanations are more often directed to the audience rather than to other characters, for the pseudo-Zhi Qian includes frequent passages of interior monologue.

That the pseudo-Zhi Qian had his eyes on the possible objections of his audience is shown most forcefully at the end of the tale when Sudāna walks out of the *Viśvantara-jātaka* and into yet another *jātaka*, one found in another collection attributed to Zhi Qian. The pseudo-Zhi Qian includes nothing of the happy ending of the narrative. Instead, once Śakra has given Mādrī back to Sudāna with the injunction that a returned gift cannot be given again, he walks to a nearby spot and transforms himself into the shape of another Brahmin. When he returns, he asks Sudāna for the gift of his eyes. As the bodhisattva is about to gouge them out with a wooden awl, Śakra stops his hand and gives back this gift as well.[39] This is the climactic scene of the well known tale of King Śibi, another former life of the Buddha.[40]

In this case again, a concordance of names seems to have justified the interpolation. Sudāna was the prince of the Śibi kingdom, while the gift of eyes was performed by King Śibi. But this is not a case of confusion. The two stories are quite distinct.

Admittedly, the pseudo-Zhi Qian here pre-emptively answers a different sort of question from his intended audience: not 'Why is Sudāna so lacking in consideration for his family?' but 'Why does Sudāna give away every-thing but himself?' There is in fact evidence, and fairly early evidence at that, to indicate that this is precisely the question a Chinese audience might ask. The *Mouzi lihuo lun* contains a discussion of the *Viśvantara-jātaka* that centres precisely on this issue. An interlocutor criticises Buddhism in the following words:

> A Buddhist scripture states that the Prince Sudāna gave his father's wealth to strangers, the kingdom's precious elephant to enemies, and [even] his wife and children to others. This respect for others over one's family members[41] is to lack ritual decorum. Loving others over one's family members is to lack virtue. Prince Sudāna was neither filial nor humane, yet Buddhists revere him. Is this not foreign?

Mouzi responds to this deluge of Chinese virtues with a list of sage kings who set aside their first wives or married without parents' consent, concluding that 'great people are not constrained by normal practices'. He continues:

> Sudāna saw the impermanence of the world and knew that worldly goods do not belong to the self. Thus he gave free rein to his giving to establish the Great Way (likely *anuttara-samyaksaṁbodhi*). His father's kingdom received his blessing, since the enemy did not invade. When he became the Buddha, his family all obtained salva-tion. If this was not filiality; if this was not humanity – then what are filiality and humanity?[42]

It is interesting to note that, by the sixth century, Chinese audiences still needed reassurance on this score. Indeed, a very similar question concerning the ultimate selflessness of such heroic acts is voiced by Ohnuma in the passage cited above. Clearly, the absence of physical sacrifice on Sudāna's part remains a question that must be addressed by anyone who relates the story.[43] None the less, the pseudo-Zhi Qian retelling confronts more particu-larly Chinese issues of familial emotional calibration as well. Though Sudāna checks Mādrī's response but once, the audience is treated to enough cues to demonstrate that Sudāna's doctrinal explanations are all that his family, or ours, might need. After each of his reiterations of this message, the family member in question is said to 'fall silent'. And through silence, they voice their consent to the truths he utters. In this context, the interpolation of the King Śibi tale merely reminds the audience that the doctrine of imperman-ence informs Sudāna's attachment to personal well-being as much as it does his attachment to members of his family.

We might fruitfully extend our analysis of family negotiation and emo-tional calibration to the rest of the scenes in our Chinese translations of the *Viśvantara-jātaka*. Possible interpolations that seem to fit these concerns appear in Sudāna's exchanges with his father and even his children. Enough evidence has been presented to demonstrate, however, that these translations were constructed to meet the expectations of Chinese audiences.

What we should take from our comparison of these Daoist and Buddhist versions of the *Viśvantara-jātaka*, however, is not this obvious observation. Instead, we should notice the ways in which reading such Daoist and Buddhist texts side-by-side, repressing attitudes brought on by the need to demonstrate influence and borrowing or find 'original texts', might bring us to a fuller understanding of both religions. In the absence of the clear concerns of the Daoist tale, unfettered as these were from the constraints of common translation, we might have noticed passages that did not fit well within the Buddhist translations and we would certainly have remarked the odd insertion of other *jātaka* plots into the tale, but we would be hard put to determine just *why* these elements were there. Without a careful comparison of similar themes in the early Buddhist translations, we might notice that Ohnuma's character-types do not match the Daoist tale, and we could easily conclude that such concessions to familial negotiation are a distinctive feature of Daoism.

As we who study Daoism strive to identify its distinctive doctrines and practices, we commonly commit this latter mistake. It is much too easy to make binary distinctions, imagining that individual heroes populate the Buddhist world, while the world of the Daoist is rooted in families. That this is not so is immediately apparent from the following anecdote from the life of Lu Xiujing (406–477), who edited and promulgated the Lingbao scriptures, as recorded by Ma Shu (522–581) in his *Daoxue zhuan*, the *Biographies of Students of the Dao*:

> Lu hid himself away on Mount Yunmeng to practise the Dao. Once, when he had come down the mountain to search for drugs, he passed by his home town and stopped with his family for a number of days. His daughter suddenly became violently ill, her life hanging by a thread, and the members of Lu's family strongly urged that he cure her. Lu said with a sigh: 'I originally abandoned my wife and children to entrust myself to the Mysterious Ultimate [the Dao]. Staying with my family is a matter no different from the passing of a traveller. How could I still have sentiments of attachment?' Then, he brushed off his robes and went straight away, without looking back. Only a day after he had left, his daughter's illness was cured.[44]

We find here no negotiation, no emotional calibration, nothing but the seemingly heartless self-assurance of the religious individual who knows that personal concerns will be resolved through transcendent deeds. Such stories of 'model giving', the religious hero as other, can easily be found in Daoist texts as well. So why were the adjustments we noticed in our Daoist retelling of the *Viśvantara-jātaka* considered necessary at all? So far, little has been said about the religious goals that might have been achieved by concessions to the demands of Chinese audiences that tales of such religious exemplars include familial negotiation and emotional calibration. Certainly, tales so told would have seemed more natural, but did they have added religious significance? The tale of Yao Jingxin, who after all was the former existence of the Celestial Worthy, suggests an answer. In his death bed instructions to his son, Yao employs the expectations of filial piety to ensure that his descendants will continue to work the fields of merit that he has opened for them through his support of the mountain-dwelling Daoist. This they cooperate to do, generating for themselves their own stores of merit.

The whole point of a field of merit, it seems, is that everyone should come to work it if they expect to enjoy its fruits. While we, as a matter of course, lack evidence, we can easily imagine members of a Chinese audience, upon hearing the exploits of a Sudāna or a Lu Xiujing, asking just what meritorious deeds the wife, son or daughter performed to justify their eventual good fortune, beyond being ignored or exploited. In retelling the *Viśvantara-jātaka*, both Buddhist and Daoist translators sought to demonstrate just what these family members might have done through altering the story, sometimes only slightly, sometimes radically. That process of audience response and authorial reaction, it seems to me, fully deserves the name 'influence'.

Notes

An earlier version of this chapter was presented as 'The Daoist Sudāna (*Viśvantara*): Jātaka Tales in the Lingbao Scriptures', at the Conference on the History of Daoism, in Honour of Liu Ts'un-yan, Canberra, Australia, 8 August 1999. I would like to thank the Humanities Research Centre of the Australian National University, Canberra, Australia, for their generous support that made possible the completion of my research on these tales. In addition, this chapter has benefited greatly from the comments and criticisms freely provided by Gregory Schopen of the University of California, Los Angeles, Mori Yuria of Waseda University and the members of the Bloomington Chinese Scriptures Reading Group, particularly Robert Campany, John McRae and Jan Nattier.

1 Stephen R. Bokenkamp, 'The Silkworm and the Bodhi Tree: The Lingbao Attempt to Replace Buddhism in China and Our Attempt to Place Lingbao Daoism', in John Lagerwey (ed.), *Religion and Chinese Society* (Hong Kong: Chinese University Press, 2004), vol. 1, 'Ancient and Medieval China', pp. 317–39.

2 The observation is Robert Darnton's. See his *The Great Cat Massacre and Other Episodes in French Cultural History* (New York: Vintage Books, 1985), p. 15.

3 For a convenient listing of sources and translations, see Leslie Grey, *A Concordance of Buddhist Birth Stories* (Oxford: Pāli Text Society, 1990), pp. 167–9.

4 T. 152, 3.7c28–11a26, story 14. Although the Pali version is widely considered the most ancient, Kang Senghui's retelling perhaps deserves that distinction. For Kang Senghui and his translation work, see Tsukamoto Zenryū (trans. Leon Hurvitz), *A History of Early Chinese Buddhism, From its Introduction to the Death of Hui-yüan* (Tokyo: Kodansha, 1985), vol. 1, pp. 151–63; Erik Zürcher, *The Buddhist Conquest of China* (Leiden: E. Brill, 1959), vol. 1, pp. 51–5; Ren Jiyu (ed.), *Zhongguo fojiao shi* (Beijing: Zhongguo shehui kexue yuan chubanshe, 1985), vol. 1, pp. 428–39. The Six Pāramitās, also translated as the 'Six Perfections' or the 'Six Transcendent Virtues', are (a) giving, (b) moral conduct,

(c) forbearance, (d) vigorous striving, (e) contemplation and (f) wisdom. Kang Senghui places the tale of Sudāna in the first section on 'giving'.

5 T. 171, *Taizi Xudanu jing*. This text has been translated by Édouard Chavannes, *Cinq centes countes et apologues* (Paris: Ernest Leroux, 1910–34), vol. 3, pp. 362–95.

6 T. 153, *Pusa benyuan jing*. Reference to this scripture first appears in the Sui-period catalogues of *Fajing* (T. 2146, 55.144a15) and Fei Changfang (T. 2034, 49.57a23). For these catalogues and their usefulness in determining false attributions, see Kyoko Tokuno, 'The Evaluation of Indigenous Scriptures in Chinese Buddhist Bibliographic Catalogues', in Robert E. Buswell Jr (ed.), *Chinese Buddhist Apocrypha* (Honolulu: University of Hawai'i Press, 1990), pp. 31–74. An additional indication of the late date of this text is the opening phrase *Wo xi ceng wen* ('once long ago, I heard'). There is no credible attribution of a scripture containing this phrase to any time prior to the late fourth or early fifth centuries, and even the earliest of these are suspect (Jan Nattier, personal communication, 12 January 2002). Unclear to me is the epithet given to Sudāna in this translation: *yiqie chi* 'Upholder of All'. I can only speculate that it was adopted to make for Sudāna the claim that he maintained all of the six Pāramitās, rather than only the first. For the possibility that this translation might have been based on an Indian recasting of the Sudāna story, see n. 43. The reader should be aware that I have regularised the names of the characters in this tale throughout. Were I to explore the source of Chinese transcriptions of the characters' names, this would be a different sort of essay.

7 Erik Zürcher, 'Buddhist Influence on Early Taoism: A Survey of Scriptural Evidence', *T'oung Pao*, 66 (1980), 84–147, pp. 102–4.

8 DZ 325. On this text, see Anna Seidel, 'Le sūtra merveilleux du Ling-pao Suprême, traitant de Lao Tseu qui convertit les barbares (Le manuscrit S. 2081)', in M. Soymié (ed.), *Contribution aux Études de Touen-houang*, vol. 3, PEFEO, vol. 135, pp. 332–6, and Stephen R. Bokenkamp, 'The Yao Boduo Stele as Evidence for the "Dao-Buddhism" of the Early *Lingbao* Scriptures', *Cahiers d'Extrême-Asie*, 9 (1996–7), 54–67.

9 Among other similarities, this text was not to be kept secret, but was to be given away (at least to Buddhists). The early references to this scripture include a critical appraisal of its message that the Celestial Worthy had been born as a commoner, to be found in the *Suishu*, 'Jingji zhi' (Beijing: Zhonghua shuju, 1991), 35: 1094.

10 DZ 325, 21b.

11 DZ 325, 17a–18a. See Zürcher, 'Buddhist Influence', pp. 90–1.

12 DZ 325, 16b1–5.

13 For these tales, see T. 152, vol. 3: selling one's body, story 10, 5a ff; feeding oneself to a tiger, story 4, 2b; cutting off one's flesh to feed a bird, story 2, 1b ff; killing oneself to feed beasts (fish), story 3, 1c; sending wife and child into servitude, story 6, 2c–3c; giving one's head as an act of generosity, story 5, 2b, and story 11, 6a–6c. All of these appear in the section of the work devoted to the pāramitā of dāna 'giving'.

14 For further interesting parallels between Lingbao accounts of karma and retribution and those of Kang Senghui's *Liudu jijing*, see Kamitsuka Yoshiko, 'Reihōgyō to shoki kōnan bukkyō – inga ōhō shisō o chūshin ni', *Tōhō shūkyō*, 91 (1998), 1–21, pp. 11–13.

15 Reiko Ohnuma, *Dehadāna: The 'Gift of the Body' in Indian Buddhist Narrative Literature*, PhD dissertation, University of Michigan, 1997, p. 122.

16 The citation is from Ohnuma, p. 140. See also pp. 121–51 for her discussion of these issues.

17 Ohnuma, p. 99. She explains this tension as arising between the kind of self the bodhisattva seeks to deny – that self caught up in worldly obligations – and the self he wishes to privilege, responsible for its own salvation.

18 DZ 325, 12a10–b7.

19 The term was suggested to me by Jan Nattier in our weekly reading group.

20 The descriptive metaphors I employ here owe much to Marcel Mauss's *The Gift: Forms and Functions of Exchange in Archaic Societies* (London: Cohen & West, 1970).

21 See particularly Gregory Schopen, 'Filial Piety and the Monk in the Practice of Indian Buddhism: A Question of "Sinicization" viewed from the Other Side', *Bones, Stones, and Buddhist Monks, Collected Papers on the Archaeology, Epigraphy, and Texts of Monastic Buddhism in India* (Honolulu: University of Hawai'i Press, 1997), pp. 56–71; originally published in *T'oung Pao*, 70 (1984), 110–26.

22 My own limitations need to be noted at this point as well. I have no knowledge of Sanskrit, Pali or Tibetan and so must rely on the published work of others for versions of the tale in these languages. Since Buddhologists who have published on the Sudāna story as it appears in Sanskrit, Pali and Tibetan tend to be more interested in tracing 'original versions' than in attempting to account for why the tale is told differently in each instance, these prove serious shortcomings. The kind Buddhologists who have commented on this chapter cannot be held responsible for my inability to track the story further. If any missteps on my part here spur others to fuller investigations of this fascinating tale in all its recensions, including the Daoist version, I shall be content.

23 Jampa Losang Panglung, 'Preliminary Remarks on the *Uddānas* in the *Vinaya* of the *Mūlasarvāstivādin*', in Michael Aris and Aung San Suu Kyi (eds), *Tibetan Studies in Honour of Hugh Richardson* (Oxford: St John's College, 1979), pp. 229–30; and *Die Erzählstoffe des Mūlasarvāstivāda-vinaya Analysiert auf Grund der Tibetischen Übersetzung*, Studia Philologica Buddhica Monograph Series, vol. 3 (Tokyo: Reiyukai Library, 1981), pp. 40–1, 109. I am grateful to Gregory Schopen for directing me to these studies.

24 None the less, it must be pointed out that the summaries of these versions that I have consulted do not provide a level of detail that would be necessary to make comparisons concerning the possible Chinese interpolations I analyse below. For another useful comparative table on plot elements within various Pali, Sanskrit and Tibetan versions of the tale, see Kabita Das Gupta, *Viśvantarāvadāna, Eine Buddhistische Legende: Edition eines Textes auf Sanskrit und auf Tibetisch, Engeleitet und Übersetzt* (Berlin: Freien Universität Berlin, 1977), pp. 15–28. Das Gupta, who is aware of only Shengjian's translation into Chinese, notes (p. 32) that it is very different from the versions she has compared, but does not go into further detail.

25 On marriages of alliance among elite families, see Patricia Buckley Ebrey, *The Aristocratic Families of Early Imperial China: A Case Study of the Po-ling Ts'ui Family* (Cambridge: Cambridge University Press, 1978) and also her introduction to Rubie S. Watson and Patricia Buckley Ebrey (eds), *Marriage and Inequality in Chinese Society* (Berkeley: University of California Press, 1991), pp. 11–14.

26 The following exchange appears at T. 152, 3.8b29–c19.

27 T. 152, 3.10a15–27.

28 For the scene in which Mādrī determines that she will accompany Sudāna in the Pali tale, see Margaret Cone and R. Gombrich, *The Perfect Generosity of Prince Vessantara* (Oxford: Clarendon Press, 1977), pp. 18–19. For the version of the Gilgit manuscripts, see Das Gupta, p. 69. Here the only promise that Mādrī makes is that she will not come to regret it if they have to be separated in the future. Yijing's account is found in his *Genben shuo yiqie youbu binaiye posengshi*,

T. 1450, 24.181c15–28. In this version, Sudāna does assert that he is determined to give all he owns and Mādrī is made to promise that she will not be a source of vexation on this account, but here as well there is no prior mention of the gift of wife and children.

29 I have no information on what these names were meant to transliterate.

30 T. 171, 3.422c13–21.

31 One compelling theory is that this scripture was first translated by Lokakṣema (*fl.* 180) and later revised by Zhi Qian, who added the rhymed portions. I am grateful to Jan Nattier for tracking down these names and providing information on this text.

32 T. 152, 3.47c20–48b24.

33 T. 1428, 22.785a2–23. Another version containing this vow is found in T. 190, *Fo benxing jijing* (3.666c28–667b1), Jñānagupta's collection of the former lives of the Buddha, translated during the Sui Dynasty. Earlier translations, such as Zhi Qian's *Foshuo taizi ruiying benqi jing*, T. 185, 3472b29–473a21, include seven flowers, but not Māṇava's clarification that she should understand that he will in future lives give away 'wife and children'. Of the versions of this story I have surveyed so far, Shengjian's interpolation seems to be the earliest to mention this retort.

34 Gregory Schopen (personal communication, 23 February 2002).

35 In fact, it was Shengjian's version of the tale that warranted inclusion in Dao Shi's (*fl.* 656–668) *Fayuan zhulin*, T.2122, 53.879b25–882b19. Thus, it must have served as source text for countless oral retellings of the Sudāna story through the Tang period at least. This is probably why Chavannes chose to translate it rather than Kang Senghui's abbreviated version.

36 T. 153, 61a20–22.

37 T. 153, 60b21–22. This response accords more fully with the Sanskrit and Pali versions.

38 T. 153, 60a2–38.

39 T. 153, 61b2–32.

40 The version attributed to Zhi Qian appears in the *Zhuanji baiyuan jing*, T. 200, 4.218b10–c14. Here Śakra takes on the appearance of an eagle to beg the king's eyes for food, but in other versions he takes on the form of a Brahmin. See Ohnuma, pp. 333–6, for summaries of these various versions in Sanskrit and pp. 1–3 for a retelling of the tale.

41 Although *qin* 'intimates' is a word that commonly refers only to one's parents, it can also refer to the immediate family as opposed to more distant relations. Here, since both the father and the wife and children are mentioned, I adopt the translation 'family members'.

42 *Hongming ji*, T. 2102, 52:3c28–4a13.

43 This was true within the Indian cultural sphere as well. The *Maṇicūḍāvadāna* describes the extreme gifts of a King Maṇicūḍa, whose gifts match Sudāna's in every respect, except that the story ends with him giving his own flesh and finally the jewel attached to his cranial protuberance (thus his name) to a demon disguised as Śakra. See Das Gupta, pp. 35–6 for a summary of this story. It is unclear to me what relationship, if any, this tale might have with the translation of the pseudo-Zhi Qian. That it was the direct source of the pseudo-Zhi Qian's seems unlikely, since, judging by Das Gupta's summary, there are many discrepancies of important detail. But, even if this was his source, the pseudo-Zhi Qian must have altered it to include an incident more familiar to his audience, since the Sanskrit version Das Gupta explores does not involve the gift of eyes.

44 This passage is from the *Daoxue zhuan* as reconstructed in Chen Guofu, *Daozang yuanliu kao* (Beijing, Zhonghua, 1963), vol. 2, p. 466.

5

VISIONS OF EVIL

Demonology and orthodoxy in early Daoism

Christine Mollier

Daoism's indifference to doctrinal and conceptual questions has frequently been overstated. Praxis, it has often been said of Daoism, largely over-shadows dogma. It is true that its conception of this world and the next, and its ontological and moral approach, have never been the subject of scholastic treatises. But although it is unrivalled as a source of meditation techniques and alchemical methods, thaumaturgy and exorcism, Daoism has still concerned itself with theological reflection. While unquestionably a religion of rites and formulae, it is nonetheless a religion in the full sense of the term: it is a model for structuring time and space, socially and cosmically, and it has as its foundation ethical values that constitute its *raison d'être* as well as its identity.

Demonology lies at the heart of medieval Daoism's concerns. Falling within the domain of eschatology, it is a complicated and highly charged domain in which the important questions of moral dualism, salvation and post-mortem retribution are played out. Often imprecise, written between the lines and submerged by a mass of materials concerning ritual practices (personal or collective), its conceptions are difficult to define, especially as they are enmeshed in religious currents and the contingencies of social and historical events. Fluctuating between violent intolerance and qualified indulgence in relation to gods and spirits, Daoist orthodoxy was to have considerable difficulty in finding a permanent position. The contractual and legislative order that the Daoism of the first centuries wanted to impart to its relationship with the visible and invisible world reinforced the bureaucratic concerns of ancient funerary beliefs and wove them into a more fully conceptualised ideological and soteriological web. Through the centuries Daoism would become an increasingly moralistic force under the influence of Buddhism. The marked dualism of the Way of the Celestial Master would serve as an ideological weapon for the sects that were developing in the wake of this first Church in southern China at the time of the Six Dynasties. Driven by similar messianic hopes, they conveyed similar theologies. Exclusivism, ethnocentrism and elitism were their pressure points.

Demonic obsessions

When Daoism set about dealing with evil, demonological conceptions were already strongly anchored in the Chinese mentality and exorcism practices had long since proven themselves. Insidious and monstrous entities, emanations of death and incarnations of evil, the demons (*gui*), kept on terrorising the living on a permanent basis. They welled up everywhere, they could take any form, and merely to refer to them aroused a macabre horror. For traditional religion, every being and every thing incorporating breath energies (*qi*) of the earthly kind, ones that are heavy and morbid, is potentially capable of becoming 'spirit', in deified (*shen*) or demonised form. The demons are animals, plants, minerals, old objects and so on, but the most feared and the most prolific are undoubtedly the spirits of the departed (the *gui* of demons is a homonym of the *gui* that means 'return') who met their death prematurely through violence, accident or illness. For man, in the image of the cosmos, is composed of heavenly *qi* that are subtle and pure, and of earthly *qi*, opaque and demonic. He is therefore congenitally inhabited by demons. The constituents of this demon-share, innate in everyone, are first our seven earthly souls, the *po*, that are opposed to the *hun*, souls that are heavenly and divine. As essential components of human nature, the seven souls, the *po*, constitute our inherent evil, our innate morbidity. The more exceptional the fate of an individual, the more his demon-share and what remains of his liberated vital essence (*jing*) will change him into a powerful creature after his death.

According to one of the oldest legends, the haunting of the *gui*, and the attempts to conjure away the evil of which these demons are the cause, go back to mythical times. When Yu the Great, the creator of Chinese civilisation, had the universe and its inhabitants figured on nine sacrificial cauldrons, he was careful to have the evil beings represented on them as well. In revealing the image of the demons, an undesirable but nevertheless integral part of humanity, Yu meant to warn men of the harm they could do. The idea has persisted. The knowledge of the secret identity of the forces of evil enables the knower to master them or to eliminate them.

The oldest known manual of Chinese exorcism, which was discovered among the archaeological materials of Shuihudi and brought to light in China in the 1970s, already testifies to the extraordinary strength of demonism in ancient China. The document, inscribed on bamboo slips and excavated from a tomb of the third century BCE, reveals the extent to which the Chinese of the Warring States period were past masters in the art of unearthing demons of all kinds. This manual proposes an exorcism that anyone can do at home, with whatever is at hand, and requiring the help of neither a shaman nor a qualified specialist in demonism.[1]

Exorcism was not, however, in those distant times, any more than in later periods, the fruit of a demon mania that affected the simple-minded or the illiterate masses, victims of hallucinations born of their superstitions and their fantasies. Problems with demons were taken very seriously and treated at all levels, individual and collective, and in all social strata. Exorcism had as much to do with the ad hoc therapeutic formula as with affairs of state. By the first century BCE the demonographic manuals (unfortunately now lost) were preserved with great care in the imperial libraries in the same way as the occult works, which were so highly prized, concerning divination or astrology.[2] The grand ceremonies of exorcism, the Nuo, celebrated at the Han court and lasting until the Tang, were part of the official cult. They were organised at the end of each year under the aegis of the masked shamans, the *Fangxiang*, who were responsible for expelling the harmful powers of the past year and for purifying the country in readiness for the institution of the new calendar. The Nuo were true imperial exorcisms.[3] Being conducted at the highest social echelons, they give an idea of the importance and seriousness accorded to demonological beliefs in ancient China.

The law of the Dao

As for many other aspects of religious life, when it came to demons or exorcism techniques, Daoism did not have anything basic to invent. The rich demonological tradition extending back more than six centuries that had preceded it had laid down the key principles.

The Daoists tapped this well of beliefs and ancestral practices and adapted the ancient exorcism manuals. Their demonological inventories retained the naive and disordered character of their predecessors, but also, more than anything else, their didactic vocation: to teach the basic prophylactic and offensive measures against demons. However, the exorcistic vocation of the Daoists went well beyond the restricted and above all pragmatic framework of this earlier demonography. It established itself in a political context of theocratic conquest that marked the rise and foundation of religious Daoism. Demonological conceptions were from that time inscribed in a globalising system, a theology. They were the defining element of the anthropological and apocalyptic eschatology of medieval Daoism. The formulae against demons became adjuncts of a more ambitious project of exorcism, which aimed for the salvation of humanity and the ordering of the universe. This was a religious programme of cosmic dimensions, expressed by divine voice, and revealed and orchestrated by the personified Dao. Through its vision of good and evil, Daoism imposed an orthodoxy and assured its authority.

The legend that traditionally establishes the organisation of the Celestial Masters, the first Daoist church, takes its origins back to the second century. This legend marks the setting in place of a theology whose foundations would remain basically unchanged in its later currents. It is a divine revelation that institutes Daoism as a historic religion. In 142 CE the god Laozi returns to earth to save humanity and establish the first Daoist institution. This second coming takes place in the kingdom of Shu (the present Sichuan–Shaanxi).

It was in a stone chamber on Mount Quting in the Commandery of Shu that Lord Lao [in 142 CE] met the Daoist Zhang Daoling . . . and said to him: 'The people of this generation have no respect for the right and the true, but fear depraved demons. It is for that reason that I have proclaimed myself "Lord Lao newly appeared".'[4]

'Lord Lao newly appeared' (*Xinchu Laojun*) conveyed the new religion to his chief priest, the first Celestial Master, Zhang Daoling. As representatives on earth of the cosmic god incarnate, the mission of the Daoist prophet and his descendants was to guarantee the instruction and the salvation of the world by conveying the way of Orthodox Unity (*zhengyi*):

Lord Lao conferred on Zhang the title of 'Master of the Orthodox and Unified *qi* of the Three Heavens of the Great Mysterious Capital' and conveyed to him the 'Way of the Sworn Alliance of Orthodox Unity' . . . He repealed the era of the Six Heavens and of the Three Ways to bring in that of the Three Heavens of Orthodox Unity.[5]

The religious revolution instituted by this messianic event saw itself not only as ethical, but as cosmic as well. As a kind of supra-celestial mandate, the proposed orthodoxy could not be conceived without a total restructuring and purification of the universe. The new cosmic order of the Three Heavens (*santian*), the epoch of good, had forever to supplant the bygone era of the Six Heavens (*liutian*), the reign of death and evil. The former was thereafter synonymous with the religion of Orthodox Unity, the latter with the demonic way. The Daoist institution presented itself as the one and only guarantor of the new universal order, as the absolute manager of men and gods and as the supreme legislator of the demons. Each individual, according to the rules of this rigid cosmic-ethical dualism, had to keep to his place within the world mega-administration and thus contribute to the maintenance of this universal hegemony.

The fundamental principles of Daoist orthodoxy, the orthodox religion (*zhengjiao*), are precisely enunciated in an anonymous commentary on the catechism of the famous Daoist theologian Lu Xiujing (406–477). *Lu xiansheng daomen keliie*, the *Abridged Code of Master Lu for Entry into the Dao*, aims to regulate the life of the faithful by teaching them the basic commandments:

The Masters of the Sworn Alliance do not receive any money; the gods receive neither food nor drink. This is what is called the Pact of Purity . . . All divinatory practices or hemerological consultations are forbidden, whether it be to get a house set up or make a grave secure, to move house or to undertake a journey or any matters of this nature . . . To renounce the thousands of spirits and myriad supernatural forces, all the heavenly and earthly deities, and worship the

Lord Lao and the [first] Three [Celestial] Masters: this is what is called the orthodox religion.[6]

Against the forces of evil

By depriving the gods of food and drink the Daoists were drawing up a programme of vast scope. They were tolling the death knell of traditional Chinese religion and proclaiming for themselves a new ideal of the divine that they also meant to impose on others. Their gods, and they only, were superior beings, released from all earthly and carnal needs, free from biological contingencies and exempt from animality. The gods of the Dao do not eat or drink. They are pure gods, immaterial and ethereal, emanating from the cosmos of the Three Heavens composed of subtle and refreshing pneumas. Their abode, far, far away from the decay of death, and far too from the here and now, is in the stars and the heaven-caves, those microcosmic paradises hidden in the heart of the holy mountains. 'Their laws', insists Ge Hong:

> are different and their nobility is of the highest. It is therefore quite clear that neither the dishes and liqueurs of stinking rats, nor the prostrations of the common people can persuade them to come down here below . . . They cannot be moved by clever speeches nor solicited by fine gifts, that much is certain.[7]

The 'other gods' are those who are pathetically encumbered by anthropomorphic attributes that chain them to a nagging desire for food and honours. Made of flesh and blood, they demand flesh and blood to live. The obsessive determination of the Daoists to bring about the disappearance of the sub-gods from the traditional pantheon thus led them, by a cruel logic, to envisage depriving these undesirables of their essential needs, in short to make them die of hunger. That is indeed the dictum of the *Santian neijie jing*, the *Scripture of the Esoteric Explanations of the Three Heavens*: 'People must not give themselves up to vain and illicit sacrifices to the demons and the heterodox spirits. If they desist, the demons will have neither food nor drink.'[8]

Considered as unworthy of the True Way, the religion of the day with its immolations of animals was definitively ostracised. The late Rolf A. Stein, in a masterly article, has shown how this Daoist war was waged unflaggingly throughout the medieval period and up into the Song.[9] The Daoist moralists acrimoniously labelled the cults of this 'polytheism' or 'paganism' in the Chinese style as 'vulgar', 'lewd' or 'pernicious' (*susi* or *yinsi*), or indeed as a 'religion of demons' (*guidao*), employing heterodox methods (*daofa*) or worse still sorcery (*wugu*).

The new Daoist orthodoxy would not rest until it had eradicated its hated double: the timeless cult practices of China, the religion without name, shared by the whole society and now, for want of a better term, termed 'popular religion'. The cults that ordered the daily life and the calendar of the local communities were declared heretical. This condemnation of popular cults (those of the people) was not a new phenomenon in medieval China. The religious activities of the peasant masses had always been subject to control and even persecution, on the part of governments ever suspicious of their possible subversion. But the arguments that the Daoist moralists used against the spirit cults were of a quite different nature from those wielded by the imperial authorities. It was not so much, as it was for the latter, to safeguard ethics and public order that the Daoists conducted their struggle, but in the name of theological legitimacy. Their normative and coherent vision of the world and of the sacred was presented as a radical alternative to the fragmented and muddled experience of the divine and to widespread idolatry.

Moreover, the proponents of this religious renewal systematically demonised the gods of the traditional Chinese pantheon and vehemently condemned bloody sacrifices.[10] The position they adopted was extreme. To deny this basic prerogative of the sacrificial cult was tantamount to severing the vital nerve of Chinese religion as a whole: popular devotion as well as the official religion of the state practised since High Antiquity. In the eyes of the Daoists, the veneration of the ancestors and the euhemerism in honour of aristocratic families were considered merely as pretexts for pouring blood on the altar in reverence to obsolete and profane gods. Daoism radically opposed the traditional process of deifying famous people who had died with a fierce demonisation of the important figures of this world, past and present. Exceptional historical figures, national or local, were particularly targeted by the Daoist moralists, who wanted to eliminate any trace of them.

The campaign of denigration led by the Daoist apologists against traditional religion also fixed its sights on ancillary and complementary practices, namely divinatory techniques. Daoism absolutely refused to authorise the services of diviners, geomancers, prophets and other technicians who communicated with the gods. Divinatory methods, indispensable preliminaries to the religious ceremonies of the sacrificers, were, like the ceremonies themselves, declared contrary to the good practice of the Dao. Medicine, as another para-religious activity, was equally subject to Daoist disapproval.

The gods of the traditional pantheon were universally decreed to be wicked. They were relegated *en bloc* to the rank of 'expired emanations of the Six Heavens' (*liutian guqi*). Torn from their pedestals, they were hurled unceremoniously into those celestial but still shadowy spheres, cosmic dumping grounds of death and evil. But weren't most of them departed souls who had been deified? Belonging to the kingdom of decomposition and putrefaction, they were logically sent back to the element from which they came: the Yin universe of death where they were forced to remain. The Law of the Dao was intransigent in this respect. The reign of the pathological cults had been conclusively brought to an end. That of the Dao and its true gods was proclaimed.

The Daoist gods were cosmic gods that no shaman of the people and no officiant of the imperial liturgy would know how to honour. Only the legitimately ordained Daoist Masters could propitiate them and were empowered to do so. It was no longer by slitting the throats of domestic animals, but by sending prayers and written petitions in the right and proper way, that they sought the support of those powerful celestial entities who were in charge of maintaining universal order and the management of the human realm.

There is no doubt that the offensive led by orthodox Daoism to denigrate its opponents would have had, if it could have been fully realised, a cataclysmic effect on established conventions. It urged nothing less than a profound reform in the relations between men and gods, a fundamentally different view of the world. As part of the offensive, it was decided to declassify and to expunge in one fell swoop the multiple secular deities, by which are to be understood *all* the gods: the spirits of nature and the lares, the spirits of the stars, of the mountains and rivers, of the trees and rocks, of the plants and springs, the divinities of the earth and of the great walls. This redefinition of the sacred excluded the deities and spirits, indiscriminately and en masse, thereby shaking the entire universe, for the lives of men and the principles of nature were thoroughly regulated by these same invisible entities. But this indictment of the divine by Daoism went even further. The very foundations of national and local history were endangered by undermining sacrosanct ancestral cults. Legendary heroes, important political and military figures, supreme demiurges and mythological beings, dynastic ancestors and elders of the clan in the glorious past were one and all consigned to oblivion; in short, all those who having died were consecrated by the cult and were the precious milestones of Chinese civilisation, the beacons of its long history and of its collective memory. For the Daoists, the departed souls of high society, far from being the incarnation of wise and beneficent deities, were perceived as supremely harmful beings. The more wide-ranging their role when living, the more dangerous they were after their death. Especially cruel and demanding, by virtue of their strong personality and the brutal interruption of their exceptional existence, they possessed a potent excess of energy, of unconsumed vitality, which turned them into creatures who at all costs had to be pacified or kept at bay. These terrible demons, often impressive military chiefs in their lifetimes, were actually, in the world of the dead, the leaders of huge armies of demon soldiers, of subordinates who caused countless and often fatal injuries.[11] The cults dedicated to these figures, extending to the highest social echelons, were just as reprehensible as the vulgar and superstitious practices of peasant religion. In any event they were related. These gods from the most elevated strata of the society, who had been fed until satiated on the blood of the sacrificial victims, were of no higher worth than the deities propitiated by the sorcerers of the people. Indeed, their illustrious origins made them even fiercer demons.

In the guise of attacking departed heroes, the great men of the nation deified by the official cult, Daoism was pointing its finger at the representatives of corrupt governments. Not without a certain demagogy, it became, in short, the defender of oppressed peoples, the victims of official exactions and the evils of the world. Like their departed equivalents, important politicians were held in large measure responsible for the universal breakdown.

In taking upon itself the absolute right to censure the gods, a right reserved until then by the state, and in criticising the imperial authorities in so barely veiled a way, the Daoism of this early period showed an incredible arrogance motivated by utopian convictions and theocratic ambitions.

Interdiction and authority

Daoism reserved the right and the power to define what, in beings and rites, was or was not 'correct' (*zheng*). It presented itself as the orthodox religion and opposed everything that was 'vulgar' (*su*), 'bad' (*e*), 'demoniacal' (*yao*), 'contrary' (*dao*) or 'perverse' (*xie*). Coercion was brought to bear at the level of the mundane as of the divine. The living and the dead, the faithful and the gods, were obliged to respect the rules pronounced by the deified and all powerful Dao. Moral and ethical norms were ratified. Commandments and interdictions were promulgated for the benefit of the faithful. Moral and ethical standards were precisely defined. The codification of behaviours and strict rules stipulating what was permitted and what was forbidden were an essential part of the definition of the new Daoist orthodoxy and its moral landscape. Rules of initiation were laid down. The Daoists intended their authority to be equally exercised over the post-mortem world. The departed were, in the same way as the living, placed under a legislative regime. Likened to troublemaking demons of all kinds, they were consigned to the shadowy realm of the Six Heavens, the colossal pandemonium of 'expired energies', and they were enjoined not to cross its boundaries. Death, synonymous with the demoniacal, was the evil that had to be contained and combated at any cost. The dualism advocated by the sect of the Celestial Master verged on fundamentalism. By instituting a radical distinction between the living and the dead, between the forces of good and evil beings, it attempted to place a *cordon sanitaire* between the sinner and the elect, the initiated and the 'pagan'. The cosmic conquest was conducted through a holy war that, on the pretext of getting rid of the superannuated gods, in fact aimed to appropriate the whole of the religious landscape.

This legislation served to plug the permeable barriers that separated the space of the living from that of the dead. Blurring these boundaries was, more than anything else, a sign of serious disturbance, in the same way that transgression, whether moral, ethnic or social, was perceived as a blatant manifestation of universal decadence.

The Daoist institution took on the appearance of an authoritarian and censorial magistracy. It legislated and codified, regulating the conduct of the living and of the deities. The Pact of Purity (*qingyue*) concluded by the Celestial Master was itself testament to the contractual nature of the relations that the Daoists wished to maintain with supernatural forces. The capitulation of the gods, validated by the oath they had taken to accept unconditionally their new circumstances (in particular the renunciation of food offerings), was the basis on which this relationship was meant to operate.

The Celestial Masters promulgated veritable decrees for the benefit of the invisible world in order to try to put an end to this confusion and to impose the rules of orthodoxy. There was no longer any question of the demoniacal spirits wandering between the two worlds in search of an existence guaranteed by the living. By hardening the juridical and penal aspect of the relations that they meant to establish with morbid and demoniacal forces, the Daoists made themselves the sovereigns of the moral order. To identify, note down, mollify or eradicate these creatures of the invisible world, to ratify their beneficial or harmful status, to proclaim their right to veneration or threaten them with expulsion: these were the basic functions of the Daoist Master. Demons had to be detected without fail and their misdeeds diagnosed; it was especially important that their names be registered and as detailed a list as possible of their distinguishing marks be supplied. There is no doubt that the exceptional zeal, bordering on the obsessional, displayed by the Daoists in classifying and curbing these hundreds and thousands of demoniacal creatures sprang from their resolve to be absolute masters in matters of exorcism. Daoism proclaimed itself as the only way to wage battle with the forces of evil, to combat them and to repair the damage they caused. Under the authority of the upholders of the Way, the demons were subject, like anyone else, to the regime of laws and contracts. To impose perfect order in this world and the next, the Daoists reprimanded and inveighed, threatened and exhorted. The exorcism manuals of antiquity began to look like legal codes.

The medieval apocalypses show more clearly than anything else the fierce desire of the Daoists to establish themselves as the regulators of the cosmos and the universal destroyers of evil. Whether they came out of the organisation of the Celestial Master or from the southern sects that were developing on its margins around the fifth century, these eschatological revelations accorded a critical position to demonology. For all these Daoist currents were imbued, in a more or less obvious way, with a sense of anticipation of the end of the world in which conceptions of evil took on an intensity never before matched.

Demonological taxonomies

The *Nüqing guilü*, the *Demon Statutes of Nüqing*, is unquestionably the greatest demonological catalogue of medieval Daoism. Issuing from the organisation of the Celestial Master, the version that has come down to us dates from the fourth to the fifth centuries, but the core of the work is probably earlier. The *Demon Statutes* aims at strict regulation of the behaviour and morality of the living,[12] but its primary intent is to exercise authority over the world of the dead and all manner of spirits, to achieve supreme power over the creatures of evil. Revealed by the incarnation of the Dao, the Highest Great Dao, to the first Celestial Master, Zhang Daoling, the *Demon Statutes of Nüqing* makes of the latter the supreme exorcist, the chief of all the spirits and demons:

> The Highest Great Dao . . . conferred on the Celestial Master, Zhang Daoling, these *Demon Statutes* . . . which show the names of all the demons and all the spirits of the universe as well as their capacity for good or for ill. Power was thus delegated to him over the demons and spirits so that no one would act intemperately.[13]

The text resembles an enormous set of police records listing everything that the imagination can conceive of in the way of demons.[14] The task is meant to be exhaustive, and it is huge: 'in this world', say the *Statutes*, 'for every living person there are ten thousand demons'.[15] With unshakeable determination, the *Statutes* provide endless lists of these potential troublemakers. There are those who have perished in accidents of all kinds, those who were murdered or starved, or who died in prison. There are sorcerers (*wushi*), delinquent ex-Daoists (*buzheng daoshi*)[16] and high-ranking soldiers killed on the field of honour. And there are demons of the stars, of the sixty days of the cycle, of the six decades and of the twelve months, of the five directions, of the five elements, of the five colours, of the five tastes, of the Yin and the Yang, of the mountains, of the seas, of the rivers great and small, of the mineral kingdom (stones, metals), of the plant kingdom (trees and plants) and of the animal kingdom (parasites, insects, tigers, leopards, foxes, snakes, tortoises, birds, monkeys). There are also demons of the house (lavatories, wells, hearth, bed), demons of graves, demons of all sorts of objects (weapons, musical instruments, old bones, carts, pillars, clothes) – and more. Some demons are the object of particular attention, as, for example, the sixty demons who govern each of the days of the sexagesimal cycle.[17]

Through this spectacular taxonomic display it can be seen that the modalities of space and time are wholly manipulated by the evil beings, who must be ceaselessly kept in check and held at bay. With punctilious zeal, the *Demon Statutes* present dossiers on the demons, revealing for almost every one of them their name or nickname, as well as details concerning their physiognomy and clothes. This is the case, to cite just one example, of the pair of female spirits of menstruation and of pregnancy, which the experienced woman will not fail to recognise: the first couple is completely clothed in green and is three feet in height, while the second, dressed all in black, only measures, to be exact, 3.3 inches![18] For the demons of the five directions, the author or authors have made the decision to carry the concern for detail to the point of furnishing the names of all their family (father and mother, brothers, relations and grandparents). They are all flying creatures who are in fact nothing but vile spreaders of poisons.[19] By providing the maximum of information about 'names and forenames, clothes, colour and height' of the demonic evil-doers in this way, the work makes it possible to pinpoint each of them quite easily and to achieve optimal control.[20] Among the methods of exorcism the heckling (*hu qi ming*) of the identified demon is one of the most often recommended.[21]

The Daoist sects that developed on the fringes of the organisation of the Celestial Master, and were active around the fourth and fifth centuries in southern China, similarly applied themselves to tracking down demons. The sect of the Emperor of the North (Beidi) and that of the *Dongyuan shenzhou jing*, the *Scripture of the Divine Incantations of the Grotto Chasms*, also produced their exorcistic catalogues. The first has given us, among other things, a demonological calendar entitled *Dongzhen taiji Beidi ziwei shenzhou miaojing*, the *Marvellous Scripture of the Divine Incantations of the Purple Tenuity of the Northern Emperor of the Highest Summit of Deep Perfection*. The work makes detailed predictions about the catastrophes caused by the invasion of the demons in the course of the nine years of the sexagesimal cycle preceding the flood at the end of the Great Kalpa.[22] The second sect, that of the Grotto Chasms, which produced the great apocalypse of medieval Daoism, the *Dongyuan shenzhou jing*, another major source for medieval demonology, conveys an even more dramatic image. The descriptions that are given of the demons also reveal their great diversity and their monstrousness: cyclops demons with three heads, demons with vertical eyes and mouth, or red noses, or with three feet and a dozen hands, two-headed or one-armed demons, or those with huge headless bodies. Most of them are armed with clubs, daggers or ropes. They infiltrate everywhere: in mountains and rivers, woods and earth. They poison food and water.[23] They invade the heavens and the ten directions of the universe and take all kinds of forms, human or animal. Some change into women in order to kidnap babies. Others turn themselves into fish ogres, giant birds, insects or deer. There are giants as well as Lilliputians. Every kind of demon *ad infinitum* is listed and unmasked.

Despite all this, the concern of the *Scripture of the Grotto Chasms*, unlike the *Demon Statutes*, is not of a taxonomic nature. The demons are denounced quite haphazardly without any attempt at classification and with a compelling sense of urgency. The feeling of terror conveyed by the book comes as much from the disjointed narration of these nightmarish visions as from the extravagant number of demons that are proclaimed. For the *Dongyuan shenzhou jing*, the problem seems to be more quantitative than qualitative. The extraordinary proliferation of the demons is the indisputable precursor of the imminence of the final days:

> The great evil-working kings of the Three Heavens, leading four hundred and eighteen thousand creatures, spread red abscesses; those of the Six Heavens, numbering eighty thousand, order seven million spirits to sow white abscesses; those of the Nine Heavens, numbering six hundred thousand, unleash a hundred and eighty million of them to propagate black abscesses; those of the Thirty-Six Heavens, the chiefs of eighty thousand million spirits, spread green abscesses.[24]

The numbers invoked are mesmerising. It is a question of seizing the imagination. Evil spreads like an uncontrollable contagion. Thousands of millions of demons are spoken of, the abodes of hell overflowing on to earth in order that their denizens commit horrifying deeds, inflicting suffering and misfortune on all. Massive invasions of these packs of havoc-wreaking spirits arrive to abduct children and old folk, to infiltrate houses, to kill wrongdoers as well as the innocent, to suck the blood of people and domestic animals. The descriptions given of them by the *Scripture of the Grotto Chasms* echo a conspicuous collective paranoia: 'The exterminating spirits with red heads will come! Their king, ten thousand measures tall, will order thirty-six thousand million of them to travel the world, armed with red clubs, to attack human beings whom they will hunt down night and day.'[25]

The proliferation of evil

The demons make terror rule. All the evils of the world are laid at their door. Violence, barbarian invasions, raids, exoduses, punishments, imprisonment, loss of livestock and harvests, corruption and calumnies are among their abominable misdeeds. They destroy the harmony of families, spread social disorder and bring failure. The henchmen of evil will yield to nothing. But it is in the area of disease that the extent of their noxious influence is greatest.

He who does not know how to protect himself against demons inevitably falls prey to illnesses that are always interpreted, if not as the wages of sin, then at least as the result of personal negligence. For the Daoists, in general terms, the attack by demons was due above all to the carelessness of those who disregarded the practices of longevity and revelled in immorality and lustfulness. They thereby left their body weakened and vulnerable to external miasmas, to the sanctions of the censor gods, as well as to the death-laden germs they harboured within themselves. The congenital presence of demoniacal elements in each human being explains the permeability of the body to external pathogenic elements caused by conditions in the familial or social environment. If we have no choice but to get along with the cursed and irreducible parts of ourselves that are our demon-souls, the *po*, there are other demoniacal beings residing within us that should be expelled. These are the death-bringing demons, called Three Cadavers (*sanshi*). Their parasitic character explains their other name of Three Worms (*sanchong*). Situated in the three vital centres, the three Cinnabar Fields of the human body – the head, the heart region and the lower abdomen – these demon parasites are particularly noxious. They zealously set to eating away at the energies of the body in order to cause its collapse so that they can rejoin their element of affinity, the earth. It is at their invitation that the external demons come to lodge within us.

For the adepts of immortality the expulsion of these demons is the necessary preliminary condition for the purification and rectification of the body. From very early on parasitology in China has been associated with demonology. This phobia about parasites emerges quite clearly in the ancient treatise of exorcism of the third century BCE mentioned earlier and in the contemporaneous medical manuscripts of Mawangdui.[26] In them the character *chong* serves as a generic term for a set of creatures: insects, worms, snakes and other reptiles. In short it designates animal vermin. Every *chong* is considered a potential agent of disaster.[27] The relationship between demonology and parasitology is equally evident in the famous practice of sorcery called *gu*. Equated with poison, demonic force and witchcraft, the *gu* by itself could stand as the symbol of Chinese 'black magic' from High Antiquity.[28] One of the oldest and deadliest preparations of the *gu* is to place insects, snakes and other small creatures in an earthenware jar and leave them there until they devour one another. The last surviving creature, appropriately called *gu*, which concentrates within it all the noxiousness of the ingested vermin, is thought to be a formidable vehicle of bewitchment.[29]

The realm of demonic imagination connected with vermin progressively gave way to a nomenclature of parasitic diseases. Just like the deities, internal and external demons maintain relations of complicity, indeed of kinship. This emerges clearly in a work of the Tang, the pinnacle of demonic entomology: the *Taishang chu sanshi jiuchong baosheng jing*, the *Book for Expelling the Three Worms and the Nine Insects and for Protecting Life*.[30] Long before that, the first Daoists took up the principles of demonic nosography that had been handed down through the centuries. Lists of illnesses caused by the demons abound in Daoist demonology. The *Demon Statutes* expose fevers, headaches, stomach ulcers, vomiting, choking and giddiness caused by the demons.[31] Mental illnesses are also attributed to the *gui*, succubi of core being and the vital energies. Among the psychiatric symptoms cited most often we find neurasthenia, depression, alternating fits of tears and laughter, terrifying nightmares, delirium, hallucinations, children's nocturnal fears and suicide.

No fewer afflictions are recorded in the interminable predictions of epidemics trotted out by the Daoist zealots of the *Scripture of the Grotto Chasms*. It is with a sense of dread that the devastating illnesses, physical as well as psychic, that afflict humanity are described: palpitations, cramps, deafness, jaundice, diarrhoea, vomiting blood, nose bleeds, suppurating abcesses, plague, cholera, paralysis, malaria, decomposition of the genital organs; and the list goes on. No pathological torture seems to have been forgotten by the adepts of the end of the world. The demons enter directly into the organism, 'suck the vital essence and eat the blood' of their victims or, in the shape of miasmas of different colours, make people intoxicated and bring about their death:

> On earth, ninety kinds of illness strike down the sinners . . . The blue breaths sow death; the red, plague; the yellow, dysentery; the white, cholera; the black, official crackdowns.[32]
> Human beings have their body covered in pustules. Their limbs and their face become [successively] green, red, yellow, white and

black. They suffer now from cold, now from heat. [Fevers] come upon them and then disappear. Day after day they endure the worst troubles. The breaths come to pierce their heart; the abdominal region becomes quite hard. They no longer want to eat and take less and less food until they completely lose their appetite . . .

They suffer from malaria. Their eyes are cloudy. In their delirious state, their speech is demented. At times they will sing and shriek, at others sob. Their limbs are quite purulent, their breathing is spasmodic and irregular. Epidemics like this are spreading over the whole earth![33]

The roots of evil

The aim of these symptomatological tracts is to alarm. Demonology and nosography owe their emphasis in Daoism to their ethical and moral dimensions. For the faithful of the organisation of the Celestial Master, pathology and demons are indissociable from sin. Illness essentially has its aetiology in moral and religious misconduct: physical or mental, it is the most convincing sign of wrongdoing. This notion was followed to the letter by the first Daoists of the sect of the Celestial Master. It is known that the interdiction on practising medicine was one of the credos of their orthodoxy. Therapeutic treatment was limited to religious intervention alone. Offerings, petitions, talismans and especially confessions were the only recommended therapeutic practices:

> From the age of seven years, the age of wisdom, those who are ill must confess their wrongdoing, make an act of contrition and organise offerings, rituals, requests and talismans. In the case of a longstanding illness or a serious and incurable illness, refuge will be taken [in the Way] and confession will [likewise] be made [of one's sins] in order to make a recovery.[34]

All forms of medicine properly speaking were strictly prohibited by the dogma of the Celestial Master, whether it be acupuncture or the taking of remedies. Children seem to have escaped this draconian rule, until the age of seven when the first initiation took place, marking the official entry of boys and girls into the bosom of the sect.[35] The conviction that the source of illness was a moral one went as far as to endow it with the weight of an ordeal. This is what is stated very clearly by one of the codes of religious commandments of the sect, dating from the third century, the *Zhengyi fawen tianshi jiaojie kejing*: 'When the Libationers care for their patients, they do it to combat the illness. If the illness returns once it has been treated, it is because the patient is a wrongdoer. He must not then, under any circumstances, be ministered to a second time.'[36] Except for minimal differences, this ideology was to remain that of the Daoists of the medieval sectarian movements. Sins, whether they are committed by the victim himself, or whether they are inherited in the family line or from personal karma, are punished in the first place by an attack on the physical or psychic integrity of the person and by a reduction of his life capital. They create a terrain favourable to demonic infiltration. This demonisation of illness and disability, indeed of the aesthetic imperfection of the body, opened the way, as we shall see, to elitist and discriminatory conceptions in which racist tendencies can be easily detected.

To denounce evil and fight against it: such was the programme of all the movements of medieval Daoism – institutionalised or marginal – whose driving force was its apocalyptic eschatology. It fully justified Daoism's mission, proselytising or not.

The presence of evil on earth is thought of as an attack by the demonic spirits. The emergence of suffering is the proof of their proliferation on earth. In the deployments of demonic legions and the string of woes that they propagate we can see the realisation of the prophecies announcing the terrible and inescapable end of the universe in its entirety. They are the undeniable manifestation, the unarguable sign, of the imminent end of a humanity in serious decline. The evil that they spread is in effect due more than anything to a fatal moral degeneration. Instead of devoting themselves to the arts of longevity, men accumulate sins, and show no respect for religious and ethical principles.

It is not surprising, in such circumstances, as the *Demon Statutes* spell out, that the world is saturated with morbid emanations, since 'many deaths are counted but few births'.[37] It is clearly men's immorality which is at the root of the emergence of the demons in this world, the *Statutes* are pained to note in describing the age of the end (*moshi*):[38]

> On earth, men and women daily show dishonesty and ingratitude. Disasters and suffering multiply day by day. The demon-bandits under heavenly control and the five poisons are spreading. All of this comes from the absence of faith and the lapse in the practices of 'keeping to the One' and of good behaviour. [It is in this way that] human beings bring misfortune upon themselves.[39]

The same type of lamentations is proffered repetitively by the *Scripture of the Grotto Chasms*:

> The men of this world accumulate bad deeds and give no allegiance to the Law of the Dao . . . The people are in the mire . . . The demon kings spread their poisons and exterminate the righteous. Each home is struck by curses and sorrow . . . People cause each other harm. They bring about their own suffering and drag one another towards death.[40]

Furthermore, human beings no longer know how to keep to their station and their place in society. Thus, the people of the last days, as *The Scripture*

of Esoteric Explanations of the Three Heavens explains, have lost their sense
of judgement and their taste for fundamental values: 'They no longer marry
according to their race. Their sexual practices are anarchic and unclean.
They believe in false [doctrines] and reject what is authentic. The original
Dao is thwarted and perverted. Deceptions of all kinds abound.'[41]

Ambivalence and rehabilitation of the demons

If the demons are the cause, the expression and the tangible presence of evil
on earth, they are also the exterminating agents charged with its eradication. Symptoms of human degeneracy, but also the instruments of universal
purification, they are a necessary evil. This ambivalence in demonism characterises Daoist 'theodicy'.

Evil fights evil. A demon can give up his free and independent existence as
an evil creature to take on the more subservient but certainly nobler role of
valet or soldier of the Dao. Then he will join the ranks of the armies of the
great cause whose task it is to purge the world of this evil assemblage of
which, only yesterday, he was a part. The disapproval earned by the male-
volence of the demon comes above all from the fact that he is not counted,
not officially included in the divine plan. His heresy comes from his margin-
ality, from his alterity. He is a 'wild divinity' (*yeshen*) or 'independent divinity' (*sishen*) who acts on his own and gives himself pompous titles such as
'great deity', 'general', 'sire' or 'lady'. Thus, when they move collectively,
these wild demons obey their own hierarchy. Regrouped into hordes, the
most important demons summon reinforcements, getting their subordinates
to carry out their exactions. The division between the 'good' and the 'bad'
demon is a question of status and title. The destructive demon passes from
the paltry state of 'other deity' to that of 'correct demon' as soon as he
leaves the uncertain camp of anarchy and evil for the more reassuring but
also more limiting one of righteousness and adherence to the norm. Now
placed under the tutelage of the Dao, he is recorded, inspected, enlisted and
engaged under oath in the exhausting work of intercessor between the two
worlds. He becomes an official servant of the Dao who entrusts him with a
position in keeping with his abilities and his talents: soldier, general, government official, chief, king, executioner or henchman. As the beneficiary of a
promotion scheme valid for the whole of the Daoist system of bureaucracy,
he has to be rewarded for his good and loyal service by an advancement in
the hierarchy. There are some who even go as far as to leave the post-
mortem administration to be enrolled on the Register of life and to be
admitted among the elect.[42]

In the state of emergency that characterised the pre-apocalyptic situation,
the Dao tries desperately to make itself heard among the implacable ones,
the demons who refuse to enter the ranks. It appeals to them directly by
'oral decrees' (*kouchi*). This is their ultimatum: either they accept rehabilitation, submit and renew their vow to become loyal and devoted servants of
the Highest Great Dao, or they will be annihilated, literally crushed. Over

and over they are told: 'Make haste to obey the Law' (*jiji ru lüling*), a stereotypical formula that is inspired by the legal language in force since the Han. The Dao multiplies injunctions, threats and inducements with regard to rebellious or reluctant spirits. Its numerous exhortations are accompanied by threats of capital punishment. The orders of the Dao are not to be taken lightly: 'You, great evil kings', says the *Scripture of the Grotto Chasms*,

> you are [lost] along [the way] to perdition. You do nothing but spread your plagues and afflict the mass of humans . . . Or else you put the hearts of men into disarray and bring it about so that they become the victims of trials, and are unjustly punished and imprisoned. You torment the entire populace. It is you, evil kings, who are the instigators of all these misfortunes! . . . If you, evil kings, refuse fidelity to the great Law and if you persist in persecuting the Masters, you will be hurled headlong into the water, or into the fire! All will be decapitated, your heads will be smashed into eighty pieces! Make haste to gather your spiritual forces! You must not go against my orders in inflicting pestilential illnesses and in spreading disorder among the good people here below! Make haste to obey my law![43]

Every means is employed to bring the spirit demons who remain stubbornly on the margins to submission. The recalcitrant ones are warned again and again that their heads will be smashed to smithereens if they disobey the laws, a punishment no doubt looked upon as fatal by those demons who are always waiting to take shape again in the world of mortals.

Like the initiated, the demons can be receptive to the holy word and able to conform to it by making an act of contrition, and to take up the cause of goodness by swearing an oath. The touching plea of the forces of evil is expressed like this: 'Since time immemorial we others have worked only evil and acted against the Dao. Today we have heard the word of the Revered Celestial One and we want to observe it and put it into practice.'[44] Should we see in this free demonic expression conceded by the Dao to the agents of evil a pedagogic impulse or even a proselytising strategy? The first step towards conversion would thus be shown by means of these direct testimonies of sincere repentance on the part of the demons. If those who represent evil in all its power, who on the face of it would not seem to be endowed with empathy and a moral sense, are so easily brought back into the fold by the camp of righteousness, there seems to be hope for all. Moreover, the example they have set for others to follow, which can be so easily formalised, is child's play.

Demonising the living

The apocalypses of medieval Daoism leave a strong feeling of ambivalence. Does the Dao really intend its message to be heard just by creatures of the other world? In fact, in the guise of relentlessly pursuing the demons, it makes an appeal to all who are in the process of being relegated to the realm of evil. It brings to their senses those human beings doomed to perdition who refuse to hear the holy word and turn their back on the Law. There is no doubt: the message is meant for everyone; it is a matter of saving all of humanity in its death throes. The good and the evil, the living and the dead, sinners along with the innocent must be converted. In appearing to call upon the spirits of the invisible world, the Daoists aimed to reach the 'pagans'. Unyielding infidels tend to become synonymous with demons. The Daoists of the movement of the Celestial Master, in the first centuries CE, aptly used the expression 'revenant forced labourers' (*guizu*) for the faithful who were not yet initiated.[45] The label of 'demon' or, worse still, 'walking corpse' (*xingshi*) was applied to all those who did not keep to the one and only way to salvation, to those who did not 'enter the Dao'.[46] It signified the exogenous element, outside the religious community. Like the deities of the shaman cults and the dynastic gods relegated to the camp of evil, the sinners and outsiders saw themselves, while they were alive, dispossessed of their human prerogatives and overwhelmed with demonic attributes usually re-served for the souls of the dead. 'Demon' was no longer a term reserved for the dead or for exhausted or animist energies, it was also applied to living beings who were declared to be outside the norm. Miscreants, heretics and barbarians were the target of demonisation campaigns zealously conducted by the partisans of an autochthonous and unique religion. As elements outside the community of the righteous, they were logically considered as pathogenic and noxious. The marked dualism of the prophetic sects of medieval Daoism rendered the sinner diabolical to the point of making him sub-human.

Idiot, sinner, troublemaker, one who is evil or vulgar or unable to be converted: all are expressions signifying those humans who are destined to endure the torments of the hells and to be reborn along the ill-favoured paths of reincarnation, those to whom the door of immortality is closed. They have inherited a 'bad heart' and carry inside them the seeds of evil. They refuse the divine teaching. The misdeeds that they committed in their past lives or that they inherited from their deceased parents or their an-cestors are their own. The sins that they incur are of a moral nature – lack of filial piety, lustfulness, greed, duplicity, hypocrisy, theft, vengeance, murder and so forth – but above all there are those that result from religious im-piety: lack of respect for the Law of the Dao, contempt for the holy books, blasphemy, refusal to be initiated, wrongdoing and harm to the faithful, unlawful or improper use of the sacred writings, sacrilege against the Daoist Masters, membership in spirit cults. The Daoist moralists draw up the lists of offences and retributions. As potential demons who will come to swell the ranks of the hells, sinners suffer during their lifetimes from afflictions of all kinds. Punishment is in the first instance immediate and terrestrial. It comes in the form of various misfortunes: accidents, illnesses, poverty, sterility. Afterwards, the effects are felt into the world beyond, the sorrows of this life continuing after death. Sinners fall into the hells where they purge their wrongdoing. As it is said in the *Taishang Lingbao Laozi huahu miaojing*, the *Marvellous Scripture on Laozi's Conversion of the Barbarians of the Most High Numinous Treasure*, their fate is identical to that of criminals sentenced by the courts and imprisoned.[47] At the end of seemingly interminable periods of expiation, they reappear on earth in one of the Eight Unfavourable Conditions of existence. The greatest sinners are reborn as one of the Six Domestic Animals: 'they eat grass, drink water and serve as food for men', announces the *Scripture of the Grotto Chasms*. Or they may become malevolent demons, or then again beings possessing 'a human aspect, but bereft of feelings', since they lack one of the six sensory organs. 'Their existence is one of unspeakable suffering.'[48] Issuing from hell, they are destined to go back there, and what is more, to drag their offspring along with them in this infinite chain of luckless destinies.

For the faithful of the Way of the Celestial Master, health and salvation go hand in hand and are ensured by the observation of religious rules and by morally irreproachable conduct. The invalid who is not curable by ritual means is categorically relegated to the status of 'evil being'.

The adherence to religion and a religious ethic are what determines a man's condition, ontologically and genetically. The wholeness of the body and perfect health are prerequisites to progressive advancement along the path of longevity and salvation. Initiation, the entry into the Dao, reveals and confirms that one has the qualities of the elect, and indeed of those destined for immortality. In the case of people who are out of the ordinary, this is shown by particular marks on the body (*xiang*), such as markings of the constellations, the lines of the hand, beauty spots or coloured spots on the skin, or by invisible features such as having the skeleton of an Immortal, a red marrow, blue liver or green kidneys.[49]

By the same logic, those who refuse to be converted are considered as genetically incapable of salvation. These miscreants also bear external signs of their demonic nature and their animality. They might be crippled, handicapped, hunchbacked or mentally defective. Some have hare lips, or have no feet and hands. Others have a 'deer's head' and are so hideous that just seeing them 'causes an attack of vomiting'.[50] Those who do not bear such conspicuous signs of their diabolical nature are still blemished by it: they are blind or deaf or dumb or without a sense of smell. Their hidden monstrosity, which results in 'their having a human form, without having human feelings' (*you renxing wu ren zhi qing*), relegates them just the same to the ranks of the demoniacal and the bestial. Illness, physical or mental handicap and even ugliness are the stigmata of sin. The reduction of the sub-human to the animal became all the more meaningful as the Daoists began to incorporate Buddhist theories of karma into their soteriological system. Rebirth in the different species of the animal kingdom (from mammals through to insects) was thought of as one of the most dreadful punishments for committing a sin.

The sinner was not the only one to be stripped of his human dignity and to be decked out in zoomorphic peculiarities. The foreigner, the 'barbarian', was also subject to demonisation. In the bitterness of the centuries of disunion of the Six Dynasties (220–589), the Chinese, already prey to myriad autochthonous demons, found themselves assailed by even more fearsome demonic beings from abroad. The already considerable demonic pantheon was endowed with a surplus of categories of demon deities imported from India: the Brahman kings (*dafan tianwang*), the vajra divinities (*jingang*), the *raksha* (*luosha*), who were man-eating demons, and the famous 'demon kings' (*mowang*).[51] Positioned ambiguously, these gods fluctuated between the clan of the good and divine, and that of evil, the demoniacal. Their foreign origin turned them into exotic entities armed with special powers. The demon kings in particular, the sinicised *māra-(deva)-rāja*, who were mostly anonymous, and without a well-defined identity, but sometimes graced with unusual 'pseudo-Sanskrit' names, deposed the indigenous demonic race. The *mowang* had the greatest responsibilities in the kingdom of evil. They assumed the role of supreme commanders of the demonic armies, relegating the traditional Chinese *gui* to inferior ranks. Their collusion in heresy and violence made them terrifying creatures. The afflictions they caused were innumerable.

This massive migration of Buddhist demons into the Daoist pantheon can undoubtedly be explained by the growing influence of the Mahāyāna on Chinese religion. It was one of the numerous borrowings made by Daoism from the great rival tradition. But as well as that it must be seen as a religious epiphenomenon of historical circumstances. The sociohistorical causes to which it can be attributed are wide-ranging. For several centuries China had been besieged by invaders who were just as frightening as the demons but much less virtual. They scourged the country with fire and bloodshed and forced exoduses of the population. In the Chinese imagination, the barbarian demons and the demonic barbarians were one and the same. The country at that time was completely dominated in the north by the fierce nomadic tribes who had come from Central Asia, a situation that helped to sharpen the sense of ethnic and cultural superiority of the Chinese and to render the enemy truly diabolical. Evil lay in difference, in alterity. The Daoists of the organisation of the Celestial Master viewed the incursions of the barbarians and the demonic raids in the same light:

From foreign countries, beyond the borders, [come] the barbaric hordes. As if possessed, they advance at the head of their diabolical and rebellious people. They change themselves into poisonous winds that rise up to heaven. Big or small, these demon-barbarians invade our world in their hundreds of thousands of millions to devour the blood and the vital essence of human beings. They go forth, their hair in disarray. Now that they are infiltrating the countryside, what recourse do you have? The disorder spread by their foot-soldiers and their troopers is beyond telling.[52]

Appearances are not deceptive: the dishevelled hair sported by these arrogant foreigners and their ability to change themselves into pestilential winds are the diabolical signs attributed to demons since Antiquity.[53] These myriads of barbarians also shared with the demons a taste for blood and anarchy.

No Daoist work better bears witness than the *Scripture of the Grotto Chasms* to the acute xenophobia that stirred up the Daoist sectarians in medieval times. Over and over again the book predicts the swarming incursions of the barbarians. They come from all sides: there are the Liao from the west, the Dingling from the Ordos, the Wuwan from the north-east (southern Manchuria) and the terrifying peoples from the north, the Toba and Xianbei tribes, the Proto-Mongols who are described as the Six Barbarians (Liuyi). During the dreadful apocalyptic years, declares the holy scripture, the barbarians relentlessly persecute the people, who are plunged into despair.[54] It is a tragic prophecy spelled out like a litany. Indeed, the barbarians are right there, on Chinese soil. They have violently invaded the north of the country, driving the people into exile in the south. And to the Daoists of this southern diaspora, the monstrousness of these demon barbarians knows no limits! Cyclops with two or three heads, monsters with vertical eyes, or with three feet, or giants with black tails, horned and in all colours – the invader comes in the most deviant of forms. The fruit of imaginations made feverish by fear and violence, these visions of the alien more readily conjure up monstrous beasts than human beings. And the texts are unambiguous about this. When the foreigners from the countries bordering China are not reduced outright to vile teratological creatures, they are seen as men who are not quite human. As the *Scripture on Laozi's Conversion of the Barbarians* explains, all they can then do is fall down to the way of the Six Kinds of Animals, where they transmigrate during thousands of Kalpa.[55] This dehumanisation of the foreigner is spelled out even more bluntly by a Daoist work of the Tang: the barbarians belong to the 'race of animals', they have neither mind nor conscience, they drink blood and walk about naked, they are wild and sybaritic.[56] Any fraternisation with these inferior races or, worse, any interbreeding between the Han people and the foreign tribes have long been seen as a symptom and a source of serious disturbance by the adepts of the Dao:

> Since the creation of the world (the separation of heaven and earth), there have been on the periphery of China, [the ethnic groups of] the Yi, Qiang, Man, Rong and Di who constitute the furthest limits of the country. Each group, when it came to marriage, used to keep to its own race. Each, as to religion, used to hold to its own truth. There was no interbreeding and confusion. (But since the Han . . .), the living and the dead (the demons) have been interacting . . . The populations live in a state of promiscuity. Chinese and foreigners intermix.[57]

The safeguarding of ethnic purity thus became a theological crusade. This aspiration to maintain the race was, to a certain extent, one of the aims of the organisation of the Celestial Masters. The 'seed-children', *zhongzi*, ritually conceived during the ceremonies of Union of the *qi* of the *Yellow Book* practised by couples numbered among the faithful under the direction of a Master, were perfect beings, immortals. This precursor of eugenicism was to foster the creation of the chosen people, the 'seed-people' (*zhongmin*), the genetic stock of the new messianic humanity.[58]

The demonic nature of the non-Chinese would remain the focus of Daoist denunciations. Under the Song, it was no longer as much the peoples of the North who played the role of the scapegoats for evil, but the ethnic minorities in the south of China. Stories and legends were circulated about the bizarre practices and supernatural powers of their 'sorcerers' (*wu*) whose morals were suspect. 'Demoniacal emanations are particularly numerous among the hundred tribes of the region south of the Yangzi', as a Daoist text of the time put it.[59] Daoism was the chosen way by which death's designs could be vanquished. The will to promote orthodoxy on the part of the Daoists, great experts in exorcism, was therefore motivated by a powerful desire to suppress these rival sorcerers, but it was also patently in line with the policy at the time to sinicise the colonised populations in the south of China.[60]

Concluding remarks

It would be pointless to try to judge the impact that the deformation and demonisation of the gods by the first Daoist theologians had in concrete terms and the extent to which it actually came up against pervading religious sentiments. However dogmatic this beginning phase might have been, and however severe the manifestations of intolerance and violence that flowed from the Pact of Purity, in real terms its application appears generally to have been nothing more than a devout wish on the part of rigid zealots who were unaware of its actual impact.

With the exception of several historically verified cases during the medieval period and under the Song, when Daoist hostility towards popular 'superstitions' had as a direct or indirect consequence overt violence against the sanctuaries of the 'minor deities' and of their shamans and seers,[61] the battle waged against pernicious gods and the sacrificial cults that honoured them was limited to the theological domain. A more moderate and nuanced approach became necessary as soon as the first attempts to apply the intransigent doctrine of the Pact of Purity were made; that is, as soon as Daoism took on the dimensions of a national religion. Ideological views were now softened considerably.

Consensus was to some extent dictated by historical circumstances. The fall of the capital Luoyang, in 311, brought in its train a major upheaval in the religious geography of China. Driven on by these dramatic political occurrences, the Way of the Celestial Master emerged from its local and sectarian framework to spread throughout the whole Empire. In the north as in the south, it had, from the fourth and fifth centuries, penetrated every level of Chinese and non-Chinese society alike. For example, in the north of the country, then under 'barbarian' rule, the renewal of the first Daoist church was promoted by the most prestigious of its foreign dynasties, the Northern Wei (386–534). The eminent Celestial Master Kou Qianzhi (d. 448) subjected the pre-existing Daoist religion to severe structural and ethical reform, stripping it in order to make it worthy of the Confucian ideal and to raise it up to the level of a highly influential Buddhist code of ethics.[62] The ideological rigidity of the Daoist theocracy that Kou succeeded in establishing for several decades (425–451) resulted in terrible repressions directed against the rival religions of Buddhism and traditional religion. The decree promulgated in 444 at Kou's instigation ordered the destruction of 'innumerable' sanctuaries dedicated to 'inferior deities' (*xiaoshen*). However, Kou and his powerful protectors, probably alerted to the dangers of this demonisation of all the gods and the eradication of popular religion, added a restrictive clause to this decree: fifty-seven places of worship would be legally authorised to remain.[63] In the view of the cunning politicians who supported him, this allocation of a share to the rival non-Daoist sanctuaries ought to have been enough to satisfy popular fervour, while ensuring perfect security and an optimal control of the places of worship that were so often suspected of nurturing popular rebellions.

Contemporaneously, in the south of the country, Daoist orthodoxy came up against vicissitudes of another kind. The great Chinese families of the north, converts for generations to the Way of the Celestial Master, emigrated under the pressure of the barbarian invasions to a southern land that to their eyes was highly exotic. Daoism, which in this way was promulgated in the area south of the Yangtze, in the region of the Jiangnan, came into contact with a culture steeped in spirit beliefs and 'shamanism' that from then on it was obliged to reckon with.[64] The sheer force of these southern beliefs, the dynamism of the cults, not to mention the need to curry favour with the state,[65] together provided the impetus for a theological reorientation and an inevitable moderation with regard to the gods who were once demonised. Influenced by the new eschatological perspective of Mahāyāna Buddhism, the great southern currents of institutionalised Daoism adopted a more complex and lenient stand towards the dead and the spirits.

The deceased-as-demons, whether famous or not, who had been irrevocably cast out by the moralists of the Way of the Celestial Master, thus made their reappearance. The pantheon of the Shangqing movement, the great mystical current of southern China, saw the return in force of deities that until then had been expelled. The rehabilitated deceased were integrated into a high-ranking post-mortem administration: former sovereigns, virtuous politicians and renowned military men, whether they had died in former times or only recently, became officials of the underworld. In his work *Zhen'gao*, the *Declarations of the Perfected*, the famous promoter of the movement, Tao Hongjing (456–536), drew up a list of historical personages and celebrities of antiquity occupying positions at different levels in the offices beyond the grave.[66] The dead waited on the dead in the world beyond, which was now given a clearer conceptual basis. To pass from the status of general, minister and even emperor to that of a simple demonic officer in the underworld might, unquestionably, have appeared ridiculous, even scandalous. But such were the stakes for the rehabilitation of the departed who had national standing: official recognition in the post-mortem bureaucracy or banishment to the marginal and humiliating ranks of heterodoxy.

The other great Daoist movement of southern China, the Lingbao current, deeply permeated by the eschatological conceptions of Mahāyāna Buddhism, for its part multiplied the ways and means to post-mortem salvation, and the chances of achieving it. The destiny of men, little by little liberated from their genealogical shackles, was determined on a more individual basis by the system of karmic retribution and its heavy moral apparatus. The diversification of the underworld and the different paths to rebirth offered unheard of choices to the departed. The idea of universal compassion and salvation tended to free death from its terrifying aspects. The demonised souls of the dead then became the vehicles of what, until then, had been unimaginable hopes. Evil was no longer just confined to the context of sectarian alienation. It was now dealt with by a liturgy addressed unconditionally to all and capable of ensuring personal as well as communal liberation.

Translated by Stephanie Anderson

Notes

1 Donald Harper, 'A Chinese Demonography of the Third Century BC', *Harvard Journal of Asiatic Studies*, 45 (1985), 459–98.
2 Donald Harper, 'Spellbinding', in Donald S. Lopez Jr (ed.), *Religions of China in Practice* (Princeton, NJ: Princeton University Press, 1996), pp. 241–50.
3 Derk Bodde, *Festivals in Classical China* (Princeton, NJ: Princeton University Press, 1975), pp. 75–138.
4 *Santian neijie jing* (DZ 1205), 1:5b.
5 *Santian neijie jing*, 1:6a.
6 *Lu xiansheng daomen kelüe* (DZ 1127), 8a. On this work, see Lai Chi-tim, 'The Opposition of Celestial-Master Taoism to Popular Cults during the Six Dynasties', *Asia Major*, 11 (1998), 1–20; and Peter Nickerson, 'Abridged Codes of Master Lu for the Daoist Community', in Lopez, *Religions of China in Practice*, 347–59.
7 *Baopuzi neipian* (Wang Ming (ed.), Beijing: Zhonghua shuju, 1985), 9:171.
8 *Santian neijie jing*, 1:6a.
9 R. A. Stein, 'Religious Taoism and Popular Religion from the Second to the Seventh Centuries', in Holmes Welch and Anna Seidel (eds), *Facets of Taoism* (New Haven, CT: Yale University Press, 1979), pp. 53–81.
10 Stein, 'Religious Taoism and Popular Religion'.
11 The *Nüqing guilü* (DZ 790) mentions the 'decapitated generals' on the battle field (*wutou huaijun*), among whom are cited Zhang Yuanbo (or Zhang Shao) and Zhong Shiji (or Zhong Hui), generals-in-chief who died on the field of honour in

the third century (1:2a and 6:1b–2a). Other 'generals of conquered armies' (*baijun sijiang*) are also singled out by the *Scripture of the Divine Incantations of the Grotto Chasms* (*Dongyuan shenzhou jing*, DZ 335, ch. 6). Among them can be recognised great political and military figures of Chinese history, see my *Une apocalypse taoïste du Ve, siècle. Le Livre des incantations divines des grottres abyssales* (Paris: Collège de France, Institut des Hautes Études Chinoises, 1990), p. 125.

12 It contains a list of twenty-two commandments to be observed by faithful (3:1a–3b). The seventeenth commandment forbids adherence to demonic cults, and the killing of living beings including birds. Its violation is punished by a reduction in the lifespan of the guilty. The *Xuanlu lüwen* (DZ 188), a breviary of religious and moral laws promulgated by the organisation of the Celestial Master, stipulates as well, in the first of its thirteen rules, the interdiction of propitiating demon-spirits. In this case, infractions are punished by a five year diminution of life.

13 *Nüqing guilü*, 1:1a–b.

14 This sort of demonological recording is not new. The ancient exorcism manuals involve the same system of cataloguing. In them a great variety of demons is denounced by name in terms that reveal their nature and diversity. Certain names by themselves betray the origins or the malevolent potential of the offender; in other cases the misdeeds for which they are responsible are stipulated (see Harper, 'Spellbinding').

15 *Nüqing guilü*, 2:4b.

16 *Nüqing guilü*, 4:1b.

17 These are the wayward and murderous demons who have the power to fly over distances of a thousand leagues; their body is human and covered in red hair, and they are without eyes (*Nüqing guilü*, 1:1a, 7b). Other medieval demonological handbooks also mention the demons who dominate the temporal divisions. The *Chisongzi zhangli* (DZ 615, 3:30a), for example, presents a list of the demons who govern the twelve months, while the *Dongyuan shenzhou jing* reveals the identity of demons that arise at each decade of the sexagesimal cycle: spirits of floods, spirits with red turbans, spirits with black faces and feet, spirits of ropes and of walls who infiltrate among people to inflict plagues on them by changing themselves into red birds (Mollier, *Une apocalypse taoïste*, p. 125).

18 *Nüqing guilü*, 4:3b.

19 *Nüqing guilü*, 6:2b–3a.

20 *Nüqing guilü*, 1:8b.

21 *Nüqing guilü*, 2:5b.

22 DZ 49. Christine Mollier, 'La méthode de l'Empereur du Nord du mont Fengdu, une tradition exorciste du taoisme médiéval', *T'oung Pao*, 8 (1997), 331–85.

23 *Dongyuan shenzhou jing*, ch. 9; Mollier, *Une apocalypse taoïste*, p. 135.

24 *Dongyuan shenzhou jing*, ch. 1; See, Mollier, *Une apocalypse taoïste*.

25 *Dongyuan shenzhou jing*, ch. 1; See, Mollier, *Une apocalypse taoïste*.

26 For insects associated with demonology, see Donald Harper, *Early Chinese Medical Literature: The Mawangdui Medical Manuscripts* (London and New York: Kegan Paul International, 1998), pp. 74–5.

27 Harper, 'Spellbinding', p. 243.

28 The *gu* is already mentioned in the manuscripts of Mawangdui. Represented pictographically by three insects above a dish, the character *gu* is, in the fourth century BCE, defined etymologically as 'insects in a receptacle' (*Zuozhuan*, cited by Harper, *Early Chinese Medical Literature*, note 5, p. 300).

29 The oldest description there is of the making of the *gu* dates back to the sixth century; cf. Paul U. Unschuld, *Medicine in China: A History of Ideas* (Berkeley: University of California Press, 1985), p. 48, who cites H. Y. Feng and J. K. Shryock, 'The Black Magic in China Known as Ku', *Journal of the American*

Oriental Society, 55 (1935), 1–30, pp. 7–8. Carmen Blacker, *The Catalpa Bow: A Study of Shamanistic Practices in Japan* (London: Allen & Unwin, 1975), shows that the practice is still to be found in Japan.

30 DZ 871. This little treatise offers a gallery of portraits of the Seven Demonic Souls and of the Three Worms that reside in the human body, as well as nine other sorts of parasites, amoebae and cockroaches designated by the generic term of Nine Insects (already mentioned by Ge Hong, *Baopuzi*, ch. 4). The pathologies that they cause human beings are the object of detailed descriptions. The iconography devoted to each of these entities leaves no doubt about their malevolent leanings. If two of the *po* souls appear in anthropomorphic guise (a man and a woman elegantly dressed in court attire) and could, by this deceptive dress, easily be taken for 'good' deities, the five other souls for their part openly display their demonic nature: three are monstrous humans, two are strange creatures made from a sort of human leg with bulging muscles, one topped with the head of a bird, the other with that of a human monster. The protozoan aspect of the Three Worms also confirms the affinity between demons and parasites of the human body. The Worm of the Middle Cinnabar Field, situated in the region of the heart, takes on the appearance of a monster with the look of a cocoon-like dog, while the Worm of the Lower Cinnabar Field, in the lower abdomen, presents itself like two of the *po* souls, in the appalling guise of a human leg with a cow's head.

31 *Nüqing guilü*, 1:8a.
32 *Dongyuan shenzhou jing*, ch. 1; Mollier, *Une apocalypse taoïste*, p. 101.
33 *Dongyuan shenzhou jing*, ch. 1; Mollier, *Une apocalypse taoïste*, p. 104.
34 *Santian neijie jing*, 1:6b.
35 The capacity for introspection and speech that confession requires no doubt explains this restriction.
36 *Zhenyi fawen tianshi jiaojie kejing*, 18b.
37 *Nüqing guilü*, 1:8a.
38 *Nüqing guilü*, 6:1a.
39 *Nüqing guilü*, 3:1a.
40 *Dongyuan shenzhou jing*, 1.1b; Mollier, *Une apocalypse taoïste*, p. 95.
41 *Santian neijie jing*, 1b.
42 *Nüqing guilü*, 6:2a.
43 *Dongyuan shenzhou jing*, ch. 1; Mollier, *Une apocalypse taoïste*, pp. 104–5.
44 *Dongyuan shenzhou jing*, ch. 1; Mollier, *Une apocalypse taoïste*, p. 106.
45 *Xiang'er*, Dunhuang ms. S.6825; the translation is from Stephen R. Bokenkamp, in Bokenkamp, with a contribution from Peter Nickerson, *Early Daoist Scriptures* (Berkeley: University of Califonia Press, 1997), pp. 35–6. See also R. A. Stein, 'Remarques sur les mouvements du taoïsme politico-religieux au IIe siècle ap. J.C.', *T'oung Pao*, 50 (1963), 1–78, p. 42.
46 The *Zhongshan yugui fuqi jing* as presented in *Yunji qiqian* (60:13b) explains that the 'moving skeletons and walking cadavers' (*xingshi zougu*) mean those who live in ignorance of the Dao. For the *Shenzhou jing* (ch. 9), the 'walking cadavers' are those who give themselves over to heterodox cults and also scorn the practices concerning immortality, heedless of the Three Worms, the demons who live inside them (Mollier, *Une apocalypse taoïste*, p. 135).
47 Anna Seidel, 'Le Sutra merveilleux du Ling-pao supreme', in Michel Soymié (ed.), *Contributions aux Études de Touen-houang*, vol. 3 (Paris: École Française d'Éxtrême-Orient, 1984), pp. 305–52.
48 *Dongyuan shenzhou jing*, 3:5a.
49 *Shangqing housheng daojun lieji* (DZ 442), 9b–11b; Bokenkamp, *Early Daoist Scriptures*, pp. 356–9.

50 *Dongyuan shenzhou jing*, 10:4b–5a.
51 *Mo* is the Chinese transcription of Māra, the prince of evil in the Indian sources.
52 *Nüqing guilü*, 5:1b–2a.
53 Harper, 'A Chinese Demonography', pp. 476, 493.
54 *Dongyuan shenzhou jing*, ch. 9; Mollier, *Une apocalypse taoïste*, p. 140.
55 Seidel, 'Le Sutra merveilleux'.
56 *Taishang dadao yuqing jing* (DZ 1312), 1:27a–30b; K. M. Schipper, 'Purity and Strangers: Shifting Boundaries in Medieval China', *T'oung Pao*, 80 (1994), 61–81, p. 80.
57 *Santian neijie jing*, 1:5a–b.
58 Mollier, *Une apocalypse taoïste*, pp. 175–6.
59 'Great Rituals of the Jade Room', *Wushang xuanyuan santian yutang dafa* (DZ 220), 27:5a–5b, cited by Judith Boltz, 'Not by the Seal of Office Alone: New Weapons in Battles with Supernatural', in Patricia Ebrey and Peter Gregory (eds), *Religion and Society in T'ang and Sung China* (Honolulu: University of Hawaii Press, 1993), pp. 241–305, p. 272.
60 Boltz, 'Not by the Seal of Office Alone', pp. 271–2.
61 Stein, 'Religious Taoism and Popular Religion'.
62 Richard Mather, 'K'ou Ch'ien-chih and the Taoist Theocracy at the Northern Wei Court, 425–451', in Anna Seidel and Holmes Welch (eds), *Facets of Taoism: Essays in Chinese Religion* (New Haven, CT: Yale University Press, 1979), pp. 103–22.
63 Mather, 'K'ou Ch'ien-chih'.
64 Peter Nickerson, 'Shamans, Demons, Diviners and Taoists: Conflict and Assimilation in Medieval Chinese Ritual Practice (c. AD 100–1000)', *Taoist Resources*, 5 (1994), 41–66; and Poul Anderson, 'Talking to the Gods. Visionary Divination in Early Taoism (The Sanhuang Tradition)', *Taoist Resources*, 5 (1994), 1–24.
65 Tao Hongjing, the notable figure of the intellectual and religious elite of the Shangqing movement, had a personal relationship with the emperor (Liang Wudi). Until the twelfth century, moreover, the patriarchs of the Shangqing continued to benefit from imperial support. His confrère of the Lingbao current, the equally famous Lu Xiujing (406–477), similarly enjoyed imperial patronage and the protection of the aristocrats who had come from the north (Michel Strickmann, 'The Mao Shan Revelations: Taoism and the Aristocracy', *T'oung Pao*, 63 (1977), 1–64).
66 DZ 1016, ch. 15 and 16.

6

BETWEEN KARMIC
RETRIBUTION AND
ENTWINING INFUSION

Is the karma of the parent visited
upon the child?

Maeda Shigeki

In the chapter entitled 'Turn your heart [to Buddhism]' in *Yanshi jiaxun*, the *Family Instructions for the Yan Clan*, it says:

> Good or evil acts bring disastrous or fortunate consequences. The Nine Schools and the Hundred Philosophers all agree upon this theory. Are the Buddhist scriptures alone to be held as untrue and unreliable? In the premature death of Hsiang T'o and Yen Hui, the cold and hunger of Yüan Hsien and Po I, the happiness and longevity of T'ao Chih and Chuang Ch'iao, and the riches and power of Ch'i Ching and Huan T'ui, if the actions of their previous life are examined and their next life is considered, these will be found to agree [with the principle of retribution].[1]

This seems to seek for a solution to the unreasonable nature of fate in the Buddhist theory of karmic retribution. It also says:

> Nowadays, people, if poor, humble, sick or sorrowful, without exception blame themselves for not cultivating virtuous deeds in a former life. From this point of view, how can one not prepare for a good place in a future life? When one has a son or grandson, it is simply an addition of living beings in the universe; in what does it concern his personal affairs [in the future]?[2]

This implies that good and bad karma is understood as a burden borne by the individual. Despite this, as we see in the following passage, 'The cases when men who are fond of killing have received retribution at their death or in disaster to their offspring are so numerous that they cannot be listed in detail, but for the time being several are set forth here in conclusion.'[3] Yan Zhitui posits 'disaster to their offspring', and gives the following example: 'The Liu family of Chiang-ling sold eel broth as their business. Later on a child was born with a head like an eel's, while from the neck down it was like a human being.'[4] Here the child of a person who sells eels is born with the head of an eel; that is, the karma, which should by rights have as its subject the individual, is repaid upon that person's child. What can be the reason behind the slippage between the Buddhist interpretation we saw above, and this perception of reality?

Of course this perception is not Yan's alone, but can frequently be seen in fictional works of around this time; it is found here and there in *Fayuan zhulin* and in the 'Retribution' section of *Taiping guangji* from Chapter 119 onwards, and there are too many examples of it to enumerate here. Needless to say, this understanding of the subject not as an individual but in terms of 'family' is a thoroughly Chinese transformation of the Buddhist doctrine, and one could dismiss it as no more than a distorted perception that developed from traditional Chinese thought such as that expressed in the passage in the *Wenyan* commentary to the trigram *kun* in the *Yijing*: 'a family that accumulates virtue will certainly be rewarded greatly, while a family that accumulates wrong deeds will certainly be visited with an abundance of troubles'. However, I wish here to call into question the process by which this transformation reached the point we have seen above.

Previous scholarly studies have already documented the development of the concept of retribution in various works, but it seems to me that there has not as yet been sufficient work done on the contrast between the concept of retribution to be found in Chinese traditional philosophy and in Daoism.[5] It is my belief that it is above all in the transformations found in the Daoist idea of retribution as it developed through a consciousness of Buddhism that we may reach an understanding of how the Chinese understood and perceived the theory of karmic retribution.

The traditional concept of retribution

Fengfa yao by Xi Chao of the Eastern Jin, a work that is a measure of the level of understanding of Buddhism attained by intellectuals during the Six Dynasties, has this to say about the theory of fate:

> The Ancients used to say: 'The flourishing of [a family of] military specialists does not last longer than three generations', and [the general] Ch'en P'ing also said: 'Since I have often devised secret stratagems, my sons and grandsons will not prosper.' The instruction to be derived from [such sayings] is truly worth being propagated. However, [karmic retribution works otherwise]: the [tyrants of] Ch'i and Ch'u enjoyed their [royal] heritage for many generations, whereas [sages like] Yen [Hui] and Jan [Keng] never obtained a glorious

recompense from their offspring [both died prematurely]. All this is clearly evident from factual cases [in history], and we do not need any deductive reasoning to elucidate this. Moreover, Kun was banished whereas [his son] Yü was raised [to the rank of minister]; tadpoles and frogs [though related] have different forms. That the four punishments do not extend to [the culprit's relatives] has been a constant rule for a hundred generations. When a sage monarch rules the world there are already no excesses [in the application of punishments] – how much less [do they occur] in the mysterious response of nature! Not to take the circumstances into consideration, but to cause punishments and rewards to be applied in a disorderly way so that good and evil are without distinction is to violate the true principles most seriously.

Moreover, when the Ch'in instituted the punishment involving the whole family, the [actual] perpetrator was still regarded as the principal [criminal], and only after the principal criminal had undergone punishment, it was inflicted on the others. [However], not to have the offence visited on the person [of the offender], but to have the disaster visited extend to his relatives – that would be a way of legislation not only intolerable to the sacred scriptures, but also certainly rejected by [the legalist philosophers] Shen [Pu-hai] and Han [-fei tzu]. Hence it is said in the *Ni-huan ching*: 'When the father has done wrong, the son will not suffer in his place; if the son has done wrong the father will not suffer either. [Karma is such that] the one who does good automatically reaps happiness, and that he who does wrong automatically undergoes its baleful results.' How perfect are these words! They agree with the heart and accord with reason.[6]

First, karmic retribution is asserted to be a matter of the individual, not of the family. As with Yan Zhitui we find a discussion of the unfairness of the relationship between the ups and downs of fortune, and good and bad deeds, as seen in examples from the classics, with a final statement made through a quotation from *Nihuan jing*. The concept of retribution found in the opening lines, 'the flourishing of [a family of] military specialists does not last longer than three generations', is general and Xi Chao says somewhat sarcastically, perhaps in response to the tendency to interpret the Buddhist theory of 'retribution over three ages' through an extension of this type of thinking, that the utilisation of this pre-existing concept may be useful for the spread of Buddhist teaching but it is a misunderstanding.

In the work called *Yudao lun*, by Sun Chuo of the Eastern Jin, who predates Xi Chao, we find:

If we examine the proofs of rewards and punishment from ancient times until the present, that all of them arise from a cause is clearly recorded. How can this be hidden? Thus, the sons and grandsons of a house [grounded on] secret strategies will not prosper and generals of the third generation are obviously shunned by families of the Way.[7]

When we see this theory being used in support of Buddhism, we realise that the interpretation of the theory of retribution over three generations was achieved by means of this pre-existing philosophy.

Later, Hui Yuan wrote in more detail in *Sanbao lun*:

> The sutras say that there are three types of karmic retribution. The first is retribution in this life, the second is retribution in the next life, the third is retribution in future lives. Retribution in this life is when good or evil committed in this body is repaid in this body. Retribution in the next life is when they are received in the life to come. Retribution in future lives is when they are received only after passing through two, three, a hundred or even a thousand lives. There is no ruler [to decide] what is received – it certainly arises from the mind. Mind has no fixed controller but responds to stimuli. The response may be fast or slow, so the retribution may come sooner or later. Although [those that come] sooner and later are different, all must respond to the events encountered, and may be strong or weak. Thus, though light and heavy are different, there is natural punishment or reward. This is a summary of the three kinds of karmic retribution.[8]

The three kinds of karmic retribution are present retribution, retribution in the next life and retribution in future lives. No doubt this last, ill-defined teaching in particular answered to the diversity of problems concerning the relationship between the believer's right and wrong actions in their present life and the fluctuations of fortune, the unfairness of fate and the question of the existence of a Heavenly Way.

This understanding of the matter was already apparent to people of the Eastern Jin, and it would be common sense to assume that it gradually spread in subsequent ages. However, we can infer that the imagination of the general believer found it impossible to transcend the 'retribution over three generations' type of understanding of karmic retribution seen earlier.

The antecedent that Xi Chao invokes at the beginning of the passage cited above is similar to the 'three generations of military men are those whom families of the Way shun', found in the 'discussion' to the biography of Geng Yan in *Hou Hanshu*, 10, the commentary of which, in turn, cites the biography of Wang Jian in *Shiji*, 73. This commentary says, 'A general of the third generation must surely be defeated since so many have been slaughtered. Their descendants will receive ill luck.'[9] This latter is based on the Family Records of Prime Minister Chen in *Shiji*, 56, where we find, 'At first Chen Ping said, "I have executed a great many secret schemes which are prohibited by families of the Way. If my descendants' [prospects] were to be destroyed, that would be final. They would never be able to rise again due to the secret calamities I have caused." '[10] We may find references in *Zuozhuan* to examples of ghosts haunting living people, but this is not an idea limited to China alone. More redolent of the characteristics of Chinese thought is the use of the concept of 'family', and the numerical consciousness seen in the 'three' of 'three generations' (*sandai*). This latter also brings to mind a possible conceptual connection with the 'three ages' (*sanshi*) of Buddhism.

The 'three ages' brings to mind the story of a man of Song, in *Huainanzi*, 18, which immediately precedes the famous story of the 'Horse of the Old Man from the Frontier'.

There was once a man of Song who loved good conduct – it had not been neglected in his household for three generations. One day a white calf was inexplicably born to a black cow, and when he asked an elder the reason for it, the elder replied, 'This is a lucky omen. You must make an offering to the gods.' A year passed, and then inexplicably the father lost his eyesight. The cow again bore a white calf. The father urged his son to go to the elder and ask the reason. But the son replied, 'Last time, we obeyed the elder's words and you lost your sight. Why should we ask him again?' The father said, 'The teachings of a sage may appear mistaken at first, but later prove correct. This matter has not yet reached its conclusion, so you must go and ask again.' So the son went to ask the elder once more. The elder said, 'This too is a lucky omen, and you should make another offering to the gods.' When the son returned and reported these words to his father, the father said, 'You must obey the elder.' Another year passed, and this time it was the son who inexplicably lost his sight. Then Chu invaded Song and encircled the town. Children were exchanged for food, and human bones were broken for cooking, and when all the hale adults had died, the old and the sick and the children all climbed the walls and defended the town fiercely without surrendering. The king of Chu was furious, and when the town fell he killed all those who had defended it. Only this father and son escaped, because owing to their blindness they had not climbed the walls to defend the town. As soon as the fighting was over and the siege was relaxed, they could see again. Thus do calamity and good fortune visit men by turns, but the time of their changing is hard to perceive.[11]

This tale seems to support the idea that it was not simply with the *Yijing* that the notion 'if virtue is accumulated [in a household], blessings will overflow [to future generations]' stopped, but that it was somewhat more widely disseminated.[12] There is a legend in *Youming lu* by Liu Yiqing of the Liu Song that provides material to support the idea that *Huainanzi*'s way of thinking was inherited by later generations. In summary, it is as follows:

In the fifth year of the Yongping reign period [62 CE] of Emperor
Ming of the [Eastern] Han, Liu Chen and Ruan Zhao of Yanxian
lost their way deep in Tiantai shan, and unintentionally arrived at
the home of two female immortals. The two female immortals
behaved just as if these men were old friends and for ten days they
received luxurious treatment. When they said that they wanted to
go home, the women said, 'It is an accumulation of good fortune
(*sufu*) that has drawn you here. Why should you want to go home?'
and so they stayed another half year. But they nevertheless wished
to return home. The women said, 'This is sin drawing you. What
can we do?' but they showed them the way home. When they returned, there was no one they knew, and when they enquired they
discovered that they were meeting their descendants of seven generations. These two disappeared somewhere again in the eighth year
of the Taiyuan reign period of the Jin, [383].[13]

The 'sufu' concept expressed in this story is evidence of the continuation
of the 'blessings will overflow if virtue is accumulated' idea in traditional
thought into the medieval period.

To return to the previous discussion, when Xiang Kai memorialised
the Emperor Huan – recorded in Xiang's *Hou Hanshu* biography – we find,
'I have heard that when those who have committed no crime are killed,
and when capable men are executed, calamities will extend for three generations.'[14] The commentary to this passage cites Huangshi gong's *Sanlüe*
thus: 'Misfortune will extend to three generations to him who injures the
capable; he who conceals the capable will himself suffer harm; blessings will
flow to the sons and grandsons of him who employs the capable; the fame
of him who disparages the capable will be incomplete.'[15] This does not have
any specific connection with Buddhism but is criticising the unnecessary
severity of the punishments of Emperor Huan. Later this same memorial
does touch on Buddhism, and on the theory of the conversion of the barbarians by Laozi. It is, thus, an important work in the history of Chinese
Buddhism, revealing the form it took in its early period, so one can sense
some connection.

He had one other aim: the submission of *Taiping qingling shu*, the fundamental religious text of the Taiping Dao, one of the original Daoist organ-
isations. In the extant *Taiping jing*, which is considered to preserve vestiges
of this work, we find the theory of *chengfu*, or inherited burden, which has
long been an object of study.[16]

The Daoist theory of retribution

Let me introduce the theory of inherited burden in the *Taiping jing*,
which has been touched on by earlier studies. In the *Jia* section of *Taiping
jingchao*, in the section called 'Instructions on the explanations of *chengfu*',
we find:

In human activities there are some who work hard to do good, yet the results are evil. Others work hard to do evil but the results are good. This is not because those who claim themselves worthy do not speak the truth. When someone strives to be good but evil results, this is because he receives and transmits the mistakes of his ancestors. Disasters flow down from the past to the future accumulating and coming to harm that person. The one who acts in an evil way but that results in good, this is the accumulated great merit of his ancestors that comes and flows down to that man.[17]

In other words, if one does good and as a result gains evil, or the opposite, this is because one is 'inheriting the burden' of the merits and demerits of one's ancestors.

In the section called 'Instructions of the explanation of the *Shici shu*' in the 39th chapter of *Taiping jing* we find:

'Cheng' relates to 'before' and 'fu' relates to 'after'. 'Cheng' is the ancestors' acting in accordance to the Heavenly Will that they originally received. They lost it bit by bit. They did not know this themselves and continued to employ it day by day, accumulating [evil] over a long time and gathering up a great deal. Now, people born later, on the other hand, innocently concealed their crimes and in their turn received disasters. Thus, that which happens before is 'cheng' and that which happens after is 'fu'. In the case of 'fu', the disasters that flow derive not from the governance of an individual but from a later lack of balance. Those who live before put a load on the back of those who come later. This is why it is called 'fu' [i.e. to put a load on the back]. Thus 'fu' is the ancestors putting a load on the back of those born later. The sick have inherited this burden as it is said that disasters and harm have not yet been able to be properly cut off. That which is 'cut off' arises again. I am honoured to receive this book from Heaven. This Dao is able completely to cut off [inherited burden].[18]

Our forebears who possessed the Heavenly Will had no sin, but this Heavenly Will was gradually lost, sinful elements accumulated and in the course of time this descended upon those who are faultless today. Natural disasters are not called down by the misgovernment of a single ruler, but are also the result of inherited burden. The Celestial Master received this book from heaven, and the attempt to sever the process of inherited burden is based on it.

This idea is found in various places in *Taiping jing*. According to Kamitsuka Yoshiko's research, inherited burden is not simply a part of the philosophy of *Taiping jing* but is related to its fundamental doctrine, whereby this accumulation of individual sin eventually leads to natural calamities afflicting the whole of society.[19] 'Since heaven and earth first formed, the inherited burden of rulers and subjects'[20] now causes 'calamities to flow down to

MAEDA SHIGEKI

those born later with increasing frequency',[21] and *Taiping jing*, as a text, is used to cut short this effect, outlives this chaotic period and incurs and encourages the *qi* of great peace. Kamitsuka explains this by means of the Han theory of calamities and does not discuss Buddhism, but I feel that one can sense the theory of karma in the way the concept of inherited burden relates to individual sin. Perhaps, at a point when the traditional ideology of 'Heaven and Earth are infinite' was being swayed by the theory of calamities (which was based on the rotation of the five virtues), people came across the concept of the kalpa. Perhaps, around this time, they also heard of the theory of karmic retribution. Could not the notion of inherited burden have arisen as an expression, in Chinese terms, of the idea that even though the world comes to an end this is subject to cyclic rotation? One is led to the idea of Buddhism as an 'impact' that drew together traditional Chinese concepts once distinct from each other.

Xiang Kai came to the imperial court bearing the scriptures of original Daoism, and spoke of calamities, of 'the inevitability of defeat after three generations' and of Buddhism. Buddhism in its earliest transmitted form was close at hand for such intellectuals as him.

The word *chengfu* is a special term, not inherited by other Daoist texts, but similar ideas abound. Their occurrence is too numerous to specify here, so I will limit myself to introducing the main works in which they may be found. Take, for example, the *Baopuzi neipian*, where we find:

> If goodness is despised and killing is approved ... following the seriousness of the affair, the Director of Destiny snatches away a *suan* or a *ji*. When the *suan* periods are finished, the person dies. If the person has evil intention but there is no trace of evil actions, a *suan* is deducted. If someone is injured by evil actions, a *ji* is deducted. If someone kills themselves before their *suan* and *ji* are finished the calamities will flow to their sons and grandsons. Everyone who interferes with or snatches away someone else's goods will have their wife, children and household included in the calculated deduction, to the extent of their deaths – but these may not happen straight away ... Thus, the Daoists say that he who wrongly kills another will himself be killed by a weapon.[22]

I find in this a typical example of the Chinese preoccupation with the family in its view of retribution. This notion is one that eventually found its way into *Zhen'gao*, the collection of revelations that Xu Mi and his son received in conversation with the realm of the immortals at the beginning of the Taihe period of the Eastern Jin (366). For example:

> Xi Hui's father killed several hundreds of innocent persons, seizing their property and treasures. The criminal investigation was very serious. The aggrieved came endlessly to bring their complaints. The Celestial Officers long ago announced punishment. According

108

to the law, Hui's family should all be eradicated. Since his cultivation of virtue has been estimable, he alone has been allowed to escape. But how can his children and grandchildren remain healthy? Hui should be able to maintain the years allotted him by heaven, but he is still far from the way of transcendence.[23]

Xi Hui's father, Xi Jian, killed a great number of innocent people and appropriated their property, and owing to this profound sin the spirits of the dead appealed to the Celestial Officers, pleading for retribution. Yet, although according to the law this sin is deserving of the obliteration of the clan, Xi Hui's own virtue saves him from retribution. But how could his descendants escape it? Hui lived out his lifespan, but it is said that he was far separated from the Way of the Immortals. It was Xi Jian who created the evil consequences but the ghosts of those sacrificed sought vengeance on the son. The Celestial Officers, who manage the moral principles of the human realm in the realm of the dead, intervened and, although the results of the evil are turned on the son Xi Hui, he escapes thanks to his virtue. Yet the retribution is then turned on the next generation. The Xi Jian of this story may be that Xi Jian, a powerful minister at the beginning of the Eastern Jin, who led thousands of refugees from the north, and wandered unaided for three years, finally reaching Jiangnan. The son Xi Hui may be Xi Yin, with the courtesy name Fanghui. According to the same set of biographies in chapter 67 of *Jinshu*, he and his sister's husband Wang Xizhi and others abstained from grains and practised the arts of Huang-Lao. His son, in turn, was Xi Chao, in whose biography we find that 'Yin served the Way of the Celestial Masters but Chao believed in the Buddha'. Xi Chao died in 377, predeceasing his father.

In *Zhen'gao* this situation is called 'demonic infusion' (*guizhu*), 'tomb infusion' (*muzhu*), 'grave mound infusion' (*zhongzhu*), etc., and one prays for its dissolution by performing the ritual of sending up a petition to Heaven.[24]

It is difficult to imagine that this kind of concept would suddenly have arisen in this period; one could postulate that it might have originated in the Way of the Celestial Masters, but to judge from the fact that Ge Hong, who could scarcely be called a religious man, describes a curse falling on one's descendants in *Baopuzi* in a way that implies that such things were a matter of common knowledge, it cannot be thought to be anything unusual. It must have developed at some previous time, as a vague theory capable of explaining the illogicality of the relation of good and evil to fortune and misfortune. No doubt, although it is not *directly* related to the Buddhist concept of karmic retribution, it can be considered to have been brought into being by conservative and traditional people who could not divorce themselves from the belief that fate was connected to family.

In the twenty-ninth section of the *Xiang'er* commentary to the *Laozi* we find: 'If one uses weapons to settle matters, the killing will not stay within bounds. The misfortune and disaster will return to your own body and to those of your children and grandchildren.'[25] This does not use the expression 'three ages', but does say that in military families where slaughter has been excessive, repayment will be visited on descendants. Such things are no doubt a faithful inheritance of the tradition of Daoists.

Examples of the reception of the theory of karmic retribution in Daoism

After the pronouncements of *Zhen'gao*, from around the fifth century there appeared the early period of what are called the 'Old Lingbao Scriptures'. I have previously drawn attention to the fact that in these we find the Buddhist theory of samsara and non-extinction included as a means to longevity.[26] The theory of samsara is the basis of the theory of karmic retribution, and no doubt through its introduction there were occasions when there was felt to be a contradiction with the concept of retribution in its original form. Among the old Lingbao scriptures there is a book that discusses karmic retribution with a density of example not seen elsewhere. This is the *Taishang dongxuan lingbao sanyuan pinjie gongde qingchong jing*. A passage at the end questions the validity of the explanation of Daoist demonic, and other kinds of, infusion, seen above, and its separation from the recently popular theory of karmic retribution. This explicitly reveals the instabilities of the old concept of retribution and vividly speaks of the perplexities concerning the Daoist idea of karmic retribution.

> The Lord of the Dao bowed and said:
> I dare ask the Celestial Worthy: There are rankings of meritorious deeds, ranks for those to be saved and distinctions of high and low, but which aspect has priority? Does the blame incurred by previous generations stop with their bodies or does it flow down to infect children and grandchildren? Are the evils one commits visited upon one's own body, or do they rise up to obstruct those who have already died? ... Some scriptures and accounts say that the evil committed in one's previous life causes disaster to flow down upon the descendants. Others say that the major transgressions one commits rise up to obstruct the departed ancestors. Yet other scriptures say that each good or evil deed we do finds karmic retribution; good and bad fortune, life and death, are all due to this root of fate. If this is so, then the retribution for all good and evil is visited through karma on a single body. There should thus be no further talk of [evil deeds] 'flowing down' or 'rising up to obstruct'.
> But again scriptures say, 'If one does not establish merit to rescue the banished cloudsouls, they will have no means to gain release. Once merit has been established, birth and death will be transcended.' Now if each misdeed has its karmic recompense, those who have committed evil will upon death sink away for thousands of kalpas, bound into the darkness. How can they have the means to establish karmic merit to redeem themselves? But if descendants establish

this merit for them, then there is no difference between this idea
and the idea that [demerit] might 'flow down' or 'rise up to obstruct'.
This is what, in my ignorance, I really cannot understand.[27]

Here the Lord of the Dao questions the Celestial Worthy: does the karma
one earns in a past life come to rest in one's present self, or is retribution
visited on descendants? If you do evil, will you yourself receive the retribution, or will it go backwards to cause obstructions to your dead ancestors?
In some scriptures it says that if one's ancestors commit evil, calamity will
befall one's descendants. Others say that if one's own offences accumulate
they will return to obstruct dead ancestors. Yet a third sort say that each act
of good and evil has its own karmic recompense, and that this lies at the
root of everyone's life and death and good and bad fortune. However, if
repayment of good and evil comes back to each individual, how does this
accord with this theory of 'flowing down' or 'rising up to obstruct'?

Furthermore, notes the Lord of the Dao, scriptures say that there is no
way to rescue and release the banished cloudsouls of previous lives except
through virtuous deeds. However, since one who performs evil deeds will
sink for endless kalpas after death and be bound in the darkness, how can
one create great merit and redeem oneself? On the other hand, if descendants can create merit that can work backwards to save their own ancestors,
doesn't this come down to the same thing as 'flowing down' or 'rising up
to obstruct'? The Lord of the Dao admits he does not fully comprehend
this situation.

The text continues:

> Then, the Celestial Worthy delightedly answered:
> . . . Heaven and earth cycle like the wheel of a chariot. The life of
> human beings is obliterated as surely as a shadow follows its form –
> it is difficult to find the end of such things. Pneuma follows pneuma
> continuously, each giving birth to the next through causation. Good
> and evil, good fortune and bad – all have their root of fate. This
> is not due to heaven, not to earth and also not to humanity, but
> is born from the heart. The heart is what is spiritual. The self is not
> in the human form. The self is born from the self-actualisation of
> void nothingness. Due to its karmic causes, it is entrusted to the
> womb, transforms and is born. Thus the self's birthing father and
> mother are not the father and mother that originally gave birth to
> the self. The self's true father and mother are not to be found here.
> But the birth parents love their offspring and are thus accorded
> the highest honour. From them one receives the kindnesses of hav-
> ing a place to entrust one's karma and of nurturance in this life.
> Thus it is only proper ritual recompense that one calls them 'father
> and mother'.
> But the form the self receives is not the form of the self. The form
> is just a dwelling place or lodging for the self. The self, in entrusting

itself to the form, gives existence to what is non-existent. This is why those who join with the Dao have no further form. 'Were I without form, what trouble would I have? The only reason I have trouble is because I have a body.' The ten thousand troubles arise from the body; while the bodiless enter into that which is so of itself.

When one establishes one's practice and joins with the Dao, the body and the bodily spirits are unified. When these are unified, this is the true [perfected] body. This return to the father and mother who originally gave birth to the self is to complete the Dao. Within the Dao there will be no further trouble then and one will not die. If one is obliterated and crosses over [nirvana] the spirits will depart and the body will not return to ash. Then the entire body will return to its origin, never departing from it.

But, when one commits the myriad transgressions and dies, this is called 'death'. Death is obliteration and destruction. The self then returns to a father and mother and entrusts itself to the womb. As long as the karma of these transgressions is not exhausted, one will never return to the true father and mother. [Instead] the spirits will join the ranks of those who labour in the earth, the body will become dust and ashes. The dust and ashes will fly up to become ghosts. The cloudsouls and bodily spirits, released, will eventually merge with these ghosts, transforming to become one again and being reborn as a human being. For such as these, neither the body nor the bodily spirits will depart. In this way, good and evil are both visited upon the body. How can the blame fall on ancestors or descendants?

From prior to the kalpa cycle of Dragonic Magnificence to that of Red Clarity, according to the old texts, birth and death entirely resulted from [the actions of] a single person. There was no 'flowing down' or 'obstructing those above'. Good and evil stopped with the individual and each put his own body as forfeit. But, after the age of Red Clarity and into the age of the Higher Monarch, people's hearts became evil. Men and women were impure and envy, strife and mutual injury arose among them. Since their hearts were not sincere, they began to call upon their ancestors above and their descendants below for surety in making oaths to one another. Thus the spirits [of ancestors and descendants] were announced as hostage. When they did not keep faith and broke their oaths, [their family members] were bound and taken before the Three Officers, where they were condemned to act as officials among the shades. Above, their ancestors were obstructed; while below it flowed down upon descendants, bringing calamity on all. Old and young implicated one another, so that they were not released until the heavens came to an end, thus causing calamity to descend upon entire lineages.

Here, the Celestial Worthy makes an extended speech concerning the Daoist version of samsara. He uses the passage 'Were I without form, what trouble

would I have? The only reason I have trouble is because I have a body',
from the thirteenth section of *Laozi*, to say that one transcends the parents
who gave birth to you in this world and returns to one's true and original
parents, in other words to the emptiness of nature (or 'self-actualisation of
void nothingness'). Further, from before the kalpa of Dragonic Magnificence to the kalpa of Red Clarity, each individual's life and death and
fortune and misfortune resulted from their actions, and there was no concept of this reaching to ancestors or descendants. However, in the kalpa of
Higher Monarch people's hearts degenerated into evil, and they began to
speak of 'flowing down' or 'rising up to obstruct' (which is used here to
mean the demonic and other sorts of infusion seen above), and made moral
oaths to the gods. Yet though they uttered them, they did not keep faith,
and instead brought calamities on their entire lineage. This was downgrad-
ing the theory of retribution to something along the lines of an expedient.

> The way of Great Benevolence gives highest priority to saving others.
> No meritorious deed goes unrewarded; no virtue is not transferred;
> none who keeps faith is not saved; none who observes the practices
> does not become Transcendent. The establishment of merit is for
> heaven and earth, for the sun, moon and stars, for the ruler, for
> commoners, for the ancestors, for those in one's family, for all the
> myriad forms of life and only finally for one's self. The scriptures
> say, 'Whoever wishes to save himself must first save others. I vow not
> to be saved until all persons are saved.' This is widespread bene-
> volence, unlimited in scope and admired by the people of heaven.
> How could it be merely on behalf of the seven generations of one's
> own family! Good and evil deeds need not be extended to others,
> but when it comes to good deeds, if one is favoured with good
> karma and in full sincerity takes the blame on one's self, heaven is
> moved by this singleness of purpose, and both the human and the
> spirit world open up. And how could [such deeds] not reach those
> who have given birth and nurturance to one? Because of the deep
> love they held, how could one not greatly establish merit in order to
> save them and to provide recompense to their orphaned souls?
> From the era of Dragonic Magnificence to that of Red Brilliance,
> none of those who have achieved the Dao, who now appear in grace,
> their families exalted and whose karmic inheritance will extend to
> their next life, has not reached this state as recompense for assemb-
> ling meritorious actions that have moved all of the heavens. As for
> those who have achieved release from the karmic blame that kept
> them in the realms of enduring night in the nine dark regions, none
> has not done so through merit.

In other words, one does not practise virtue for the sake of oneself alone. If
one wishes to be saved, one must first save others, if the masses are not
saved, one cannot oneself be saved, and even more is this the case with

parents and ancestors. Virtue moves the heavens, while retribution reaches to the realms of enduring night in the nine dark regions. This is an attempt to reach a Mahayanist solution to the assertion that prayers for the salvation of the soul are not at odds with the theory of retribution by making heaven the intermediary.

This *Taishang dongxuan lingbao sanyuan pinjie gongde qingchong jing* appears to be the work listed in *Lingbao jingmu* as '*Sanyuan jiepin*, one volume. Revealed. The *Juanmu* refers to it as *Taishang dongxuan lingbao sanxuan pinjie.*'[28] This latter catalogue was created by Song Wenming, who relied on Lu Xiujing's *Sandong jingshu mulu*; thus *Taishang dongxuan lingbao sanyuan pinjie gongde qingchong jing* is one of the old Lingbao scriptures. 'Revealed' (*chu*) or 'already revealed' (*yichu*) is used in this context in relation to the idea that some scriptures are 'still hidden in the palace of Heaven'; in other words that have 'not yet been revealed' (*weichu*). The *Sandong jingshu mulu* was presented to the throne 'by decree' in 471 so the *Taishang dongxuan lingbao sanyuan pinjie gongde qingchong jing* must have been available to Lu Xiujing before this time.

However, in the recovered fragments of Ma Shu's Chen period *Daoxue zhuan* we find the following anecdote in the biography of Lu Xiujing:

[Master Lu] went into reclusion on Waterfall Peak of Mount Lu to practise the Dao. Emperor Ming of the Song, desiring to expand the teachings of the Dao, widely sought out those renowned for virtue. He delighted in the style of the Master and ordered him to be summoned. In the third month of the third year of Grand Beginnings (467), he ordered Regional Inspector of Jiangzhou, Wang Jingzong out of the capital to urge with all ritual propriety that [Lu respond] . . . The Master first reached Jiujiang, where the Prince of Jiujiang asked him of the relative strengths and differences between Daoism and Buddhism. The Master replied, 'In Buddhism, it is "*liu qin*";[29] in Daoism, the Jade Sovereign. These are but different roads that arrive at the same place.' The prince pronounced this a skilful answer. When [Lu] arrived in the capital, the scribe Ji Linzi was ordered [by the emperor] to have Lu stay in his rear hall . . . The emperor then ordered the Minister over the Masses Prince of Jian'an, [Liu Xiuren] and the Prefect of the Masters of Writing, Yuan Can (420–477) to hold a banquet [for Lu] at the Buddhist Guangyan Temple, inviting worthies, scholars from the court and notable gentlemen of the age. At that time, the lofty disputations of Gentlemen who discoursed on the Mysteries flowed like rivers; the counterarguments of eminent *śramaṇa* jutted forth like lances as the teachings of Li [Laozi] and Shi [Śākyamuni] were brought into dispute, with each side seeking to deride the other. The Master [Lu] expressed his principles in conciliatory phrases, calmly dissolving the quarrel and blunting its sharp edges. The princes and lords all applauded him, while those [holding opinions] both distant and near [to his] submitted in defeat . . . Within a period of ten days, [Lu] was again invited to a gathering at the Hall for Inviting Worthies of the Imperial Hualin Park. The emperor himself attended and all of the princes and lords assembled . . . [One of] the lords asked, 'I have never heard of Daoists speaking of the "two ages".' The Master answered: 'The scripture states: "Do you not yet know whose child I am? My image preceded the Thearchs." Since there is here a "before" and an "after", clearly there is a "present". And the *Zhuangzi* states: "Now births, now deaths." Both of these passages explicate the "three ages". It is just that the words are succinct and their significance profound, so that those of the world have until now been unenlightened as to their meaning.' The members of the court wished that he be ennobled, but Lu paid them no heed. The emperor then built the Chongxu Guan in the northern outskirts of the city to honour him . . . The flourishing of the teachings of the Dao began with this.[30]

This material is from the Chen period, but the specification of the date (the third year of the Taishi, or 'Grand Beginning', reign period, 467) and the appearance of real people, such as the Emperor Ming (r. 465–472) and Yuan Can (420–477) – and Wang Jingzong is perhaps Wang Jingwen – lends credibility. In addition, there is a realistic feeling to the answers and the questions received from the Prince and his Lords before Emperor Ming and the hundred officials at the Guangyan Temple. This being the case, there are problems in Lu Xiujing's view that Buddhism and Daoism can be unified through the words of the *Xici* commentary to the *Yijing*, and particularly in the answer to the question on the two ages (could this be a mistranscription of three ages, or does it mean that in Daoism only the present life is spoken of, not the two ages of past and future?), where reference is made to the fourth section of *Laozi* and the 'Sorting that evens things out' chapter of *Zhuangzi*.

Sandong jingshu mulu was submitted to the throne in 471, four years after the dialogue translated above. This is precisely the time when Lu Xiujing was collecting the Lingbao scriptures, which were re-formed with an infusion of Buddhist philosophy and extensively expound the three periods. Why are the Lingbao scriptures not mentioned?

Perhaps he thought it was as yet too early to bring them to the attention of the world, or perhaps there was at that time no record of the *Sanyuan pinjie*, and Daoists of a later period added it. Or perhaps, in the midst of the experiences described above, Lu Xiujing was overwhelmed by the convincing nature of the karmic theory of retribution and felt painfully the need to introduce it into Daoism, and spent these four years adding to the final part.

Part of the end of the record of *Sanyuan pinjie* is quoted in *Wushang biyao* from the Northern Zhou, so we know it was completed before this time.[31] But was it not the best of possible opportunities for Lu Xiujing to gain new knowledge when he debated with the best of the age (including monks) in the capital? It is only through debate that comparative theories can occur. As we know from the case of Yan Zhitui, it is surely the case that a different culture is not as much understood and disseminated down the ages as dramatically interpreted and received by cultural advocates.

Sanyuan pinjie concludes with a stereotypical expression common in general in Daoist scriptures but hardly suitable in this case. It says: 'If you treat [the teaching of the Celestial Worthies] lightly, calamity will extend to extinguishing your clan.'[32]

So what has he just been talking about at such length? Surely this slip reveals that the work was written without any real comprehension of the theory of karmic retribution, while the author was aware of Buddhism, and aimed to somehow include it. This slip and that of Yan Zhitui are equivalent. This is why one cannot entirely dismiss the possibility that it was Lu Xiujing himself who wrote it – but the opposite may also be the case.

Finally, let me jump to another era, namely the end of the Tang and the Five Dynasties, to examine the story 'Xu Zhu performs a Yellow Register Ritual for his Father', from Du Guangting's *Daojiao lingyan ji* found in *Yunji qiqian*.[33] This is a suitable tale from which to learn in what way later perceptions changed.

> Xu Zhu of Gaoping was a native of Lianshui. Official duties caused him to move to Qingzhou. He was wealthy, and had three children, but two of them were hunchbacks, and the youngest had a growth like a cangue on his neck, so all who saw them were amazed. Zhu was at the time in eager pursuit of advancement in life, a proud and arrogant man, who would dismount from his carriage and move straight to banquet, and in speech and behaviour would pander to his audience. Nevertheless, he was one who enjoyed desires that did not accord with the norms of the social world. It did not much disturb him to see his hunchback children, but the strange growth on his other child's neck induced him to melancholy, and his path to success suddenly petered out. So he went to a Daoist temple on Mount Donghai, and consulted a Daoist on the matter, who said: 'The illness of your three children is neither your fault nor caused by the sin of the children themselves. It must surely be the actions of karma. In this case it is not what Daoists call karma – the illness is the result of your ancestor's karmic deed. The crimes of forebears have flowed to the descendants. In previous generations of your family there must have been someone who was cruel in his application of the criminal law, rough in his whipping, an official without sympathy for those he dealt with, one who did not pity those in jail. Such a person would feel the urge to deal out punishment in excess of the stipulations of the law, and cruelly to execute people. Retribution for this has reached your children.'
> Zhu wept copiously and said, 'What you say is true. My late father became an official in the court of the Empress Wu when the world

was in disarray and slander triumphed. All the princes of the Li clan were executed, the imperial family were swept away and laws were made to condemn all virtuous members of the court to punishment. They suffered in fear of execution, were tortured, and those who could not bear the pain were thrown into prison, where they died in the cangue. Wu Yizong, Lai Junchen, Zhou Lizhen and Li Yifu received special favours from the Empress and time and heaven turned to their tune [that is, they ran the country according to their will], so that all feared them. The kind and benevolent were considered cowards, while the rough and cruel were thought to be able officials. It was the spirit of the times that blocked the path of compassion and caused the decay of righteousness. My late father's position was a humble one, and he lacked authority, but he was called an able official. He held many large trials, and although by and large he kept within the law, if this present retribution is as you say, and there is proof that it is so, I wish to erase this sin, and remove this grudge. What should I do?'

The Daoist replied, 'In order to save your late father, you must hold a Lingbao Ritual for the Release of those in Peril. To free the living and the dead from suffering, you must hold a Yellow Register Ritual.'

To summarise the remainder of the story, it tells how this Xu Zhu then did as he was told and held the rituals, and the gods, accompanied by over a thousand heavenly warriors and several hundred officials, called on the Xu household, bringing with them Xu Zhu's father Xu Xuanzhi, and announced that the ceremonies had been effective and the father's sin was erased. The father was reborn in a heavenly realm owing to Xu Zhu's conversion to Daoism. One month after they departed, the deformities of all three children disappeared. Xu Zhu finally became a Daoist, read the scriptures, refined his *qi*, and abstained from eating grains.

This miraculous tale suggests that in the Daoism of Du Guangting's time there was accepted acknowledgement of the difference between the Daoist idea of retribution and the traditional one, and reflects the strange state of affairs whereby the response of the Daoist to the suffering of everyday people was a traditional one despite recognition of the fact that it differed from the Daoist idea of retribution. Could this Daoist, or Du Guangting, have understood the nature of this retribution that was visited upon this 'family'?

Conclusion

In the sixth chapter of the *Yanshi jiaxun*, 'Customs and Manners', we read:

According to unorthodox books, after a man's death there is a day on which his soul returns and on such a day all his sons and grandsons would run away, no one daring to stay at home. Charms are drawn on tiles and plates to prevent the return. On the day for carrying the coffin to burial, fires are lighted and ashes are spread on the doorway to repel the family ghost. A petition is sent up to Heaven to sever the connection with such a calamity.[34]

This describes the custom of sending up petitions upon returning home after a funeral, and cutting the entwining infusion (*zhulian*). Wang Liqi in his commentary to *Yanshi jiaxun* cites the *Shiming* of Liu Xi of the Later Han in its section giving 'explanations of diseases', where it says 'Infusion disease: one person dies. If another person gets it, their *qi* will be poured into them.' Wang comments that this is, 'in other words, today's "infectious disease"'.[35] When infectious diseases were raging, surely more than one person would die in families of similar physical type living together. This sort of thing must have been the origin of the entwining infusion concept that later became widespread. This is the demonic infusion that we saw above under a different name, where the parent's karma was visited on the child.

Yan Zhitui, however, rejects this custom. 'Things like these are not in accord with human feelings, while persons following such practices are regarded by Confucianists as sinners who should be condemned.'[36] We glimpse in these values how an aristocrat who by nature was a Confucian-style intellectual, who by experience held 'pure conversation' to be vain and fruitless, who had no taste for metaphysical 'dark learning', was nevertheless converted to the foreign religion of Buddhism. And we may see, in the fact that this was not true of Yan Zhitui alone, the standard of Chinese understanding.

Translated by Meredith McKinney and Benjamin Penny

Notes

1 Wang Liqi (ed.), *Yanshi jiaxun* (Beijing: Zhonghua shuju, 1993), 16:385. Translations from this work are taken from Teng Ssu-yü, *Family Instructions for the Yen Clan by Yen Chih-t'ui* (Leiden: E. J. Brill, 1968). This passage can be found on pp. 145–6. On Yan Zhitui and his *Yanshi jiaxun*, see Utsunomiya Kiyoyoshi, 'Ganshi kakun kishinhen oboegaki', in his *Chūgoku kodai chūseishi kenkyū* (Tokyo: Sobunsha, 1977); Katsumura Tetsuya, 'Ganshi kakun kishinhen to enkonshi o megutte', *Tōyōshi kenkyū*, 26, 3 (1967); Yoshikawa Tadao, 'Gan Shisui ron', in his *Rikuchō seishishi kenkyū* (Kyoto: Dohosha, 1984); 'Rikuchō Zuitō ni okeru shūkyō no fūkei', *Chūgoku shigaku*, 2 (1992); 'Chūgoku rikuchō jidai ni okeru shūkyō no mondai', *Shisō*, 4 (1994); Kominami Ichirō, 'Gan Shisui "enkonshi" o megutte', *Tōhōgaku*, 65 (1983).
2 *Yanshi jiaxun*, 16:395; *Family Instructions*, p. 148.
3 *Yanshi jiaxun*, 16:399; *Family Instructions*, p. 149.
4 *Yanshi jiaxun*, 16:401; *Family Instructions*, p. 149.
5 See Yamazaki Hiroshi, 'Rikuchō Zuitō jidai ōhō shinkō', *Shirin*, 40, 6 (1957); Akizuki Kan'ei, 'Sangen shisō no keisei ni tsuite – dōkyō no ōhō shisō', *Tōhōgaku*, 22 (1961); 'Rikuchō dōkyō ni okeru ōhōsetsu no hatten – kyōri tenkai tsuiseki no

itsu shiron', *Hirosaki daigaku jimbun shakai*, 33, *Shigakuhen*, 55; Nakajima Ryuzo, 'Chūgoku ni okeru bukkyō uke-ireru no zentei', in his *Rikuchō shisō no kenkyū: shitaifu to bukkyō shisō* (Kyoto: Heirakuji shoten, 1985); 'Dōkyō ni okeru innensetsu uke-ireru no itsu sokumen' in *Araki Kyōju taikyō Chūgoku tetsugakushi kenkyū ronshū* (Fukuoka: Ashi shobō, 1981).

6 *Fengfa yao*, T.2102:87b. The translation comes from Erik Zürcher, *The Buddhist Conquest of China: the Spread and Adaptation of Buddhism in Early Medieval China* (Leiden: E. J. Brill, 1972), p. 169. Zürcher's translation regards the citation from *Nihuan jing* as ending with 'will not suffer either'. In this article I follow the punctuation of the author [editor's note].

7 *Yudao lun*, T.2120:16c.

8 *Sanbao lun*, T.2120:34c.

9 *Hou Hanshu*, 19:715; *Shiji* (Beijing: Zhonghua shuju, 1982), 73:2341–2.

10 *Shiji*, 56:2026.

11 *Huainanzi honglie jijie* (Liu Wendian (ed.), Taipei: Taiwan shangwu yinshuguan, 1978), 18:8b–9a.

12 *Yijing*, kun:19.

13 This anecdote from *Youming lu* survives in various Tang and Song *leishu*.

14 *Hou Hanshu*, 30b:1077.

15 *Hou Hanshu*, 30b:1078.

16 See Tang Yongtong, 'Du taiping jingshu suojian', *Guoxue jikan*, 5, 1 (1935), Ōfuchi Ninji, 'Taihei kyō no shisō ni tsuite', *Tōhō Gakuhō*, 28, 4 (1941).

17 *Taiping jing hejiao* (Wang Ming (ed.), Beijing: Zhonghua shuju, 1979), 28–34:22. This translation is partly based on that of Barbara Hendrischke, 'The Concept of Inherited Evil in the *Taiping jing*', *East Asian History*, 2 (1991), 1–30, p. 10.

18 *Taiping jing hejiao*, 39:70.

19 Kamitsuka Yoshiko, 'Taihei kyō no shōfu to taihei no riron ni tsuite', in her *Rikuchō dōkyō shisō no kenkyū* (Tokyo: Sobunsha, 1999).

20 *Taiping jing hejiao*, 37:54.

21 *Taiping jing hejiao*, 48:151.

22 *Baopuzi neipian*, 6:126–7.

23 *Zhen'gao* (DZ 1016), 8:5b.

24 *Zhen'gao*, 7:16b, 10:14b.

25 *Laozi xiang'er zhu jiaozheng* (Rao Zongyi (ed.), Shanghai: Shanghai guji chubanshe, 1991), p. 38. This translation comes from Stephen R. Bokenkamp, with a contribution from Peter Nickerson, *Early Daoist Scriptures* (Berkeley: University of California Press, 1997), p. 129.

26 See Maeda Shigeki, '"Tonkōhon" to "Dōkyōhon" no sa-i nitsuite – ko "Reichōkei" o chūshin toshite', *Tōhō Shūkyō*, 84 (1994).

27 The following passages come from the *Taishang dongxuan lingbao sanyuan pinjie gongde qingchong jing* (DZ 456), 32a–35b, translation by Stephen R. Bokenkamp.

28 Dunhuang ms, P.2861–2, 2256. See Ōfuchi Ninji, 'On Ku Ling-pao Ching', *Acta Asiatica*, 27 (1974), 39.

29 The exact meaning of '*liuqin*' is obscure. Bokenkamp observes that it 'seems to mean literally "tarrying in China", but since it is recorded that the auditors all thought this a cunning response, we must suspect a pun'. He assays the possibility (based on a suggestion from John McRae) that at the time it 'may have sounded like . . . one common transliteration of Vairocana'. However, both he and Stephan Peter Bumbacher (*The Fragments of the Daoxue zhuan* (Frankfurt am Main: Peter Lang, 2000), p. 211) concur that *liuqin* and the Jade Sovereign are equivalents in Buddhism and Daoism, respectively. See Stephen R. Bokenkamp, 'Lu Xiujing, Buddhism and the First Daoist Canon', in Scott Pearce,

Audrey Spiro and Patricia Ebrey (eds), *Culture and Power in the Reconstitution of the Chinese Realm, 200–600* (Cambridge, MA: Harvard University Press, 2001), pp. 181–99, 319.
30 Chen Guofu, *Daozang yuanliu kao* (Beijing: Zhonghua shuju, 1985), p. 467, translation by Stephen R. Bokenkamp.
31 *Wushan biyao* (DZ 1138), 34:8b.
32 *Taishang dongxuan lingbao sanyuan pinjie gongde qingchong jing*, 38a.
33 *Yunji qiqian* (DZ 1032), 121:4b–5b.
34 This translation is based on that of Teng Ssu-yü, with alterations. See *Yanshi jiaxun*, 6:98, *Family Instructions*, p. 36.
35 *Yanshi jiaxun*, 6:102.
36 *Yanshi jiaxun*, 6:98, *Family Instructions*, p. 36.

7

EARLY DAOIST MEDITATION
AND THE ORIGINS OF
INNER ALCHEMY

Fabrizio Pregadio

According to one of the scriptures belonging to the Taiqing, or Great Clarity, tradition, after an adept receives alchemical texts and relevant oral instructions from his master, he withdraws to a mountain or a secluded place to perform purification practices. He establishes the ritual area, demarcates it with talismans for protection against demons and wild animals, and builds a Chamber of the Elixirs (*danshi*) at the centre of this protected space. To start compounding the elixir, he chooses a favourable day based on traditional methods of calendrical computation. When all ritual, spatial and temporal conditions are fulfilled, he may finally kindle the fire. Now he offers food and drink to three deities, and asks that they grant the successful compounding of the elixir:

> This petty man, (*name of the adept*), truly and entirely devotes his thoughts to the Great Lord of the Dao, Lord Lao and the Lord of Great Harmony. Alas! This petty man, (*name of the adept*), covets the Medicine of Life! Lead him so that the Medicine will not volatilise and be lost, but rather be fixed by the fire! Let the Medicine be good and efficacious, let the transmutations take place without hesitation, and let the Yellow and the White be entirely fixed! When he ingests the Medicine, let him fly as an immortal, have audience at the Purple Palace (Zigong), live an unending life and become an accomplished man (*zhiren*)![1]

The Great Lord of the Dao (Da Daojun), Lord Lao (Laojun, or Laozi in his divine aspect) and the Lord of Great Harmony (Taihe jun) are not mentioned together in other alchemical texts. They are, instead, referred to as a group of deities in an early manual on Daoist meditation, the *Laozi zhongjing* (the *Central Scripture of Laozi*). One of the sections of this text devoted to the main gods who live both in heaven and within the human being contains this passage:

The Lord of the Dao is the One (Yi). He is the Emperor on High of the August Heaven (Huangtian shangdi) and is the central star of the Northern Asterism of the Central Ultimate (*zhongji beichen*). He resides above the Nine Heavens, ten thousand *zhang* on high, within the Palace of the Purple Chamber (Zifang gong) in the Great Abyss (*taiyuan*). He is clothed in five-coloured garments and wears the Headgear of the Nine Virtues (*jiude zhi guan*). Above him is the five-coloured glow of the cloudy pneumas of Great Clarity. Underneath a nine-layered flowery canopy, Laozi and Great Harmony attend upon him at his left and his right.

The text continues by giving details on the Lord of the Dao, including his names, bodily features, garments, spouse (the Jade Woman of Mysterious Radiance of Great Yin, Taiyin Xuanguang Yunü) and location within the human being – under another flowery canopy within another Palace of the Purple Chamber, i.e. the gallbladder. His two attendants, Lord Lao and Great Harmony, are described separately in the next two sections of the *Central Scripture*.[2]

While at first it might seem unusual that a text on *waidan* and a text on meditation mention the same three gods, this and the other shared details in the passages quoted above – the references to the heaven of Great Clarity and to a Purple Palace, or Palace of the Purple Chamber – are less surprising if one considers that both texts circulated at the same time, the third century, in the same area, the Jiangnan region south of the lower Yangzi River. These parallels invite us to look more closely at the relation between alchemy and meditation, and especially at the role played by traditions based on meditation practices in the transition from *waidan* or 'external alchemy' to *neidan* or 'inner alchemy'.

From *Waidan* to *Neidan*

The influence of meditation in the shift from *waidan* to *neidan* has been noted in several studies, and the importance of the Shangqing (Highest Clarity) tradition of Daoism has often been emphasised in this context. About twenty-five years ago, Michel Strickmann looked at the place of *waidan* within Shangqing, and remarked that this tradition moved the focus of alchemy from the actual compounding of elixirs to 'a sequence of symbolic procedures within a diffused frame of pharmacochemical reference'.[3] A few years later, Isabelle Robinet observed repeated instances of alchemical imagery in her work on the Shangqing revealed literature, and suggested that the Shangqing meditation practices not only played a crucial role in the rise of *neidan* but actually anticipated many of its features.[4] The relation between meditation and *neidan* has also been examined in studies by Sakade Yoshinobu and, most recently, by Katō Chie. While Sakade has clarified how *neidan* compares to the two main types of Daoist meditation (visualisation of inner gods and 'inner contemplation' or *neiguan*),[5] Katō has shown that some facets of *neidan* practice are adumbrated in a text as early as the *Central Scripture of Laozi.*[6]

In the present study, I examine the role played by meditation in relation to the main feature in the development of Chinese alchemy: the shift of emphasis from the world of gods and demons to the impersonal principles that fashion and regulate the functioning of the cosmos and the human being. The broad traits of this shift may be formulated as follows. The earliest extant *waidan* sources, belonging to the Taiqing tradition, are distinguished by two related features. First, the elixirs are compounded, not only to obtain longevity and immortality but also to receive the protection of divinities and to ward off demons and other dangers. Second, the alchemical process is described without having recourse to the abstract emblems of correlative cosmology. The few instances of methods based on cosmological configurations are not predominant in the Taiqing sources as a whole, whose recipes include a large variety of ingredients; when they occur, they reproduce simple patterns – either Yin and Yang, or the Five Agents (*wuxing*) – and do not make it possible to represent sequences of cosmological planes and the hierarchical relations that subsist among them. There is, more exactly, no intent in using the alchemical process for this purpose. In their own domain, the contemporary texts on meditation share both of these features. These sources are primarily concerned with the divine world existing both in the outer heavens and within the human being. Accordingly, they require an adept to visualise the inner gods, feed them with essences and pneumas found in his own body, and invoke them so that they stay with him and allow communication with the gods of the outer pantheon. Like the Taiqing sources, moreover, the early meditation texts do not discuss the different cosmological states that mark the extension of the Dao into the cosmos, and do not resort to correlative cosmology to frame the practices that they describe or to expound their meaning.

The shift of emphasis mentioned above happened in parallel with the rise to prominence of the *Zhouyi cantong qi*, or *Token for the Agreement of the Three According to the Book of Changes*, the main Chinese alchemical scripture. The date and the main features of this work, and its relation to *waidan* and *neidan*, are discussed later in this study. Here it is sufficient to note that, under its influence, a large number of texts, dating from the Tang period onward, describe the compounding of an 'outer' or 'inner' elixir based on two emblematic substances, Authentic Lead (*zhenqian*) and Authentic Mercury (*zhenhong*). With considerable innovation in language and in the underlying notions, the new *waidan* and *neidan* texts associate the elixir and its ingredients (metals and minerals in the former case, the primary constituents of the cosmos and the human being in the latter) with cosmological principles, and systematically ground the alchemical process in patterns of emblems that include Yin and Yang, the Five Agents, the trigrams and hexagrams of the *Book of Changes*, the Celestial Stems and the Earthly Branches, the twelve pitchpipes, the twenty-eight lunar mansions and so forth. These emblems serve to relate the alchemical process to the major

features of the cosmos – especially its temporal cycles – and, more importantly, to represent different cosmological states that the adept traces in a
sequence contrary to their hierarchical order.[7] In this form of *waidan*, the
ritual features of the earlier Taiqing tradition are discounted; and in *neidan*,
there is no more need to rely on the deities of the inner pantheon in order to
approach those of the outer heavens. In the new traditions of both *waidan*
and *neidan*, in fact, gods and demons are virtually forgotten.[8]

The comparable shift of emphasis that occurs in the outer and inner
practices from the Tang period onward is related, therefore, to the adoption
of a new doctrinal model that underlies both. This shows that the *neidan*
tradition cannot be seen merely as an 'inner' version of *waidan*, or as created
ex nihilo after the *Cantong qi* had favoured the development of a new form
of *waidan*. Taking this into account, the process that preceded the creation
of a text like the *Cantong qi*, and the rise of the related inner practices,
acquires much more importance for understanding the nature and history of
neidan than its borrowings from the language and terminology of *waidan*.
The first purpose of the present study is to trace some aspects of this process. As we already know, at its origins lie the meditation practices of
Shangqing Daoism and, even earlier, those described in a text such as the
Central Scripture of Laozi; some sources quoted below actually allow us to
trace it as far back as the second century. All these sources, as we shall see,
use identical or similar alchemical images and terms in relation to the visualisation of inner gods and the circulation of inner pneumas and essences.
To examine their role in the process that led to the rise of *neidan*, I briefly
survey some features of early *waidan*, and then look at examples of the use
of alchemical imagery in early meditation texts, at the inner pantheons and
the related practices described in two important third-century sources and
at the integration and expansion of this legacy by Shangqing Daoism.

The second purpose of this study is to present some initial comments on
the nature of the *Cantong qi* and its relation to the earlier meditation practices, on one hand, and to the Tang and later forms of alchemical practice,
on the other. As I have said, and as we shall see in more detail below, this
scripture performed the historical task of replacing one doctrinal model
with another. The *Cantong qi*, none the less, bears clear traces of traditions,
practices, images and terminology related to meditation. This is not unex-
pected, since the received text took shape in the same region, and at
approximately the same time, in which the main sources examined in this
study circulated.[9] The explicit and unquestionable criticism to which the
Cantong qi subjects some aspects of those traditions and practices signals,
though, a firm intent to distinguish its own doctrines from theirs. The
examples drawn from the pre-Shangqing and Shangqing sources on meditation allow us to place this attitude in its historical context.

As will be clear, I refer here to *neidan* in an inclusive way and not to a
specific period of its history, or to a specific lineage. In the context of current studies on Chinese alchemy, even a broad outline such as this might
contribute to our understanding of the nature of this complex tradition and

its relation to other traditions within Daoism. There are, none the less, three related issues that complicate the survey attempted here. First, there seems to be no way of fixing a precise date for the shift of emphasis from gods and demons to impersonal principles within the history of Chinese alchemy. The available evidence shows that the transition had already happened by 500 CE, but in this and similar cases, major changes in systems of doctrine and practice occur within individual lineages or local groups before they invest larger segments of a tradition.[10] Second, the lineages or local groups that accomplished this process cannot, at present, be exactly identified. Further work on the history of Daoism in the Six Dynasties may provide clues to their identity; until then, one can only sketch an outline, in the hope that this may help to identify who actually was involved in the relevant processes of change. Third, these processes took place under the influence of multiple factors; besides meditation, these include, in varying degrees, the doctrines of the *Laozi* (quoted several times in the *Cantong qi*), Han cosmological lore, Six Dynasties Daoist revelations, Buddhist teachings and practices, classical medical theories and self-cultivation techniques. The processes of change examined here, moreover, should be seen against the background of the historical and social changes that affected Jiangnan during the Six Dynasties. While this study touches on some of these factors, it makes no attempt to examine them in a comprehensive way.

Great Clarity

A brief outline of the Taiqing, or Great Clarity, tradition of *waidan* will serve to identify the main features it shares with meditation. This tradition evolved in Jiangnan during the third and fourth centuries. Hagiographic and pseudo-historical sources place at its origin the revelations received by Zuo Ci on Mount Tianzhu (Tianzhu shan, in present-day eastern Anhui) at the end of the second century.[11] The three writings that Zuo Ci obtained form the textual core of the Taiqing legacy; they are the *Taiqing jing* (the *Scripture of Great Clarity*), the *Jiudan jing* (the *Scripture of the Nine Elixirs*) and the *Jinye jing* (the *Scripture of the Golden Liquor*). These texts describe the alchemical process as a sequence of stages that include the transmission of scriptures and oral instructions from master to disciple, the preliminary purification practices (*zhai*), the establishment and protection of the ritual area, the choice of an auspicious time for starting the fire, the heating of the ingredients in the crucible, the offering of the elixir to the gods and finally the ingestion of the elixir.[12]

The main benefit granted by the Taiqing elixirs is immortality, sometimes described as incorporation into the celestial hierarchies. In one of the relevant passages, the *Golden Liquor* mentions two other major deities:

> If you take one ounce each of Gold Water (*jinshui*, i.e. the Golden Liquor) and Mercury Water (*hongshui*), and drink them facing the sun, you will immediately become a Golden Man (*jinren*). Your

125

body will turn into pure light and will grow feathers and wings. On high you will put in motion Original Essence (*yuanjing*) on behalf of [the Real Man of] the Central Yellow (Zhonghuang [zhenren]) and the Great One (Taiyi).[13]

As we shall see, both gods are also mentioned in the *Central Scripture of Laozi*. Besides immortality, the Taiqing elixirs confer longevity, grant the power of summoning gods and warding off demons and spirits, heal various ailments, offer protection from wild animals and brigands and award powers such as walking on water or retrieving spent coins.

The alchemical medicines, however, do not need to be ingested to provide their benefits. One can use them as protective or apotropaic devices merely by carrying them in one's hand, or at one's belt, in order to send off demons and other calamities.[14] Moreover, one can employ the alchemical 'gold' to make dishes and cups; in this case, it is eating and drinking from those vessels that confers immortality.[15] In the Taiqing tradition, therefore, the elixir is valued, not only as an actual medicine that confers ascension to Heaven after ingestion, but also for its ritual and symbolic properties. As we shall see, the early texts devoted to meditation practices represent the elixir in the same way.

Alchemical imagery in early meditation practices

Although the origins of alchemical imagery in China are often associated with the Shangqing school of Daoism, there is evidence to suggest that Shangqing in this respect did not innovate, but developed earlier traditions. Later in this study we shall look at relevant examples found in the *Central Scripture of Laozi* and in another text related to meditation practices transmitted during the third century. Even before them, sources antedating the Shangqing revelations of 364–370 by exactly two centuries contain brief hints of this concern.

One of these sources, the *Inscription for Laozi* (*Laozi ming*) of the year 165, describes Laozi in his divine form:

> He joins the radiance of the Sun and the Moon,
> and is at one with the five planets;
> he goes in and out of the Cinnabar Hut (*danlu*),
> and rises from and descends into the Yellow Court (*huangting*).[16]

These verses depict Laozi as a divine being existing at once in the outer cosmos and in inner space: the Cinnabar Hut and the Yellow Court are names of the upper and the lower *dantian*, or Cinnabar Fields, respectively located in the regions of the brain and the abdomen. Also important for our present subject is the image of 'joining the radiance of the Sun and the Moon', which suggests an affinity with practices mentioned in the *Central Scripture* (and later with *neidan* methods) that we shall examine below.

126

Moreover, one can hardly read this passage without noticing the association between the Cinnabar Hut and its homophone, the alchemical stove or 'elixir furnace' (*danlu*).

Both the *Inscription for Laozi* and a second epigraph dating from 165, the *Stele to Wang Ziqiao* (*Wang Ziqiao bei*), also contain the earliest mention of a term that later would become prominent in *neidan*, namely *dantian*. The *Inscription* uses this term to mean the lower Cinnabar Field and places it alongside Purple Chamber (*zifang*), a name for the gallbladder analogous to those we have seen above, Purple Palace and Palace of the Purple Chamber. These verses of the *Inscription* again refer to Laozi in his divine aspect:

> He regulates the Three Luminaries (*sanguang*),
> and the Four Numina (*siling*) are to his sides;
> he maintains his thoughts on his Cinnabar Field
> and on the Purple Chamber of the Great One.[17]

As in the passage of the *Central Scripture* quoted above, the *Inscription* defines the Purple Chamber as the residence of the Great One (according to the *Central Scripture*, 'the Lord of the Dao is the One'). Moreover, the *Inscription* associates both the Purple Chamber and the Cinnabar Field with meditation practices (Laozi 'maintains his thoughts', *cunxiang*, on these loci, i.e. visualises them). The *Stele to Wang Ziqiao* does the same, telling the story of a local magistrate who had a temple built in homage to this immortal after unusual events had occurred near his tomb in Ye (present-day central Henan). At that time, says the *Stele*, 'some strummed zithers and sang of the Great One; others practised meditation by passing through (*li*) their Cinnabar Fields'.[18]

In the late second century, another text related to the divinised Laozi, the *Scripture of the Transformations of Laozi* (*Laozi bianhua jing*), again mentions the Yellow Court. This time Laozi talks about himself, saying:

> I flow in cycles (*zhouliu*) through the Four Oceans,
> and according to the seasons appear in the Yellow Court.[19]

The Four Oceans (*sihai*) also are loci of the inner body (heart, kidneys, brain and spleen), through which Laozi – or, rather, the adept meditating on him as an inner god – goes in a cyclical motion.[20]

From the late second century also comes the first allusion to the 'inner embryo', another notion that would become distinctive of *neidan*. Somewhat unexpectedly, it is found in the *Xiang'er* commentary to the *Laozi*, written around the year 200 and produced within the milieu of the Way of the Celestial Masters (Tianshi dao). Commenting on the sentence *you zhi yiwei li, wu zhi yiwei yong* of the *Laozi*, which the *Xiang'er* understands as '[those who] have something regard its profit; [those who] lack it regard its utility', the commentary criticises the belief that one can find the Dao or the One by meditating on one's own inner body, saying:

Those who regularly practise false arts in the mortal world have established glib and deceptive arguments, basing themselves on this perfected text (i.e. the *Laozi*)... They say that nurturing the embryo (*peitai*) and refining the physical form (*lianxing*) should be like making clay into pottery.[21]

The *Xiang'er* states its argument more precisely in another passage:

Now, where does the Dao reside in the body of a person? How can a person hold it fast? The One does not reside within the human body... Those who forever practise false arts in the mortal world point to [one of] the five viscera and call it 'the One'. They close their eyes and practise meditation, hoping by these means to seek good fortune. This is wrong. They depart even further from life in so doing.[22]

The One, according to the *Xiang'er*, fundamentally resides 'outside Heaven and Earth', and when it enters the human body, it does so by 'coming and going' (*wanglai*, i.e. changing positions) within it.[23] Therefore, according to this text, it cannot be identified with or localized in any inner organ.

Early mentions of the inner gods

Both the *Xiang'er* and other contemporary sources document, for the first time, another topic with which the present study is concerned, namely the belief that the human being is the residence of inner gods. As shown by the passage quoted above from the *Xiang'er*, the generation of the inner embryo is achieved through practices focused on the five viscera (*wuzang*), which are the temporary residences of the One. Around the same time as the *Xiang'er*, the *Taiping jing* (*Scripture of Great Peace*) gives the earliest descriptions of deities dwelling within these loci of the inner body. A passage of this work reads:

The subtle spirits (*jingshen*) of the four seasons and the Five Agents are, within, the subtle spirits of the five viscera of man and, outside, the subtle spirits of the four seasons and the Five Agents... Their colour corresponds to the colour of the seasons of Heaven and Earth... They have periods of growth and decline that follow the rhythms of the seasons.[24]

Another passage gives details on practices specifically related to the gods of the viscera: 'Meditate (*sinian*) on the gods (*shen*) of the five viscera; depict (*hua*) their coming and going (*wanglai*), and see their moving around. You can talk to them... Thus you will know good and bad fortune'.[25] The term translated as 'depict' in the above passage is likely to refer to creating 'mental pictures' of the inner gods as they move within the inner body. That the word *shen* is meant here in the sense of anthropomorphic deities is also shown by the fact that one can 'talk' to them, presumably by means of invocations similar to those quoted later in the present study. Also worthy of attention is the statement that the purpose of these practices is knowing 'good and bad fortune', which matches the 'seeking good fortune' of the *Xiang'er*.

Neither the *Xiang'er* nor *Scripture of Great Peace* mentions the names of the inner gods. These are found for the first time in an apocryphon or 'weft text' (*weishu*) approximately dating from the same period as the texts examined above. One of the extant fragments of the *Longyu hetu* (*River Chart of the Dragon-fish*) names the deities of the hair, the ears, the eyes, the nose and the teeth, followed by two short sentences on a meditation practice.[26] The same names appear in a longer list found in the *Lingbao wufu xu* (*Prolegomena to the Five Talismans of the Numinous Treasure*), a work dating from the fourth or early fifth century but known to reflect, among others, the apocryphal traditions of the late Han period. Since the *Prolegomena* mentions the five gods in the same order as in the fragment of the *Dragon-fish*, and continues with details on the same meditation practice summarised there, it may preserve the original passage of the *Dragon-fish*.[27]

Taken together, the works quoted above show that alchemical imagery was used in relation to meditation practices as early as the mid-second century, and that the notion of an embryo generated within one's inner body already existed by the beginning of the third century. Related contemporary sources mention the existence of deities residing within the human being – the Great One and Laozi himself among them – and give their names.

Traces in the *Inner Chapters*

The step is not a major one from the notion of an embryo generated within one's inner body to the idea of producing an 'inner elixir'. Indeed, as early as the fifth century a scripture belonging to the Lingbao (Numinous Treasure) corpus states that 'the Golden Elixir is within your body' (*jindan zai zi xing*).[28] Below, we examine the main identities and differences between the two notions; but to follow the process that led to the statement of the Lingbao scripture, we should first look at sources that developed the ideas and terminology seen in the texts quoted above.

Traces of two of these sources, both of which are now lost, appear in passages of Ge Hong's (283–343) *Inner Chapters* (*Neipian*). The initial verses of one of them read:

> The One resides at the North Pole,
> in the midst of the abyss.
> In front is the Hall of Light (*mingtang*),
> behind is the Crimson Palace (*jianggong*).
> Imposing is the Flowery Canopy (*huagai*),
> great is the Golden Pavilion (*jinlou*)![29]

Another passage, whose prosodic form is different and therefore is likely to derive from a different text, refers to inner essences circulated and joined by the adept in meditation:

> Under Initial Green (*shiqing*) the Moon is with the Sun:
> the two halves ascend together and combine to become one.
> Exiting from the Jade Pond (*yuchi*), it enters the Golden Chambers
>   (*jinshi*);
> it is as large as a pellet, as yellow as an orange,
> and has a delicious taste within, as sweet as honey.
> If you are able to obtain it, beware not to lose it:
> once gone you could not chase it, and it would be extinguished (*mie*).
> The pure and white pneuma, utterly subtle and rarefied,
> ascends to the Obscure Barrier (*youguan*) by bending and twisting
>   three times,
> and the middle Cinnabar [Field] (*zhongdan*) shines incomparably;
> when it is established in the Gate of Life (*mingmen*), your bodily
>   form will know no end.
> Profound! Wondrous! And difficult to investigate.[30]

These poems contain several terms that appear in contemporary texts related to meditation and in later texts related to *neidan*, including Hall of Light (the upper *dantian* or one of its 'chambers'), Crimson Palace (the middle *dantian*), Flowery Canopy (the eyebrows and, again, the upper *dantian*), Jade Pond (the mouth), Golden Chambers (the lungs), Obscure Barrier (the space between the kidneys) and Gate of Life (the lower *dantian*, or a locus in its region). In the second poem, moreover, we find another reference to joining essences associated with the Sun and the Moon. There is no exact match of terms, on the other hand, between the two poems and the sources examined above. All these texts, none the less, share the use of images (palaces, halls, courts, chambers) that refer to the view of the human body as a bureaucratic administration, and of other images (fields, huts) that refer to the view of the body as an 'inner landscape'.[31]

The mention of the One in the first poem quoted above suggests that these descriptions were related to the practice of 'guarding the One' (*shouyi*), which Ge Hong reckons as the superior way of transcendence in his time, together with alchemy. He distinguishes between two types of practice. The first, which he calls 'guarding the Authentic One' (*shou zhenyi*), consists in visualising the features that the One, as an anthropomorphic deity, takes within the human being. A well known passage of the *Inner Chapters* gives details on the practice:

> The One has surnames and names, clothes and colours. In men it is
> nine tenths of an inch tall, in women six tenths. Sometimes it is in
> the lower Cinnabar Field, two inches and four tenths below the
> navel. Sometimes it is in the middle Cinnabar Field, the Golden

Portal (*jinque*) of the Crimson Palace below the heart. Sometimes it is in the space between the eyebrows: at one inch behind them is the Hall of Light (*mingtang*), at two inches is the Cavern Chamber (*dongfang*) and at three inches is the upper Cinnabar Field.[32]

Like Laozi does in the *Inscription* and in the *Transformations*, and like the gods of the viscera do in the *Great Peace*, in this passage the One moves from one Field to the other, followed in its motions by the adept in meditation. The second type of practice, which Ge Hong calls 'guarding the Mysterious One' (*shou xuanyi*), results in multiplying one's body or making it invisible to demons and other dangerous creatures.[33] The benefits afforded by the two practices, however, are the same. Guarding the Authentic One allows an adept to 'communicate with the gods' (*tongshen*) and confers protection against demons and other dangers. Similarly, by guarding the Mysterious One, an adept will be able 'to see all the numina of heaven and the spirits of earth, and to summon all the deities of the mountains and the rivers'.[34]

The *Central Scripture of Laozi* and the *Scripture of the Yellow Court*

The analogies among the sources examined above show that a set of cognate meditation practices existed by the third century, and that a codified terminology was used to describe them. Both the practices and the relevant terminology continued to be transmitted in the subsequent centuries, first within traditions related to meditation, and later within traditions related to *neidan*. The two main sources that document the relation of these traditions to both *waidan* and *neidan* are the *Central Scripture of Laozi* and a cognate text that also circulated in Jiangnan during the third century, the *Huangting jing* (*Scripture of the Yellow Court*). One detail is sufficient to indicate the extent of their continuity with the sources examined above. In its descriptions of the inner body, the *Central Scripture* mentions the Yellow Court, the Cinnabar Field and the Purple Chamber, i.e. three of the four terms found in the two epigraphs of 165 CE.[35] The *Scripture of the Yellow Court* mentions the Hut, the Yellow Court and the Cinnabar Field in one of its two versions, and all four terms in the other.[36]

The *Central Scripture* and the *Yellow Court*, however, differ from each other in important respects. The *Central Scripture* is a text in prose containing factual and relatively clear instructions concerned with loci of the inner body, visualisations to be performed on certain days and at certain hours and invocations to be addressed to the inner and outer gods. The speaker of the text is the divine Laozi, a detail significant in itself given the role that he performs in some of the sources quoted above. Most scholars agree in dating the *Central Scripture* to the early third century, although it has been suggested that it may date from around 500. In this connection, it is worthwhile to consider that the *Central Scripture* repeatedly mentions the Great

Clarity as the residence of the highest gods of the outer pantheon. This suggests that the text, or at least most of it, does indeed date from before the Shangqing revelations, when the Great Clarity lost its status of most exalted celestial domain and was replaced by other heavens in this role.[37]

The *Yellow Court*, which is spoken by the Great Lord of the Dao (Da Daojun), is a work in verse, written in an allusive language hardly suitable for learning or performing actual practices. One might define it as the poetical version of a meditation manual, and indeed it appears clear that its first purpose is to portray, in an aesthetically charming form, traditions that were cherished by the learned elite of Jiangnan.[38] This description applies to both received versions of the *Yellow Court*, known as 'Outer' (*wai*) and 'Inner' (*nei*). Although the respective status and date are still debated among scholars, for our present purposes it is sufficient to note that the 'Outer' and the 'Inner' versions do not substantially differ from each other as far as their language and imagery are concerned. All verses of the 'Outer' version appear in the 'Inner' version (which is about two times longer), unaltered, with minor changes or with amplifications. The main distinction between the 'Inner' and the 'Outer' text is that while the former discloses the names and locations of the inner deities, these details are missing (with one exception to be mentioned below) in the latter. Also worthy of note is the fact that whereas the 'Inner' version was formally incorporated into the Shangqing corpus, and contains occasional references to Shangqing doctrinal features, the names of its inner gods are not the same as those found in the original Shangqing revealed sources. This suggests that even though the 'Inner' version was composed based on the 'Outer' version after the Shangqing revelations of 364–370, it substantially reflects traditions that were current before that time.[39]

Two inner pantheons

Both the *Central Scripture* and the *Yellow Court* enjoin adepts to visualise the deities who reside within themselves, and to feed both them and the loci in which they reside with their own inner essences and pneumas. These deities perform multiple related roles: they serve as administrators of the body, allow the human being to communicate with the major – and in several cases corresponding – gods of the outer pantheon and personify the formless Dao or abstract notions such as Yin and Yang and the Five Agents. Especially in the latter aspect, they are 'images' (*xiang*) playing an intermediary function 'between the world of sensory realities and the world of the unknowable'.[40] As their disappearance is one of the major indicators of the transition to *neidan*, the main features of the inner pantheons reflected in these two texts deserve attention before we examine other aspects of their practices.

The *Central Scripture* mentions an impressive number of gods. Their size is often said to be only 'nine-tenths of an inch' (which is also the size of the One according to the *Inner Chapters*), and they often superimpose each other in the same loci of the body. This is especially true of the minor gods, whose dwellings and names are often identical or similar to those given in the *River Chart of the Dragon-fish* and in the *Prolegomena to the Five Talismans of the Numinous Treasure*.[41] This suggests that the apocryphal traditions of the Han period contributed to the forming of one layer in the text of the *Central Scripture*. The existence of several textual layers explains the repetitions that occur throughout this work, sometimes even within individual sections.

The major gods, instead, are essentially transformations of a single sovereign deity, the Supreme Great One. He is the Original Pneuma (*yuanqi*) spontaneously issued from the Dao, and appears under varying names and forms, including Yin–Yang dyads, in different cosmic domains and inner loci. The appearances of the Supreme Great One are mutually related by their designations as the father, the mother or the son of each other, and often by the name of the respective spouse: four of the gods listed below, in particular, are married to the Jade Woman of Mysterious Radiance of Great Yin, whose name is sometimes abbreviated into Jade Woman or into Mysterious Radiance. These major gods are described in the first twelve sections of the text and are mentioned again in other sections. Some details that concern them are summarised below.

1 The Supreme Great One (Shangshang Taiyi) 'is the Father of the Dao (*dao zhi fu*) and exists before Heaven and Earth'. The anonymous author of the *Central Scripture* attributes to Laozi these words about this god: 'I do not know his name(s)' (*wu bu zhi qi ming*); the same sentence is found in *Laozi* 25, which continues: 'I style it Dao, and if I am forced to give it a name, I call it Great'. The Supreme Great One, in fact, is the only major god for whom the *Central Scripture* gives no alternative names. He has 'the head of a man and the body of a bird, and his shape is similar to a rooster'. His residence is 'above the Nine Heavens, within the Great Clarity', but he also dwells 'just above your head, nine feet away from your body'.

2 The Most High Original Lord of the Ultimateless (Wuji Taishang Yuanjun) is 'the son of the Supreme Great One; but actually he is not his son, for he comes spontaneously from Original Pneuma'; that is, from the same pneuma that is his father. Above, he resides in the heaven of Great Tenuity (Taiwei); within the human being, he is 'just above your head', but he can also be visualised in the upper *dantian* ('the space between the eyebrows').

3–4 The Queen Mother of the West (Xiwang mu) and the King Father of the East (Dongwang fu) reside in heaven in the Northern Dipper, on earth on Mount Penglai (Penglai shan) and Mount Kunlun and within the human being in the right and left eyes, respectively. They are the father and the mother of a child who lives between the eyes, in a location that corresponds to the upper *dantian*. The King, who is equated with the Sun, is also known as Fu Xi; the Queen, who is equated with

133

the Moon, is also called Great Yin, Mysterious Radiance and Reclined Jade (Yanyu).

5–7 The Lord of the Dao (Daojun), as we have seen in a passage quoted above, is the One (Yi). He resides in the heaven of Great Clarity, and within the human being he is in the gallbladder. His spouse is the Jade Woman of Mysterious Radiance of Great Yin. As we already know, the Lord of the Dao is attended on his left by Lord Lao (Laojun) and on his right by the Lord of Great Harmony (Taihe jun). These two gods also stand to the left and the right of each human being; their spouses are the Pure Woman (Sunü) and the Jade Woman (Yunü).

8 The Lord of the Muddy Pellet (Niwan jun) is the god of the brain, the upper *dantian*. He is also known as the Old Man of the Southern Ultimate (Nanji laoren, on whom see the next section).

9 The Southern Ultimate (Nanji) resides in the planet Mars on high, and in the heart (the middle *dantian*) within the human being. 'He is the Supreme Great One', or another of his multiple forms. Like the Lord of the Dao, his spouse is the Jade Woman.

10 The Minister of Education (Situ gong), the Minister of Works (Sikong gong), the Controller of Destiny (Siming), the Metropolitan Commandant (Sili xiaowei), the Controller of the Registers (Silu) and the Chamberlain for Law Enforcement (Tingwei) reside in the kidneys. Together, these six gods 'rule on recording the faults of the human being, reporting above to the Emperor on High of the August Heaven, the Most High Lord of the Dao' (who is the Most High Original Lord of the Ultimateless; see under 2 above). Therefore the *Central Scripture* advises: 'You should constantly visualise them, so that they delete your name from the Records of Death (*siji*)' and enter it in the Jade Calendar of Long Life (*changsheng yuli*).

11 The Yellow Old Man of the Central Ultimate (Zhongji Huanglao) resides in the Central Dipper (*zhongdou*) in heaven, and in the Yellow Court (the lower *dantian*) within the human being. He is also called Real Man of the Central Yellow (Zhonghuang zhenren); we have already met him under this name in a passage of the *Golden Liquor*. The *Central Scripture* also states that this god, under the name Supreme Lord of the Central Ultimate (Shangshang zhongji jun), is the Dao itself.[42] His spouse is variously called Empress (*huanghou*), Pure Woman and Jade Woman of Mysterious Radiance of Great Yin.

12 The Red Child (Chizi) lives in the stomach. He is the son of the Yellow Old Man and of the Jade Woman of Mysterious Radiance.

The inner pantheon depicted in the 'Inner' version of the *Yellow Court* is different and, in a numerical sense, more modest that the one of the *Central Scripture*. Here the main groups of deities are the following:

1 Seven gods who live in different parts of the head: hair, brain, eyes, nose, ears, tongue and teeth.[43]

2   The gods of the five viscera – heart, lungs, kidneys, liver and spleen – and of the gallbladder, which in the *Yellow Court* and other texts represent all the 'six receptacles' (*liufu*).[44]

3   The gods of the *dantian*, namely the Great One who resides in the upper *dantian*; White Origin (Baiyuan) and Blossomless (Wuying, also called the Lordling or Gongzi), who reside in two chambers of the upper *dantian*; and the Peach Child (Taohai, also known as Peach Vigour or Taokang), who resides in the lower *dantian*.[45]

4   The twenty-four *jing*, which are 'luminous spirits' (*mingjing*) arranged into three groups of eight.[46]

Using a terminology that refers to the underlying bureaucratic view of the human body, each of the six main inner organs (five viscera and gallbladder) is called in the *Yellow Court* a 'department' (*bu*) and is managed by a deity who resides in a 'palace' (*gong*) within that organ. The single deities, who are identified by their names and the colours of their garments, rule on the organ that hosts them and supervise the corresponding function in the body.

Nourishing the gods, receiving nourishment from the gods

Nourishing the gods of the inner pantheon and the loci in which they dwell is essential to ensure that the gods are maintained (*cun*) in their locations, perform the bureaucratic and biological functions that lie with them, allow communication with the outer deities and guarantee the alignment of the individual with the impersonal forces on which life depends. In both the *Central Scripture* and the *Yellow Court*, accordingly, meditation on the inner gods is combined with the visualisation of nutritive essences and pneumas that adepts drive through the body and deliver to the gods in the five viscera, the three *dantian* and other organs. Both Shangqing and *neidan* would incorporate these practices and much of the attached imagery.

In particular, the *Central Scripture* often instructs adepts to circulate within their body a 'yellow essence' (*huangjing*) and a 'red pneuma' (*chiqi*) that respectively represent the Moon and the Sun. Adepts should merge them with each other and then ingest them:

> Constantly think that below the nipples are the Sun and the Moon. Within the Sun and the Moon are a yellow essence and a red pneuma that enter the Crimson Palace; then again they enter the Yellow Court and the Purple Chamber. The yellow essence and the red pneuma thoroughly fill the Great Granary (*taicang*).

In this practice, the yellow essence and the red pneuma are moved through the Crimson Palace (heart), the Yellow Court (spleen) and the Purple Chamber (gallbladder), and finally reach the Great Granary (stomach). The purpose is to nourish the Red Child, the deity residing within the Great

135

Granary.[47] In another instance, the yellow essence and the red pneuma are joined and then ingested:

> The saintly man dissolves the pearls; the worthy man liquefies the jade. For dissolving the pearls and liquefying the jade, the method is the same. Dissolving the pearls means ingesting the essence of the Sun: the left eye is the Sun. Liquefying the jade means feeding on the essence of the Moon: the right eye is the Moon.

The related practice consists of lying down and repeatedly visualising the yellow essence and the red pneuma that descend from one's eyes and enter one's mouth, so that they may be swallowed. Doing so makes one's spirit (*shen*) bright, and one 'discerns throughout the eight directions'.[48]

The *Yellow Court* mentions the same essences and pneumas, saying, for instance:

> Circulate the purple (*huizi*) and embrace the yellow (*baohuang*)
>   so that they enter the Cinnabar Field;
> an inner light in the Abyssal Chamber (*youshi*) illuminates the
>   Yang Gate (*yangmen*).

Here the two pneumas are circulated and guided to the upper *dantian*, while the Gate of Life (or Yang Gate) in the lower *dantian* is visualised as irradiated by a light issuing forth from the kidneys (the Abyssal Chamber).[49]

There are clear associations between the essences and pneumas of the Sun and the Moon, delivered by the adept of the *Central Scripture* to his inner gods, and the Yin and Yang essences and pneumas that a *neidan* adept circulates in his body to compound the elixir or nourish the 'inner embryo'. These associations are explicit when the *Central Scripture* refers to visualising the pneuma of the Sun descending from the heart and the pneuma of the Moon arising from the kidneys; the adept should 'join them making them one, and distribute them to the four limbs'. An analogous practice is performed by a *neidan* adept when he joins the Fire of the heart and the Water of the kidneys.[50] Analogies with the alchemical process are also apparent in relation to another major source of nourishment for the inner gods and their residences, namely the adept's own salivary juices. Their main function is to aid the ingestion of essences and pneumas, but they are also used to 'irrigate' (*guan*) the inner organs and, as we shall see presently, to feed the gods.[51] To denote these juices, the *Central Scripture* and the *Yellow Court* use terms derived from *waidan* or having alchemical connotations, such as Mysterious Pearl (*xuanzhu*), Jade Sap (*yujiang*), Jade Blossom (*yuying*), Jade Pond (*yuchi*), Jade Liquor (*yuye*), Golden Nectar (*jinli*) and even Golden Liquor (*jinye*). Other sources refer to them as Divine Water (*shenshui*), White Snow (*baixue*) and Golden Essence (*jinjing*), all of which are also synonyms of ingredients of *waidan* elixirs. These terms suggest that in providing superior nourishment to the adept and his inner gods, the salivary juices are seen as performing a function similar to the one that the elixirs, or their ingredients, play in *waidan*. The analogies of essences, pneumas and salivary juices with *waidan* end where those with *neidan* begin: the adept nourishes himself and his gods not through the ingestion of 'external' substances, but through components of his own inner body; he finds the vital ingredients within himself, and their ingestion takes place internally.

Similar dual associations with both *waidan* and *neidan* are manifest in another feature of the methods of the *Central Scripture*. Although offering nourishment to the gods is the rule, in some cases it is the adept who asks the gods to deliver nourishment to him. To do so, he utters invocations that recall the one pronounced by the Taiqing alchemist in a passage quoted above. Now, however, he does not ask the gods to favour the compounding of the elixir. He asks, instead, that they dispense an elixir to him:

> The highest god is styled Lord Great One of Original Radiance (Yuanguang Taiyi jun) . . . Below he resides within the heart of human beings. At dawn and at midday, on the *jiawu* and the *bingwu* days, always call him and say: 'Old Man of the Southern Ultimate, Lord Great One of Original Radiance! I want to obtain the Dao of long life of the Divine Elixir of the Great One!'[52]

In an invocation he addresses to Master Yellow Gown (Huangchang zi), the father of the Red Child, he asks to receive 'medicinal liquor' (*yaojiu*) and other nurture: 'Master Yellow Gown! Master Yellow Gown! Real Man of the Yellow Court, reside in me! Summon for me medicinal liquor, dried pine-seeds, rice, and broth of millet, so that I can eat and drink of them! Let them come right now!'[53] Similarly, the adept invokes Double Indigo, the god of the liver who is none other than Lord Lao himself, as follows:

> Flesh Child (Rouzi), Double Indigo (Lanlan)! Be my friend, stay here and be my envoy! I want to obtain the Divine Elixir of the Great One and ingest it! Let me live a long life! Do not leave my body! Constantly reside within the Palace of the Purple Chamber, joined with the Dao![54]

If the term 'inner elixir' was not already charged with other meanings and associations, it could be an appropriate definition for the nourishment that the inner gods are invited to provide. Indeed, whether its elixir is 'outer' or 'inner', the *Central Scripture* regards alchemy and meditation as equivalent when it states: 'If you cannot ingest the Divine Elixir and the Golden Liquor, and do not labour to become skilled in meditation (*sinian*), you merely bring suffering upon yourself.'[55]

The Red Child and the inner embryo

As we have seen, leading the yellow essence and the red pneuma to the stomach provides nourishment to the Red Child. This god, who is also known as Child-Cinnabar (Zidan), is called the 'self' (*wu*) or 'the master of one's real self' (*zhenwu zhi shi*), and is the innermost deity residing within the human being. Like the Supreme Great One, he is a transformation of the primordial pneuma emanating from the Dao. The *Central Scripture* describes him as follows:

> The self is the son of the Dao; this is what he is. Human beings also have him, not only me. He resides precisely in the ducts of the stomach, the Great Granary. He sits facing due south on a couch of jade and pearls, and a flowery canopy of yellow clouds covers him. He wears clothes with pearls of five hues. His mother resides above on his right, embracing and nourishing him; his father resides above on his left, instructing and defending him.[56]

The Child's mother is the Jade Woman of Mysterious Radiance. Through the nourishment that she provides, the Child 'feeds on yellow gold and jade dumplings, and ingests the Divine Elixir and the fungus-plant (*zhicao*)'. But the Child should also be nourished by the adept: 'He feeds on the yellow essence and the red pneuma, drinking and ingesting the Fountain of Nectar (*liquan*)', another name of the salivary juices produced during meditation practices. The Child's father, whose task is 'instructing and defending' his son, is the Yellow Old Man of the Central Ultimate, god of the Yellow Court. The *Central Scripture* often calls him Master Yellow Gown (Huangchang zi), a name that derives from a term used in the *Book of Changes* (*Yijing*) and that may have entered the *Central Scripture* through the Han apocryphal literature.[57] Both the Red Child, under the name of Child-Cinnabar, and Yellow Gown are also mentioned in the 'Inner' version of the *Yellow Court*, while the 'Outer' version grants Child-Cinnabar the honour of being the only deity mentioned by name in the entire text.[58]

The alchemical imagery associated with the nourishment of the Red Child – gold, jade, the Divine Elixir itself – does not need to be emphasized again. Another point, instead, calls for attention, namely the relation of the Red Child to the inner embryo of *neidan*. The Child of the *Central Scripture* resides within oneself since one's birth; he is not generated through the adept's practice, but by other gods who are his parents; and he receives nourishment and guidance from his own mother and father, the adept's task being one of support. This differs from the inner embryo as an image of the inner elixir, conceived and generated by the *neidan* adept himself through his practice. But the relation between the Red Child and the inner embryo is more complex than this annotation might suggest, for the image of the embryo changes according to the understanding of *neidan* itself: while some *neidan* authors emphasise the notion of 'generating' and 'raising' the inner embryo through practices performed for this purpose, others refer to the embryo, and the elixir itself, as an image of one's own authentic self and of one's inherent awakened state. Both ways of seeing have affinities with the image of the 'inner child' as it appears in the *Central Scripture* and (as we shall see shortly) in Shangqing Daoism. On the one hand, nourishing the Red Child in meditation and generating and raising the embryo in *neidan* are achieved through similar practices – by joining essences and pneumas related to the Sun and the Moon in the former case, or to Yin and Yang in the latter. On the other hand, the 'inner child' and the inner embryo are both representations of the 'real self' (*zhenwu*), which, just like the Red Child in the *Central Scripture*, is innate in everyone and is raised by the same forces that sustain life – represented by the Child's parents in the *Central Scripture*, and by one's 'original Father and Mother' (*yuanfu, yuanmu*) in Shangqing – but also requires one's continuous sustenance and nourishment.

With regard to the first view, we should also note that the notion of generating an inner embryo is not a *neidan* innovation. As we have seen, the *Xiang'er* commentary already alludes to practices for 'nurturing the embryo'. The 'Inner' version of the *Yellow Court* also instructs adepts to generate a 'body' (or a 'person', *shen*) in their own inner womb:

> By coagulating the essence and fostering the womb (*yubao*), you
>   will generate a body by transformation (*huasheng shen*);
> by detaining the embryo (*liutai*) and causing the essence to stop,
>   you will live a long life.[59]

While this passage has no correspondence in the 'Outer' version, it is hard to establish whether it reflects an influence of Shangqing meditation practices, where the image of generating an inner embryo appears in different forms and contexts. Even in this case, earlier traditions provided *neidan* with the representation of an 'inner being' that personifies one's authentic self, with the notion of generating that being in one's inner body and, in relation to the latter notion, with a model for the practices required to accomplish that task.

Dantian: Cinnabar Fields and Fields of the Elixir

In several passages quoted above, we have met mentions of the three *dantian* or Cinnabar Fields. The *Central Scripture* is the first source that describes the lower *dantian* in detail, saying:

> The Cinnabar Field is the root of the human being. It is the place where essence and spirit are stored, the origin of the five pneumas (*wuqi*) and the Storehouse of the Red Child (*chizi zhi fu*). Men store it in their semen, and women in their menstrual blood. It rules on generating children and is the gate of the joining of Yin and Yang. It is three inches below the navel, attached to the Caudal Funnel

(*weilü*), and is the root of the two kidneys. Within the Cinnabar Field the centre is red, the left is green, the right is yellow, above is white and below is black. It is within a space that measures four inches, square (like Earth) and round (like Heaven).[60]

The passage ends by stating that the god of the *dantian* 'has the surname Kong, the name Qiu and the style Zhongni'. The god of this locus of the body is, therefore, none other than Confucius himself. As has been noted, this is likely to be a further element that reveals the relation of the *Central Scripture* to the Han apocrypha, sometimes deemed to have been written by Confucius to expound the meaning of the Classics.[61]

As we have seen, early meditation texts describe the three *dantian* as the abodes of the One in the human being, or of other gods who are transformations of this supreme deity. In particular, the *dantian* are inhabited by youthful lads (*tongzi*): the Red Child himself in the upper *dantian* (according to the *Yellow Court*), the son of the Queen Mother and the King Father also in the upper *dantian* and Peach Child in the lower *dantian*. In another case, the adept of the *Central Scripture* invokes the Lords of the Sun and the Moon, and asks that they help him to nourish two 'little lads' in the middle and the lower *dantian*:

> Effulgent Lord, Original Yang (Jingjun Yuanyang)! Join your virtue with me! Let us nourish together the little lad within the Crimson Palace! . . . Lord of the Moon, Child-Light (Yuejun Ziguang)! Join your virtue with me! Nourish the little lad within my Cinnabar Field![62]

In *neidan*, instead, the *dantian* are the three main loci of inner transmutation, where the elixir, or the 'inner child', is generated, nourished and progressively moved upward, in a process described in some texts as the 'egress of the spirit' (*chushen*) through the sinciput. I will not attempt, though, to examine the similarities and differences between meditation and *neidan* in relation to the *dantian*, and will merely focus on two terminological remarks.

First, although several dozens of names and synonyms are attested for the three *dantian*, most texts apply the term Cinnabar Field, or *dantian*, specifically to the lower Field (as in the passage just quoted), and call the middle one Crimson Palace, or *jianggong*, and the upper one Muddy Pellet, or *niwan*. The theory that the term *niwan* originated as a phonetic transcription of *nirvana* appears to have no foundation, as this meaning is not attested in the dozen or so occurrences of this term in the Taishō Buddhist canon. The earliest sources that mention the term *niwan* to mean the upper *dantian* are, to my knowledge, the *Central Scripture* and the *Yellow Court*.[63] Interestingly, a passage in Ge Hong's *Inner Chapters* lists *niwan* as a synonym of an unidentified substance used in *waidan* (possibly the mud used for luting the crucible).[64] As in several other cases, therefore, the use of this term in *neidan* texts appears to derive from an earlier use in *waidan*, attested around

300 CE; the contemporary texts on meditation were the agents of its transmission from *waidan* to *neidan*.

The second remark concerns the use of the term *dantian* itself in meditation and *neidan* texts. As shown by the description in the *Central Scripture* quoted above, the *dantian* is denoted as 'cinnabar' with reference to the colour of its inmost part. This peculiarity is deemed to be so important as to overcome the canonical associations between directions and colours: the centre of the *dantian* is red, while yellow – normally associated with the centre – is the colour of its right side. In *neidan*, instead, *dantian* is used in a sense closer to 'field of the elixir' than to 'cinnabar field', for these are the three loci involved in the compounding of the inner elixir. At the basis of both ways of understanding this term is the root meaning of the word *dan* as 'essence', in the sense of reality, principle, nature and authenticity. The colour cinnabar (*dan*) and in general the colour red partake of this meaning, as also do the mineral cinnabar (*dan*) and the elixir (also *dan*). Neither the mineral cinnabar nor the elixir, however, is originally involved in the notion of *dantian*. Just as the *dantian* in the *Central Scripture* is the storehouse of male and female essence (*jing*, i.e. semen and menstrual blood), so in *neidan* it is the 'field' where one grows and collects the elixir, the human being's authentic essence.[65]

From the Great Clarity to the Highest Clarity

We may now leave the *Central Scripture of Laozi* and the *Scripture of the Yellow Court*, which have guided us along the greater part of this study, and look at the role that Shangqing played in the transition to *neidan*. As this stage in the history of Daoist meditation has already been studied extensively,[66] it will be enough to provide some examples of the Shangqing adaptation of two of the themes discussed above – the image of the 'inner child' and the practices associated with the Sun and the Moon – and briefly comment on the influence that Shangqing had on the decline of *waidan*.

Methods of visualisation of the deities of the inner pantheon, and chants addressed to them, form the subject matter of the *Dadong zhenjing* (the *Authentic Scripture of Great Profundity*), the main Shangqing text.[67] Although this pantheon differs from the ones of the *Central Scripture* and the *Yellow Court*, the 'inner child' plays within it the same central role. The *Great Profundity* ends by describing how an adept generates an inner 'divine person' by coagulating and ingesting pneumas that descend from his upper *dantian*:

> Visualise a five-coloured purple cloud entering within you from your Muddy Pellet. Then ingest that divine cloud with your saliva. It will coalesce into a divine person (*shenshen*), wrapped in a five-coloured, purple, white and roseate round luminous wheel. The god is inside the wheel. Below he spreads himself within your entire body, distributing his pneuma to your nine openings and coagulating it over the tip of your tongue.

Revealing the identity of the 'inner child' more explicitly than does the *Central Scripture*, the *Great Profundity* calls him the Venerable Lord Emperor One (Diyi zunjun), thereby equating him with the Supreme Great One of the earlier model.[68]

In other contexts, the image of the 'inner child' or the inner embryo reveals alchemical connotations different from those we have seen in the pre-Shangqing texts. One of the Shangqing revealed scriptures applies a *waidan* term, Nine Elixirs (*jiudan*), to the pneumas of the Nine Heavens (*jiutian zhi qi*) received by human beings during their embryonic development. In the view of this and other Shangqing texts, however, the gestation process also accounts for the creation of 'knots and nodes' (*jiejie*). Their function is 'holding together the five viscera', but at the same time they are responsible for one's death:

> When one is born, there are in the womb twelve knots and nodes that hold the five viscera together. The five viscera are obstructed and squeezed, the knots cannot be untied and the nodes cannot be removed. Therefore the illnesses of human beings depend on the obstructions caused by these nodes, and the extinction of one's allotted destiny (*ming*, i.e. one's death) depends on the strengthening of these knots.

To untie the 'knots of death', adepts are instructed to re-experience their embryonic development in meditation, again receiving the Nine Elixirs (the pneumas of each of the Nine Heavens) and then visualising the Original Father in the upper *dantian*, and the Original Mother in the lower *dantian*, who issue pneumas that adepts join in the middle *dantian* to generate, this time, an inner immortal body.[69]

A further set of Shangqing practices based on the image of the embryo are those performed to ensure that the souls of one's ancestors obtain release from the underworld. Through these practices, ancestors may 'return to the embryo' (*fantai*) and become 'immortals at the embryonic state' (*taixian*), obtaining, this time, rebirth in heaven. In this case too, the notion of purification underlying these practices is associated with alchemical imagery and terminology. Thanks to their descendant, ancestors can rise to the Golden Gate (Jinmen), a station in the heavenly circuit of the Sun, where they 'refine their matter' (*lianzhi*) by bathing themselves in the Water of Smelting Refinement (*yelian zhi shui*).[70]

The role of the Sun as a purifying agent is also apparent in the Shangqing practices based on the images of the Sun and the Moon. Here Shangqing clearly develops the legacy of earlier traditions where, as we have seen, pneumas and essences associated with these two celestial bodies perform a major role; here, however, the essences and pneumas are not those found within the adept's own body, but those of the Sun and the Moon themselves. In one instance, the adept meditates on the circuits of the Sun and the Moon, then visualises their essences and joins and ingests them. In another method, he

Figure 7.1 Generating the 'inner child' in meditation. *Shangqing dadong zhenjing* (Highest Clarity Authentic Scripture of Great Profundity), 6.13b.

collects their essences in a vessel containing water and a talisman, then ingests some of that water and uses the other part to wash himself. These and similar methods often end with the adept visualising himself as being ignited by the Sun and transformed into pure light.[71] Some notions related to these practices have an even deeper relation to alchemy than those seen before. As noted by Robinet, the Shangqing texts sometimes exchange the Yin and Yang qualities of the Sun and the Moon, so that each of them is said to contain an essence of the opposite sign (Yin for the Sun, Yang for the Moon). This anticipates an essential pattern of *neidan*, where the alchemical process is based on gathering Yin within Yang (Original Yin) and Yang within Yin (Original Yang) in order to join them and compound the elixir.[72] Two further common features can be identified. First, as in alchemy, here fire is the agent of purification – of matter in one case, of the human being himself in the other. Moreover, in both *waidan* and *neidan* the elixir formed by joining Original Yin and Original Yang is equated with Pure Yang (*chunyang*), the state before the separation of the One into the two. In the same way, the Shangqing practices related to the Sun and the Moon end with the adept absorbing himself into the Yang principle, represented by the Sun.

Shangqing also influenced the history of alchemy in another significant way. Taking the compounding of the elixir as the starting point of some of its practices, it effectively reformulated the nature and purposes of *waidan* and used the compounding of the elixir as a metaphor to describe inner processes.[73] This attitude, which essentially is the same as the one that *neidan* has to *waidan*, was a decisive contribution to the decline in the status of *waidan* among the traditions of medieval Jiangnan, and was, indeed, at the origins of that decline. While Ge Hong, writing only a few decades before the Shangqing revelations, had promoted *waidan* and meditation as the two superior paths to immortality, the revelations of 364–370 resulted in a new hierarchical arrangement of methods and practices.[74] The *Zhen'gao* (Authentic Declarations), a work that Tao Hongjing (456–536) wrote both to systematise the Shangqing legacy and to clarify its relation to the earlier local traditions, reflects a hierarchy that places the Shangqing meditation methods first, followed by *waidan*, then by sexual techniques, circulation of pneuma (*xingqi*), *daoyin* (gymnastics) and finally by the ingestion of herbal drugs. One of the relevant passages in Tao's work ends with these words: 'If one obtains the Golden Liquor and the Divine Elixirs, one becomes an immortal with no need of other practices. If one obtains the *Authentic Scripture of Great Profundity*, there is no need for the Way of the Golden Elixir (*jindan zhi dao*).'[75] This decline in the status of *waidan* may have been one of the major reasons for the replacement of the earlier forms of alchemical practice with those based on the doctrinal model of the *Zhouyi cantong qi*.

New forms of alchemical doctrines and practices

Another indication of the decrease of importance of *waidan* among the early medieval traditions is seen in the system of the Three Caverns (*sandong*).

Created during the fifth century, this system resulted from the effort of arranging both the earlier and the contemporary Daoist traditions of Jiangnan into a unitary framework after the Shangqing and Lingbao corpora had taken shape, and after the cults and practices of the Way of the Celestial Masters had spread to that area. The low rank assigned to *waidan* among the Three Caverns fully partakes of the Shangqing outlook. The Taiqing or Great Clarity heaven, from which the *waidan* scriptures and methods are revealed and to which they grant access, lost the exalted status that it had enjoyed earlier, and became the lowest of three celestial domains, or Caverns, after those related to the Shangqing and Lingbao corpora.[76]

As it was around the same time – the fifth century – that the *Cantong qi* entered the history of Chinese alchemy, one can look at the course taken by the alchemical traditions from the last part of the Six Dynasties as a response to these changes. A remarkable feature of this response is that it occurred in part by recovering Han traditions represented by the apocryphal texts, of whose importance in relation to meditation we have had glimpses in the course of this study. As I have tried to show elsewhere,[77] a text entitled *Cantong qi* existed during the Han period; it was related to the milieu that produced the apocrypha and possibly was a 'weft text' itself. The transmission of this original *Cantong qi* did not suffer major breaks after the end of the Han period and continued, like that of other apocrypha, in Jiangnan, where the *Cantong qi* came in touch with the traditions that we have surveyed. The received text is the result of alterations and additions made as part of this process. As we know it today, the *Cantong qi* is related to the development of two new forms of practice: a new variety of *waidan* that relies on the abstract emblems of correlative cosmology instead of ritual, and a new variety of inner practice that relies on those same emblems instead of meditation on the inner gods.

While this is not the place to dwell in detail on the contents of this complex text, some remarks are in order at least on one point. Although it incorporates fragments of both *waidan* and *neidan* practices, the *Cantong qi* is not primarily concerned with either *waidan* or *neidan*, and not even with 'alchemy' per se. Using a language remarkably different from that of the earlier sources on *waidan* or meditation, it purports to illustrate the bond that exists between Non-being (*wu*) and Being (*you*), or the absolute and the relative. To do so, it borrows from correlative cosmology various patterns of emblems – Yin and Yang, the Five Agents, the trigrams and hexagrams of the *Book of Changes*, the Celestial Stems and Earthly Branches and so forth – and uses them to represent the ontological and cosmological states that define the extension of the Dao into the cosmos, with the intent of explaining their nature and mutual relations.[78]

The ultimate purpose is to show that change, the main feature of the world of form, is owed to the operation of the formless Dao as it manifests itself. Alchemy comes into play, so to speak, at a later stage, namely when the *Cantong qi* offers its way to 'return to the Dao'. But besides being extremely allusive, descriptions of processes related to either *waidan* or *neidan* form only a fraction of the whole text. The task of describing alchemical methods, whether 'inner' or 'outer', is left to commentaries and other works that apply the same emblems to the compounding of the elixir. The purpose, in this case, is to follow the ontological and cosmological stages that intervene between the Dao and the 'ten thousand things' in a sequence contrary to their hierarchical arrangement, and therefore revert to the higher states of being.

In this context, the inner gods serve no more. In their intermediary function between the Formless and the forms, they are replaced by other 'images' (*xiang*), namely the emblems of correlative cosmology and the alchemical symbols proper.[79] Some of these images correspond to those represented earlier as anthropomorphic deities: it is not difficult to see, for instance, the relation that occurs between the Original Pneuma of the Dao that changes itself into the cosmos and the Supreme Great One of the *Central Scripture* who is that very pneuma; or even between the inner elixir and the inner Red Child who is one's own inner 'self'. However, the 'speculative gnosis' that forms an essential aspect of the discourse of the *Cantong qi*, and that relies on correlative cosmology as a tool for explaining the relation between the Dao, the cosmos and the human being, is absent in the traditions represented by the early texts on meditation, as it is also in Shangqing. Even some clusters of terms that recur in the *Cantong qi* show how its adept is not interested in meditating on the deities that reside within himself any more. Instead, he surveys (*can*), examines (*cha*), investigates (*kao*), explores (*tan*), enquires (*ji*) and inspects (*shen*); he gauges (*cun*) and measures (*du*); he reflects (*si*), ponders (*lü*), infers (*tui*) and assesses (*kui*). This is not mere intellectual activity and takes place, instead, through 'contemplation' (*guan*).

Despite this, the *Cantong qi* uses terminology also found in the *Central Scripture*, the *Yellow Court* and the Shangqing texts. For instance, it borrows from the *Yellow Court* the phrase that describes the centre of the human being ('square and round and with a diameter of one inch') and applies it to the elixir itself; this is one of about four or five dozen terms and expressions shared by the two texts.[80] A similar sentence, as we have seen in a passage quoted above, is found in the *Central Scripture of Laozi*, and here again it is one of several instances of shared images and phrases. In most cases, though, the actual meanings of the terms, or the sense in which the *Cantong qi* uses them, are different. An example found in a section concerned with the principles of inner cultivation illustrates how the text borrows earlier images and terms and uses them in relation to impersonal notions. On three occasions, the *Central Scripture* instructs its adepts to visualise their inner essences and pneumas, saying that those essences and pneumas should 'moisten and impregnate' (*runze*) several organs of the body.[81] The *Cantong qi* uses the same expression with a change of focus: what is 'moistened and impregnated' is not the viscera of the adept

in meditation, but the cosmos itself when Original Pneuma expands throughout it from the centre:

> Gradually 'from the Yellow Centre it pervades the veinings (*tongli*)',
> moistening and impregnating it reaches the flesh and the skin . . .
> The One thereby covers all,
> but no one in the world knows it.[82]

In another passage, the action of 'moistening and impregnating' is performed by the Sun and the Moon, when they join to each other at the end of
each time cycle and release their 'nurturing fluids' (*ziye*, a compound formed
by two terms that in the *Central Scripture* and other texts define the salivary
juices):

> Between the last day of a month and the first day of the next,
> they join their tallies and move to the Centre.
> In chaos, vaporous and opaque,
> female and male follow each other:
> their nurturing fluids moisten and impregnate,
> emanating and transmuting, they flow and pervade.[83]

This passage provides another example of the incorporation and modi-
fication of earlier symbolic forms in the *Cantong qi*. In the meditation texts,
as we have seen, essences and pneumas associated with the Sun and the
Moon are joined and ingested by the adept. In the *Cantong qi*, the passage
just quoted is found in a section concerned with the *najia* (Matching Stems)
cosmological pattern, which this work uses to formulate one of its most
important doctrines. Being the main emblems of the two complementary
principles in the cosmos, the Sun and the Moon respectively harbour the
essences of Original Yin and Original Yang of the precosmic state. Their
conjunction, which occurs at the end of each monthly cycle when they 'join
their tallies and move to the Centre', causes Original Yin and Yang to
couple and generate the next time cycle. While these cycles are responsible
for the existence of change, in the views of the *Cantong qi* they are also
necessary for Original Yin and Yang to be constantly present in the cosmos,
rising and descending through the temporal cycles.[84]

As one could expect, these changes in the use of earlier terms and images
are accompanied in the *Cantong qi* by statements about practices that are
not derived from its doctrines. The last example that I provide of borrowed
terms and expressions is one of those that reveal the attitude of the *Cantong
qi* in this respect. In a section of the *Central Scripture*, visualising the inner
gods of the viscera and directing essences and pneumas from one to another
is called *lizang* or 'passing through the viscera'.[85] This expression, as we
have seen, also appears in the *Stele to Wang Ziqiao* in relation to the three
Cinnabar Fields, and is attested by several other Han and later sources,

including the 'Outer' version of the *Yellow Court*.[86] The *Cantong qi* uses the term *lizang* in a passage devoted to asserting the superiority of its doctrines compared to meditation and other practices:

> This is not the method of passing through the viscera, contemplating within (*neiguan*) and concentrating on something;
> of treading the Dipper and pacing the asterisms (*lüxing bu douxiu*),
> using the six *jia* (*liujia*) as chronograms (*richen*);
> of sating yourself with the nine-and-one (*jiuyi*) in the Way of Yin
> (*yindao*), fouling and tampering with the original womb (*yuanbao*);
> of ingesting pneuma till it chirps in your stomach, exhaling the
> upright and inhaling the external and evil.
>
> By being sleepless day and night,
> and from month to month never taking a pause,
> daily your body becomes tired and exhausted:
> you are 'vague and indistinct', but look like a fool (*chi*).
>
> Your hundred channels (*baimai*) churn like a cauldron,
> unable to clear and to settle;
> piling up soil you make space for an altar,
> and from morning to sunset reverently make offerings.

All this, concludes the *Cantong qi*, becomes pointless when 'you leave your bodily form to rot'.[87]

Two different meditation practices are mentioned in this passage: visualisation of the viscera (*lizang*) and 'treading the Dipper and pacing the asterisms' (*lüxing bu douxiu*), an expression that alludes to the Shangqing methods of 'pacing the celestial net' (*bugang*).[88] Besides them, 'six *jia*' refers to calendrical deities, in particular those of the divination method of the 'orphan-empty' (*guxu*), which in one of its applications allows adepts ritually to exit the cycle of time and the directions of space.[89] 'Way of Yin' is a term associated with sexual techniques, and 'nine-and-one' refers to 'nine shallow and one deep' penetrations in intercourse. 'Making offerings' obviously alludes to rites performed in honour of minor deities and spirits. The last sentence in the first paragraph, as well as the first two lines in the second quatrain, refer to breathing practices.

We have here, in other words, a sample of methods that were current during the Six Dynasties: different meditation practices, breathing techniques, sexual techniques and rites addressed to minor supernatural beings. The *Cantong qi* is not content with criticising these methods but refers to them with irony. 'Exhaling the old and inhaling the new' (*tugu naxin*), a common expression that denotes ingesting pneuma, is overturned into 'exhaling the upright and inhaling the external and evil' (*tuzheng xi waixie*). Pneuma is ingested 'till it chirps (*ming*) in your stomach'. The adept who devotes himself to these practices is 'vague and indistinct' (*huanghu*); in the *Laozi*, this expression denotes the Dao itself, but in the *Cantong qi*, that adept 'looks like a fool'.[90]

Conclusion: the fate of the inner gods

After seeing, in the earlier sections of this study, several examples of the use of alchemical imagery in relation to inner processes, one question is inevitable. Are we already dealing, before the development of practices related to the *Cantong qi*, with 'inner alchemy'? The answer to this question depends on how one evaluates the processes of change that we have surveyed, and especially the innovations reflected in and promoted by the *Cantong qi*.

Reckoning that the elixir is to be found within, and in general shifting the associated images to an inner plane, does not characterise *neidan* per se. *Neidan* reiterates and magnifies here the process of 'interiorisation' of earlier notions and practices that had already distinguished Shangqing Daoism,[91] and of which we have seen examples of an even earlier date. Taking this into account, the main feature that distinguishes *neidan* from earlier traditions is the replacement of a codified system (the pantheon of inner gods) with another codified system (correlative cosmology) both to construe the relation of the human being to the Dao and to frame the stages of one's practice. The *Cantong qi* is the main text that inspired this change. Under its influence, a comparable change invests *waidan* with an abstract framework at practically the same time, or slightly before. Thus, an earlier model, represented by the Taiqing tradition with its ritual approach to the compounding of the elixir, is replaced by a new model also based on correlative cosmology.[92]

With this shift, the whole outlook changes remarkably. I believe, therefore, that there is much value in Isabelle Robinet's suggestion of applying the term *neidan* to traditions that, besides representing their goal as the compounding of an 'inner elixir', use not only language and notions directly pertaining to alchemy, but also language and notions drawn from the system of correlative cosmology.[93] The shift mentioned above, however, can fully be appreciated if one looks at the doctrines incorporated into the *Cantong qi* as distinct from *neidan* as a practice. The change occurs first at the doctrinal level; the new practices result from grafting earlier methods – in particular, the forms of meditation that we have surveyed – into the new doctrines. Only in this way is it possible to account for the same pattern of change that is apparent in *waidan*, where the grafting of an earlier form of practice (the methods of the Taiqing tradition) on to new doctrinal foundations results in a remarkably different way of making the elixir: an earlier variety of methods based on a variety of ingredients is replaced by a single model, based on the conjunction of only two ingredients (lead and mercury) that represent Original Yin and Original Yang.

One of the several points that remain to be investigated is the fate of the inner gods after other traditions replaced the pre-Shangqing and Shangqing meditation practices, and the relation of these traditions to *neidan*. From the Tang period onward, visualisation of the inner deities is superseded by Buddhist-inspired *neiguan* (inner contemplation) and by *neidan*. As in *neidan*, the inner gods have no real function in the *neiguan* techniques. The *Neiguan jing* (Scripture of Inner Contemplation) mentions some inner gods in its opening passages, but the text is not involved with them: those passages briefly introduce a 'model' of the inner body that an adept perceives through the enlightened state of his mind and spirit. The text is entirely concerned with this state, and the inner gods play no direct or indirect role in its attainment.[94] *Neidan*, as we have seen, discards the inner gods in an even more radical way. But do the inner gods really vanish, never to appear again?

Although many of the doctrinal and historical links remain to be explored, it is noteworthy that the inner deities have continued to perform a role until the present day in a different context, namely Daoist ritual. The few examples that follow might serve to establish a possible historical sequence. As we have seen, an important source incorporated into the Lingbao corpus but reflecting earlier traditions, the *Prolegomena to the Five Talismans*, mentions several inner gods and describes meditation practices. Not long later, a text related to the codification of Daoist ritual that occurred under Lingbao auspices, the *Ershisi shengtu* (*Charts of the Twenty-four Life-givers*), lists the inner gods that the priest despatches to heaven to submit petitions to the outer gods. Although their names are not the same as those given in pre-Shangqing or Shangqing sources on meditation, their locations correspond almost exactly with those that these and other works populate with inner gods: these deities are the twenty-four *jing* or 'luminous spirits' that also play a role in the *Scripture of the Yellow Court* and in Shangqing meditation.[95] At a time that is the heyday of the traditions surveyed above, thus, the inner gods accomplish in ritual one of the main functions they perform in meditation, namely relating the human being – in this case, the priest, and through him the whole community that he represents – to the gods of the celestial pantheon.

At the same time and in the same context, the main Lingbao text, the *Duren jing* (the *Scripture of Salvation*), enjoins adepts to ask the Lord of the Dao (Daojun) that he summon forth several inner divine beings from within their body before they may recite this text.[96] The same invocation is pronounced in the early Lingbao funerary rite[97] and reappears, in a slightly modified form, in the thirteenth-century *Shangqing lingbao dafa* (the *Great Rites of the Highest Clarity and the Numinous Treasure*), a work associated with the Daoist lineages of the Song period but embedded in the Lingbao tradition. It is still pronounced in present-day ritual during the rite of the Lighting of the Burner (*falu*).[98] In the version of the *Great Rites*, the priest addresses the Lord of the Dao, asking him to:

> summon forth from within your servant's body the correct spirits of the Three Pneumas (*sanqi*), the Controllers of Destiny, Fortune, Works and Judgement, as well as the two lords Taokang and Jingyan . . . the officers of merit of the three and the five, the agents on the left and right, the jade lads in charge of the incense, the jade lasses who transmit what is said, the keepers of the talismans of the Five Emperors and the officers of the incense in charge today, thirty-two individuals in all, to report what I say.[99]

Taokang – whom we have already met above as a god of the lower *dantian* – and Jingyan are mentioned together in another early Lingbao scripture that gives the names of the inner gods.[100]

Other examples concern the 'inner child'. In a twelfth-century text on the rite of Salvation through Refinement (*liandu*), the priest performs an inner meditation aimed at releasing the souls of the deceased from the underworld. In particular, he visualises a 'child' (*ying'er*) within his lower *dantian* and then moves him to the central and the upper *dantian*, where the 'child' becomes the Supreme Emperor of Primordial Commencement (Yuanshi shangdi). The assistant spirits of this deity enter Fengdu, the administration of the underworld that the priest visualises between his own kidneys, to release the souls imprisoned there.[101] A similar inner practice is performed in the present day during the rite of the Land of the Way (*daochang*). Here the priest concentrates on his twenty-four 'luminous spirits', then visualises a 'child' in his own lower *dantian* and moves him to the central and the upper *dantian*. Transformed into a Real Man (*zhenren*) dressed in red, this deity submits a petition to the gods of the Golden Portal (Jinque), which – like Fengdu in the example above – is also interiorised and symbolically located in the pearl-shaped pin of the priest's crown.[102]

Whether the priest, in visualising the 'inner child' within his Cinnabar Fields, is practising a form of inner alchemy, or whether he is performing the practices of early Daoist meditation under a different context that provides them with a different meaning, is a point that would require attention but that cannot be discussed within the limits of the present study. The examples shown above suggest, though, that just as Shangqing played a crucial historical role in handing down earlier meditation traditions to *neidan*, Lingbao played a similar role in passing them to Daoist ritual, where they survive to the present day.

Neglected by the *Cantong qi*, and replaced by other images in the *neidan* practices associated with it, the inner gods, thus, continue to perform the task of relating our world to the world above us.

Notes

This study develops some themes examined in the final chapter of my *Great Clarity: Daoism and Alchemy in Medieval China* (Stanford, CA: Stanford University Press, 2005). I am grateful to Monica Esposito, Elena Valussi and Carl Bielefeldt for their valuable criticism and suggestions.

1 *Huangdi jiuding shendan jingjue* (DZ 885), 1:3a. In translating 'covets the Medicine of Life' I read *yao* for *le*.

2 *Laozi zhongjing*, sec. 5–7. The Purple Chamber is identified as the gallbladder in sec. 37. Here and below I refer to the section numbers in the text of the *Laozi zhongjing* found in *Yunji qiqian* (Seven Lots from the Bookcase of the Clouds; DZ 1032), *j.* 18–19. The independent edition in the Daoist Canon (DZ 1168) is virtually identical to the text in the *Yunji qiqian* but is entitled *Laojun zhongjing* (Central Scripture of Lord Lao).

3 Michel Strickmann, 'On the Alchemy of T'ao Hung-ching', in Holmes Welch and Anna K. Seidel (eds), *Facets of Taoism: Essays in Chinese Religion*

(New Haven, CT: Yale University Press, 1979), pp. 123–92. See especially pp. 169–78; the quotation above is from p. 178.

4 Isabelle Robinet, *La révélation du Shangqing dans l'histoire du taoïsme* (Paris: École Française d'Extrême-Orient, 1984), vol. 1, pp. 176–80.

5 Sakade Yoshinobu, 'Zui-Tō jidai ni okeru fukutan to naikan to naitan', in Sakade (ed.), *Chūgoku kodai yōsei shisō no sōgōteki kenkyū* (Tokyo: Hirakawa shuppansha, 1988), pp. 566–99.

6 Katō Chie, '*Rōshi chūkyō* to naitan shisō no genryū', *Tōhō shūkyō*, 87 (1996), 21–38.

7 It should be noted that this description applies to 'alchemy' in the conventional sense of the term. The same emblems, alchemical or cosmological, can also be used to represent the identity of the Dao and the cosmos, or the absolute and the relative, without distinction between *waidan* and *neidan* and, indeed, without the need for either. The *Cantong qi* is primarily concerned with the exposition of this doctrine, while the related *waidan* and *neidan* texts discuss its application in the sphere of the practice. I return to this point below.

8 On the two *waidan* subtraditions outlined above see Pregadio, 'Elixirs and Alchemy', in Livia Kohn (ed.), *Daoism Handbook* (Leiden: E. J. Brill, 2000), pp. 165–95 (especially pp. 179–85). The 'three' in the title of the *Cantong qi* is explicated by several commentators as Daoism, the system of the *Book of Changes* and alchemy; by others as Heaven, Earth and humanity.

9 See Pregadio, 'The Early History of the *Zhouyi cantong qi*', *Journal of Chinese Religions*, 30 (2002), 149–76.

10 As I show in the article cited in the previous note, around 500 CE the *Cantong qi* is mentioned for the first time in relation to the compounding of elixirs in a *waidan* context; this suggests that by that time at least its doctrinal principles were applied to alchemy. Whether forms of *waidan*, on the one hand, or inner practice, on the other, based on the same doctrines as those incorporated in the *Cantong qi* existed before that time is, at present, impossible to ascertain historically. To my knowledge, no extant source contains traces of such practices.

11 I am grateful to James Robson for discussing the location of Mount Tianzhu with me. This name refers to different mountains, a feature related to the shifts of location of the southern sacred mountain (Nanyue). In 'Elixirs and Alchemy' (p. 167), I mistakenly identified Tianzhu as one of the mountains in the Taishan range of Shandong.

12 The *Great Clarity* survives in fragments quoted in the *Taiqing jing tianshi koujue* (DZ 883), compiled not later than the mid-seventh century. The *Nine Elixirs* is included in the *Huangdi jiuding shendan jingjue* (see note 1 above), a *waidan* compilation written for Tang Gaozong (r. 649–683). The *Golden Liquor* is extant in the *Baopu zi shenxian jinzhuo jing* (DZ 917) with a commentary dating from *c*.500 CE. On these and other Taiqing texts see Pregadio, *Great Clarity*.

13 *Baopu zi shenxian jinzhuo jing*, 1:7a–b.

14 *Huangdi jiuding shendan jingjue*, 1:13b.

15 *Baopu zi shenxian jinzhuo jing*, 1:6b–7a. The final part of the first method in the *Nine Elixirs* (*Huangdi jiuding shendan jingjue*, 1:5b) also refers to the malleability of alchemical gold, which suggests that casting tools was one of its uses.

16 See Anna Seidel, *La divinisation de Lao tseu dans le Taoïsme des Han* (Paris: École Française d'Extrême-Orient, 1969), pp. 47–8, 128.

17 See Seidel, *La divinisation de Lao tseu*, pp. 44, 123. The Three Luminaries are the Sun, the Moon and the five planets. The Four Numina are the emblematic animals of the four directions (green dragon for the east, vermilion bird for the south, white tiger for the west and turtle-snake for the north).

18 See Seidel, *La divinisation de Lao tseu*, pp. 58–9; and Donald Holzman, 'The Wang Ziqiao Stele', *Rocznik Orientalistyczny*, 47, 2 (1991), 77–83, p. 79. On the term 'passing through' in relation to meditation practices, see below, pp. 147–8.
19 See Seidel, *La divinisation de Lao tseu*, p. 69.
20 The *Huangdi neijing lingshu* (Congshu jicheng edn), sec. 33, defines the Four Seas as the Ocean of Blood (*xuehai*, heart), the Ocean of Pneuma (*qihai*, kidneys), the Ocean of Marrow (*suihai*, brain) and the Ocean of the Five Grains (*wugu zhi hai*, spleen). The same list of the *Huangdi neijing* is found in one of the *neidan* works included in the late thirteenth- or early fourteenth-century *Xiuzhen shishu* (DZ 263), 21:2a. The *Laozi zhongjing*, sec. 37, states that 'the stomach is the upper ocean' and 'the abdomen is the lower ocean'.
21 Rao Zongyi, *Laozi xiang'er zhu jiaozheng* (Shanghai: Shanghai guji chubanshe, 1991), p. 14; Stephen R. Bokenkamp, with a contribution from Peter Nickerson, *Early Daoist Scriptures* (Berkeley: University of California Press, 1997), p. 92. The *Laozi* sentence is found in sec. 11 of the current text. I quote Bokenkamp's translation, which renders it according to its understanding in the *Xiang'er*. More often, the sentence is interpreted as meaning 'the benefit lies in what is there, but the use lies in what is not there', an aphorism illustrated in the *Laozi* by the examples of the empty space in a vase or in a room, and later borrowed by the *Cantong qi* to support the notion that Non-being (*wu*) is the function (or 'operation', 'use', *yong*) of Being (*you*).
22 *Laozi xiang'er zhu*, p. 12; trans. Bokenkamp, *Early Daoist Scriptures*, p. 89.
23 *Laozi xiang'er zhu*, p. 12; trans. Bokenkamp, *Early Daoist Scriptures*, p. 89.
24 Wang Ming, *Taiping jing hejiao* (Beijing: Zhonghua shuju, 1960), 72:292; translated from the Chinese by Isabelle Robinet, *Taoist Meditation: The Mao-shan Tradition of Great Purity* (Albany: State University of New York Press, 1993), p. 64.
25 *Taiping jing*, 71:283; see Robinet, *Taoist Meditation*, p. 65.
26 Yasui Kōzan and Nakamura Shōhachi (eds), *Isho shūsei* (Tokyo: Meitoku shuppansha, 1971–88), vol. 6, p. 93. See Anna Seidel, 'Imperial Treasures and Taoist Sacraments: Taoist Roots in the Apocrypha', in Michel Strickmann (ed.), *Tantric and Taoist Studies in Honour of Rolf A. Stein* (Brussels: Institut Belge des Hautes Études Chinoises, 1981–5), vol. 2, pp. 291–371, p. 322; and Robinet, *La révélation du Shangqing*, vol. 1, pp. 29, 63.
27 *Lingbao wufu xu* (DZ 388), 1:21a–b. A similar list of inner gods, whose origin could be the same as the ones in the *Dragon-fish* and the *Prolegomena*, is quoted as coming from the *Dongshen jing* in *Wushang biyao* (DZ 1138), 5:12b–15b; see John Lagerwey, *Wu-shang pi-yao: Somme taoïste du VIe siècle* (Paris: École Française d'Extrême-Orient, 1981), pp. 79–80. *Dongshen jing* refers to the corpus attached to the *Script of the Three Sovereigns* (*Sanhuang wen*), which represents another textual and ritual tradition that incorporates the lore of the apocrypha.
28 *Bawei zhaolong miaojing* (DZ 361), 2:13a; see Isabelle Robinet, *Taoism: Growth of a Religion* (Stanford, CA: Stanford University Press, 1997), p. 228.
29 Wang Ming, *Baopu zi neipian jiaoshi* (second revised edn, Beijing: Zhonghua shuju, 1985), 18:324.
30 *Baopu zi*, 6:128. Initial Green is the first stage of life after the joining of Original Yin and Yang. A few lines before this passage, the sentences dealing with the 'two mountains' (*ershan*) are also related to meditation practices. A fourth relevant passage is in *Baopu zi*, 5:111. See James Ware, *Alchemy, Medicine and Religion in the China of AD 320: The Nei P'ien of Ko Hung (Pao-p'u tzu)* (Cambridge, MA: MIT Press, 1966), pp. 120–1 and 99–100, respectively.
31 As shown by illustrations of the inner body as a mountain with peaks, watercourses and palaces, and even more by the well known *Neijing tu*, there is no

FABRIZIO PREGADIO

contradiction between the two representations, which do not constitute alternative models. See Catherine Despeux, *Immortelles de la Chine ancienne: Taoïsme et alchimie féminine* (Puiseaux: Pardès, 1990), pp. 194–8, on the body as a mountain, and Despeux, *Taoïsme et corps humain: Le Xiuzhen tu* (Paris: Guy Trédaniel, 1994), pp. 44–8, on the *Neijing tu*. On the 'inner landscape', with particular reference to the *Central Scripture*, see Kristofer Schipper (trans. Karen C. Duval), *The Taoist Body* (Berkeley: University of California Press, 1993), pp. 100–12.

32 *Baopu zi*, 18:323. Although Ge Hong mentions only the first three chambers, their names match those given in later sources, which describe nine. The third and central one is the upper *dantian* proper.

33 *Baopu zi*, 18:325–6; Ware, *Alchemy, Medicine, and Religion*, pp. 305–6.

34 *Baopu zi*, 18:326.

35 *Laozi zhongjing*, sec. 3, 11, 17, 25, 27, 30 and 36 for the Yellow Court; sec. 3, 17, 20, 23, 26, 32, 35, 36, 45 and 50 for the Cinnabar Field; sec. 3–5, 11, 19, 23, 28, 36, 37, 39 and 40 for the Purple Chamber.

36 *Huangting jing*, 'Inner' version, sec. 2 for the Hut and the Cinnabar Field, sec. 4 for the Yellow Court and sec. 23 for the Purple Chamber; 'Outer' version, 32a and 54b for the Hut, 29a, 30a and 53b for the Yellow Court and 29b and 30b for the Cinnabar Field. References to the *Huangting jing* here and below are to the section number of the 'Inner' version and the page number of the 'Outer' version as found in *Yunji qiqian*, 11:1a–12:27b and 12:28a–56b, respectively.

37 The *Central Scripture* mentions the heaven of Great Clarity in sec. 1–3, 5, 13, 32 and 55. The approximate date of the text is also indicated by passages shared with the *Lingbao wufu xu*; compare *Wufu xu*, 1:18b–19b with sec. 34 and 35, 1:20b–21a with sec. 14 and 37, 1:21a–b with sec. 26 and 1:21b with sec. 21 and 22. Other evidence for a late Han date is provided by Kristofer Schipper in his 'The Inner World of the *Laozi zhongjing*', in Huang Chun-chieh and Erik Zürcher (eds), *Time and Space in Chinese Culture* (Leiden: E. J. Brill, 1995), pp. 114–31, especially pp. 118–19. Maeda Shigeki, however, has suggested that the shared passages derive from a third shared source, and has dated the *Central Scripture* to around 500 CE; see his '*Rōshi chūkyō* oboegaki' (Notes on the *Laozi zhongjing*), in Sakade, *Chūgoku kodai yōsei shisō no sōgōteki kenkyū*, pp. 474–502, especially pp. 491–7. The relation between the *Central Scripture* and the *Prolegomena* is examined in detail by John Lagerwey, who also accepts a late Han date for the *Central Scripture*; see his 'Deux écrits taoïstes anciens', *Cahiers d'Extrême-Asie*, 14 (2004).

38 Obviously, those who had received the transmission of the relevant practices could decipher the terminology and imagery of this work, but the text as we have it is primarily a literary work. This is also suggested by the fact that the 'Inner' version states four times that it should be recited (*yong*) or chanted (*song*) rather than used for meditation practices. See sec. 1 ('This is called a Jade Writ and deserves to be studied in detail / If you recite it ten thousand times, you will rise to the Three Heavens'), sec. 21 ('By meditating on and reciting this Jade Writ, you will enter into Highest Clarity'), sec. 24 ('Why would you not ascend a mountain and chant my Writ?') and sec. 36 ('Perform ablutions to reach complete purity, and discard fat and spicy food / Enter the Chamber, face east and chant this Jade Book'). Isabelle Robinet's views on this text were unambiguous: the *Yellow Court*, she wrote, 'was not written to expose or explicate anything' (*Taoist Meditation*, p. 58).

39 The issues surrounding the relation of the two versions to each other cannot be approached within the limits of the present study. Here I can only note that the

154

traces of a Shangqing influence on the 'Inner' version do not go much beyond
the mentions of the heaven of Highest Clarity (Shangqing; see the previous
note) and of the *Dadong zhenjing* (see sec. 36). As I remark below, it is unclear
whether the allusion to generating an 'inner body' in the 'Inner' version reflects
a direct Shangqing influence.

40 Robinet, *Taoist Meditation*, pp. 48–54; the quotation is from p. 50.
41 See Robinet, *La révélation du Shangqing*, vol. 1, pp. 29, 63.
42 *Laozi zhongjing*, sec. 39: 'The Dao is the self (*wu*); he is the Supreme Lord of the
    Central Ultimate'.
43 *Huangting jing*, 'Inner' version, sec. 8.
44 *Huangting jing*, 'Inner' version, sec. 9–14. A verse in sec. 14 reads: 'The Palace
    of the Department of the Gallbladder is the essence of the Six Receptacles'. On
    the gallbladder as representing the 'six receptacles', see Robinet, *Taoist Medita-
    tion*, pp. 66–7, and Despeux, *Taoïsme et corps humain*, pp. 110–12.
45 *Huangting jing*, 'Inner' version, sec. 9, 11, 15, 17 and 20. Other texts describe
    White Origin and Blossomless as also related to the lungs and the liver, respect-
    ively. See Bokenkamp, *Early Daoist Scriptures*, pp. 384–5, and Despeux, *Taoïsme
    et corps humain*, pp. 135–8.
46 The *Yellow Court* does not give details on the twenty-four *jing*. On their loca-
    tions and names in texts belonging or attached to the Shangqing and Lingbao
    corpora, respectively, see Mugitani Kunio, '*Kōtei naikei kyō* shiron', *Tōyō bunka*,
    62 (1981), 29–59, pp. 46–8; and Wang Ming, '*Huangting jing* kao', in *Daojia he
    daojiao sixiang yanjiu* (Beijing: Zhongguo shehui kexue chubanshe, 1984), pp.
    324–71, pp. 340–3.
47 *Laozi zhongjing*, sec. 11.
48 *Laozi zhongjing*, sec. 39. For similar practices see especially sec. 21, 30 and 34–
    36. Katō Chie provides an excellent guide to reading these and related passages
    in her '*Rōshi chūkyō* to naitan shisō no genryū'.
49 *Huangting jing*, 'Inner' version, sec. 2.
50 *Laozi zhongjing*, sec. 51. On the corresponding *neidan* practice, see Despeux,
    Taoïsme et corps humain, pp. 152–8.
51 On the role played by the salivary juices in the practices of the *Scripture of the
    Yellow Court* see Robinet, *Taoist Meditation*, pp. 90–4.
52 *Laozi zhongjing*, sec. 25.
53 *Laozi zhongjing*, sec. 11.
54 *Laozi zhongjing*, sec. 28. The note with the variant name of the god is found in
    the text. On this passage see Kristofer Schipper, 'Le Calendrier de Jade: note
    sur le *Laozi zhongjing*', *Nachrichten der Deutsche Gesellschaft für Natür- und
    Völkerkunde Ostasiens*, 125 (1979), 75–80, pp. 77–8.
55 *Laozi zhongjing*, sec. 21. The same sentence, without the reference to meditation,
    is in the opening passages of the *Scripture of the Nine Elixirs*; see *Huangdi jiuding
    shendan jingjue*, 1:1a. See also sec. 38 of the *Central Scripture*, which says: 'If
    you constantly ingest pneuma, you will obtain a long life and be a Divine
    Immortal. If you visualise the gods and ingest the elixir, you will become a Real
    Man'.
56 *Laozi zhongjing*, sec. 12. The initial part of this passage defies a proper transla-
    tion, for Laozi (the speaker of the *Central Scripture*) refers to himself in both
    the first and the third persons. He introduces himself as 'I' (*wu*) and says that
    he resides in every human being ('human beings also have me', i.e. 'him'); he
    is, therefore, one's own 'self' (*wu*) represented by the Red Child. For similar
    statements, see sec. 23 ('Child-Cinnabar, Original Yang, is the self'), 37 ('the
    stomach is the Great Granary, the residence of the Prince, the hut of the self'),
    37 ('Child-Cinnabar is the self') and 39 ('the Dao is the self').

57 See Schipper, 'Le Calendrier de Jade', p. 76. The Red Child's father is also called Lingyang ziming, a name that in *waidan* is a synonym of mercury.
58 *Huangting jing*, 'Inner' version, sec. 13, 17 and 35; 'Outer' version, 34a. The Red Child also appears as Zidan in *Lingbao wufu xu*, 1:13a. On his images in the *Central Scripture*, see Maeda, '*Rōshi chūkyō* oboegaki', pp. 488–90, and Lagerwey's study quoted in note 37 above.
59 *Huangting jing*, 'Inner' version, sec. 20.
60 *Laozi zhongjing*, sec. 17; see also Despeux, *Taoïsme et corps humain*, pp. 75–6. On the physiology and the imagery of the Caudal Funnel, a point at the level of the coccyx, see Despeux, *Taoïsme et corps humain*, pp. 81–5. The corresponding passage in the independent edition of the *Central Scripture* in the Daoist Canon (DZ 1168) has *jilü* (lumbar vertebra) for *weilü*. I am grateful to Monica Esposito for providing me with details on this passage.
61 Schipper, 'Le Calendrier de Jade', p. 76.
62 *Laozi zhongjing*, sec. 34 and 35. These passages also appear in the *Lingbao wufu xu*, 1:18b–19b.
63 *Laozi zhongjing*, sec. 2, 8 and 22; *Huangting jing*, 'Inner' version, sec. 7, 9, 21 and 25. The term does not appear in the 'Outer' version of the *Huangting jing*.
64 *Baopu zi*, 16:287–8; Ware, *Alchemy, Medicine, and Religion*, p. 270. The luting mud is usually called *liuyi ni* (Mud of the Six-and-One) or *shenni* (Divine Mud). Sealing the mouth of a crucible with mud in *waidan* is called *feng*; the synonym given in the *Baopu zi* is *fengjun niwan*.
65 On the meanings and associations of the word *dan*, see Pregadio, *Great Clarity*, chapter 4.
66 See especially Robinet, *Taoist Meditation*, and Robinet, *La révélation du Shangqing*, vol. 1, pp. 161–85.
67 On this third major inner pantheon, after those of the *Central Scripture* and the *Yellow Court*, see Robinet, *Taoist Meditation*, pp. 100–3, and Mugitani Kunio, '*Daidō shinkyō sanjūkyū shō o megutte*', in Yoshikawa Tadao (ed.), *Chūgoku ko dōkyōshi kenkyū* (Kyoto: Dōhōsha, 1992), pp. 55–87 (especially pp. 75–82). On the deities mentioned in another revealed Shangqing scripture, the *Lingshu ziwen*, see Bokenkamp, *Early Daoist Scriptures*, pp. 284–5, 326–7.
68 *Shangqing dadong zhenjing* (DZ 6), 6:13b–14a.
69 This view of the gestation process and its re-enactment in meditation is the topic of the *Shangqing jiudan shanghua taijing zhongji jing* (DZ 1382). The passage quoted above is found at 3a–b. On this text see Robinet, *Taoist Meditation*, pp. 139–43, and *La révélation du Shangqing*, vol. 1, pp. 78–9, and vol. 2, pp. 171–4. Other Shangqing sources locate the nodes in twelve loci of the body. On the Shangqing views of the embryo, and their relation to earlier descriptions of the gestation process, see Katō Chie, 'Tai no shisō', in Noguchi Tetsurō (ed.), *Dōkyō no seimeikan to shintairon* (Tokyo: Yūzankaku shuppansha, 2000), pp. 100–19; on the 'nodes' see pp. 106–12.
70 See Robinet, *La révélation du Shangqing*, vol. 1, pp. 172–3.
71 See Robinet, 'Randonnées extatiques des taoïstes dans les astres', *Monumenta Serica*, 32 (1976), 159–273 (especially pp. 159–219), and the summary in *Taoist Meditation*, pp. 187–200. Other examples are given by Sakade, 'Zui-Tō jidai ni okeru fukutan to naikan to naitan', pp. 157–60.
72 Robinet, 'Randonnées extatiques', pp. 178–84, and *Taoist Meditation*, pp. 193–5. This view of the alchemical process is also shared by the *waidan* texts based on the *Cantong qi*.
73 For discussions of relevant texts see Strickmann, 'On the Alchemy of T'ao Hung-ching', and Pregadio, *Great Clarity*, chapters 3 and 8. One of the main sources in this respect is translated by Bokenkamp in *Early Daoist Scriptures*,

pp. 331–9; see also Bokenkamp's remarks on the relation between *waidan* and alchemical imagery at pp. 289–95.
74 Robinet, *La révélation du Shangqing*, vol. 1, pp. 35–48. On Ge Hong's views of the relations among alchemy, meditation and other practices prevalent at his time in Jiangnan, see Pregadio, *Great Clarity*, chapter 7.
75 *Zhen'gao* (DZ 1016), 5:11b.
76 On the main features of the Three Caverns system see Bokenkamp, *Early Daoist Scriptures*, pp. 190–4; on its doctrinal origins and antecedents, see Robinet, *La révélation du Shangqing*, pp. 75–85.
77 See Pregadio, 'The Early History of the *Zhouyi cantong qi*'.
78 As elsewhere in Daoism, this ontology is also a cosmogony: the same hierarchical states can be arranged into a 'chronological' sequence to form a description of how the cosmos takes shape. This is important for alchemy, as the compounding of the elixir can be associated with different cosmogonic stages, sequentially traced in reverse.
79 To a certain extent, a similar change of focus characterises the formation of correlative cosmology itself in the third to second century BCE. Michael Puett has noted an early instance in relation to the cosmology of the *Taiyi shengshui*, a late fourth-century BCE manuscript from Guodian. He remarks: 'In this cosmology, natural phenomena are not controlled by individuated spirits. Rather, the authors of this text appropriated divinities and spirits and made them into cosmological forces . . . any attempt to manipulate the spirits of the world through divination and sacrifices would be useless within such a cosmology'. For a similar reason, the same could be true, according to the *Cantong qi*, for meditation on the inner gods. See Puett, *To Become a God: Cosmology, Sacrifice, and Self-divinization in Early China* (Cambridge, MA: Harvard University Asia Center, 2002), pp. 160–4 (quotation from p. 163).
80 *Huangting jing*, 'Inner' version, sec. 7; *Cantong qi*, sec. 7. On these borrowings see Pregadio, 'The Early History of the *Zhouyi cantong qi*', and *Great Clarity*, chapter 12. References to the *Cantong qi* here and below are to the redaction by Chen Zhixu (1289 to after 1335), usually entitled *Zhouyi cantong qi fenzhang zhu* and available in several editions and reprints, including those of the *Siku quanshu* and the *Daozang jiyao*.
81 *Laozi zhongjing*, sec. 26, 28 and 42.
82 *Cantong qi*, sec. 6. The phrase within quotation marks comes from the 'Wenyan zhuan' of the *Book of Changes*, on the *kun* hexagram.
83 *Cantong qi*, sec. 18.
84 The description of the moon cycle is the main focus of sec. 4 and 18, but the joining of the Sun and the Moon as generating the time cycles is mentioned in several other sections of the *Cantong qi*. For a brief description of the *najia* and other time cycles employed in the *Cantong qi*, see my 'The Representation of Time in the *Zhouyi cantong qi*', *Cahiers d'Extrême-Asie*, 8 (1995), 155–73.
85 *Laozi zhongjing*, sec. 26: 'If you want to practise the Dao, you should first of all pass through the viscera and see their deities'.
86 *Huangting jing*, 'Outer' version, 37a: 'Pass through the five viscera in contemplation, and observe their patterns (*jiedu*) / When the six receptacles are cultivated and controlled, they are as untainted as white silk'.
87 *Cantong qi*, sec. 8. The first part of this passage is in prose, followed by two quatrains in five-character verses.
88 See Robinet, *Taoist Meditation*, pp. 187–225. Other redactions of the *Cantong qi* read *neishi* (inner observation) for *neiguan*; this term is used in various sources in relation to visualisations of the viscera.

89 See Ngo Van Xuyet, *Divination, magie et politique dans la Chine ancienne* (Paris: Presses Universitaires de France), pp. 194–6; and Marc Kalinowski, *Cosmologie et divination dans la Chine ancienne: Le Compendium des Cinq Agents (Wuxing dayi, VIe siècle)* (Paris: École Française d'Extrême-Orient, 1991), pp. 217–19.
90 Similar warnings about the performance of incorrect practices, or the incorrect interpretation of certain notions and terms, will continue in later traditions related to the *Cantong qi*, sometimes becoming even more radical. I plan to devote a separate study to this topic.
91 Robinet, *La révélation du Shangqing*, vol. 1, pp. 74–80.
92 In *waidan*, this change is reflected in the adoption of mercury and lead as the two metals that, in their refined or 'authentic' state, respectively represent Original Yin and Original Yang. These two metals are the main *waidan* emblems adopted in *neidan*.
93 Robinet, 'Original Contributions of Neidan to Taoism and Chinese Thought', in Livia Kohn (ed.), *Taoist Meditation and Longevity Techniques* (Ann Arbor: University of Michigan, 1989), pp. 297–330 (especially p. 301); see also *Taoism: Growth of a Religion*, p. 217.
94 See Livia Kohn, 'Taoist Insight Meditation: the Tang Practice of Neiguan', in Kohn (ed.), *Taoist Meditation and Longevity Techniques*, pp. 193–224, p. 205.
95 See Bokenkamp, *Early Daoist Scriptures*, pp. 458–60, and Wang Ming, '*Huangting jing* kao', pp. 340–3.
96 See Bokenkamp, *Early Daoist Scriptures*, pp. 385, 414.
97 *Wushang biyao*, 51:3b; Bokenkamp, 'The Purification Ritual of the Luminous Perfected', in Donald S. Lopez Jr (ed.), *Religions of China in Practice* (Princeton, NJ: Princeton University Press, 1996), pp. 268–77 (see p. 273). See also Lagerwey, *Wu-shang pi-yao*, pp. 158–9.
98 John Lagerwey, *Taoist Ritual in Chinese Society and History* (New York: Macmillan, 1987), pp. 121–3; Schipper, *The Taoist Body*, pp. 96–7.
99 *Shangqing lingbao dafa* (DZ 1221), 39:2a and 39:4a–b. See Lagerwey, *Taoist Ritual*, pp. 155–9, whose translation I have quoted with minor changes to match the terminology used above.
100 *Ziran jiutian shengshen zhangjing* (DZ 318), 10a.
101 See Judith Boltz, 'Opening the Gates of Purgatory: A Twelfth-century Taoist Meditation Technique for the Salvation of Lost Souls', in Strickmann (ed.), *Tantric and Taoist Studies*, vol. 2, pp. 487–511. A different version of the same rite is translated in Lagerwey, *Taoist Ritual*, pp. 233–4. On the interiorisation of Fengdu, see Despeux, *Taoïsme et corps humain*, pp. 97–9.
102 See Lagerwey, *Taoist Ritual*, p. 132, and Schipper, *The Taoist Body*, pp. 96–7.

8

THE DYNAMIC DESIGN

Ritual and contemplative graphics in Daoist scriptures

Franciscus Verellen

The reverence in Chinese civilization for written characters and cosmic diagrams finds expression in Daoism in a variety of ritual documents and designs that are thought to be endowed with transformative and efficacious powers. Written memorials, confessions and sacred symbols known as 'talismans' (*fu*) form the main media for communication with the unseen world. In the ritual propitiation of divine and demonic forces, the offering of such carefully calligraphed, formal compositions takes the place of the blood sacrifices in China's common religion. Talismanic writings incorporate written characters, or designs suggestive of Chinese characters, side-by-side with other graphic elements. Illegible as mundane texts, they are destined to sway divine bureaucracies. For the liturgical specialist, they constitute dynamic ritual instruments. In addition, pictures in scriptures serve another fundamental religious purpose: the mental representation of the unseen world for contemplative or evidential purposes. Showing, for example, the landscapes of paradises and hells or the likenesses of gods and saints, or the effects that ritual or devotional acts produce in the beyond, illustrated scriptures inform us how believers were intended to imagine articles of faith and doctrine.

The following observations are based on a survey of the illustrations in the Daoist canon of the Ming, the *Da Ming Daozang jing* or *Zhengtong Daozang*.[1] Commissioned by the Yongle Emperor in 1406, this massive collection was issued under the reign of the Zhengtong Emperor in 1445. The woodblock-printed engravings reproduced in this chapter are taken from the Wanli reprint of 1598 and the facsimile reprint of 1926. It should be noted at the outset that it is often impossible to assign a precise date or attribution to graphic materials in the *Daozang*, which in many cases did not originate with the works they illustrate. Since at least early Tang times (618–907), successive editions of the Daoist canon featured a twelve-fold generic classification system (*shier lei*) that included beside essentially textual compilations of scriptures, records and manuals, two categories titled 'Sacred Symbols' (*shenfu*) and 'Efficacious Diagrams' (*lingtu*).[2] Although these two categories assign a special place to graphic representations, overall there is no clear demarcation between textual and graphic materials in the *Daozang*. The *shenfu*, based on the celestial writing of scriptural revelation, are used as essentially graphic talismans in ritual; *lingtu*, representations of cosmic symbols such as the Eight Trigrams, likewise feature in scriptures and in written ordination registers (*lu*). Some entire scriptures function as talismans.[3] The scriptures, moreover, are transmitted to adepts in conjunction with associated diagrams, registers and talismans. Graphic representations are embedded in many of the scriptures in the Daoist canon. These designs can be descriptive or prescriptive, serving as models for the production of ritual documents or talismans. Our selection is discussed under the headings of 'Visualization', 'Pictorial metaphor' and 'Dynamic symbols'. The examples range from representations of concrete entities to increasingly abstract concepts, from static depictions to dynamic designs. A recurring theme is the interlocking relationship between textual and graphic elements in Daoist documents, where diagrams complement discursive description and words form part of the diagrammatic designs. The Daoist belief in the authority of the written word is common to Chinese civilization as a whole. It is founded on a conception of the written character as the ultimate magic graph.[4]

Visualization

The simplest form of pictorial aids to visualization depicts an actual object or procedure, enhancing a less satisfactory discursive account with the immediate visual grasp afforded by an image. The visible side of ritual is a common subject of such graphics in the Daoist canon. A typical example is the illustrations of ritual vestments for male and female priests of different grades in 'The Regulations for the Practice of Daoism in Accordance with the Scriptures of the Three Caverns', an early Tang work setting out standards and observances for Daoist religious activities like 'the production of icons' and 'the copying of scriptures' and including regulations for the performance of ritual.[5] The illustration of the Zhengyi register in Figure 8.1, the 'Secret Register of the Most High for Obtaining Release from Sundry Spells and Incantations' issued by the Forty-fourth Heavenly Master Zhang Yuqing (d. 1427),[6] shows the performance of an exorcistic ritual. In his left hand the priest holds a bowl filled with water, in his right a sword. The seven stars of the Dipper are to be visualised on such occasions. Here they are shown as part of the talismanic design on the left that, together with the sword and lustral water, constitutes the exorcist's essential equipment. Other features of ritual performance that are objects of similar illustrations in the Daoist canon include altar arrangements, funeral banners, musical notations for hymns and choreographies for ritual dance steps.

Beside ritual in the strict sense, many Daoist methods and techniques gave rise to 'how-to' diagrams of a plainly practical nature. The example in Figure 8.2 is from a medical work on the circulation of *qi*-energy in the body, the 'Arcanae of the Circulation of Qi in the Fundamental Questions

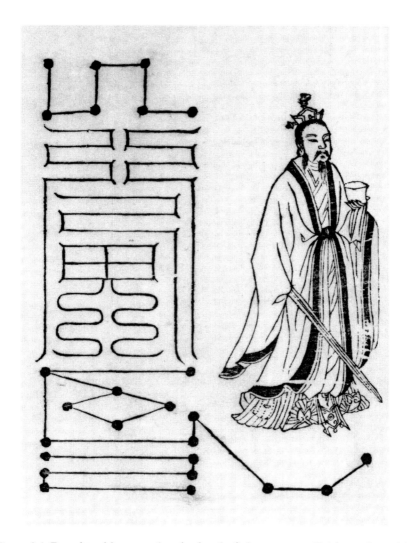

Figure 8.1 Exorcist with a sword and a bowl of charm water. *Taishang zhengyi jie wuyin zhouzu bilu* (*c.*1400) 2a–b, Ming edition of 1598. Courtesy of the Bibliothèque nationale de France (Chinois 9546/1200).

[of the Yellow Emperor]' (1099) by Liu Wenshu.[7] Depicting the phasing of the Five Agents (wood, fire, earth, metal and water) and the Six Humours (heat, humidity, dryness, cold, wind and warmth) through the sexagesimal cycle, it could also be used as a mnemonic aid for counting in the cycle of sixty using one's ten fingers.[8]

The theory and practice of the gymnastic exercises 'Eight Lengths of Brocade Method' (*baduan jin fa*) are discussed and illustrated in a compilation of texts on physiological self-cultivation and breathing exercises titled

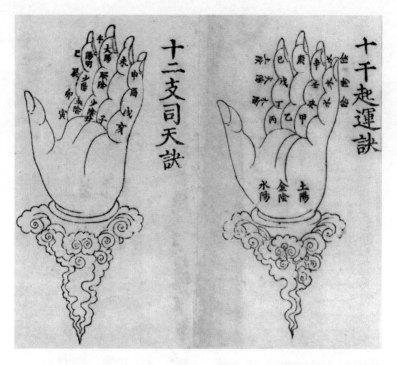

Figure 8.2 Arrangement of the Heavenly Stems and Earthly Branches on the hand. *Suwen rushi yunqi lun'ao* (1099) 1.2a, Ming edition of 1598. Courtesy of the Bibliothèque nationale de France (Chinois 9546/1010).

'Miscellany Digest' (*Zazhu jiejing*), which forms part of the collection 'Ten Books on the Cultivation of Perfection' (*c*.1400).[9] The method depicted there is a development of the ancient tradition of *daoyin*, gymnastics, and the representation of the exercises continues an early pictorial convention known from the '*daoyin tu*' silk painting discovered in Tomb no. 3 at Mawangdui (186 BCE).[10] Many other medico-physiological procedures are subjects of similar visual representations: moxibustion loci (places for applying moxa on the skin), different types of body sores and so on.

Another richly illustrated type of practice is divination. An example can be seen in the popular manual for meteorological prediction, 'The Atmospheric Agents of Rain and Shine'.[11] The pictures resemble modern meteorological symbols. At the same time, they too evoke traditional iconographical conventions, such as the depiction of 'haloes' surrounding celestial bodies in the Mawangdui chart on divination by astrology and meteorology.[12] The pre-modern spheres of scientific and religious thought are of course seldom truly discrete. Technical in nature, 'The Atmospheric Agents' uses empirical observations of celestial bodies, winds and clouds, as well as calendrical calculations, for an essentially religious end: the prevention of evil influences associated with violent weather conditions. Not surprisingly, technical illustrations in the *Daozang* in proto-scientific areas like medicine, botany, alchemy, metallurgy and astronomy are generally inspired by religious objectives such as healing, divination or the production of magical elixirs, swords and mirrors. A rare exception in the Daoist canon is found in the 'Illustrated and Expanded *Materia Medica*' (1116) by Kou Zongshi.[13] It depicts two techniques for winning salt from sea water – one by evaporation in a cauldron, the other in a salt marsh. An apparently purely practical illustration, this would not have been out of place in a technical manual on those subjects.

The category of pictorial hagiography – images depicting gods, sages or saints, and their legends – covers dissimilar representations ranging from portraits to icons and straddling the functions of illustration and visualization. At the mainly illustrative end of the spectrum one could cite the 'Portraits of Ten Masters of the Mysterious Origin',[14] an album of drawings by the celebrated painter Zhao Mengfu (1254–1322). The original work is dated 1286 and was executed at the request of Zhao's Daoist master, the Southern Song and early Yuan commentator and philosopher Du Daojian (1237–1318).[15] The portrait of Zhuangzi, for example, served as a commemorative likeness of a historical personage, while forcefully capturing the artist's personal vision of the sage's spirit.[16] The transmission of Zhao's work, like all pre-Ming graphics in the Daoist canon, depended on the skills of mostly anonymous copyists and engravers. Among other noteworthy portraits in the Daoist canon might be mentioned those of a primordial-looking Laozi, depicted as 'Undifferentiated Beginning' (Hunyuan),[17] and of a Liezi in billowing robes that adorns the *Daozang* edition of the philosophical work of that name.[18]

The semi-historical Lü Dongbin, from Yuan times onward one of the popular group of Eight Immortals, is among the most depicted saints of Daoist iconography. A portrait in his illustrated hagiography 'Records of the Patriarch Lü'[19] shows Lü Dongbin standing beneath the sun and the moon, beside his birth (literally, 'descent') and ascension dates (see Figure 8.3). Between the two columns representing these dates is a diagram of the Three Terraces (Santai) constellation of fate and a talisman, probably Lü's Talisman of Personal Destiny (*benming fu*). The latter incorporates the character for 'five', evoking his ascension date in the fifth month.

A subcategory of this genre is the narrative pictorial hagiographies in the *Daozang*, such as the 'Faithful Illustrations with Eulogies of the Imperial Chamberlain of Shangqing and Zhenren of Tongbo'. This album by the Tang court Daoist and Shangqing patriarch Sima Chengzhen (647–735) depicts the deeds of the immortal Wangzi Jin in eleven scenes.[20] Each episode begins with a narrative account and a description of the corresponding illustration, noting items of clothing, palaces and paraphernalia, followed by a eulogy and the illustration itself. For example, in Scene 8 (14a–b), Wangzi Jin is seen descending from Heaven to take up his post as governor of Mount Tongbo in the Tiantai shan range of Zhejiang. The saint's new residence was the 'grotto-heaven'[21] situated directly beneath Sima's Tongbo

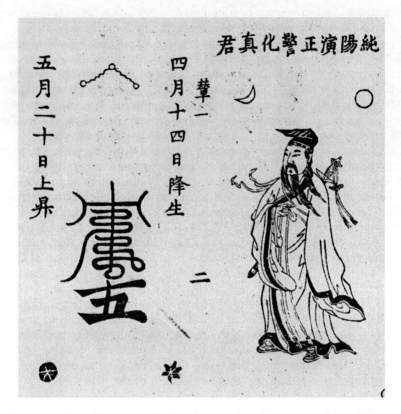

Figure 8.3 Lü Dongbin with his birth and ascension dates (sixteenth century). *Lüzu zhi* 1.1b.

Guan temple. The latter was Sima Chengzhen's residence, constructed in 711 on imperial orders in the patriarch's honour. Another remarkable example of the narrative type of pictorial hagiography is the illustrated episodes from the hagiography of Xu Xun (239–336) in the 'Life of the Grand Astrologer Xu',[22] including such popular scenes as 'Xu Xun smelting the iron pillar' and 'Xu Xun rising up to Heaven'.

The depiction of the Emperor of the Pole Star in Figure 8.4 belongs even less equivocally to the area of iconic representation. It is taken from the 'Register of the Lord of the North Pole, Subduer of Evil Spirits Whose Divine Spells Annihilate Demons' (*c.* 1400),[23] another ordination document issued by the Heavenly Master Zhang Yuqing. It shows the god as emperor and ruler of the Fengdu hells in the North, surrounded by an entourage of officials.

The imperial administrative metaphor underlying this kind of generic representation of deities allowed their orderly accommodation in the ever-expanding pantheon by means of the attribution of official ranks, titles, vestments, etc. The idea of a correspondence between the administrative

Figure 8.4 The Emperor of the Pole Star. *Taishang beiji fumo shenzhou shagui lu*
(*c.*1400) 8b–9a, Ming edition of 1598. Courtesy of the Bibliothèque
nationale de France (Chinois 9546/1198).

systems of this world and of the beyond, and hence the bureaucratic metaphor for depicting the pantheon, is one of the most enduring constants in
the evolving Chinese worldview.[24]

The visualisation of gods is a problematic issue in Daoism, as in many
religions. The Daoist reasoning on this question is nevertheless distinctive.
Images were not forbidden, as in the biblical prohibitions, on the grounds of
being overwhelmingly awesome or objects of idolatrous worship, i.e. falsely
representing non-existing entities.[25] Instead, developing the *Laozi's* insistence
on the ineffability of the Dao and the inadequacy of language for grasping
metaphysical truths, an early commentary affirmed the *a priori* invisibility
of the Dao, the deities within the body and the spirits of the organs, and
even forbade attempts to visualise them.[26] As a rule, however, meditative
visualization constituted an accepted practice, while images were simply
considered immaterial. The section on making icons in the Tang manual
'Regulations for the Practice of Daoism', cited above, states that ideal images of deities were formless and colourless and that no more than fleeting
manifestations of the gods could be captured in pictures.[27] In fact, early
Daoism had no need for icons. Its visionary iconography relied on meditative techniques to make cosmic deities manifest and to actualise the hidden
gods within the body. Paradoxically, however, as everywhere in the history
of religious art, the desire for contemplative vision provided a major motivation for making material images.[28] After the arrival of Buddhism in the
China of the Eastern Han (25–220), Daoists became interested in making
icons as aids to meditation and as objects of a developing cult of image

worship.[29] By that time, Buddhism had long overcome its own, differently motivated opposition to the production of Buddha images and deployed an elaborate religious iconography to great missionary effect through large parts of Asia. Daoism responded in kind. From the period of the Northern and Southern Dynasties (386–589) onwards, images of gods multiplied, especially statues of Laozi and the Heavenly Worthies (*tianzun*). In time, individual icons and depictions of the pantheon were produced as mural paintings in temples, as hanging scrolls for liturgical use and as portable statuettes and hand scrolls for private worship. These developments are reflected in the hagiographic illustrations of the Daoist canon.

Another category of scripture illustrations in the *Daozang* is epistemological in nature. It shares with Chinese philosophical and cosmological diagrams the aim of rendering abstract structural principles intelligible through visual means. Figure 8.5, from the 'Shangqing Illustrations of Precious Mirrors for Prolonging Life' of the Tang period,[30] is on the face of it an illustration of an object: a bronze mirror used for magical, ritual and apotropaic purposes.

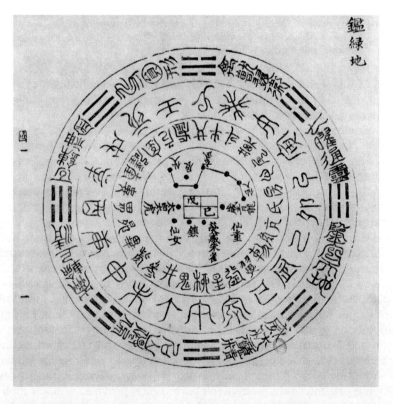

Figure 8.5 Magic mirror. *Shangqing changsheng baojian tu* (Tang) 1a–b, Ming edition of 1598. Courtesy of the Bibliothèque nationale de France (Chinois 9546/426).

Thanks to archaeology, we know that objects like this, featuring near-identical designs, indeed existed.[31] Thus the original object already comprised a depiction of the sky and the universe, including star maps, diagrammatical representations of cosmological theory and text elaborating on the significance of these images. The mirror's decorative and cosmological elements include the Northern Dipper, Polaris, five planets and constellations of the circumpolar region, surrounded by the four emblematic animals in the centre. The first ring from the centre gives the names of the twenty-eight stellar lodges, followed in the next ring by the twelve stations of Jupiter. The names of the latter are interspersed with eight of the ten Heavenly Stems. The two missing stems, *wu* and *ji*, standing for Centre and Earth, are found among the circumpolar constellations in the central circle. The outer ring shows the Eight Trigrams, their diagrammatical representations alternating with eight four-character verses describing the mirror, the figures depicted among its decorative design, the mirror's apotropaic power and its particular use as protection against demons when walking in the mountains.[32]

Figure 8.6, depicting Water as the elemental substance of the universe, is taken from the treatise on Inner Alchemy by Lin Yuan titled 'On the Spirit of the Valley' (preface dated 1304).[33] The fundamental place of water in Daoism is evident from the pronouncements of the *Laozi* regarding its enduring power and adaptability. The recent discovery of the fourth-century BCE Guodian *Laozi* manuscript brought to light an associated text titled after its opening line, 'The Great One Engendered Water (*Taiyi shengshui*)'. This short treatise confirms that water was the first element in early Daoist cosmogony, Taiyi being equated with Dao or primordial chaos.[34] The inscription in the present diagram begins with the words 'The Heavenly One Engendered Water (*Tianyi shengshui*)', a variant of the Guodian phrase.[35] Other examples among numerous representations of this nature in the *Daozang* include the cosmic diagram showing the emblematic animals of the four directions in the 'Shangqing Register for the *Instructions on the Emanations from the Labyrinth*',[36] or the depiction of man and the universe, with the multiple correspondences between the body and cosmic energies, in 'Diagrams of Proven Methods for the Cultivation of Perfection',[37] both from the Tang dynasty. The famous Diagram of the Great Ultimate (*Taiji tu*) also appears in various shapes and forms in the canon,[38] suggesting that this kind of visualisation was also intended, as in the wider Chinese tradition, as an epistemological tool for the exploration of philosophical abstractions.

An equally current type of Daoist diagram depicts the mental projection of microcosms and sacred spaces. A familiar example shows the 'Inner Landscape (*neijing*)', i.e. the microcosm within the human body, with symbolic representations of the gods residing there, its cosmological structure and alchemical processes. This 'side view' (*cemian tu*) is from the introduction to the 'Illustrated Phrase Glosses on the Yellow Emperor's Classic on the Eighty-One Difficulties' (1269) by Li Jiong.[39] It shows the inner topology of the body with physiological and alchemical captions and illustrations. A corollary to the vision of a microcosm within the body is the inner re-creation

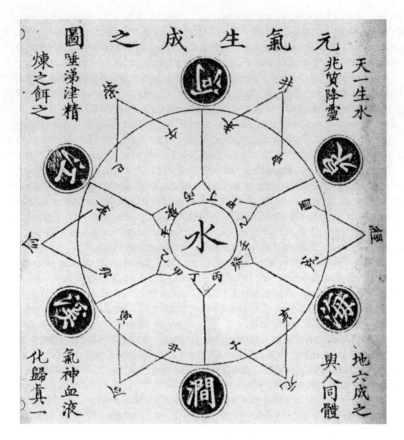

Figure 8.6 Water as primordial element and its devolution. *Gushen pian* (fourteenth century) 2.9a.

of the universe in 'Illustrations of the Return of the Golden Liqueur to the Cinnabar Field.' The first stage of this exercise shows the meditative visualisation of Heaven and Earth emerging from primordial chaos.[40] Such images belong to another tradition of Daoist visual representation, also closely connected with contemplative technique: the projection of microcosms and the mental recreation of remote, idealised or mythical places.[41]

The depiction of the palaces of Heaven in the 'Illustrated Pantheon of the Three Spheres',[42] a guide to the universe by the Northern Song official and Daoist liturgist Zhang Shangying (1043–1121), shows the residence of the supreme deity, the Jade Emperor atop the *axis mundi*, surrounded by the Thirty-two Heavens represented as palatial halls. Other examples of the visualisation of stellar palaces include countless visions of the Dipper stars in the *Daozang*[43] and the often reproduced Daoist choreographies for executing ritual dance steps by treading the stars of the Dipper and other constellations.[44]

Figure 8.7 The map of Man-Bird Mountain. *Xuanlan renniao shan jingtu* (Six
Dynasties) 5a, Ming edition of 1598. Courtesy of the Bibliothèque
nationale de France (Chinois 9546/431).

The 'true form (*zhenxing*)' representations of the Five Sacred Mountains
and other holy sites, suggesting mystical visions of esoteric topographies,
also belong in this category.[45] Figure 8.7, taken from the 'Map of the Book
of the Mysterious Contemplation of Man-Bird Mountain',[46] a geography of
an imaginary mountain inhabited by hybrid spirits, is a striking example.

Others, in addition to the classic 'true forms' of the Five Sacred Mountains themselves,[47] include ostensible maps or landscape depictions of such
mythical sites as Fengdu or the Ten Islands. The 'true map' of the Fengdu
underworld reproduced in the liturgical compendium 'Standard Rituals of the
Supreme Yellow Register Retreat' (*c.*1223)[48] was intended for visualisation
in the course of rituals of salvation. The mountain and seascape rendering
the Three Isles and Ten Continents of the Blessed in 'Diagrams of the Great
Ultimate and Primordial Chaos for the Cultivation of Perfection' (Song)[49]
served the visualisation of these blessed places in meditation. It shows the
Purple Residence of the Taiwei zhenjun in the foreground, with the remaining
nine islands in clusters of three beyond.

We began with an illustration of ritual paraphernalia. For the illustrator, an appealing aspect of ritual is that it operates across the boundary between the visible and the invisible worlds. Daoist priests perform an invisible and inaudible interior ritual in parallel with the public, exterior one. Their liturgy involves journeys to the underworld and into the heavens, the transmission of documents from this world to the next and the slaying of invisible demons with sword and lustral water. While the implements and substances used look the same in both spheres, their nature is transformed by consecration, and the purpose they serve translated on different planes. Consider Figure 8.8, showing musical instruments used in Heaven, from a commentary

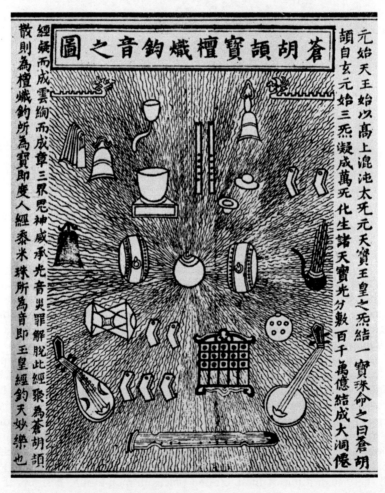

Figure 8.8 Instruments for Heavenly Music. *Yuqing wuji zongzhen Wenchang dadong xianjing zhu* (1309) 1.22b.

dated 1309 by Wei Qi to a ritualised version of the Great Cavern Scripture revealed to Wenchang in Sichuan.[50]

These instruments look for all the world like those used by earthly musicians. Similarly, emissaries carrying petitions from the altar to their divine addressees in rituals for the salvation of the dead are no different from their counterparts employed by the civil administration.[51] The same reliance on familiar reality in representations of the supernatural can be found in accounts of the invisible that refer to pictorial conventions ('it looked just like a painting of hell'). Such references invite us to picture the invisible on the basis of our experience of viewing art.[52] Like the bureaucratic metaphor alluded to above, these representations of the invisible world assume a single, organic and seamless order embracing the human, the natural and the supernatural domains. A corollary of this interconnectedness is that ostensible representations of the invisible world can offer us rare glimpses of a mundane reality that, in the eyes of a traditional artist or writer, would not have merited a depiction as such.

Guides to devotional practice and lay initiation also seek to provide the adept with mental pictures of the invisible benefits of devotion, the effect that religious acts have in the beyond or, conversely, the dangers and blessings emanating from the spirit world that affect mortals. For example, a Tang manual on the transmission and recitation of the *Laozi*, the 'Illustrated Instructions on the Principal Visualizations of the Most High Lord Lao', shows mental evocations of gods in the course of transmission rituals, as well as adepts meditating or predicating on the *Daode jing*. One picture shows a visitation from Heaven rewarding an adept for assiduous recitations of the scripture.[53] Similar illustrations of contemplative practices can be found in meditation manuals and registers, e.g. the series of nine images showing the stages of the 'whirlwind (*huaifeng*) meditation' in the Six Dynasties 'Jade Scripture of the Golden Flower'[54] or the picture of a meditating Daoist in the 'Register of Flying Steps of the Six Stars Governing Fate'.[55] This last text, about practices connected with the cult of the Southern Dipper (Nandou), the imaginary constellation of Long Life, also includes an illustration of 'meditating on the Dipper while reclining' (4b–5a). Dream visions are illustrated and interpreted in the 'Precious Register of Purple Yang of the Career Controller Wenchang', another register issued by the Heavenly Masters of Longhu shan in Jiangxi. The document provides aids to visualisation, including eight dream apparitions of animals, monsters and strange occurrences (*yingmeng*) that could be used in career divination.[56] The visualisation in Figure 8.9 is from a register for invoking the dragons of the Ten Heavens in the Tang collection of illustrated Shangqing registers for lay devotees already cited.[57] It shows a highly satisfied adept having successfully commandeered such a celestial mount.

Pictorial metaphor

Metaphoric, allegoric and emblematic representations are common features in religious iconography. An area noted for distinctively Daoist metaphors

Figure 8.9 Marshalling the Dragons of the Ten Heavens. *Shangqing qusu jueci lu*
(Tang) 7a–b, Ming edition of 1598. Courtesy of the Bibliothèque nationale
de France (Chinois 9546/1373).

of both the discursive and the pictorial kinds is Inner Alchemy (*neidan*).
Contemplative practices had always been an important component of Chinese
alchemy. From the Tang onward, as these practices became increasingly
autonomous and even the predominant discipline, Inner Alchemy continued to couch its theories in the language and imagery of laboratory or
Outer Alchemy (*waidan*). This produced a dense, metaphoric idiom. While
the *Daozang* also contains illustrated technical manuals for the actual
laboratory,[58] more often its ostensible references to processes and ingredients stand metaphorically for mental, psycho-physiological and spiritual
entities.

A remarkable case is the 'Alchemical Diagrams to Master Shangyang's
Essentials of the Elixir'.[59] Master Shangyang, the author of this collection,
was Chen Zhixu (b. 1290), a prominent Daoist and leader of a syncretic
branch of the Quanzhen movement, incorporating elements of Southern

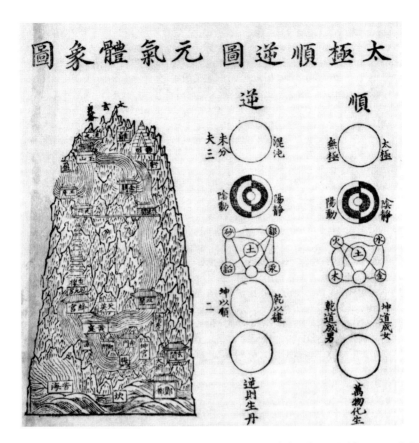

Figure 8.10 The progressive and regressive dynamics of the Great Ultimate and the representation of Original Qi as a body. *Shangyang zi jindan dayao tu* (*c.*1331) 3a, Ming edition of 1598. Courtesy of the Bibliothèque nationale de France (Chinois 9546/1054).

Lineage (Nanzong) Daoism and Chan Buddhist teachings. The first example, on the right of Figure 8.10, depicts the principles of progression and regression in Inner Alchemical theory. The natural processes of progression, on the far right, result in giving life, or 'the incarnation of the myriad creatures'; regression, on the other hand, is an alchemical reversal of such temporal processes as ageing, 'engenders the elixir', i.e. immortal life. The left half of the diagram portrays Original Qi as the flow of streams in a mountain, representing the circulation of vital energy (*qi*) in the body. Another diagram in the same work (8a) shows the emblematic dragon and tiger representing the cosmic principles of Yang and Yin as symbols of the corresponding forces in alchemical and physiological processes. On a different metaphoric plane, the 'Collection on the Return to Perfection' by Wang Jie (*fl.* 1331–1380), the first chapter of which deals with the formation of the 'immortal embryo', analyses the graphs of the characters for 'mind' and 'mystery' as symbols for Inner Alchemical principles.[60]

A common pictorial metaphor represents the spirits of the Five Viscera (*wuzang*) as the emblematic animals of the five corresponding directions of space.[61] Souls and other psycho-physiological agents are typically pictured as spirits or demons, such as the Three Corpses (*sanshi*) in the 'Scripture of the Most-High for the Protection of Life through the Elimination of the Three Corpses and the Nine Worms' (Five Dynasties?), a compendium on the causes of death and decay, including demons and germs.[62] The same richly illustrated text (2b–3b) depicts the Seven *po*-Spirits (*qipo*) as a series of fantastic monsters.[63] One of the most graphically striking images of the collection is shown in Figure 8.11.

As a rule, we find a tendency to visualise real and imaginary life forms in the natural world – whether microbes, animals or plants – as spirits, i.e. in terms of their spiritual essence as opposed to their physical aspect. To the extent that this 'spiritual essence' is hidden behind the world of phenomenal appearances, and that its apprehension constitutes a mystical or esoteric insight, we are dealing here with a concept analogous to the idea of 'true form' (*zhenxing*) encountered above. Botanical depictions in the *Daozang* also bear this out; for example, in the 'White Cloud Immortal's Song of Divine Herbs',[64] an illustrated repertory of medicinal plants, or in the 'Catalog of *zhi* – Fungi', mythical mushrooms of Long Life.[65]

Daoist animal allegories frequently feature the ox, the mount or draught animal used by Laozi when he left China for the West (i.e. Central Asia). The Final Way of the Return of the Chariot (*huiju bidao*) in the illustration below is named for the ox-drawn vehicle that conveyed the adept to the foot of the mountain whence he was to ascend as an immortal. The Final Way of the Return of the Chariot was the highest stage of Daoist initiation, attained after having received the complete scriptures of the Shangqing corpus. In the depiction in Figure 8.12, from the 'Shangqing Register for the *Instructions on the Emanations from the Labyrinth*',[66] the master's departure is allegorised by the abandoned ox and chariot.

Buffalo and chariot are also pictured as an allegory representing the relationship of body and soul, or *xingming*, in 'Daoism as Integration of the Myriad Dharma',[67] a collection of the writings of Mu Changzhao, a Daoist of the Southern Tradition (Nanzong) around the time of the Yuan conquest of the Southern Song. As the title of the work suggests, Mu was a syncretist, well versed in Quanzhen, Buddhist and Chan teachings. The Quanzhen term *xingming*, current also with various connotations in Confucian and Buddhist philosophy, here suggests a combination of human nature, vitality and destiny: the enduring Self, shown as a flaming chariot, tethered to its mortal Being, the buffalo.

'Taming the Horse of the Mind', an allegory of spiritual discipline, has a number of avatars in Chinese religious culture. An example in the *Daozang*

174

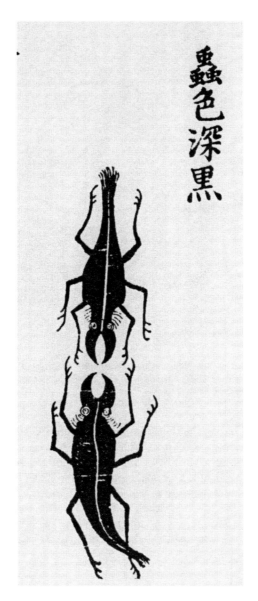

Figure 8.11 Pathogenic agents in the body. *Taishang chu sanshi jiuchong baosheng jing* (Five Dynasties?) 14a.

is found in the 'Three Essentials for the Cultivation of the Perfection According to the Superior Vehicle' by Gao Daokuan (1195–1277), a Quanzhen master in the lineage of the twelfth-century patriarch Ma Danyang. This work includes Gao's illustrated didactic poem 'Song of the Three Methods'

Figure 8.12 The chariot of the final return. *Shangqing qusu jueci lu* (Tang) 24a–b, Ming edition of 1598. Courtesy of the Bibliothèque nationale de France (Chinois 9546/1373).

(*Sanfa song*), which likens the disciplining of the mind (*xin*) and of human nature (*xing*) to the training of a horse.[68] The allegory was current in Quanzhen Daoism and constituted a variant of the Training of the Buffalo in Chan Buddhism and of the Bridling of the Horse of the Will (*yima*), the latter popularised in the novel *Journey to the West*. In Quanzhen-inspired Yuan poetic drama (*zaju*), the horse appears, in the manner of the Inner Alchemical metaphors discussed above, as an anatomical personification of the Daoist Yellow Court (*huangting*), i.e. the central organ of the heart or mind (*xin*).[69]

Dynamic symbols

Beliefs in the dynamic and transformative potential of images are a part of Europe's classical heritage, as well as China's. Greek and Roman apprehensions of the supernatural qualities of statues and *icones symbolicae* resurfaced in different phases of European cultural history. Renaissance art theory, exemplified by Marsilio Ficino, whose Florentine Academy led the Platonic revival in fifteenth-century Florence, rediscovered the powerful and quasi-magical properties of symbolic images. The nineteenth century, reacting against the rationalism of seventeenth- and eighteenth-century Enlightenment Europe, once again became absorbed with the primitive, irrational substrate of both ancient Greek and Renaissance thought.[70]

The examples discussed in this section can be considered as the quintessential designs of Daoism: the dynamic, magical graphs that the *Daozang* terms 'sacred symbols' and 'efficacious diagrams'. These designs constitute symbols in the dual sense that they are material objects used to represent something invisible, and also tokens used for identification and empowerment. They are 'efficacious' because they are deemed to possess transformative powers and to embody or confer the authority to command results. Although several different categories of such symbols can be distinguished,[71] the examples below have a common grounding in the Chinese written word. In the Daoist cosmogony, the Chinese ideogram had evolved from the cosmic medium of revelation itself; that is, congealed primordial ether. Calligraphy was consequently the privileged medium for communicating with the gods.[72]

The Daoist idea that writing was at the origin of the universe was given special prominence in the Lingbao scriptures and the myths explaining their revelation at the end of the fourth century. When Lu Xiujing (406–477) devised the fundamental structure of the Daoist canon in three receptacles, these were named after the Three Caverns (*sandong*) from which the three primordial *qi* emerged, engendering the creation of the 'myriad beings' out of Chaos.[73] Preceding this cosmogony, True Writs (*zhenwen*) appeared spontaneously, fixing the emerging cosmic order in place.

The Lingbao 'Scripture on the Real Writs of the Five Ancients of the Primordial Beginning' (*c.*400)[74] reproduces these True Writs in a 'celestial script' (*tianwen*) resembling seal script (*zhuanwen*) (Figure 8.13). For each of the five directions, four groups of characters are inscribed in celestial palaces. They record the names of adepts destined for immortality, guarantee the cosmic order, hold demons in check and control floodwaters. These writs are complemented by *fu*-talismans for the five directions, derived from the mythical Five Talismans of the Divine Treasure (*Lingbao wufu*).[75]

Graphic symbols called *fu*, the term commonly translated as 'talisman', probably played a role in Chinese religious practice from an early date. The currently available archaeological evidence stretches back to the Warring States period. If the writing used in *fu* was associated with Creation itself, the original magico-ritual use of *fu*-talismans is attributed to the culture heroes at the dawn of Chinese civilisation. According to early legends, attested by Qin and Han archaeological finds, the Yellow Emperor used a *fu* to obtain divine help in a military campaign, while Yu the Great employed the Five Talismans of the Divine Treasure to control the Flood. *Fu*-talismans found in Han tombs were used for healing[76] and in political prognostication. Although during the Six Dynasties graphic standards for the production of *fu* began to emerge, from the Sui to modern times the growing complexity of Daoist ritual led to a multiplication of the forms and liturgical uses of *fu*-talismans.[77] The latter phase, in particular, is abundantly documented in the Ming *Daozang*.

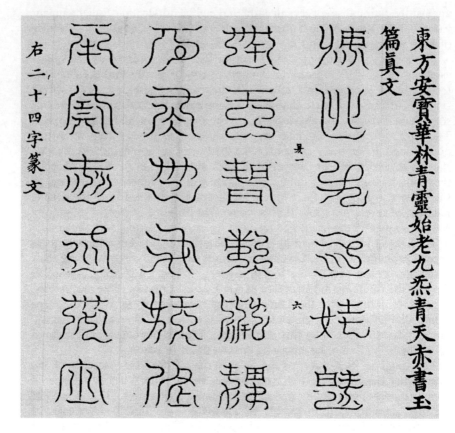

Figure 8.13 The True Writ of the East. *Yuanshi wulao chishu yupian zhenwen tianshu jing (c.*400) 1.7b–8a.

Fu-talismans are tokens of authority and function as letters of command addressed to demons and deities.[78] In addition to communication and control, talismans serve protective and curative purposes. The 'Lingbao Scripture on the Diagrams of the Twenty-four Vital Energies' (*c.*400),[79] for example, represents the vital energies. The Twenty-four Spirits of these energies in the body are arranged in three hierarchical groups of Eight Effulgences (*bajing*). This book presents models of twenty-four *fu* with which the adept could invoke and command the corresponding spirits in the three spheres of the body.

Written in the celestial script of the True Writs, talismans, like archaic Chinese seal script, can only be partially deciphered by the untrained eye. In addition, talismans contain graphic elements such as diagrams of constellations drawn, in the way of Chinese star maps, as small discs connected by straight or curved lines.[80] The 'Cloud Case with Seven Labels', a Northern Song anthology of books from the seven divisions of the Daoist canon, devotes a chapter to Daoist calligraphic styles. In it, the section titled 'talismanic characters' (*fuzi*) defines the following distinctions between the pictorial representation (*tuxiang*) and written elements in talismans (*fushu*), using language reminiscent of the theory of images and writing of the Book of Changes (*Yijing*):[81]

> Talismans (*fu*) assume the configurations of the clouds and the stars, writing (*shu*) delineates the meanings of units of discourse, while pictures (*tu*) represent the shapes of divine transformation. Thus the written element inside talismans is of a pictorial nature, and the pictorial aspect of writing serves both figurative and phonetic functions.[82]

In some talismans the pictorial element predominates. The Talisman of Heisha in Figure 8.14 is an example from the 'Shangqing Correct Method of the Heart of Heaven',[83] the twelfth-century compilation of Tianxin methods of exorcism by the Southern Song scholar-official Deng Yougong. The three fundamental talismans of the Tianxin zhengfa school – the *Sanguang fu*, the *Tiangang fu* and the *Heisha fu* – constitute the core of the book. Heisha, the Black Killer, here seen carrying his authorization in the form of the character *chi* for 'command', was the chief officer of the Emperor of the North (Beidi). The latter presided over the Department of Exorcism (Quxie yuan), which comprised the priests of the Heart of Heaven movement. Note that even in this essentially pictorial talisman the crucial element is a word, held in the figure's hand as an emblem of authority. Specimens of talismans transmitted in the *Daozang*, many of them of spectacular design,[84] are legion.

The religious use of seals (*yin*) is also attested by archaeology from the Warring States period onward. Seals too were emblems of authority, ritual instruments and implements for stamping characters, images or talismanic designs. As apotropaic objects, they were worn on belts or buried in tombs. Their engravings included the names of deities or demons and the titles of the practising priest or exorcist. Perhaps the oldest direct antecedents of the seals found in the *Daozang* are those recovered among other 'tomb-quelling' objects (*zhenmu wu*) and texts from Han tombs.[85] As apotropaic instruments, they are in the same class of Daoist ritual implements as mirrors and swords. As tokens of authority and writs of command, seal impressions can be printed and used much like talismans.[86] As Michel Strickmann pertinently observed, seals were engraved in reverse relief, the reverse image revealing, like the reflection in a mirror, the 'true form' of invisible entities.[87] Many seal inscriptions contain the character *tong*, meaning to 'penetrate', and are used as media for communicating with the unseen world. An example can be seen in the 'Scripture of the Most High on Efficacious Seals for Communicating with Mystery'.[88]

The specimen of an exorcistic seal in Figure 8.15 is taken from 'The Essentials of the Practice of Perfection According to the Orthodox One

FRANCISCUS VERELLEN

Figure 8.14 Talisman of Heisha. *Shangqing tianxin zhengfa* (late twelfth century) 3.6b, Ming edition of 1598. Courtesy of the Bibliothèque nationale de France (Chinois 9546/561).

Canon',[89] a Tang compendium of miscellaneous physiological practices and healing methods, including diagnostics and exorcistic treatments (*xingjin*) by means of a seal. Beside talismanic designs, this seal contains some recognizable elements: the seven stars of the Northern Dipper (Beidou) on the right, the six stars of the Southern Dipper (Nandou) on the left, the

Figure 8.15 Seal for use in exorcism. *Zhengyi fawen xiuzhen zhiyao* (Tang) 19b, Ming edition of 1598. Courtesy of the Bibliothèque nationale de France (Chinois 9546/1252).

character *shan* for 'mountain' on top, *ri* for 'sun' in the middle and the words and diagrams for the Three Terraces (Santai) constellation in the upper left and right hand corners. The text thus illustrated includes a detailed description of the seal technique in healing and its rationale:

> For saving lives in peril of death, there is nothing better than seals. In ancient times, Fan Li practised this, and caused mountains to crumble, rivers and seas to flow backwards, spirit-powers to tremble with fear, and thunderclaps to resound. With seals one can

181

smelt metal and polish jade, restore vital breaths and bring back the ether-souls [to reanimate corpses]; how much more easily, then, can one heal the sick by these means![90]

Conclusion

In conclusion, even comparatively straightforward types of visual representation in the Daoist canon, such as illustrations of existing objects and practices, tend to operate on multiple cognitive planes and to involve an intricate relationship with words: the picture illustrates a text and at the same time incorporates verbal elucidations of itself. An example is the illustration of a Tang bronze mirror in Figure 8.5: a ritual object, it is itself a mandala-like diagram of the universe that resorts to words to explain its graphic design and significance.

The religious objective of rendering the unseen world visible (mythical places, hells and paradises, the invisible side of ritual and so on) relies on pictorial aids to inner visualisation. The representations, meanwhile, are frequently based on the familiar sights of the phenomenal world, suggesting an organic unity across the different spheres. Written descriptions also refer to graphic depictions as aids to the imagination. Daoist affirmations regarding invisibility and ineffability (*wuxing wuming*) notwithstanding, the arts of both discursive and pictorial representation flourished in the pages of the Daoist canon. The Daoist tendency to focus on the essential nature or spirit of a thing, hidden to mundane eyes, had an appreciable influence on Chinese aesthetics and theories of representation in art (*jingshen, qiyun*).[91]

The esoteric language and imagery of Inner Alchemy, deceptively posing as operative or laboratory alchemy, is a major source of pictorial metaphors in the *Daozang*. Animal allegories in the Daoist canon, like 'Taming the Horse of the Will' and 'Buffalo Chariot Representing Body and Soul', translate textual allegorisations to a pictorial plane.

True Writs, talismans and seals are dynamic symbols with transformative powers used in healing, exorcism and ritual. Thanks to the authority of the written word in China, the graphs of written characters are regarded as the ultimate efficacious designs of Daoism. In illustrated scriptures, there is no clear distinction between text and image: the words themselves are graphs and the scriptures as a whole are considered to have the transformative efficacy of the talismans they embody.

Notes

1 These remarks originated as a talk delivered in San Francisco in April 2001 at the symposium organised by Stanford University and the East Asian Art Museum on the occasion of the exhibition 'Taoism and the Arts of China'. They are offered here as a tribute to Professor Liu Ts'un-yan's pioneering research on the Daoist canon, published in 'The Compilation and Historical Value of the *Tao-tsang*', in Donald D. Leslie, Colin Mackerras and Wang Gungwu (eds), *Essays on the Sources for Chinese History* (Canberra: Australian National University

Press, 1973), pp. 104–19, and his numerous studies of works in the canon. For illustrations mentioned but not reproduced below, the reader is referred to *The Taoist Canon: A Historical Companion to the Daozang*, edited by Kristofer Schipper and Franciscus Verellen (Chicago: University of Chicago Press, 2004). I am indebted to my co-editor for stimulating discussions on the subject of Daoist graphic materials.

2 The twelve genres are: Fundamental Writings (*benwen*), Sacred Symbols (*shenfu*), Exegeses (*yujue*), Efficacious Diagrams (*lingtu*), Annals (*pulu*), Precepts (*jielü*), Solemn Rites (*weiyi*), Techniques (*fangfa*), Miscellaneous Arts (*zhongshu*), Hagiography (*jizhuan*), Hymns (*zansong*) and Memorials (*biaozou*).

3 For instance, the 'Esoteric Writs of the Three Sovereigns' (*Sanhuang neiwen*) and the 'True Form of the Five Sacred Peaks' (*Wuyue zhenxing tu*). On celestial signs as revelatory writing, see Anne-Marie Christin, *L'image écrite ou la déraison graphique* (Paris: Flammarion, 1995).

4 See Jonathan Chaves, 'The legacy of Ts'ang Chieh: The written word as magic', *Oriental Art*, 23 (1977), 200–15.

5 *Dongxuan lingbao sandong fengdao kejie yingshi* (DZ 1125), 5:5a–b.

6 *Taishang zhengyi jie wuyin zhouzu bilu* (DZ 1217).

7 *Suwen rushi yunqi lun'ao* (DZ 1022).

8 A comparable image in a Southern Song commentary on the Book of Salvation (*Duren jing*) by Chen Chunrong illustrates a breathing exercise correlating the body's vital energy (*qi*), as measured through the pulse, with the 'heavenly clock-work' of the Northern Dipper. See *Taishang dongxuan lingbao wuliang duren shangpin jingfa* (DZ 93), 1:6a.

9 *Xiuzhen shishu* (DZ 263), 19:4a–5b. For a translation of the text, ascribed to the immortal Zhongli Quan, see Henri Maspero (trans. Frank Kierman), 'Methods of "Nourishing the Vital Principle" in the Ancient Taoist Religion', in his *Taoism and Chinese Religion* (Amherst: University of Massachusetts Press, 1981), pp. 547–8.

10 See the reproduction in Fu Juyou and Chen Songchang, *Mawangdui Han mu wenwu* (Changsha: Hunan chubanshe, 1992), p. 148.

11 *Yuyang qihou qinji* (Song/Yuan, DZ 1275), 3b–4a.

12 Reproduced in Fu and Chen, *Mawangdui Han mu wenwu*, p. 155. See also the Dunhuang ms S. 3326, a military divination manual of *qi*-formations, reproduced and discussed in Jean-Pierre Drège, 'Du texte à l'image: les manuscrits illustrés', in Jean-Pierre Drège (ed.), *Images de Dunhuang: dessins et peintures sur papier des fonds Pelliot et Stein* (Paris: École Française d'Extrême-Orient, 1999), pp. 123–4.

13 *Tujing yanyi bencao* (DZ 769), 3:7b–9a, 9a–b.

14 *Xuanyuan shizi tu* (DZ 163).

15 On Zhao's Daoist inclinations, see Lu Renlong, 'Zhao Mengfu yu daojiao: jianlun song mo yuan chu daojiao fazhan de yixie tezhi', *Shijie zongjiao yanjiu*, 3 (1991), 24–34.

16 *Xuanyuan shizi tu*, 8a.

17 In *Daofa zongzhi tu yanyi* (DZ 1277), 1:4a.

18 *Chongxu zhide zhenjing* (DZ 668), 1a.

19 *Lüzu zhi* (16th century, DZ 1484), 1:1b. This work is part of the Supplement to the Daoist canon, *Xu Daozang*, which was added to the Zhengtong canon in 1607.

20 *Shangqing shi dichen Tongbo zhenren zhen tuzan* (DZ 612).

21 On the visionary conception of these places, see F. Verellen, 'The Beyond Within: Grotto-heavens (*dongtian*) in Taoist Ritual and Cosmology', *Cahiers d'Extrême-Asie*, 8 (1995), 265–90.

22 *Xu taishi zhenjun tuzhuan* (DZ 440). See also the reproductions in S. Little, *Taoism and the Arts of China* (Chicago and Berkeley: The Art Institute of Chicago and University of California Press, 2000), pp. 314–17, and discussion in Kristofer Schipper, 'Taoist Ritual and Local Cults of the T'ang Dynasty', in Michel Strickmann (ed.), *Tantric and Taoist Studies in Honour of R. A. Stein* (Brussels: Institut Belge des Hautes Etudes Chinoises, 1985), vol. 3, pp. 812–34.

23 *Taishang beiji fumo shenzhou shagui lu* (DZ 1215).

24 See David N. Keightley, 'The Religious Commitment: Shang Theology and the Genesis of Chinese Political Culture', *History of Religions*, 17 (1978), 211–25.

25 See Alain Besançon (trans. Jane Marie Todd), *The Forbidden Image: An Intellectual History of Iconoclasm* (Chicago: The University of Chicago Press, 2000), pp. 63–108.

26 The Xiang'er Commentary (Later Han?) to the *Laozi*. See Jao Tsung-i, *Laozi Xiang'er zhu jiaozheng* (1956, revised reprint edition Shanghai: Shanghai guji chubanshe, 1991), pp. 17, 19.

27 *Dongxuan lingbao sandong fengdao kejie yingshi* 2:1a–5b. Cf. Florian Reiter, 'The Visible Divinity: The Sacred Icon in Religious Taoism', *Nachrichten der Gesellschaft für Natur- und Völkerkunde Ostasiens*, 144 (1988), 51–70.

28 See the chapter '*Invisibilia per visibilia*: Meditation and the Uses of Theory', in David Freedberg, *The Power of Images: Studies in the History and Theory of Response* (Chicago: University of Chicago Press, 1989), pp. 161–91.

29 See Franciscus Verellen, "Evidential Miracles in Support of Taoism': The Inversion of a Buddhist Apologetic Tradition in Late T'ang China', *T'oung Pao*, 78 (1992), 256–7.

30 *Shangqing changsheng baojian tu* (Tang, DZ 429).

31 See, for example, the specimen preserved in the American Museum of Natural History, New York, reproduced in Little, *Taoism and the Arts of China*, p. 140.

32 See Edward H. Schafer, 'A T'ang Taoist Mirror', *Early China*, 4 (1978–9), 56–9.

33 *Gushen pian* (DZ 252).

34 See Donald Harper, 'The Nature of Taiyi in the Guodian Manuscript *Taiyi sheng shui* – Abstract Cosmic Principle or Supreme Cosmic Deity?', *Chūgoku shutsudo shiryō kenkyū*, 5 (2001), 1–23.

35 See Sarah Allan and Crispin Williams (eds), *The Guodian Laozi: Proceedings of the International Conference, Dartmouth College, May 1998* (Berkeley, CA: Institute of East Asian Studies, 2000), pp. 162–71. On Taiyi and Tianyi as constellations in early *fu*-talismans, see Wang Yucheng, 'Wenwu suojian zhongguo gudai daofu shulun', *Daojia wenhua yanjiu*, 9 (1996), 269–70.

36 *Shangqing qusu jueci lu* (DZ 1392), 10b.

37 *Xiuzhen liyan chaotu* (DZ 152), 15b.

38 See, for example, the 'integral representation' in *Zhouyi tu* (12th/13th c., DZ 157), 1:1a.

39 *Huangdi bashiyi nanjing zuantu jujie*, 'Xulun' (DZ 1024), 4a–b.

40 *Jinyi huandan yinzheng tu* (DZ 151), 2b.

41 On this type of mental representation, see my 'The Beyond Within'.

42 *Sancai dingwei tu* (c.1222, DZ 155), 10b–11b.

43 For example, in *Shangqing jinque dijun wudou sanyi tujue* (Six Dynasties, DZ 765), 1a–b.

44 See, for example, the choreography for the Pace of Yu and for Pacing the Celestial Mainstay and Flying on the Terrestrial Filaments (1116) in *Taishang zhuguo jiumin zongzhen biyao* (DZ 1227), 8:3b, reproduced in Little, *Taoism and the Arts of China*, p. 200. Cf. Edward Schafer, *Pacing the Void: T'ang Approaches to the Stars* (Berkeley: University of California Press, 1977), pp. 238–42.

45 See Kristofer Schipper, 'Gogaku shinkei zu no shinkō', in Yoshioka Yoshitoyo and Michel Soymié (eds), *Dōkyō kenkyū, vol. 2* (Tokyo: Shorinsha, 1967), pp. 114–62, and the same author's 'The True Form – Reflections on the Liturgical Basis of Taoist Art', *Sanjiao Wenxian*, 4 (2005).

46 *Xuanlan renniao shan jingtu* (Six Dynasties, DZ 434).

47 See reproductions of the ink rubbing of 1604 from the Zhongyue miao stele at Songshan, now in the Dengfeng Bureau of Cultural Relics, Henan, in Little, *Taoism and the Arts of China*, p. 358, and of the rubbing of 1682 from a stele in Xi'an, now in the Field Museum of Natural History, in Munakata Kiyohiko, *Sacred Mountains in Chinese Art* (Urbana and Chicago: Krannert Art Museum/ University of Illinois Press, 1991), p. 113.

48 *Wushang huanglu dazhai licheng yi* (DZ 508), 40:5b.

49 *Xiuzhen taiji hunyuan tu* (DZ 149), 8a.

50 *Yuqing wuji zongzhen Wenchang dadong xianjing zhu* (DZ 103). The scripture explicated in this work is *Taishang wuji zongzhen Wenchang dadong xianjing* (DZ 5).

51 *Wushang huanglu dazhai licheng yi* (1223, DZ 508), 39:16b–17a. Such messengers also feature in liturgical scrolls; see Caroline Gyss-Vermande, 'Les messagers divins et leurs iconographie', *Arts Asiatiques*, 46 (1991), 96–110.

52 At the same time, they imply the authentication of conventional representations ('the invisible world really does look like that'). Cf. Stephen Teiser, '"Having Once Died and Returned to Life": Representations of Hell in Medieval China', *Harvard Journal of Asiatic Studies*, 48 (1988), 433–64, and my 'Evidential Miracles in Support of Taoism'.

53 *Taishang laojun da cunsi tu zhujue* (early Tang, DZ 875), 23b–24b.

54 *Dadong jinhua yujing* (DZ 254), 7a–10a.

55 *Shangqing dantian sanqi yuhuang liuchen feigang siming dalu* (DZ 675), 3a.

56 *Gaoshang dadong wenchang silu ziyang baolu* (15th c., DZ 1214), 3:11b–12b.

57 DZ 1392.

58 See, for example, the illustrations of an alchemical altar and a furnace for the extraction of mercury in 'Requisite Knowledge for the Alchemical Laboratory' by Wu Wu (preface dated 1163), *Danfang xuzhi* (DZ 900), 5a and 7a.

59 *Shangyang zi jindan dayao tu* (DZ 1068).

60 *Huanzhen ji* (pref. 1392, DZ 1074), 1:1a.

61 See, for example, the representations of the Dragon Spirit of the Liver in *Huangting neijing wuzang liufu buxie tu* (848, DZ 432), 10a, and of the Tiger Spirit of the Lungs in *Siqi shesheng tu* (late Tang, DZ 766), 12a–b. See also the illustrated version of the Tang 'Book of the Hidden Period and the Karma Body of the Yellow Court' (*Huangting dunjia yuanshen jing*, DZ 873) in *Yunji qiqian* (DZ 1032), 14.

62 *Taishang chu sanshi jiuchong baosheng jing* (DZ 871), 8b.

63 See Jean Lévi, 'The Body: the Daoists' Coat of Arms', in Michel Feher *et al.* (eds), *Fragments for a History of the Human Body* (New York: Zone, 1989), pp. 105–26.

64 *Boyun xianren lingcao ge* (late Tang/Five Dynasties, DZ 932), 17a–b.

65 *Taishang lingbao zhicao pin* (Song? DZ 1406), 2a.

66 DZ 1392. See also above.

67 *Xuanzong zhizhi wanfa tonggui* (*c.*1300, DZ 1066), 1:10a–b.

68 *Shangcheng xiuzhen sanyao* (DZ 267), 1.

69 See Glen Dudbridge, *The Hsi-yu Chi: A Study of Antecedents to the Sixteenth-century Chinese Novel* (Cambridge: Cambridge University Press, 1970), pp. 171–2.

70 The art historian Aby Warburg (1866–1929), for example, pioneered a new, psycho-anthropological approach to the study of symbols. See Ernst H. Gombrich, *Symbolic Images: Studies in the Art of the Renaissance 2* (Oxford: Phaidon Press, 1972), pp. 123–95, and his *Aby Warburg: An Intellectual Biography*

(London: The Warburg Institute, 1970), ch. 14 and passim. On comparable phenomena in China and elsewhere, see Hubert Delahaye, 'Les antécédents magiques des statues Chinoises', *Revue d'esthétique*, nouvelle série, 5 (1983), 45–53; Mircéa Eliade, *Images et Symboles: Essai sur le Symbolisme Magico-religieux* (Paris: Gallimard, 1952).

71 See Li Yuanguo, 'Lun daojiao fulu de fenlei', *Zongjiao xue yanjiu*, 2 (1997), 39–47.

72 See Laszlo Legeza, *Tao Magic: The Secret Language of Diagrams and Calligraphy* (London: Thames and Hudson, 1975), and Lothar Ledderose, 'Some Taoist Elements in the Calligraphy of the Six Dynasties', *T'oung Pao*, 70 (1984), 246–78.

73 See *The Taoist Canon*, introduction.

74 *Yuanshi wulao chishu yupian zhenwen tianshu jing* (DZ 22). Cf. the specimen of 'celestial script' preserved in the Dunhuang ms P. 2865 of the *Taishang lingbao dongxuan miedu wulian shengshi miaojing* (7th/8th c.), Bibliothèque Nationale, reproduced in Little, *Taoism and the Arts of China*, p. 206.

75 See *Taishang lingbao wufu xu* (DZ 388). Cf. Stephen Bokenkamp, 'Sources of the Ling-pao Scriptures', in M. Strickmann (ed.), *Tantric and Taoist Studies in Honour of R. A. Stein* (Brussels: Institut Belge des Hautes Etudes Chinoises, 1983), vol. 2, pp. 454–6.

76 See Donald Harper, *Early Chinese Medical Literature: The Mawangdui Medical Manuscripts* (London: Kegan Paul, 1997).

77 See the historical survey by Wang Yucheng, 'Wenwu suojian zhongguo gudai daofu shulun', *Daojia wenhua yanjiu*, 9 (1996), 267–301.

78 On corresponding functions of tallies and seals in secular government, see Mark Edward Lewis, *Writing and Authority in Early China* (Albany: State University of New York Press, 1999), pp. 28–35.

79 *Dongxuan lingbao ershisi sheng tujing* (*c.*400, DZ 1407), 7a.

80 See 'Lun daofu de jiegou yu bifa', *Zongjiao xue yanjiu*, 2 (1998), 8–13.

81 See Lewis, *Writing and Authority in Early China*, pp. 262–78, and Haun Saussy, 'The Prestige of Writing: Letter, Picture, Image, Ideography', *Sino-Platonic Papers*, 75 (1997), 4–5.

82 *Yunji qiqian*, compiled by Zhang Junfang (*fl.* 1005–1028, DZ 1032), 7:5a.

83 *Shangqing tianxin zhengfa* (DZ 566).

84 See Legeza, *Tao Magic*, and Little, *Taoism and the Arts of China*, e.g. the 'Talisman for Summoning the Nine Transformations of Great Obscurity', reproduced in Little, 106.

85 See the historical survey by Liu Zhaorui, 'Zaoqi daojiao yongyin kaoshu', *Daojiao xue tansuo*, 8 (1994), 58–83. On tomb-quelling writs, see Anna Seidel, 'Traces of Han Religion in Funeral Texts Found in Tombs', in Akizuki Kan'ei (ed.), *Dōkyō to shūkyō bunka* (Tokyo: Hirakawa, 1987), pp. 21–57.

86 See Judith Boltz, 'Not by Seal of Office Alone: New Weapons in Battles with the Supernatural', in P. Ebrey and P. Gregory (eds), *Religion and Society in T'ang and Sung China* (Honolulu: University of Hawaii Press, 1993), pp. 241–305.

87 Michel Strickmann, 'The Seal of the Law: A Ritual Implement and the Origins of Printing', *Asia Major*, third series, 6, 2 (1993), 1–84, p. 6.

88 *Taishang tongxuan lingyin jing* (Song? DZ 859), 1a. The title, which appears slightly garbled, contains elements of the name of the Lingbao talisman *Xuandong tongling fu*, mentioned in *Taishang tongling bashi shengwen zhenxing tu* (4th c., DZ 767), 2:11b–12a.

89 *Zhengyi fawen xiuzhen zhiyao* (DZ 1270).

90 Strickmann, 'The Seal of the Law', pp. 12–13.

91 See Ding Ruomu, 'Daojiao yu zhongguo hua lüelun', *Daojia wenhua yanjiu*, 9 (1996), 347–73.

PART TWO

9

WAS CELESTIAL MASTER ZHANG
A HISTORICAL FIGURE?

Liu Ts'un-yan

1

The question of whether Celestial Master Zhang Ling who was active at the
end of the Eastern Han, and who was sometimes called Zhang Daoling, was
a historical figure is rarely raised. He appears in all the general histories and
textbooks, but it is in the traditional histories such as the *Hou Hanshu*,
Sanguo zhi and *Huayang guozhi* that evidence that Zhang was a real historical figure is found.[1] Apart from these standard and unofficial histories,
Zhang naturally appears in Daoist literature. There he is a towering figure
and many biographies of him exist.[2] These biographies are generally
hagiographical in nature, and blend a limited amount of historical data with
a large amount of embellishment. If we consider them as literary creations
or as 'scriptures' that are grounded in belief rather than historical evidence,
then their value as historical texts is clear and we need not spill ink over
them. However, if such a text is to be regarded as a useful historical source,
then a coherent argument with supporting evidence should be provided.
When working with hagiographies it is best to arrange all available accounts
into chronological order as a genealogical relationship between them is usually clear. Later hagiographies, for example, often appear to make claims
that are baseless when checked against the standard histories when in fact
they are based on earlier hagiographic accounts. For instance, the *Lishi
zhenxian tidao tongjian* compiled by Zhao Daoyi during the thirteenth century includes an entry for Celestial Master Zhang that occupies an entire
chapter and is the most detailed biography available. It states that 'he was
recommended in both the "Capable, Good, Sincere and Upright" category
and that of "Spoke Frankly and Admonished Unflinchingly"', and that
'When Emperor He assumed the throne, he summoned [Zhang] with the
third rank seal of office and a four-horse chariot to become Grand Mentor,
and later enfeoffed him as Marquis of Ji County.'[3]

These details of Zhang's life are not found in the historical biographies.
In Zhang's biography in *Sandong qunxian lu*[4] – an earlier collection of hagiographies compiled by Chen Baoguang of Jiangyin[5] in 1154 – the phrases

'he was recommended as "Capable, Good, Sincere and Upright"' and 'third rank seal of office' can both be found. However, it does not place him in the 'Spoke Frankly and Admonished Unflinchingly' category, and although it has 'bestowed the third rank seal of office on him, but he did not accept', Chen Baoguang placed these events at the time of Emperor Zhang of the Eastern Han (76–89) rather than Emperor He (89–106).

As far as the phrase 'enfeoffed as the Marquis of Ji County' is concerned, the Tang dynasty work *Sandong zhunang* by Wang Xuanhe cites a passage from the *Zhang tianshi ershisi zhitu* that includes the phrase 'In the first year of the *yuanhe* reign period he was made the Minister of Works and enfeoffed as the Marquis of Ji County.'[6] However, the *yuanhe* reign period (84–87) belongs to the reign of Emperor Zhang. Thus, the later records clearly follow the earlier records – and if the earlier ones are unreliable, the later ones that employ them and make modifications according to the imperatives of their own time will be just as unverifiable.

In much the same vein the *Lishi zhenxian tidao tongjian* states that Zhang Daoling 'was the eighth generation descendant of Zifang [Zhang Liang] the Marquis of Liu'.[7] This follows the *Sandong qunxian lu* which says that he 'was the sixth generation descendant of the Marquis of Liu', although the later text has, of course, inserted two more generations. However, Song Lian's 1376 preface to the *Han tianshi shijia* compiled by Zhang Zhengchang, the forty-second Celestial Master, says that 'the lineage in the *Shijia* begins with Wencheng [Zhang Liang], the Marquis of Liu, and there are no records of anyone before him'. Song suggests that by 'gathering the clan's collected writings to fill the gaps in this record, and employing historical methods, one can gain an outline of how the inheritance was handed down'.[8] His preface traces those who came before Zhang Liang, the Marquis of Liu, all the way back to the fifth son of Qingyang who was the son of the Yellow Emperor (Xuan Yuan of the Ji clan). Even the Zhang Zhong who appears in the *Shijing* as 'Zhang Zhong, the filial and friendly' is included to help make up an extra ten generations of ancestors.[9] It has to be said that this is quite absurd.

Zhang Liang had a son called Buyi and from Buyi to Zhang Ling there is an interval of seven generations. The names of the seven people given in Song Lian's preface differ from those given in the *Tidao tongjian*, and Song also adds a genealogy for Buyi's elder son. The record of the 'Liuhou shijia' in the *Shiji* states clearly that when Zhang Liang died his son, Buyi, was enfeoffed.[10] However, while this matches up well, this text and the 'Gaozu gongchen houzhe nianbiao', also in *Shiji*, both state that in 175 BCE Buyi committed a crime and his dukedom was abolished.[11] Scholars today have no way of ascertaining his genealogy, let alone that of his descendant Zhang Ling.[12] In fact, Zhang Ling and Zhang Buyi were unrelated to each other.[13] Song Lian, a Director General on the *Yuanshi*, couldn't avoid acting counter to historical principles when he encountered a hagiography.

One more point that needs to be clarified regarding Zhang Ling's appearance in historical works concerns the fact that in Eastern Han times there was not just one person called Zhang Ling. In chapter thirty-six of the *Hou Hanshu* there is a Zhang Ba from Chengdu in Shu.[14] This Zhang was well known for conducting research into Yan Pengzu's studies on the *Chunqiu* and the *Gongyang* commentary and in later years became a Palace Attendant and served in Henan. When he died he was buried in Liang County in Henan. His son, Zhang Kai, was also thoroughly versed in Yan Pengzu's *Chunqiu*. He tried to avoid being appointed to office: 'The Five Officials repeatedly summoned him as a candidate who was recommended as "Capable, Good, Sincere and Upright", but he did not go.'[15] Zhang Kai lived as a recluse on Mount Hongnong, and in 142 a special edict was sent by the court ordering the Governor of Henan to persuade him to take office with gifts but he 'claimed he was ill and did not take up the post'. He was, 'by nature, fond of Daoist techniques, and could create a five *li* mist. At that time there was a man from Guanxi, Pei You, who could create a three *li* mist. He saw that he was not the equal of Zhang Kai and desired to become his student but Kai avoided him and did not permit himself to be found.' In the year that Emperor Huan ascended the throne (147), Pei You made a mist and committed a robbery. When arrested he claimed that Zhang Kai had taught him how to make the mist. Zhang Kai was thus implicated and the Commandant of Justice had him incarcerated for two years. In the end, he was released for lack of evidence and allowed to go home. In 149, Emperor Huan again tried to engage him with gifts and a single-horse chariot. As before, Kai refused, saying that he had a serious illness, and he died soon after. Zhang Kai's biography says that his son was called Zhang Ling.

The biography of this Zhang Ling who was from Chengdu comes after those of his grandfather Zhang Ba and his father Zhang Kai but is rather brief. In this biography it is said that Zhang Ling was recommended as 'filial and incorrupt' when Liang Ji's younger brother, Buyi, was the Governor of Henan. Zhang later became an Imperial Secretary and during 151–152, he went to the first court celebrating the beginning of the year. Liang Ji entered the court with a sword but was loudly rebuked by Zhang Ling who ordered the Guards of the Feathered Forest and the Troops as Rapid as Tigers to disarm him. Zhang then accused him in a memorial to the throne, the result of which was that the Emperor issued an order that Liang Ji forfeit a year's salary. Such a remarkable event, if true, is certainly worth recording but no supporting evidence or related material can be found anywhere. However, in Liang Ji's biography in the *Hou Hanshu* we find a narrative account where Liang's position is precisely reversed. It says that 'In the first year of the *yuanjia* reign period [151] the Emperor [Huan] wanted to honour Ji with a special ceremony for his merit in helping him gain the throne. To this end he convened a meeting of the dukes and ministers, and together they discussed the ceremony. As a result of this an official submitted a memorial suggesting that Ji should be allowed to enter the court without the [normal] ceremonial steps, be allowed to carry his sword and wear shoes in the hall, and not be required to have his name announced in an audience – the ceremony would be like that for Xiao He.'[16] This incident is not found in the 'Annals of Emperor Huan' but as it is elaborated at such length it is unlikely to be simply made up. Eight years later, the whole of Liang Ji's family ran into misfortune. The 'Annals of Emperor Huan' pass over this as well and it is only recorded in the biography of Liang Ji but neither does this mean it was made up. Nevertheless, it provides negative evidence in support of Zhang Ling's rebuke of Liang Ji and Liang's forfeiture of salary outlined above, so its credibility must remain in some doubt.

The affairs of the Chengdu Zhang Ling are few, though in accordance with the later Daoist practice of appropriating the affairs of others as one's own, everything embraced in this way appears to become part of the original with the passing of time. This process can be seen in the way Daoist canonical texts appropriated structures and language from Buddhist works.[17] Suppose that there was, in reality, no Zhang Ling involved in the foundation of Daoism. In that case, could not the Zhang Ling that they nominated as founder quite possibly have derived from this Zhang Ling of Chengdu? The various bits of information such as Zhang Kai's native place of Chengdu in Shu, the fact that he could give a demonstration of a five *li* mist, and even that Zhang Kai's son Ling became Imperial Secretary could easily have been appropriated. Despite this, we rarely see these phenomena when we read the hagiographies today. Fifty years ago, Professor Lü Simian cited the materials on the genealogy of Zhang Ba in the footnotes to his *Qinhan shi*. First he asked, 'Could it be that [Zhang] Ling [of Chengdu] carried on his father's techniques but [Zhang] Lu added to them?' He continued: 'The records in the biography of Liu Yan in the *Hou Hanshu* and the biography of Zhang Lu in the *Sanguo zhi* give no evidence for this.' Because Lü was inclined to doubt the veracity of the accounts of Zhang Ling in Daoist historical sources he went on to say: 'Furthermore, since Ling [the son of Zhang Kai] was of the literati, he could not be so easily made use of, therefore I suspect that the supposed events pertaining to Zhang Lu's father and grandfather were invented and cannot be reliably sourced.'[18]

It is common knowledge that, aside from the reasons given above, Lü's scepticism towards Zhang Ling stems from the records of the Way of the Five Pecks of Rice in the official biographies. This is the case as, apart from the father Zhang Ling, the son Zhang Heng and grandson Zhang Lu, they include another figure, namely Zhang Xiu. This Zhang Xiu appears to be one person in the earlier records and a different one in the later records, which gives rise to scholary scepticism.[19] Lü wrote:

> The biography of Zhang Lu in the *Sanguo zhi* says: 'His grandfather, Ling, travelled to Shu and studied the Way in the Guming Mountains. He wrote Daoist texts, and with them misled the common people. From those who had received the Way he extracted five pecks of rice, and therefore he became known as the "rice thief". When Ling died, his son Heng continued propagating his Way; when Heng died, Lu continued it in his turn.' On the other hand, the commentary cites the *Dianlüe,* which says: 'During the

xiping reign period [of Emperor Ling, 172–177] demon bandits arose everywhere: Luo Yao was in the Three Capital Districts. During the *guanhe* reign period [178–183] Zhang Jue was in the east while Zhang Xiu was in Hanzhong. Luo Yao taught the people the Method of Vanishing, Zhang Jue was for the Way of Great Peace while Xiu propagated the Way of the Five Pecks of Rice.' The 'Annals of Emperor Ling' in the *Hou Hanshu* say, 'In Autumn, in the seventh month of the first year of the *zhongping* reign period [184], Zhang Xiu, the sorcerer of Ba Commandery, rebelled and plundered all the counties in the commandery.' The commentary to this cites Liu Ai's [*Han Ling Xian erdi*] *Ji* that says: 'At that time the sorcerer Zhang Xiu was healing the sick in Ba Commandery. Those who were cured paid with five pecks of rice, so he became known as the Master of the Five Pecks of Rice.' So, therefore, the Way of the Five Pecks of Rice comes from Zhang Xiu and not Zhang Lu.[20]

The word 'sorcerer (*yaowu*)' used in this passage is a common term in historical biographies, referring to people of unorthodox belief or involved in religiously inspired insurrections, so there is nothing odd about this usage. The problem is that there was another, later, Zhang Xiu who appeared when Liu Yan was the Provincial Governor of Yizhou. This Zhang Xiu commanded troops in an attack on Hanzhong that was led by Zhang Lu. After the commandery had fallen, he was killed by Zhang Lu. However, the biographical records fail to mention whether or not the Zhang Xiu who led the troops was also the sorcerer from Ba Commandery who had risen in revolt. This touches on the question of who first propagated of the Way of the Five Pecks of Rice. If we cannot clarify this question, then other doubts that arise in research into the history of Daoism will have to remain unresolved. What makes it difficult for us is that the biographies and records from this chaotic period of history are extremely unclear, particularly with regard to dates and places.

The Yellow Turban rebellion led by Zhang Jue began in 184 and this dating poses no problems. Pei Songzhi's commentary to Zhang Lu's biography in the *Sanguo zhi* notes that during the *guanghe* period (178–184, one or two years before the rebellion began) Zhang Jue was in the East while Zhang Xiu was in Hanzhong. The situation had been fermenting for many years before Zhang Jue actually rose in rebellion – this is familiar to everyone who has read the histories. Equally, it is clear that the sorcerer Zhang Xiu raised troops in Ba Commandery in the same year of 184, according to the 'Annals of Emperor Ling', only a few months after the Yellow Turban rebellion had begun. However, it is difficult to know if Zhang Ling and his son Heng were already active in Sichuan in this period because their activities remain obscure, as most historical accounts are vague or very brief. This is because the historical record concentrates on the activities of Zhang Lu and not on his two forebears. Zhang Lu relied on Liu Yan for his rise in the early period of his activities. Liu Yan was from the Han imperial clan and although he was initially appointed to office in Luoyang, he sought a pretext to go to a distant province to escape the chaos. In the fifth year of the *zhongping* reign period of Emperor Ling (188) 'the designation Regional Inspector was changed and that of Provincial Governor was re-established',[21] at Liu's own suggestion, and he was made the Provincial Governor of Yizhou.[22] In the sixth month of that year the Yellow Turban uprising of Ma Xiang occurred there, and the Regional Inspector, Qie Jian, as well as the Governor of Ba Commandery, Zhao Bu, were killed. However, before long, Ma Xiang was defeated in battle and was killed by Jia Long at Qianwei. Jia Long was the Attendant Official of Yizhou and had despatched a welcoming party for Liu Yan when the latter came to take up office. The administrative seat of Yizhou was Luocheng (present day Guanghan in Sichuan), but upon arrival Liu Yan moved the administrative seat, first to Mianzhu, on account of Qie Jian's being killed, and then later to Chengdu.

The account of Zhang Xiu raising troops in Ba Commandery in the 'Annals of Emperor Ling' is very brief. The ambiguity in this description is rarely encountered in the basic annals, as other rebellions generally come to some conclusion, whether in success or failure. The only supplementary historical materials to hand are Pei Songzhi's commentary to Zhang Lu's biography in the *Sanguo zhi*, and the commentary of Li Xian to Liu Yan's biography in the *Hou Hanshu*, both of which cite the *Dianlüe* of Yu Huan of the Wei. The 'Annals of Emperor Ling' under the seventh month, autumn, of the first year of the *zhongping* reign period (189) records that 'Zhang Xiu, the sorcerer in Ba Commandery, rebelled'. Below that entry is Li Xian's annotation citing Liu Ai's *Ji* which says, 'At that time the sorcerer Zhang Xiu was healing the sick in Ba Commandery.' This passage is the one cited by Lü Simian, above, and is also the one Pei Songzhi and Li Xian both cited from the *Dianlüe*. However, Li Xian's citation may have been copied incorrectly, as there appear to be errors and words missing.[23] However both of these records, taken from the *Dianlüe*, say that, 'Zhang Xiu was in Hanzhong.' Liu Ai's *Ji* however, says that Zhang Xiu was a medium from Ba Commandery.[24] Now, at the end of the Han, Yizhou had both a Hanzhong Commandery and a Ba Commandery.[25] Since Liu Ai's *Ji* refers to Ba Commandery and since this agrees with the 'Annals of Emperor Ling', we may provisionally conclude that there was a Zhang Xiu active in Ba Commandery in Sichuan. This Zhang Xiu is probably the Zhang Xiu who accompanied Zhang Lu when he attacked Hanzhong.[26] The difficulty here is that we have no records that can verify where Zhang Xiu's rebellion took place, what type it was, how he could also have become Zhang Lu's companion and how he could either directly or indirectly have become affiliated with Liu Yan. Even though he might have surrendered and pledged allegiance to Liu Yan, the histories leave out this intervening period and simply retain the capture of Hanzhong and Zhang Xiu's subsequent death at the hands of Zhang Lu.

Of the three generations of the Zhang family, the only figure given a clear account in historical biographies is Zhang Lu. He was a man notable in his time who forcibly occupied an entire region and who initiated the rise of the Celestial Masters sect of Daoism. So it was not a matter of luck that 'he commanded Han[zhong] and Ba [commanderies] by force for thirty years',[27] as the biographies record. The historical records also agree that initially he was the 'Major who Oversees Morality' in the party of Liu Yan. This position was not one of the usual prescribed offices so, in all likelihood, it was newly established. Now, the *Bajun taishou fanmin* stele, which was erected in 205 (and which is included in the *Lishi* of Hong Kuo of the Southern Song), has similar titles such as 'Chief Commandant who Assists Morality' and 'Colonel who Honours Morality'. Hong Kuo's colophon says 'These were all hastily established by Liu Yan', which expresses it well.[28] In Liu Yan's biography in the *Hou Hanshu* it says 'The mother of Zhang Lu of Pei was enchanting and knew the Way of the Ghosts. She came and went from [Liu]Yan's residence and so decided that Lu should be the "Major who Oversees Morality".' It appears that the position which Zhang Lu obtained came from his mother's actions and that, aside from her particular knowledge of the Way of the Ghosts, her influence with Liu Yan's family was due to her being 'enchanting', a word I examine below. However, the word 'so' (*sui*) plays a pivotal role in this short passage. Liu Ban of the Northern Song maintains in his *Donghan shukan wu* that it is superfluous, that other writers do not employ it and that it is probably a printing error.[29]

The events surrounding Zhang Lu and Zhang Xiu being sent to attack Hanzhong where Su Gu was the Grand Administrator are recorded in Zhang Lu's biography in the *Sanguo zhi*, Liu Yan's biography in the *Hou Hanshu*, the 'Hanzhong zhi' in the *Huayang guozhi* and the third part of the 'Xianxian shinü zongzan' in the same text. The three sources all agree on the major points, but the *Huayang guozhi* narrative also describes some strategic errors made by Su Gu in battle, how his subordinates Zhao Song and Chen Tiao engaged Zhang Xiu in battle and almost captured him, and finally how both Zhao and Chen were killed in action. The circumstances of the battle have little to do with our main subject of Zhang Lu and I will not go into them. Here are the relevant sentences from Zhang Lu's biography in the *Sanguo zhi* and Liu Yan's biography in the *Hou Hanshu*:

> Liu Yan, being the Provincial Governor of Yizhou, made [Zhang] Lu the 'Major who Oversees Morality'. With the 'Major of a Separate Division', Zhang Xiu, they went to attack the Grand Administrator of Hanzhong, Su Gu. Lu made a surprise attack on Xiu and killed him and captured his army.[30]

> [Liu Yan] thereupon made Lu the 'Major who Oversees Morality'. Then [Lu] with the 'Major of a Separate Division', Zhang Xiu, took the troops and fell upon and slew Su Gu, the Grand Administrator of Hanzhong. They cut off the Xie valley and killed his envoy. Thus Zhang Lu obtained Hanzhong. Then he killed Zhang Xiu and incorporated his army.[31]

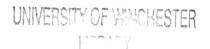

Here, both records indicate that Zhang Lu and Zhang Xiu attacked Hanzhong together. However, the 'Hanzhong zhi' of the *Huayang guozhi* says that 'Lu sent his comrade Zhang Xiu to attack [Su] Gu',[32] while the third part of the 'Xianxian shinü zongzan' says that the object of Zhao Song and Chen Tiao's counterattack was Xiu's encampment and, furthermore, that Zhang Xiu had almost been captured.[33] Thus, the *Huayang guozhi* can fill in some of the details not found in the other two records.

Zhang Xiu's position was that of 'Major of a Separate Division'. On the surface this appears to mean that he was an Assistant General whom Zhang Lu could despatch, like Wang Ping in the ninety-fifth chapter of the *Sanguo yanyi*.[34] But this may not be so, for regardless of Zhang Xiu's background his position of 'Major of a Separate Division' was high ranking or, at least, allowed close contact with his commander. Liu Yan had four children. Two of them participated in opposing the warlords Li Jue and Guo Si in battle and were killed in Chang'an during 194. His third son, Liu Zhang, inherited Yan's position. He was sent by order of the court from Chang'an to Yizhou with explicit instructions for his father. Liu Yan detained him there and would not let him return. Only the youngest son, Liu Mao, stayed by his father's side and he held the official title of 'Major of a Separate Division'.[35] Thus, Zhang Xiu's appointment as 'Major of a Separate Division', it appears, was not a setback in his career.

Zhang Lu also took over Zhang Xiu's forces, so the biographies say that he 'captured his army' or that he 'incorporated his army'. Indeed, in addition, he took up Zhang Xiu's Way of the Five Pecks of Rice. Lü Simian says that 'I suspect that Lu's methods were taken over from Xiu, particularly because he made a surprise attack on Xiu and killed him. Because he did not want to say that he was following Xiu's Way, Zhang cunningly attributed it to his paternal grandfather.'[36] While we may be hesitant to use the phrase 'cunningly attributed it to his paternal grandfather', both the *Sanguo zhi* and the *Hou Hanshu*, citing the *Dianlüe*, can corroborate that the Way of the Five Pecks of Rice was inherited from Zhang Xiu. The *Dianlüe* states:

> During the *guanghe* reign period, Zhang Jue was in the East while Zhang Xiu was in Hanzhong . . . Jue was for the Way of Great Peace while Xiu had the Way of the Five Pecks of Rice[37] . . . Xiu's method was somewhat similar to that of Jue, but in addition he made use of oratories where those who were ill would be sent to reflect on their transgressions. He also made people become Libationers who issued illicit commands. The Libationers were in charge of the *Five Thousand Character Laozi* and they made everyone familiar with it. This was called an 'illicit command'. Those who became ghost officers were in charge of making entreaties for the sick. The method of making entreaties was as follows: a record would be made of the sick person's family name and given name and then their intention to admit their guilt would be stated. This

would be copied three times, the first to be sent up to Heaven – this copy would be placed on a mountain – the second to be buried in the earth and the third to be submerged in water. This was termed the 'Hand Written Document to the Three Offices'. As a rule the sick person's family would give five pecks of rice, and so they became known as the Five Pecks of Rice Masters. In fact, this did nothing to cure the illness and was dissolute and reckless. The common people were confused and foolish and they competed with each other to serve Xiu. Later Jue was executed and Xiu also died. When Lu was in Hanzhong, because the people there sincerely prac-tised Xiu's teachings, Lu added to them and embellished them.[38]

The final two sentences show that Zhang Lu did not merely take Zhang Xiu's territory and army, he also took over the religious system of the Way of the Five Pecks of Rice. While the equivalent text of the *Dianlüe* cited in the record of Zhang Lu within the biography of Liu Yan in the *Hou Hanshu* has some minor omissions, the meaning is essentially the same. The only substantive change is that 'during the *guanghe* reign period' has been changed to 'during the *xiping* reign period', which was only five or six years earlier. The citation in the *Hou Hanshu*, the later publication, changed the date but did not change the place – suggesting that 'Hanzhong' is correct, and that it was not in Ba Commandery where Zhang Xiu rose in rebellion. So, Zhang Xiu first had several years of activity in Hanzhong, later losing his territory, and was then active in Ba Commandery, a little to the south. It was at this time that he went to attack Su Gu. He led the main force and had a base in Hanzhong, but when he attacked it was under the banner of the Provincial Governor of Yizhou of the Han dynasty – in fact, this was to recover lost territory. This is why the *Dianlüe* states that because Zhang Lu knew that many of the people of Hanzhong believed in Zhang Xiu's teachings, Zhang Lu embellished them. If Zhang Xiu had not had his base there, it would be hard to support this statement. When Zhang Xiu lost his territory in Hanzhong there was nothing in the way to block him from moving his activities southwards to Ba Commandery and even rising in rebellion. There-fore when we talk about the 'rice thief', Zhang Xiu is the prototype and Zhang Lu's Way of the Five Pecks of Rice is the second generation. The Zhang family later gained much fame and strength and the banner of the Way of the Five Pecks of Rice became the sign of their own household. Zhang Lu did his utmost to remove completely the influence of Zhang Xiu although in the end he could not thoroughly sweep it away. One revealing sentence from the 'Xianxian shinü zongzan' of the *Huayang guozhi* says: '[Zhao Song] served the Grand Administrator Su Gu. Gu was killed by the "rice thief" Zhang Xiu who hated him and this pained Song.'[39] Why did Zhang Xiu hate his opponent so much when he was acting under orders to go and snatch territory? Was it not because his enemy had earlier taken his own territory?

2

No-one doubts that Zhang Lu engaged in significant religious activity, but what of Zhang Heng and Zhang Ling? There are very few records of Zhang Heng's activities and we shall place them to one side for the moment. The generation he represented existed, of course, and must have engaged in religious activities. However, the traces that remain in the biographies concern Zhang Lu's mother. These are recounted in Liu Yan's biography in the *Hou Hanshu*: 'The mother of Zhang Lu of Pei was enchanting and knew the Way of the Ghosts. She came and went from [Liu] Yan's residence.'[40] The 'Hanzhong zhi' from the *Huayang guozhi* also states:

> [Zhang] Lu's courtesy name was Gongqi.[41] With the Way of the Ghosts he had gained the faith of the Provincial Governor of Yizhou, Liu Yan. Lu's mother looked youthful and came and went from Liu's residence. During the *chuping* reign period [190–193] he made Lu 'Major who Oversees Morality'.[42]

Zhang Lu and his mother practised the Way of the Ghosts, their family teaching. Zhang Lu's biography from the *Sanguo zhi* says, 'his grandfather, Ling, travelled to Shu and studied the Way in the Guming Mountains. He wrote Daoist texts, and with them misled the common people. From those who had received the Way he took five pecks of rice, and therefore he became known as the "rice thief". When Ling died, his son Heng continued propagating his Way and when Heng died, Lu continued it.'[43] The record in Liu Yan's biography in the *Hou Hanshu* is much the same, and merely adds the single line that Zhang Ling travelled to Shu, 'during the reign of Emperor Shun'.[44] Both records state that it was the Way of the Five Pecks of Rice that was promulgated by the Zhang family. This is something that we now can say came late in Zhang Lu's life after he had absorbed the methods and doctrines of Zhang Xiu's group. The beginnings of the Zhang family's teachings were different and their central activity was controlling ghosts; because of this it is called the Way of the Ghosts. There are several records that only mention the Way of the Ghosts rather than the Way of the Five Pecks of Rice. In the comparatively early biography of Zhang Lu from the *Sanguo zhi* we find that after mentioning the Way of the Five Pecks of Rice, the text describes Zhang Lu occupying Hanzhong, gaining enough territory to set up a separate state and gradually becoming domineering. After Liu Yan died, Zhang Lu did not heed the orders of Liu's successor, Liu Zhang, so Liu Zhang 'exterminated the household of Lu's mother'. Zhang Lu and the Chengdu side became enemies: '[Zhang] Lu thereupon occupied Hanzhong, instructed the people in the Way of the Ghosts, and styled himself Lord Teacher.'[45]

The Way of the Ghosts was the family teaching but with the acquisition of the Way of the Five Pecks of Rice, it became the basis of a new strategy. Hanzhong had a foundation of people who practised the Way of the Five

Pecks of Rice during the Zhang Xiu period, and with the backing of a new religious and political force, this branch of the Way of the Celestial Masters flourished. However, the Way of the Ghosts method handed down through the Zhang family did not disappear from the religious practice promoted by Zhang Lu – the two streams merely merged. Therefore, some records still have the old shorthand term, the 'Way of the Ghosts'. Following the citation from the 'Hanzhong zhi' that mentions Lu being made the 'Major who Oversees Morality', the text reads:

> [Lu] resided in Hanzhong, and cut off the road through the valley. Since he arrived, his actions had been tolerant and kind and he instructed people in the Way of the Ghosts. He established 'free hostels' where free rice and meat were placed; travellers could help themselves but only according to their needs. If someone took more than they needed it was said that the ghosts would make them sick. The market-traders and shopkeepers were also regulated in this kind of way. Those who broke the law would only be punished after having done so three times. Those who were studying the Way but were yet to fully believe were known as 'ghost soldiers'; later they became Libationers. The barbarians in Ba and Hanzhong mostly went along with this.[46]

Li Te's biography from the *Huayang guozhi* says that Li's,

> ancestors were originally Cong people from Dangqu in the western part of Ba. They were formidable and brave, and were commonly referred to as ghost mediums. At the end of the Han, Zhang Lu was in Hanzhong and he instructed the people in the Way of the Ghosts. The Cong people held it in high esteem. When there was great turmoil in the empire, they moved from Dangqu in the western part of Ba to Hanzhong.[47]

In Yizhou at the end of the Han, the term the 'Way of the Ghosts' was already common, which was probably a result of the influence of three generations of the Zhang family. The 'Record of Li Te' in the *Jinshu* also says that 'at the end of the Han, Zhang Lu was in Hanzhong and he instructed the people in the Way of the Ghosts. The Cong people held male and female mediums in high esteem, and often went to pay their respects to them.'[48] This record appears to have used the same sources as, or sources close to those used by, the *Huayang guozhi*. Li Te was killed in 303, however, before his time, the Grand Administrator of Yizhou, Wang Jun, claimed when he had Chen Rui of Qianwei put to death in 277, that 'at first Rui misled the people with the Way of the Ghosts.'[49] Thus, the Way of the Ghosts was a set of folk beliefs that persisted for a long time, and corresponded well with Zhang Ling's legendary ghost-controlling practices. It is, therefore, possible to divide the Way of the Ghosts and the Way of the

Five Pecks of Rice into two separate categories and regard Zhang Lu's later Way of the Five Pecks of Rice in Hanzhong as being a mixture of the old Way of the Five Pecks of Rice and the Way of the Ghosts. In later records, we see declining use of the term the 'Way of the Ghosts' until it is no longer mentioned.

Liu Yan's biography in the *Hou Hanshu* says that Zhang Lu's mother was 'enchanting'. On what basis could Fan Ye have written this apparently frivolous statement? Liu Yan's biography in the *Sanguo zhi* says, 'Zhang Lu's mother initially practised the Way of the Ghosts, she was of youthful appearance and often came and went from Liu's residence.'[50] To say that she had a youthful appearance is not to say that she was 'enchanting'; the term described someone who knew the arts of the Way and so appeared young despite being advanced in years.[51]

In the earliest records of Zhang Lu's mother in Daoist books, she holds the status of one of the *sanshi*, literally 'the three teachers'. This refers to the three figures worshipped by Daoist followers in their rituals and not to the later *sanshi* that would transmit the religious law to pupils entering into a study of the Way, namely the Scripture Teacher, the Text Teacher and the Transcendence Teacher.[52] Subsequently, these figures of the Way of the Celestial Masters – the *sanshi* – came to represent the three generations of the Zhang family, the so-called Celestial Master, the Inheriting Master and the Descendant Master, the latter being Zhang Lu. However, in Daoist books like the *Shangqing huangshu guoduyi* there are phrases addressed to them such as 'I am the disciple of the *sanshi*: the Celestial Master, the Inheriting Master and the Female Master' [53] at the invocation of the 'statement of merit' (*yangong*). In the section of the *Shangqing huangshu guoduyi* that discusses the Way of combining the *qi* of men and women – the 'application of *yin* and *yang*' – attention should be drawn to the important position of the Female Master. The first chapter of the *Yuanchen zhangjiao licheng li* says: 'I am the disciple of the *sanshi*: the Celestial Master, the Inheriting Master, the Descendant Master and the Female Master.'[54] This is an exceptional example of four figures being squeezed into three teachers. In the second chapter of Tao Hongjing's *Dengzhen yinjue*, written at the transition from the Qi dynasty to the Liang, he wrote: 'Respectfully inform the officer in charge of ceremonies for the disciples of the *sanshi*: the Celestial Master, the Female Master and the Descendant Master.'[55] Here there is no Inheriting Master but there is a Female Master. This is perhaps indicative of the importance of Zhang Lu's mother in Daoism, but I am afraid that the word 'enchanting' cannot throw any light on the matter.

The Way of the Ghosts flourished in Sichuan and surrounding areas in the area in which the south-western minorities (as we would refer to them today) lived eighteen hundred years ago. These minorities, roughly speaking, are those referred to as the 'Bandun Manyi' in the 'Biographies of the Southern Man and the South-Western Yi' from the *Hou Hanshu*,[56] however their clan arrangements and situation were possibly not as they are represented in the *Hou Hanshu*'s brief account. Regardless of the terms 'commanderies' and 'counties', these were places where the Han and Yi intermixed – the nomenclature and bureaucratic structure of the commanderies and counties derive from the Han administrative system. The Yi periodically rose up in armed rebellion and after a time would surrender. This is readily gleaned from historical works from the end of the Eastern Han. The Yi undoubtedly could have had some relationship with those who led religious insurrections such as Ma Xiang and Zhang Xiu, and could also be conscripted or employed by officials in territory under Han control. The latter situation is evident, for example, in the account of the newly appointed Grand Administrator of Yizhou, Li Yong, for the *xiping* reign period of Emperor Ling (172–177), as recorded in the 'Nanzhong zhi,' of the *Huayang guozhi*, where it states that Li 'led the Ba Commandery Bandun army and punished the enemy who were completely defeated'.[57] The subordination of Yi troops to the Han army was quite common in this region. When the two sons of Liu Yan who had been left in Chang'an joined with Ma Teng to attack Li Jue and Guo Si, 'Ma despatched five thousand *Sou* troops to his aid'. When Cao Cao attacked Jingzhou, Liu Zhang sent a delegation to pay Cao his respects, and sent others to 'accompany three hundred *Sou* soldiers and miscellaneous material for military use to Duke Cao'.[58] These '*Sou* soldiers' were actually Yi soldiers. Meng Wentong wrote an essay that mentioned the '*Wudou* [Five Pecks] *Sou*', in which he said the *Jinshu* records that a '*Wudou Sou* called Hao Suo gathered the people together and rebelled'.[59] Hao Suo was from the same camp as Liu Mangdang of Pingyang who also raised an army in rebellion; the *Jinshu* refers to him as being from a 'branch of the Hu'. This 'branch of the Hu' probably refers to the Qiang. The '*Wudou Sou*' probably indicates those of the *Sou* who believed in the Way of the Five Pecks of Rice. There were great population movements from the end of the Eastern Han, through the Three Kingdoms to the Western Jin. If Hao Suo were in military service then he would have been a *Sou* soldier – troops who frequently made their appearance in the north. Dong Zhuo's biography from the *Hou Hanshu* says that after Zhuo died, Li Jue and others besieged Chang'an and 'it was defended for eight days but then the *Sou* soldiers in Lü Bu's army rebelled and led Jue in. The city walls were breached and the soldiers sacked it.'[60]

The Way of the Ghosts was propagated by these mixed groups of Han and Yi – this can be gleaned from several scriptures of the Way of the Celestial Masters, or the Orthodox Unity Sect, written during this period. These scriptures, like other texts from such an early period, naturally may have suffered at the hands of later transmitters both through embellishment and copying errors, and we should take the time to analyse them carefully. In general, they appear particularly interested in controlling ghosts, a characteristic of works of this period. If we regard all of them as being the product of comprehensive editing during the Tang dynasty then, perhaps, there is nothing left of the original works. However, this would be unfair. From a historical viewpoint, the records relating to Zhang Lu shed light on the propagation of his doctrine and of the relationship between the Yi and

Han peoples. The 'Hanzhong zhi' of the *Huayang guozhi* says that in 200 '[Liu] Zhang killed Lu's mother and brother. Lu persuaded Du Huo, Pu Hu, Yuan Yue and others to rebel against his enemies.'[61] From this we know that the Yi leaders in Ba believed what Zhang Lu said. Zhang Lu's biography from the *Sanguo zhi* says that when Zhang Lu heard that the Yangping Pass had been lost he thought of surrendering to Cao Cao, but Yan Pu who was in charge of the Division of Merit persuaded him against doing so and said 'it would be better to rely on Du Huo and go to Pu Hu and resist with him'.[62] After Zhang Lu had surrendered to Cao Cao, the 'Annals of Emperor Wu' in the *Sanguo zhi* record that in 215 'the King of the seven-surnamed Yi, Pu Hu, and the Cong Chieftain Du Huo, brought the Yi and Cong peoples of Ba into allegiance',[63] following the example of Zhang Lu.[64] When Zhang Lu was firmly established in Hanzhong,[65] it was said that 'the Yi believed in him and the court could not deal with him militarily, so they honoured him as the Leader of Court Gentlemen Who Guards the Yi'.[66] Thus, the power of persuasion of the teaching of the Way of the Ghosts was considerable.

3

The 'Miwu jijiu Zhang Pu tizi', which was inscribed in 173, reads:[67]

> On the first day of the third month of the second year of the *xiping* reign period, Heaven made known that the ghost soldier Hu Jiu [two characters missing] had undergone transcendence and completed the Way and was mysteriously granted length of life. The Way truly has one origin and is propagated through the hundred *qi*. He decided to summon the Libationer Zhang Pu, and his students Zhao Guang, Wang Sheng, Huang Chang, Yang Feng and others, to receive the *Weijing* in twelve chapters. The Libationer made a covenant to bestow on them the Way of the Celestial Masters whose methods had unlimited power.

Despite the fact that even the punctuation in this short passage of text may be problematic, it has some sections that can be explicated.[68] The word 'students', I would venture, refers to those pupils who had already received the registers of the Covenantal Authority of Correct Unity. The figures 'Zhao Guang, Wang Sheng, Huang Chang', later became Wang Chang and Zhao Sheng in the *Zhenling weiye tu*, the *Dongzhen huangshu* and in Zhang Daoling's biography in the 109th chapter of the *Yunji qiqian* (which itself was transformed into the Ming dynasty story 'Zhang Tianshi qishi Zhao Sheng' in the *Yushi mingyan*). From this it appears that Wang Chang and Zhao Sheng were historical figures and, even more importantly, at this time the Way of the Celestial Masters already had a text called the *Weijing*. If we are inclined to accept that Celestial Master Zhang Ling was actually the author of the *Weijing*, then this provides evidence in support of statements in the *Sanguo zhi* and the *Huayang guozhi* that he 'wrote Daoist texts' and in the *Hou Hanshu* that he 'wrote talismanic texts'. However, the twelve-chapter *Weijing* is no longer extant and there are only a few fragments of it scattered throughout Daoist works that allow us to catch a fleeting glimpse into the content of the text.

Several sections of the *Zhengyi fawen tianshi jiaojie kejing*, such as the 'Yangping zhi', the 'Tianshi jiao', and in particular the 'Dadao jia lingjie', have been the subject of discussion by modern scholars. They were probably composed several years after Zhang Lu surrendered and reflect the influence of the historical circumstances of his descendants, who were by then in the territory of the Wei, one of the Three Kingdoms. Those who research the history of religions would do well to pay attention to them.

In the 'Dadao jia lingjie', there are some abstract passages of a philosophical bent:

> From heaven and earth on down everything is born and dies through the Way. The Way bestows itself by means of subtle *qi*. There are three colours, associated with the Mystic (*xuan*), the Primal (*yuan*) and the Inaugural (*shi*) *qi*. The Mystic is blue and formed heaven. The Inaugural is yellow and formed earth. The Primal is white and formed the Way.[69]

In the untitled section before the 'Daodao jia lingjie' in *Zhengyi fawen tianshi jiaojie kejing* the following passage appears:

> The Way emerged from Spontaneity and was born before heaven and earth. It is known as the Supreme (*wushang*), the Mystic and Ancient (*xuanlao*) and the Most High (*taishang*). Their three *qi* blend into one and are the Way of Orthodox Truth of Limitless Height.[70]

The mention of *qi* (in both its written forms) in these two passages is important. The second citation mentions that 'the three *qi* blend into one', although it does not say what colour the three *qi* are. For detail on this topic we can refer to the *Shangqing huangshu guoduyi*, a product of the Way of the Celestial Masters that concerns the so-called 'merging of the *qi*' of men and women. This text was somewhat inappropriately collected into the Shangqing scriptures. However, when the Shangqing sect was young and it drew heavily on the Way of the Celestial Masters, the two groups' texts and beliefs often became confused. This can be observed in Tao Hongjing's *Zhen'gao* and *Dengzhen yinjue*, written slightly later. The objective of this process may have been to elevate the deities and scriptures of the Shangqing sect while demonstrating apparent respect for the beliefs of the Way of the Celestial Masters. Thus, Celestial Master Zhang occupies a low position in the *Zhenling weiye tu*.[71] Scholars like us who are only interested in knowledge can occasionally gain illumination by juxtaposing related texts. In the section on 'Cunsi' in the *Guoduyi* it says:

Number nine: sit opposite each other. Yang is in the direction of the branch *yin*, Yin is in the direction of the branch *shen*. The seekers for salvation splay their knees and have their hands together, palm-to-palm. Yin withdraws both hands onto her knees, while Yang turns his hands over, spreads his fingers and covers one with the other. Each click their teeth together twelve times. Think on the Supreme whose *qi* is true green, the Mysterious and Ancient whose *qi* is true yellow and the Most High whose *qi* is true white. These three *qi* combine into one *hundun*, shaped like an egg. The five colours blend into yellow, and descend into the Cinnabar Field.[72]

The 'Si sanqi' section has a similar account:

Return to the left, lie face-up and think on the spirits: on the left is the Supreme whose *qi* is true green; on the right is the Mysterious and Ancient whose *qi* is true yellow; the Most High whose *qi* is true white. They pass right through the Six Jia, the Five Viscera and the Stems and Branches of my body, rising on the left and descending on the right. They circulate once through my body and return to put it in order, descending into the Cinnabar Field and ascending to Mount Kunlun.[73]

Both of these passages can shed light on the earlier citation from the 'Dadao jia lingjie'. The *Guoduyi*'s materials are heterogeneous and describe many methods for merging *qi* that are not easily understood, but what it says correlates with the Mystic, the Primal and the Inaugural *qi*s of the 'Dadao jia lingjie'. However, the text of the *Guoduyi* is not completely consistent; for example, some places show the extraneous influence of five directions theory, adding the additional colours of red and black. For instance, the 'Si wangqi' section says, 'In Spring, think on the green *qi* of the east, it enriches my body and is assisted by the red *qi*'[74] – in this way the five *qi* supplement each other but without, it seems, following any pre-determined pattern. The 'Si yigong' section says 'The Mystic and Primal green *qi* of Grand Clarity [*taiqing*] encircles one palace by rising on the left and descending on the right; the white *qi* of Grand Simplicity [*taisu*] encircles one palace by rising on the left and descending on the right; the red *qi* of Grand Incipience [*taichu*] encircles one palace by rising on the left and descending on the right; the yellow *qi* of Grand Inauguration [*taishi*] encircles one palace by ascending on the left and descending on the right.'[75] This latter passage adds the terms *taiqing*, *taisu*, *taichu* and *taishi* which are widely used in the sources. But to find important historical leads we have to pay even greater attention to detail. The 'wangqi' – or ascendant *qi* – of the 'Si wangqi' is a term that refers to the 'bagua xinwang' system that was employed by masters of prognostication in the Han. The 'Nansui' chapter of Wang Chong's *Lunheng* takes issue with much of this (see below). The 'one palace' of the phrase 'surrounds one palace' is also specialised vocabulary. Fortunately the *Guoduyi* itself says that 'the one palace is the Lower Cinnabar Field'.[76]

The very first sentence in the *Guoduyi* is 'the disciples receive the Way in their Master's parish; if they have not attained twenty they cannot perform the Ritual of Passage, if they are more than twenty when they receive the Way they must perform the Ritual of Passage immediately.' Entering the place where the religious law is propagated was called 'entering tranquillity'.[77] The figures worshipped included the Celestial Master, the Inheriting Master, the Descendant Master and the Female Master among a cluster of other spirits. This is evidence of the influence of ceremonial behaviour derived from the Way of the Celestial Masters.[78]

The focus of the *Guoduyi* is on explaining the merging of the *qi* of men and women but the *Zhengyi fawen shilu zhaoyi* is concerned with superstition and prognostication. The so-called 'ten registers (*shilu*)' of this title must refer to the Daoist registers formulated to manage the ten types of spirits that the Dao commands that ordinary people could receive. However, this text only describes one register. It explains which Spirit Lord from which heaven can appoint and dismiss people born in particular years in the cycle – and it also records more than ten types of spirits. In addition, it describes how people born in different months, and indeed in the three different ten-day periods of any one month, are all regulated by different spirits – the elements of this system are arranged in a very elaborate structure. Within this system of worship the help of the sixty spirits of the Six Jia is still required, so the text has an appendix entitled the 'Liujia liushi zhenhui jue', that gives detailed notes. In the *Guoduyi* merging the *qi* requires the assistance of the Six Jia spirits as well as the Shifu and the Shimu. The names for the Six Jia spirits are the same in both books, and also agree with two other calendrical texts of about the same period, so we will not cite from them extensively.[79] The important thing is the formula found in the *Zhengyi fawen shilu zhaoyi*: 'People born in the years *jiazi, yichou, bingyan, dingmao*, and *wuchen* are appointed by the Taiyang Lord of Taiqing in the Qingwei Heaven.'[80] Information from each of the twelve entries of the 'Qingjialu xianguan zhao' section of the *Zhengyi fawen shilu zhaoyi*, of which this example is the first, are shown in the table below. The heavens of Qingwei, Yuyu and Dachi each appear four times. The Taiyang, Tongyang and Weiyang Lords each appear twice as do the Taiyin, Tongyin and Weiyin Lords. The table thus has twelve rows and three columns with three variables on the left and six on the right (see Table 9.1).[81]

Taiqing, taixuan, taiyuan and *taishi* form the middle column of the table, each one appearing three times. The *xuan, yuan* and *shi* that we have already seen in the 'Dadao jia lingjie' are present here as *taixuan, taiyuan* and *taishi* with *taiqing* preceding them; and it will be recalled that in the *Guoduyi* we have seen the 'Mystic and Primal green *qi* of Grand Clarity [*taiqing*]'. Here the *taiqing, taixuan, taiyuan* and *taishi* are allocated different duties, and they seem to have a linking function among the three heavens and the six lords. The *taiqing, xuan, yuan* and *shi* were all originally connected but

Table 9.1 The 'Qingjialu xianguan zhao'.

Qingwei heaven	Taiqing	Taiyang Lord
Qingwei heaven	Taiqing	Taiyang Lord
Qingwei heaven	Taiqing	Tongyang Lord
Qingwei heaven	Taixuan	Weiyang Lord
Yuyu heaven	Taixuan	Weiyang Lord
Yuyu heaven	Taixuan	Tongyang Lord
Yuyu heaven	Taiyuan	Taiyin Lord
Yuyu heaven	Taiyuan	Taiyin Lord
Dachi heaven	Taiyuan	Tongyin Lord
Dachi heaven	Taishi	Weiyin Lord
Dachi heaven	Taishi	Weiyin Lord
Dachi heaven	Taishi	Tongyin Lord

joining them in a five-character title does not feel comfortable in the Chinese language, so the '*shi*' has been removed. The result is the 'Mystic and Primal Way of Grand Clarity [*taiqing xuanyuan dao*]'.

The 'Hanzhong zhi', of the *Huayang guozhi* says:

At the end of the Han, Zhang Ling of Peiguo studied the Way in the Heming Mountains in Shu where he wrote Daoist texts, and styled himself 'Mystic and Primal of Grand Clarity [*taiqing xuanyuan*]'.[82]

This final phrase is omitted from the *Sanguo zhi* and the *Hou Hanshu*. Looking for traces of evidence in Daoist works, this sentence by Chang Qu can supplement what is lacking in the official histories. Other Daoist scriptures also use the phrase 'Mystic and Primal of Grand Clarity', such as the *Zhengyi fawen jing huguo jiaohai pin*,[83] and Tao Hongjing's *Dengzhen yinjue*.[84] The former is a scripture from the Way of the Celestial Masters but some Shangqing terminology has seeped into it. Apart from traditional Celestial Masters language it also contains examples of phraseology from other groups.[85] There are two places in Tao Hongjing's book where it may be that original text has been preserved.[86] Some years ago Liu Yi's 'Mai di juan', or land-selling deed from 485 was unearthed. Its final sentence includes the phrase 'Mystic and Primal of Grand Clarity'.[87] The 'Xu Fu di juan,' recently unearthed near Changsha, includes the date 433.[88] This is some fifty years earlier than Liu Yi's 'Mai di juan' and it ends with a string of characters that includes 'Mystic and Primal of Grand Clarity' that is almost identical to Liu's deed. These particular phrases can, in my view, be traced back to the period of the *Huayang guozhi* and the 'Dadao jia lingjie' and were not corrupted in the process of transmission.

The 'Dadao jia lingjie' says 'the Way bestows itself by means of subtle *qi*' and this probably corresponds to the meaning of *wei*, 'subtle', in Zhang

Ling's *Weijing*. The term 'subtle *qi*' can be found elsewhere in works from the Han period. However, in the books of the Way of the Celestial Masters its roots can be seen in works that explicate the *Laozi*. The incomplete Dunhuang text of the *Xiang'er* commentary to the *Laozi* says:

> The Way is of the highest worthiness. It is hidden away in its subtlety.[89]

> The *qi* of the Way hide themselves away and there is no uniform distribution.[90]

> When people practise the Way and honour the precepts, the subtle *qi* return to them. These *qi* enter the innermost depths [of their bodies] and are therefore unrecognisable.[91]

> 'Subtle' refers to the fact that the *qi* of the Way are clear and transparent.[92]

> The *qi* of the Way reside in this space – clear, subtle and invisible. All blood-bearing beings receive them in reverence. [93]

> The *qi* of the Way constantly ascend and descend, active in heaven and on earth, within and without. The reason they are not seen is that they are clear and subtle.[94]

> 'Attenuated' means subtle. If from youth one follows the path of increasing subtlety, one will endure for a long time.[95]

The *Xiang'er* commentary is now universally recognised as a work coming from the 'three Zhangs' – some attribute it to Zhang Ling, others to Zhang Lu. I will try to demonstrate the relationship it has with the *Weijing*; in the future it may be possible to prove whether there is a possibility that Zhang Ling was its author.

The *Taiping jing*, which was written a little earlier than the *Weijing* and the *Xiang'er* commentary of the Way of the Celestial Masters, often uses the term 'subtle *qi*'. In some places the *Taiping jing* usage differs from that of the Celestial Masters but this question requires further analysis. However, identical or nearly identical usages are still present. These include:

> The *Yijing* is rooted in the subtle *qi* of heaven and earth and yin and yang, and it considers primal *qi* as the beginning.[96]

> In the beginning, [the Way of the sovereign, the emperor, the king and the tyrant] were brought into being by bestowing the subtle *qi* of heaven and earth; punishments should not be imposed.[97]

Being a little more specific about the 'subtle *qi* of heaven and earth' or the 'subtle *qi* of yin and yang', we can say that it is the tiny stimulus that begins

all things. This stimulus is simply a concept. To use more substantial terminology, it could be called the most minute, invisible and inaudible 'subtle
body'. The phrase 'punishments should not be imposed', means that living
things should not be punished or restrained as this would entail injury,
which would prevent further development. This subtle *qi*, and the subtle *qi*
of the 'Dadao jia lingjie', is *xuan*, *yuan* and *shi* – Mystic, Primal and Inaugural. It is a type of coloured *qi* substance that precedes the production of the
qi of heaven, earth and the Way and is coloured green, white and yellow.
Thus, these understandings and those of the 'Dadao jia lingjie' are close.
Although this type of subtle *qi* is said to be bestowed by the Way – the Way
acts as the mother which bestows *qi* – at the same time, it acts as a recipient
of a share of the subtle *qi* – so it also becomes a child. This is quite mysterious; perhaps we could say that heaven and earth are also like the Way in its
form as a child in that they are all part of the Way in its form as the mother.
So although the subtle *qi* of the 'Dadao jia lingjie' is minute, it is far from
insignificant and is identical in substance to the Way that is the mother that
produced it – and so its origin is the same as that of heaven and earth.
However in the *Taiping jing*, subtle *qi* occupies a minor place. The *Taiping
jing* refers to the terminology of the 'bagua xiuwang' system of the Han
dynasty masters of yin and yang.[98] This system defined imperial *qi*, ascendant *qi*, adjutant *qi*, extended *qi*, and subtle *qi* in such a way that the designations are graduated, and the place of subtle *qi* is below that of extended *qi*.[99]
At one point it explains that, 'subtle *qi* corresponds to minor functionaries;'
at another, 'subtle *qi* is the name for minor functionaries'.[100] This is quite
different from the purport of the 'Dadao jia lingjie' and also runs counter to
the traditional thinking of yinyang five-phase theory.

Since there are many instances in the *Taiping jing* where basic notions
surrounding subtle *qi* do not correspond with those of the 'Dadao jia
lingjie', I suspect that they may derive from some aspects of the Confucian
tradition. The phrase 'see the subtle and know the manifest' that seems
fortuitously to confirm this appears several times in the *Taiping jing* in
passages not related to those ideas.[101] It is probably the case that the 'subtle'
(*wei*) of the Celestial Masters' *Weijing* was originally influenced by the use
of 'subtle *qi*' in yinyang five-phase theory that had become intermingled
with Confucianism.

To gloss the phrase 'see the subtle and know the manifest' we can
refer to the passage from Chen Chong's memorial from the year 85, 'Three
Subtleties make one Manifestation, and are transmitted to the Three
Calendars [*santong*]'.[102] In the seventh month of the same year that Chen
submitted his memorial, Emperor Zhang issued an edict that read: 'Each
Spring the *Chunqiu* notes which month is the "ruler" [*wang*], to stress the
importance of the Three Rectifiers [*sanzheng*] and to pay heed to the Three
Subtleties.'[103]

What are the 'Three Rectifiers' and the 'Three Subtleties'? Ban Gu, in
the 'Sanzheng' chapter of his *Bohu tong*, cites the *Li Sanzheng ji*, which
says:

There are three dates for New Year's Day which alternate, with substance following pattern. What are the 'Three Subtleties'? When the yang *qi* begins to move in the Yellow Springs, its movements are subtle and it is not yet made manifest. In the eleventh month when the yang *qi* begins to nourish the roots and trunk beneath the Yellow Springs, the myriad things are red. Red is the apogee of yang *qi*; consequently the Zhou were the Heavenly Rectifiers and their colour was red. In the twelfth month the myriad things begin to sprout and are white. White is yin *qi*, therefore the Yin were the Earthly Rectifiers and their colour was white. In the thirteenth month, the myriad things become prominent; appearing at budburst they are black. Men activate them and therefore the Xia were the Human Rectifiers and their colour was black.[104]

What are referred to here as the Three Rectifiers indicate the three dynasties of antiquity: the Zhou, the Yin or Shang and the Xia. Because they took the months with the cyclical designations *jianzi*, *jianchou* and *jianyin* respectively as the first month of their years, the calendrical systems of the three dynasties were not the same. Thus, these three 'first months' are known as the Three Rectifiers as well. These three months were all during the cold season when the warm yang *qi* was weak so they were also called the Three Subtleties. This discussion is best seen in Liu Xin's *Santong li* from the end of the Western Han. The first part of the calendrical treatise of the *Hanshu* recounts Liu Xin's discussion of the Three Calendars:

The three dynasties each had their own calendar. It is clear that the Three Calendars always coincided yet they shifted the starting point. The advance and retreat of the starting point of each calendar was governed by rotation through the five phases. Thus, the three and the five embrace each other and give birth. The first month of the Heavenly Calendar begins halfway through *zi*, with the sun red as it germinates. The Earthly Calendar receives it at the beginning of *chou*, with the sun yellow as it starts its growth. Halfway through *chou* the sun is white as it sprouts. The Human Calendar receives it at the beginning of *yin* with the sun black as it puts forth shoots. Halfway through *yin* the sun is green as it becomes mature.[105]

Liu Xin's *Santong li* is deeply coloured by yinyang five-phase theory. Since it also uses the *Yijing* there is the very real possibility that it was influenced by the ideas of the slightly earlier figure of Jing Fang or even of Meng Xi. However, since the Eastern Han, nobody who explicated these theories was uninfluenced by their explanations of yin and yang and the occurrence of catastrophes. Jing Fang's biography in the *Hanshu* says that he 'allocated the sixty-four hexagrams to days and applied them in daily affairs. He took wind, rain, cold and warmth as signs.' This is a simple explanation of the theory of the *qi* of the hexagrams. These theories and stories are common in the apocrypha to the classics.[106] An apocryphon to the *Yijing* called the *Qianzuo du* says 'Three Subtleties of the Heavenly *qi* complete one Manifestation. Three Manifestations complete one Body.' Zheng Xuan's commentary reads 'Five days make one Subtlety. Fifteen days make one Manifestation.' In the second chapter of his *Hou Hanshu buzhu*, the Qing scholar Hui Dong explained the earlier citation from the edict of Emperor Zhang by saying:

> Yang begins its life at 'Winter Solstice'. The fifteen days from then until 'Lesser Cold' is one Manifestation. It is two Manifestations to 'Greater Cold' and to 'Beginning of Spring' it is three Manifestations. Therefore it is said 'three Manifestations complete one Body'. 'Winter Solstice' was the Zhou's rectification, 'Lesser Cold' was the Shang's rectification and 'Greater Cold' was the Xia's rectification. Therefore it is said, 'respect the Three Rectifiers and pay heed to the Three Subtleties'.[107]

Apart from the arguments from yinyang five-phase theory, there are also some traces of the origins of the 'Three Calendars' in comparatively early works. For example, the *Lunyu* mentions what was added and what was omitted in rites and rituals as the three dynasties, the Xia, Shang and Zhou, followed on from each other.[108] In the 'Grand Unified Calendar' of the *Gongyang* and in its explanation of why the *Chunqiu* wrote 'Spring. The first month is the ruler' as well as 'the second month is the ruler' and 'the third month is the ruler',[109] we might well see the seeds of the 'Three Calendars'.[110]

In the calendrical treatise previously referred to, when Liu Xin spoke of the Three Calendars he noted that as the sunlight changed colour there was a spectrum of five colours. The subtle *qi* of the 'Dadao jia lingjie' has only green, yellow and white, it is without red and black, but the *Guoduyi* has all five colours. The 'Siyi gong' of the *Guoduyi* uses the terms 'Grand Simplicity', 'Grand Incipience', and 'Grand Inauguration' that are also used in the apocryphal *Qianzuo du*.

In summary, the 'Dadao jia lingjie' states that the Way bestows subtle *qi*. Records from other Daoist books of this period tally with the Eastern Han Apocrypha and Confucian understandings and materials which were produced at the same time as the *Taiping jing*. The *Huayang guozhi* says that Zhang Ling, 'styled himself "Mystic and Primal of Grand Clarity"', and there is no mention of this phrase even in the usually exaggerated hagiographies. As it was unnecessary to invent it, we might perhaps regard it as reliable.

4

It has been noted, above, that the Way of the Ghosts was characteristic of the Zhang family and that control over ghosts was the central concern of the Zhengyi texts in the *Daozang*. The 'Dadao jia lingjie' has the date 255 in the text.[111] Although this is almost forty years after the death of Zhang Lu, it is still one of the earliest Daoist books that records Zhang Ling's activities.[112] It says:

> Though the Han house was thus established, its last generations moved at cross-purposes to the will of the Way. Its citizens pursued profit, and the strong fought bitterly with the weak. The Way mourned the fate of the people, for were it once to depart, its return would be difficult. Thus did the Way cause Heaven to bestow its *qi*, called the 'Newly Emerged Lord Lao', to rule the people, saying, 'What are ghosts that the people should only fear them and not place faith in the Way?' Then Lord Lao made his bestowal on Zhang Daoling, making him Celestial Master. He was most venerable and spiritual and so was made the master of the people . . . On the first day of the fifth month of the first year of the *han'an* reign period [11 June, 142], the Way created the 'Way of the Covenantal Authority of Correct Unity (*zhengyi mengwei*)' at Red-Stone Wall at Quting in Linqiong County, in Shu Commandery. Binding tallies were formed with heaven and earth, and the twenty-four parishes were established to promulgate the Mystic, Primal and Inaugural *qis* to rule the people.[113]

The phrase 'only fear them and not place faith in the Way', makes clear that in some areas of Sichuan, where the Han and Yi peoples mixed, religion amounted to belief in ghosts, and talismans and registers were used to control them. The methods employed were a matter of contention between the old-style sorcerers and the Way of the Celestial Masters. Thus, Zhang Ling's method was reformist. The name 'Way of the Celestial Masters' had already appeared on the Zhang Pu stele referred to above so the reliability of the term 'Celestial Master' is not problematic. The phrase 'promulgate the Mystic, Primal and Inaugural *qis*' also corresponds to a previously cited passage from elsewhere in the 'Dadao jia lingjie'.

However, a passage cited earlier read 'the Way bestowed subtle *qi*', whereas here it says 'the Way mourned the fate of the people, for were it once to depart, its return would be difficult'. This takes the word 'Way' and anthropomorphises it into a divinity with consciousness and the capability of action. However, it then reads 'Lord Lao made his bestowal on Zhang Daoling, making him Celestial Master.' If Lord Lao is not the embodiment of the Way, then he is subordinate to the Way and performs the will of the Way. The 'Heaven' of 'thus did the Way cause Heaven to bestow its *qi*', may be missing the word 'Master' after it. This might be surmised from the fact that it was the Celestial Master who, 'promulgate[d] the Mystic, Primal and Inaugural *qis* to rule the people'.

Lord Lao is, of course, Lord Lao, the Most High (*Taishang Laojun*). Here, however, the 'Newly Emerged Lord Lao (*Xinchu Laojun*) makes his appearance'. Naturally this 'Newly Emerged Lord Lao' is not the Celestial Master – he is rather the lofty one who can grant the authority to control people to the Celestial Master. However, by this time the Celestial Master used talismans and registers to control ghosts in order to govern. Accordingly, the Lord Lao from whom he derived his authority was not of the earlier type (such as the Laozi in Ku County to whom Emperor Huan sent palace Attendant-in-ordinary Zuo Guan in 165 to make a sacrifice)[114] but was a new manifestation who used talismans and registers and so deserves the prefix 'Newly Emerged' added to the title 'Lord Lao'. One example from the *Taishang qishiwuguan tongzilu* in the *Taishang zhengyi mengwei falu* reads: 'Receiving (insert name) Law register, I (insert name) have always had the *qi* of the ascendant spirit of the August Emperor, the Most High, the Newly Emerged Lord Lao in my body and I cannot separate myself from it.'[115] The title 'Newly Emerged Lord Lao' can also be found in the *Shangqing huangshu guoduyi*,[116] the 'Taishang sanmeng fushou yi' in the *Zhengyi fawen falu buyi*,[117] the *Santian neijie jing*,[118] and the *Sandong zhunang*.[119] In the *Zhengyi fawen falu buyi* the titles 'Newly Emerged Lord Lao' and 'Lord Lao, the Most High' appear side by side. In the *Santian neijie jing*, a scripture of the Way of the Celestial Masters dating from the beginning of the Liu-Song, the titles 'Newly Emerged Lord Lao' and 'Newly Emerged, the Most High (*Xinchu Taishang*)' are both used. In Wang Xuanhe's *Sandong zhunang* from the time of Emperor Gao and Empress Wu of the Tang, there is the 'Newly Emerged Lord Lao, the Most High (*Xinchu Taishang Laojun*)'.

The same text also says that there were five figures who came to bestow 'the ghost title to pass on down the generations' on the Celestial Master and he would 'put the ghost *qi* in order'. Apart from the 'Newly Emerged Lord Lao, the Most High', the others were the 'Archivist of the Zhou', the 'Most High August Emperor, the Central Yellow Realised Lord', Zhang Liang and 'Ziyuan of the Han, the Celestial Master's Maternal Grandfather'. The Archivist of the Zhou is the historical Laozi – he and the Newly Emerged Lord Lao, the Most High are incarnations of the same figure. The problem of 'Central Yellow' is quite complicated and will be discussed further below. The figure named Ziyuan is actually Wang Bao from Shu who was active during the reign of Emperor Xuan. His biography in the *Hanshu* says that his work, the 'Shengzhu dexianchen song', contained a number of sentences on Daoist cultivation noting that this was because, 'at the time the Emperor was favourably inclined towards immortals, so he fulfilled his expectations', which is meant sardonically. Many later hagiographies mention an immortal of the same name – perhaps his name was absorbed and employed by the Shangqing sect.[120]

Simply put, the absurd claim made in this passage is that Wang Bao and Zhang Liang were both related to Zhang Ling. However, the *Sandong zhunang* says 'I bestow on you [Celestial Master] the ghost title to pass on down the generations', to 'put the ghost *qi* in order'; the *Santian neijie jing* says 'The Most High announced to him, "The people of this generation do not hold in awe the True and the Correct, but fear [only] the deviant and the ghostly. Thus I have proclaimed myself the Newly Emerged Lord Lao".'[121] These words echo those in the 'Dadao jia lingjie' and reveal the object the Celestial Masters had in view and the goal of the Covenantal Authority of Correct Unity.

The title 'Newly Emerged Lord Lao' was still in common use in the Way of the Celestial Masters during the period of the Northern and Southern Dynasties. The previously cited 'Xu Fu di juan' begins 'By Order of the Newly Emerged Lord Lao, the Most High' while it finishes with 'Mandated by the Regulations and Ordinances of Lord Lao the Most High and the Underground Nüqing'. This is material evidence for the use of the title 'Newly Emerged Lord Lao'. However, its history can, at the very least, be traced back 180 years, to the period of Cao-Wei rule or even earlier.[122]

The passage of the 'Dadao jia lingjie' that was previously cited says 'on the first day of the fifth month of the first year of the *han'an* reign period, the Way created the Way of the Covenantal Authority of Correct Unity at Red-Stone Wall at Quting in Linqiong County, in Shu Commandery. Binding tallies were formed with heaven and earth, and the twenty-four parishes were established.' This is where 'The Way of the Covenantal Authority' was created. This is slightly different from the biography of Zhang Lu in the *Sanguo zhi*, which says that Zhang Ling 'wrote Daoist texts' (the *Hou Hanshu* states that he 'wrote talismanic texts') in the Guming Mountains (the *Hou Hanshu* and the *Huayang guozhi* both say Heming Mountains, while the *Shenxian zhuan* also has Guming Mountains but it recounts a version of the story different from the dynastic history). The influence of the historical biographies is pervasive, and authors who mention Red-Stone Wall at Quting in Linqiong County are few, although the *Santian neijie jing*[123] and the *Sandong zhunang*[124] both support this tradition. However, before the sentence 'wrote Daoist texts' (or 'talismanic texts') all three biographies say that when Zhang Ling went into the mountains in Shu his aim was to 'study the Way'. Liu Yan's biography in the *Hou Hanshu* adds that he 'travelled to Shu at the time of Emperor Shun', which makes clear the precise time he was there. We could surmise that the writing of Daoist texts (or talismanic texts) referred to in the next line took place elsewhere. The sources allow for the possibility that he left the mountain and went to another place to propagate the lessons of the Newly Emerged Lord Lao and the method of using talismans and registers to control ghosts and people after he had finished his studies. However, this is merely a tentative theory that may be drawn from a reading of the literature; it cannot stand as a firm conclusion. Fortunately, we can be confident that whether we speak of the place he studied the Way, or studied the Way and wrote texts, or where he first completed his studies before going elsewhere to write texts and pass on his teachings, Zhang Ling was active in the vast area of western Shu.

In the 'De taiqing daoren pin' section of chapter 84 of the fragmentary *Wushang biyao* (compiled during the reign of Emperor Wu of the Northern Zhou, 561–578), one passage reads:

The Realized Man of Orthodox Unity, Master of the Law of the Three Heavens Zhang Daoling studied the Way. On the first day of the fifth month of the first year of the *han'an* reign period which was a *renwu* year, an immortal official came down to the Heming Mountains and bestowed on him the teachings of the Covenantal Authority of Correct Unity, and the methods to transform and lead the people. Passed down to the present, [their bearers] are called the Celestial Masters.

His wife also attained the Way and became a female master. His grandson Lu continued to transmit the methods of the Way and Emperor Wu of the Wei [Cao Cao] honoured him as the General who Subdues the South. The *Zhenshou* refers to, 'the night liberation of Zhang who Subdues the South.' This was the Descendant Master.

There were twenty-four disciples; those who were granted instruction were Wang Chang and Zhao Sheng; the rest did not shine.[125]

This agrees with the records that say that Zhang Ling studied the Way and received the methods in the Heming Mountains. The *Zhenshou* is the *Zhen'gao* and the phrase 'the night liberation of Zhang who Subdues the South' comes from the passage referred to earlier on the topic of the year Zhang Lu died (see note 112). I should mention here in passing that Tao Hongjing was of the opinion that Zhang Lu's death was what the Daoists refer to as 'corpse-liberation'. These few records are the only ones that mention the possible site of these activities. As the location is not of great consequence to the topic under discussion, I will now move on.

The Way was received in the first year of the *han'an* reign period (142). Although resources that support this date are few, it is seldom disputed, but this point also has its strange aspects. Why is it that in these comparatively believable Daoist records, different texts are all said to have been transmitted in the same apparently important year but not on different dates? Like the 'Dadao jia lingjie', the 'Yangping zhi' is a distinct section of the *Zhengyi fawen tianshi jiaojie kejing*. It begins speaking in the voice of the Celestial Master:

This is an order for the twenty-four parishes, the lead spirit of the five *qi* and the central *qi*, the superintendent spirits on the right and left of the circulating qi of the four divisions, the head Libationers of the parishes and those in charge of sub-parishes, male and female elders who govern the people: on the first day of the fifth month of the first year of the *han'an* reign period I received the Way from the *qi* of the ascendant spirit of the First Emperor of the Han. Taking the five pecks of rice as a sign of good faith I desired that all those who were able to attain immortality should gain salvation. You are all so difficult to instruct – it is impossible to speak to you. You turn right into wrong, and make the crooked straight. How should I deal with you on this once-in-a-thousand-years opportunity?

> Obeying Lord Lao, the Most High, I have travelled among the people
> in all eight directions to select seed people but in the end found
> none among the common folk. None of you are fit to be the seeds
> of men![126]

Although this is spoken in the voice of a Celestial Master, it cannot be
from the hand of Zhang Ling. Nor can it be from Zhang Lu as in the
'Dadao jialing jie' it already has him saying 'conforming to the celestial
dispensation and the propitious times, I received the mandate to be Master
of the Kingdom'.[127] Since it says that his whole family received the favour of
the Cao-Wei regime on 1 February 255,[128] the text cannot have been written
earlier than this. Thus, saying, 'taking the five pecks of rice as a sign of good
faith', is not problematic as the text must postdate Zhang Lu's occupation
of Hanzhong. This text also makes use of Zhang Ling's voice, as in the
statement, 'I received the Way from the *qi* of the ascendant spirit of the
First Emperor of the Han'. The previously cited *Taishang zhengyi mengwei
falu* also has 'I have always had the *qi* of the ascendant spirit of the August
Emperor, the Most High, the Newly Emerged Lord Lao in my body',[129]
which brings together the names of two deities into a single form, including
one who is identical to 'the First Emperor of the Han' – this is actually Lord
Lao. This can be inferred from the sentence that begins 'Obeying Lord Lao,
the Most High, I have travelled among the people in all eight directions'.

The *Wushang biyao* also records these events as occurring in the first year
of the *han'an* reign period. The *Sandong zhunang's* account on this point is
descended from that of the 'Dadao jia lingjie'. It reads:

> during the first year of the *han'an* reign, dated *dingchou* in the cycle,
> [Celestial Master Zhang] received the Imperial edict. Appointed by
> the Most High to have responsibility for a whole region, he relin-
> quished his official duties and entered Yizhou County. That year,
> at Red-Stone Wall at Mount Quting in Lin'ang [qiong] County
> in Shu Commandery, he stilled his thoughts and gained pleasure
> in his situation. At midnight on the first day of the fifth month, a
> thousand chariots and ten thousand riders arrived.[130]

These 'thousand chariots and ten thousand riders', were, according to the
text that follows 'innumerable dragons, tigers and ghost soldiers', who were
the attendants of those who came to transmit the Law to Zhang Ling. Five
in number, the Law transmitters were the 'Archivist of the Zhou' and company, mentioned above. The reference to Zhang 'relinquish[ing] his official
duties' at the beginning of this work points to the absurdity of the hagiographies – for example, the *Sandong zhunang* states that Zhang Ling had held
the office of 'Minister of Works, enfeoffed as the Marquis of Ji County'.
This passage from the *Sandong zhunang* is cited from the *Zhang tianshi
ershisi zhitu* which agrees with early records in several places despite its
general unreliability. The dates and places it mentions are identical with
those of the 'Dadao jia lingjie' – perhaps, in fact, it derived from that text.

The *Dongzhen huangshu*, which is stylistically close to the *Shangqing huangshu guodu yi*, includes several important passages:

> In the first year of the *han'an* reign period (which corresponded to *renwu* in the cycle) and in the second year (which corresponded to *guiwei*) the Celestial Master kowtowed and received from Laozi, orally, a copy of the *Yellow Book* in eight chapters, the red *qi*, the triple *qi*, one each of the *Nine Talismans*, and the *Seven Talismans*, one *Mysterious Register*, one *Chaos Completed*, three *Middle Scripts* and one *Spirit Register*. On the twenty-fourth day (which corresponded to *yisi*) by the middle of the day, twenty-four chapters had been passed over to him and thoroughly learned. On the twenty-fourth day (which was *ji* [*yi*] *si*) [the Celestial Master] gave oral instruction to [Zhao] Sheng, [Wang] Chang, [Wang] Zhi, [Wang] Ying proclaiming the great salvation of heaven and earth and all clearly understood. He selected the people, he selected their bone structure and he selected their virtue. When they promised death as a pledge, he transmitted two chapters – their spiritual power should not be handed out rashly. The Six Jia, the five phases, the twenty-four *qi*, the nine palaces, the eight trigrams, and the *yin* and *yang*, transcending the generations, doing away with calamities, protecting the fated lifespan and taking the elixir – the eighth chapter of the *Sanwei xuwu bijing* should not be recklessly transmitted.[131]

> The Master said: '. . . If you can put things into action according to the *Mysterious Register*, *qi* becomes like a *hundun*. This yellow-and-white *qi* can either kill you or keep you alive. Cultivating your body and meditating on what is good will just keep you hankering after life and enjoying vitality. But when there is an emergency you have to put it into action. Fearing you were not clear about this, I sent down the method for putting the triple *qi* into practice, beginning in *renwu* and *guiwei* years.' In the first year of the *han'an* reign period, in the middle of the tenth day of the first month, the eight chapters, the *Mysterious Register* and the illustrated writings of *Chaos Completed* were brought forth. It was proclaimed that men and women were not to hand them out rashly.[132]

> In the middle of the seventh day of the seventh month of the first year of the *han'an* reign period, Lord Lao, the Most High, passed on the oral essentials to Zhang Ling: long life and transcending the generations, corpse-liberation, ascension to heaven in broad daylight, and the avoidance of calamities for all descendants, generation after generation. During the middle of the seventh day of the first month of the second year (which corresponded to *guiwei*), Daoling taught Zhao Sheng, Wang Chang, Wang Zhi, and Wang Ying how to put into action the *Mandate of the Yellow Book*, the

prohibitions and taboos of the nine palaces and the knowledge of what the official spirits of men and women govern. The essential words are to be found in the eighth chapter.[133]

These three extracts are interrelated and must be examined together. The *Sanwei xuwu bijing* is certainly related to the *Weijing*, which is mentioned in the Zhang Pu stele as the phrase 'Three Subtleties (*sanwei*)' is found in its title, even though that has twelve chapters and here there are only eight. At the very least, the *Weijing* was partly concerned with the merging of male and female *qi*. Aside from Wang Chang and Zhao Sheng, the Wang Zhi and Wang Ying found here were probably two of the 'twenty-four disciples' mentioned in the *Wushang biyao*.

The day that the Law was received was the seventh day of the first month of the second year of the *han'an* reign period, which was a *guiwei* year, namely 143. That year, the designation for first day of the first month was *yihai*, the seventh day would have been *xinsi*, and twenty-four days later it would have been *yisi*, so the dates are consistent.[134] Why, then, do the 'Dadao jia lingjie', the 'Yangping zhi' and the *Dongzhen huangshu*, which all have different concerns (not to mention the later *Wushang biyao* and *Sandong zhunang* with their similar accounts), all use the same year – the first year of the *han'an* reign period of Emperor Shun? Is there some reason for this?

The *Santian neijie jing*, a Celestial Masters scripture from the Liu-Song ascribed to 'Xu, the disciple of the Three Heavens', includes a section that praises Liu Yu, the founding Emperor of the Liu-Song. It mentions many propitious omens surrounding Liu receiving the mandate, several of which are corroborated in the treatise on talismans and omens from the *Songshu*. This work appears to have been compiled around 434, about ten years earlier than the 'Xu Fu di juan'. Xu was an enthusiastic adherent of the 'Orthodox Unity of the Three Heavens', and the text states quite definitely that, 'Those who revere the Way without employing the five pecks of rice cannot be considered adherents of the Way of the Covenanted Authority of Correct Unity of the Three Heavens.'[135] It also says that, 'There is the Illimitable Great Way of Grand Clarity, the Mystic and Primal [*qi*] and the Highest Three Heavens'[136] and 'Grand Nullity transformed itself into the three *qi*: the Mystic, the Primal and the Inaugural. Joined alike in undifferentiated Chaos, these three *qi* transformed to give birth to the Dark and Wondrous Jade Maiden. Once the Jade Maiden had been born, the undifferentiated *qi* coalesced in her to give birth to Laozi . . . Laozi is Lord Lao.'[137] Although this contains legendary elements, it preserves traces of early accounts of the Mystic, the Primal and the Inaugural *qi*. In this work Liu Yu is referred to as 'the Song Emperor, Liu'. Liu Yu died in the second year of his reign (422) but as the text does not use his posthumous title it must have been written while he was still alive. It praises Liu Yu's period of rule saying that 'the devouring spirits of the unofficial shrines were all swept away, the orthodox was regulated with the Way, and the old *qi* was eradicated'.[138]

The previously cited passage from the 'Yangping zhi' includes: 'Obeying Lord Lao, the Most High, I have travelled among the people in all eight directions.'[139] The *Zhengyi fawen tianshi jiaojie kejing* also includes a section called the 'Tianshi jiao' which says:

> I send out words and publish the teachings, but my heart and
> thoughts are troubled.
> Releasing *qi* to the eight extremes, I return to where I started.
> Observing the common people, the Yi, the Hu and the Qin,
> I see no seeds of men, only corpses.[140]

This is quite abstruse, but the *Santian neijie jing* offers an explanation:

> During the time of Emperor Shun (125–144), the Most High se-
> lected Court Commissioners to subdue the rule of the Six Heavens,
> to distinguish the true from the false and to make manifest the *qi* of
> the Three Heavens.[141]

It continues in a manner identical with the 'Dadao jia lingjie':

> On the first day of the fifth month of the first year of the *han'an*
> reign period, corresponding to *renwu* in the cycle, Lord Lao met
> with the Daoist Zhang Daoling in a stone chamber on Mount Quting
> in the Commandery of Shu. Lord Lao was going to bring Zhang
> with him to visit Mount Kunlun in order to propagate the doctrine
> of the Newly Emerged Most High.
>   The Most High claimed that the people of this generation do not
> hold the True and the Correct in awe, but fear [only] the evil and
> the ghostly, therefore he proclaimed himself the Newly Emerged
> Lord Lao.
>   He forthwith honoured Zhang as the 'Master of Three Heavens
> of the Correct and Unified *qi* of the Grand Mystic Metropolis' and
> entrusted to him the Way of the Covenanted Authority of Correct
> Unity.[142]

Omitting about a line and a half, the text then continues:

> After sixteen years had elapsed, in the third year of the *yongshou*
> reign period [157], which corresponded to *dingyou* in the cycle, Zhang
> went to the court of the Han emperor and made a covenant with
> the emperor and his ministers sealed with the blood of a white
> horse and with an iron tally inscribed in cinnabar as verification.
> This covenant was made by the two sides before the Three Offices
> of Heaven, Earth and Water and before the God of the Year Star
> and the Heavenly General. Both vowed that they would eternally
> employ the correct Law of the Three Heavens and not proscribe the
> people of Heaven. The people were not to wantonly carry out improper
> sacrifice to the ghosts and spirits belonging to other groups.[143]

Of course, the phrase 'Zhang . . . made a covenant with the emperor and his ministers' is not found in the histories. The 'Dadao jia lingjie' reads, 'Binding tallies were formed with heaven and earth, and the twenty-four parishes were established',[144] but the phrase 'binding tallies were formed with heaven and earth', is a standard formulation made by people in ancient times when offering a pledge. Here, the corresponding partner of the covenant could not have been the Han emperor or his ministers. However, in the few passages cited above from the *Santian neijie jing* we have: 'During the time of Emperor Shun (126–144), the Most High selected Court Commissioners to subdue the rule of the Six Heavens', 'the people were not to wantonly carry out improper sacrifice to the ghosts and spirits belonging to other groups' and 'not proscribe the people of heaven'. These phrases cannot have come out of nowhere, and almost all of these matters bear some relation to the figure of Luan Ba, who was a Daoist at the same time as Zhang Ling. The fact that such passages appear in Daoist scriptures that honour 'the Way of the Covenanted Authority of Correct Unity of the Three Heavens' cannot but lead us to suspect that, at a certain time, there may have been some relationship between the life of Luan Ba and the activities of his contemporary Zhang Ling. This may provide corroborating evidence that attests to the historical reality of Zhang Ling.

Within the *Hou Hanshu*, Luan Ba appears as an unusual figure. He had been a eunuch, and his biography in the *Hou Hanshu* says that he 'was fond of the Way. During the period of Emperor Shun he worked with the eunuchs at the Lateral Courts. He became the Prefect of the Yellow Gates, although it was not what he desired . . . Although he was in the eunuch (*zhongguan*) section, he had few dealings with the Palace Regular Attendant.' Later, his 'yang *qi* was unblocked and he begged to withdraw', so he no longer served as a eunuch. In the *Hou Hanshu* he is granted his own biography and is grouped with Du Gen, Liu Tao and others – certainly not among the biographies of eunuchs. To say 'his yang *qi* was unblocked', means that he returned to having a regular sex life. Perhaps he originally had some physiological deficiency and was never castrated. He knew techniques of the Way and should be seen as being like Zuo Ci or Gan Shi, but these figures were recorded in the biographies of *fangshi* and Luan Ba was not.

During the period from the middle of the Eastern Han to the end of the dynasty there was no lack of eunuchs who developed an interest in techniques of the Way. In July 1991 in Yanshi County in Henan a piece of the Fei Zhi stele, inscribed in 169, was unearthed.[145] On the top of the stele the accession dates of Emperors Zhang (76, *bingzi* in the cycle) and He (89, *jichou* in the cycle) appear. The combined reigns of these two emperors only amounted to twenty-nine years and we do not know whether this indicates the period of activity of the Daoist adept Fei Zhi. The text on the stele says that he 'was an Expectant Appointee at the Lateral Courts . . . when young he had held to spontaneity, when mature he had cherished unusual conduct and often remained in seclusion nurturing his ideals. He lived in the branches of a date tree and did not come down for three years. He wandered free and easy with the Way.' The Lateral Courts were where the women in the palace resided. An Expectant Appointee was a junior official serving under the Prefect of the Lateral Courts.[146] They were the people who attended to young ladies and were therefore eunuchs.

The position of the Expectant Appointees was low and so the statement on the stele that the emperor 'sent an envoy with gifts to invite him' and 'conferred vast sums of cash on him but they were politely refused', is perhaps hyperbolic. However, we may find some support for the line, '[he] often remained in seclusion nurturing his ideals' among the biographies of eunuchs: 'Wu Kang, the Junior Attendant of the Yellow Gates,[147] was skilled at prediction by watching the wind. He was widely learned and a good servant. Knowing that his knowledge would not be put to use he often pleaded illness and returned to his official lodgings, there in leisure to nurture his ideals.' The 'nurturing his ideals' of the Fei Zhi stele is perhaps close to this description.

Not long after Luan Ba returned to a regular life, he

> was selected as a Gentleman of the Palace and after promotion his fourth posting was as the Grand Administrator of Guiyang... He examined government affairs thoroughly, attended to official duties for seven years, then asked to retire on account of illness. The Regional Inspector of Jingzhou, Li Gu, recommended Ba for his achievements in administration and he was summoned and honoured as a Gentleman Consultant, and then as an Imperial Household Grandee. Along with Du Qiao, Zhou Ju and some five others, he was sent on an inspection tour through the regions and commanderies.

This 'inspection tour through the regions and commanderies' is what the *Santian neijie jing* refers to when it says 'During the time of Emperor Shun, the Most High selected Celestial Court Commissioners to subdue the rule of the Six Heavens.' This was in the first year of that emperor's *han'an* reign period. The 'Annals of Emperor Shun' in the *Hou Hanshu* record that:

> During [the eighth month of the first year of the *han'an* reign period] *dingmao* in the cycle, the Emperor despatched eight officials: the Palace Attendant Du Qiao, the Imperial Household Grandee Zhou Ju, and the Probationary Imperial Household Grandees, Guo Zun, Feng Xian, Luan Ba, Zhang Gang, Zhou Xu and Liu Ban. They travelled separately around the regions and commanderies to spread morals and manners, recommend the honest and censure the wicked.[148]

This is the real event that has been mythologized in all the Daoist records as 'I have travelled among the people in all directions'. The *Wushang biyao* quotes the *Dongxuan yuanshi wulao chishu yupian jing* as saying that in heaven many eminent spirits

> regularly, on the twenty-third of the month, ascend and meet in the Palace of Penetratingly Numinous Primal Yang on Jade Capital Mountain in the Grand Mystic Metropolis of the Numinous Jewel . . . together they would collate and compare the lengths of life on the registers of the heavenly people, dividing them into good and evil. That day [the eminent spirits] order the Grand Monad and the eight spirit envoys to descend to accompany the Three Offices in their summoning and examination, and to go throughout the world inspecting the goodness and wickedness of the heavenly people.[149]

The transmitted text of the *Yuanshi wulao chishu yupian zhenwen tianshu jing*[150] is almost the same as the *Wushang biyao* except that the twenty-third day is changed to the eighteenth day. This is a Lingbao scripture and as they were typically inclined to favour their own spirits, Lord Lao is merely rendered here as 'Cinnabar-numinous Laozi, the Red Emperor of the South'.[151] However in another place in the *Daozang* edition,[152] we can still find the title 'Lord Lao, the Most High, Supreme, Mystic and Ancient, the Illimitable Great Way of the Upper Three Heavens, Mystic and Primal of Grand Clarity'. This has a close relationship with the Way of the Celestial Masters. In Qin and Han times there were also a Grand Monad and eight spirit generals.[153] However, many related figures are reflections of the eight people who were sent out on an inspection tour around the regions and commanderies in the first year of the *han'an* reign period.

The *Santian neijie jing* refers to 'Court Commissioners' being selected. Court Commissioners, generally speaking, were those who were sent out of the court by the emperor. For instance, the biography of Zhang Rang in the biographies of eunuchs, says that at the beginning of the *zhongping* reign period of Emperor Ling (around 184) 'whenever the Emperor sought for something, a mounted attendant would be despatched with a secret edict from the imperial stable in the Western Garden. These were called Court Commissioners. This put the regions and commanderies into a panic and so [the Court Commissioners] received many bribes.'[154] These Court Commissioners were eunuchs. As a matter of fact, of the eight high officials Emperor Shun dispatched to patrol the regions and commanderies, the only person worthy of the honourable title of Court Commissioner was Luan Ba.

Luan Ba was sent on inspection to Xuzhou.

> After his return he moved to become the Governor of Yuzhang. In the commandery there were many ghosts and demons in the mountains and rivers and commoners often spent their money to make sacrifices to them. Luan Ba had always possessed techniques of the Way and was able to control ghosts and spirits. He destroyed house

sacrifices and set evil sorcerers to rights. As a result demonic anoma-
lies naturally disappeared. The common people were alarmed at
first but in the end were at peace.[155]

This passage from the *Hou Hanshu* says that 'Luan Ba had always
possessed techniques of the Way', and this led to the exaggerations in the
Shenxian zhuan and later accounts with their numerous legends. Some of
these stories were included in Li Xian's commentary to the *Hou Hanshu*.
These legends resemble stories of Lang Zong in his son Lang Yi's biography
in the *Hou Hanshu*, and also the demonstrations of prognostication by Guo
Xian and Fan Ying in the biographies of *fangshi*.

Where the text mentions the destruction of house sacrifices we should
note that these sacrifices were of two types. The first type arose from the
veneration of heroes among the people. Thus the biography of Liu Penzi in
the *Hou Hanshu* says that the soldiers of Fan Chong – that is, the Red
Eyebrows – 'advanced as far as Huayin. In the army there were commonly
mediums from Qi who would beat drums and dance in sacrifice to King Jing
of Chengyang, seeking good fortune and assistance.'[156] King Jing of
Chengyang was Liu Zhang, who was enfeoffed as the Marquis of Zhuxu at
the beginning of the Western Han during the suppression of the disorder
caused by Lü Lu and Lü Chan.[157] Alternatively such sacrifices were for
those who displayed moral behaviour or purity in administration like Zhuo
Mao, Grand Tutor at the beginning of Emperor Guangwu's reign, or Wang
Huan, who was the Prefect of Luoyang at the time of Emperor He. The
biography of Wang Huan among the upright officials in the *Hou Hanshu*
says of Wang that 'the people considered him virtuous and so established
sacrifices to the west of the Anyang Commons. At every meal offerings were
made to the accompaniment of songs and strings.'[158]

The second type of sacrifices was made to various ghosts and spirits.
When Luan Ba destroyed the house sacrifices at Yuzhang, worship at Huang-
Lao temples, which were precursors of Daoism, was, in all likelihood, already popular. The Way of Great Peace and the Way of the Ghosts, already
active in Sichuan, were probably just beginning there. Luan Ba's motives
were most likely still based on traditional Confucian teachings that ostracised mediums. That said, the Huang-Lao Way also forbade sacrifices to
various spirits. Not more than two years after the death of Emperor Shun,
Emperor Huan was brought from his marquisate to the throne at the age of
fifteen. In time he became famous as an adherent in the Huang-Lao Way. In
165 (that is, in the first month of the eighth year of the *yanxi* reign period)
he sent the Palace Regular Attendant Zuo Guan to Ku County in Henan to
sacrifice to Laozi. In the eleventh month he sent another Palace Regular
Attendant, Guan Ba, to do the same and in the seventh month of the
following year he also sacrificed to Huang-Lao at the Zhuolong Temple in
Luoyang. His belief in the Huang-Lao Way may have been influenced by
eunuchs in the palace. It is known that among the eunuchs there were some
former Daoists and that there were also those who maintained close connec-

tions with popular beliefs. It is also known that in 184, before the Yellow Turban rebellion had broken out, the Palace Regular Attendant Feng Xu, Xu Feng and others were the agents of Zhang Jue and Ma Yuanyi in the palace. Zhang Rang was also in communication with Zhang Jue, and even Emperor Ling knew about Zhang Rang's activities. This serves to show just how formidable Huang-Lao was.[159]

Huang-Lao belief was also exclusive. In the fourth month of the eighth year of the *yanxi* reign period of Emperor Huan (165), an imperial edict ordered: 'Destroy all the house sacrifices throughout the kingdoms and commanderies.' According to the biography of Wang Huan, 'during the *yanxi* reign period Emperor Huan served the Huang-Lao Way and all house sacrifices were destroyed. The only exemptions were the old temple to the Grand Tutor, Zhuo Mao, in Mi County, and the shrine to Wang Huan in Luoyang.' It should be noted that the main focus of the campaign was the sacrifices of the second type, described above. The 'Annals of Emperor Wu' in the *Weishu* of the *Sanguo zhi* says 'at the end of the *guanghe* reign period [183] the Yellow Turbans arose'. At that time, Cao Cao was the Counsellor in the vassal kingdom Ji'nan and, 'prohibited licentious sacrifices and the scoundrels fled'.[160] In 186, 'Cao assumed the Regional Governorship of Yanzhou. He advanced troops and attacked the Yellow Turbans east of Shouzhang.' Pei Songzhi's commentary cites the *Weishu* saying that the Yellow Turbans wrote Cao Cao a letter praising him: 'Earlier, in Ji'nan, you destroyed the spirit altars. Your Way is at one with the Central Yellow Grand Monad, it seems as if you understand the Way.'[161] This is evidence that the Yellow Turbans also did away with various sacrifices. In a passage from the *Santian neijie jing* cited earlier, it says that 'the people were not to wantonly carry out improper sacrifice to the ghosts and spirits belonging to other groups', and if we bring that together with Luan Ba being on an inspection tour through the counties and commanderies, as well as the period when he was debarred from holding office (see below), we can infer that Luan Ba was not unrelated to the development of the Way of the Celestial Masters.

The biography of Luan Ba continues: 'He was moved to Pei as Chancellor where he gave meritorious service. He was summoned back to the court as a Master of Writing.'[162] None of the records states in which year either of these events occurred, though they must have taken place before the death of Emperor Shun in 144. This is because Luan Ba had severely admonished the Consort Dowager Liang for attempting to destroy the graves of common people in order to erect the emperor's mausoleum. This made her furious and she threw him in jail. He was on the point of death when an earthquake intervened – instead he was given the punishment of being debarred from office and he returned home.[163]

It is not known how long Luan Ba was in office as the Chancellor of Pei nor when Zhang Ling left there. Liu Yan's biography in the *Hou Hanshu* merely says that Zhang 'travelled to Shu at the time of Emperor Shun', and does not mention the year. If Zhang Ling was still in Pei when Luan Ba was also there, then they may have had the opportunity to meet. The records in the hagiographies – such as the *Lishi zhenxian tidao tongjian* – also neglect to mention when Zhang entered Shu although it gives the period of his activities in Sichuan as being very early.[164] This is contrary to the standard histories that say that it was 'at the time of Emperor Shun'. After Luan Ba was debarred from holding office and he returned home, we can say that he did not engage in any other political activities during the entire twenty-one year period that Emperor Huan was on the throne (147–167).[165]

Luan Ba's native place, according to his biography in the *Hou Hanshu*, was 'Neihuang in Wei Commandery'.[166] Li Xian's commentary cites the *Shenxian zhuan* which says that he 'was from Shu in Ba Commandery'. The *Shenxian zhuan* is a very early hagiography and should be handled with particular care. Li Xian's annotation cites it twice, and the second instance concerns the time Luan Ba was a Master of Writing. According to this record he came late to a grand meeting at the court and when he arrived he 'drank some wine then spat it out to the south-west. An official reported to the throne that he was not respectful. When a summons was sent asking him on the matter, he kowtowed and confessed his faults, saying "I was putting out a fire in Chengdu, my native place".' This also shows that he was from Shu, and it may be that his given name of Ba relates to the name of the region. However, Chengdu was in Shu Commandery and not Ba Commandery, so such a proposition is farfetched.

There *was* a certain Liu Ba in Shu during the Three Kingdoms – an official in Shu Han who hailed from Cheng County in Lingling Commandery in Jingzhou.[167] The *Shenxian zhuan* and other hagiographies – relying on the *Shenxian zhuan* record – all state that Luan Ba was from Chengdu in Shu Commandery.[168] Only the *Lishi zhenxian tidao tongjian* uses the biography from the *Hou Hanshu* that says he was 'from Neihuang', which is annotated with, 'the hagiographies say that he was from Shu Commandery'.[169] But further on it records the fire incident as occurring 'in Chengdu city'.[170] The *Shenxian zhuan* claims to be Ge Hong's work but scholars have surmised that the original work was lost and surviving versions are the subject of later editing.[171] Further, hagiographic accounts cannot always serve as historical materials so here we must withhold judgement. For the relationship between Luan Ba and Sichuan we can still only work with hypotheses. If Zhang Ling was active in Sichuan during the twenty years when Luan Ba was back there, and if there was cooperation between them, then there ought to be traces of this to track down.

After Emperor Huan died, Emperor Ling came to the throne. The first year of the *jianning* reign period (168) was the same year that Luan Ba's fortunes took a turn for the worse and he came to a miserable end. The biography of Luan Ba says:

> When Emperor Ling came to the throne, General-in-chief Dou Wu and Grand Tutor Chen Fan were assisting in government, and so he was summoned back to court as a Gentleman Consultant. When

Fan and Wu were executed, as Ba was in their clique, he was again demoted to become the Governor of Yongchang, with the possibility of redeeming himself through meritorious service. Pleading illness he did not go but sent up an extremely critical memorial that remedied the injustice done to Chen and Dou. The Emperor was furious and issued an edict severly rebuking him. Ba was arrested and handed over to the Commandant of Justice, and he took his own life.

Dou Wu and Chen Fan had wanted to get rid of the eunuchs, however they were not powerful enough to do so and their activities did not remain secret. They were opposed by the Palace Regular Attendant and Prefect of the Yellow Gates, Wang Fu, and others who led the Troops as Rapid as Tigers and the Guards of the Feathered Forest. They could not overcome the eunuchs' power, and in the end they were killed. Emperor Ling had come to the throne through a strategy of Dou Wu's when he was only twelve or thirteen. In this time of disorder he had enthusiastically drawn his sword and was subject to the eunuchs' manipulations. Thus, when the 'Emperor was furious and issued an edict severly rebuking him,' this may have been the eunuchs inciting trouble.

Thus, Luan Ba killed himself. This was the second time he had been incarcerated, and this time he came to a tragic end. While Daoist records generally say he attained corpse-liberation (*shijie*), the *Jianjing*, cited in the *Zhen'gao*, says that, 'In ancient times, Luan Ba underwent weapon-liberation (*bingjie*), he left and went into the Linlü Mountains. After thirteen years he returned home. He is now in the Guming Red-Stone Mountains.' The commentary says 'in the *Hanshu* it says that, "Ba was the Governor of Guiyang and Yuzhang. Later he died in prison". Yet he actually took a numinous pill to achieve liberation as stated in the biographies of immortals.'[172] In the *Yunji qiqian* the 'Biography of Luan' says 'later he was executed on account of a certain matter, then he underwent weapon-liberation',[173] but the term weapon liberation is unreliable. The 'numinous pill' by which he 'achieve[d] liberation' refers to the process of being able to appear dead by taking certain medicine. By bluffing one's way through an examination of the body, it may be possible to escape with one's life. Such a case is recorded in the biography of Du Gen in the *Hou Hanshu* which says that,

the Consort Dowager [Deng] was furious, so she seized Gen and the others, and ordered them to be put inside silk bags and to be beaten to death in the palace hall. Some legal officers who heard of Du's reputation spoke privately to those who were to carry out the punishment to minimise their force. Later they took his body outside the city walls and he revived. When the Consort Dowager sent people to examine him, Gen faked his death and after three days maggots came out of his eyes. As a result of this he got away and worked as a bartender in a wine shop in the mountains of Yicheng.[174]

Luan Ba's use of a numinous pill is a supposition made by Tao Hongjing and the hagiographers and material evidence to corroborate this statement cannot readily be found, but saying that Luan Ba fled and hid in the Linlü Mountains and only came out after thirteen years does appear to imitate the biography of Du Gen, which says that 'only after fifteen years ... did he return to his native village'. The biographies of those involved in the 'Great Proscription' in the *Hou Hanshu* mention a certain Xia Fu who at the time he escaped death, 'cut his own beard and changed his appearance. He entered the Linlü Mountains and adopted a different name. He was employed in a blacksmithing family, attending the chimney amid smoke and charcoal. He looked completely worn out and after two or three years no one recognised him.'[175] Li Xian's commentary says of Linlü that 'It is now a county in Xiangzhou [present day Lin County in Henan].' These different accounts show that Luan Ba's escape was a possibility but we have no way to confirm it.

Tao Hongjing says Luan Ba 'is now in the Guming Red-Stone Mountains'. This 'now' probably indicates the period in which Tao Hongjing lived. But that is at least three hundred years after the death of Luan Ba, so he must have thought that Luan was an immortal. By contrast, he also said that Luan Ba later returned home. The Guming Mountains are in Sichuan so it seems that Tao felt that Luan Ba's native village was in Shu Commandery. Thus, Luan Ba had the opportunity to meet Zhang Ling in Sichuan during the twenty years when Luan was at home and debarred from holding office even if he did not actually achieve corpse-liberation.

5

If we now draw together the various threads of evidence from scattered materials assayed in this article, we can be relatively confident that, apart from the unreliable records in the hagiographies, there are several simple accounts in historical biographies, and an assortment of excerpts from Daoist scriptures, and archaeological excavations that, taken together, more or less prove that there was a historical figure called Zhang Ling, and that he was Zhang Lu's grandfather. He went from Peiguo to present-day Sichuan during the reign of Emperor Shun. Once there he 'studied the Way in the Guming Mountains. He wrote Daoist texts.' This comes from the biography of Zhang Lu in the *Sanguo zhi* and, except for changing 'Daoist texts' to 'talismanic texts', the material in the biography of Liu Yan in the *Hou Hanshu* is almost identical. Both biographies state that the disciples who received the Way donated five pecks of rice: 'therefore he became known as the "rice thief".' Earlier, I noted that Zhang Ling propagated the Way of the Ghosts. Meanwhile, the Five Pecks of Rice teaching represented Zhang Lu carrying on the legacy of Zhang Xiu. In Hanzhong, Zhang Lu subsequently took the Way of the Ghosts of Zhang Ling, practised it in conjunction with the Way of the Five Pecks of Rice, and thus made a new Way of the Five Pecks of Rice.

The 'Hanzhong zhi', the second chapter of the *Huayang guozhi*, does not mention five pecks of rice in relation to Zhang Ling's affairs and merely states that:

At the end of the Han, Zhang Ling of Peiguo studied the Way in the Heming Mountains in Shu, where he wrote Daoist texts and styled himself 'Mystic and Primal of Grand Clarity'. In doing so he misled the common people. After Ling's death his son, Heng, carried on his legacy, and after Heng's death his son, Lu, passed on the teachings. Lu's courtesy name was Gongqi. With the Way of the Ghosts he had gained the faith of the Governor of Yizhou, Liu Yan. Lu's mother looked youthful and came and went from Liu's residence. During the *chuping* reign, he made Lu 'Major who Oversees Morality'. [Lu] resided in Hanzhong, and cut off the road through the valley. Since he arrived, his actions had been tolerant and kind and he instructed people in the Way of the Ghosts. He established 'free hostels' where free rice and meat were placed; travellers could help themselves but only according to their needs. If someone took more than they needed it was said that the ghosts would cause them to become sick. The market-traders and shopkeepers were also regulated in this kind of way. Those who broke the law would only be punished after having done so three times. Those who were studying the Way but were yet to fully believe were known as 'ghost soldiers'; later they became Libationers. The barbarians in Ba and Hanzhong mostly went along with this.[176]

The final sentence of this section is a summary and merely says that: 'Offerings made were limited to donations of five pecks of rice, so for generations it was known as the "Way of Rice".'

The record of the *Huayang guozhi* is comparatively objective. When it refers to 'those who were studying the Way but were yet to fully believe', this refers to those who had been instructed in the techniques of controlling ghosts but who were still not proficient. They would only be called 'ghost soldiers', and were followers in the ranks of those who controlled ghosts. When promoted to Libationer they were equivalent to those who were generally called Master of the Law in later sects. The term 'Libationer' is worthy of specific research.

When Zhang Lu was in Hanzhong 'teaching the Way of the Ghosts' he promoted 'free hostels' and 'free rice'. Whether or not this was using Zhang Ling's methods of governance we still do not know, but we should remember that Zhang Ling himself had neither a territorial base nor political power. The *Weijing* of Celestial Master Zhang Ling (attested in the Zhang Pu stele of 173) made use of Eastern Han five-phase and prognosticatory theories that were to some extent connected to Confucian practices of the time. It could also have been associated with the 'merging of the *qi*' sexual practices as attested, for instance, in the *Sanwei xuwu bijing* cited in the

Shangqing huangshu guoduyi. Sanwei xuwu bijing may simply have been another name for the *Weijing* – minimally, it made use of part of the *Weijing*. The ascription of the authorship of the *Xiang'er* commentary to the *Laozi* to either Zhang Daoling or the Descendant Master Zhang Lu has long been a topic of speculation for scholars. Many scholars agree that regardless of whether it came from Zhang Ling or Zhang Lu, the Xiang'er commentary is definitely a product of the Zhang family. Likewise, the Newly Emerged Lord Lao of the records in the Daoist scriptures is a piece of terminology specifically created by the Celestial Masters.

The historical biographies state that Zhang Ling 'studied the Way in the Guming Mountains, and wrote Daoist texts' (or talismanic texts). From whom did he 'study the Way'? Did he have a master proficient in Daoist techniques? Did he write the Daoist texts or talismans and registers in conjunction with someone else? What were the popular talismans and registers during that period? The words 'Daoist texts' could perhaps refer to the *Weijing* or the Xiang'er commentary, but what about talismans and registers? Which talisman and register books were by him either with or in collaborations with others?

I have suggested that Zhang Ling and his contemporary Luan Ba may have had this sort of relationship. Their collaborations possibly took place when Luan Ba was at home while debarred from holding office and Zhang Ling was in Sichuan. The *Santian neijie jing* says that Emperor Shun sent Court Commissioners on inspection tours throughout the empire, that he advocated the destruction of sacrifices to various spirits and that he opposed debarment from office. These matters have a close connection with the activities of Luan Ba. In several Daoist scriptures there is the record of Lord Lao bestowing the position of Celestial Master on Zhang Ling during the first year of the *han'an* reign period of Emperor Shun. This possibly marks the year Luan Ba was on his inspection tour. This should be kept in mind as attention is now turned to the Way of the Ghosts of the Covenanted Authority of Correct Unity and to the more widespread talismans and registers of the Way of the Celestial Masters.

I have examined the talismans and registers left by the Covenanted Authority of Correct Unity. Among the most important texts are the *Taishang Laojun hunyuan sanbu fu*, the *Taishang sanwu zhengyi mengwei lu*, the *Taishang zhengyi mengwei falu* and the *Shangqing dongtian sanwu jin'gang xuanlu yijing*, all of which are in the *Daozang*. These books have talismans and registers of all types. Some only have talismans and no registers. It should also be noted that some parts of the texts may have been composed later than others. For example, the *Shangqing dongtian sanwu jin'gang xuanlu yijing* begins with the Celestial Worthy of Primordial Commencement (Yuanshi tianzun). In the *Dongxuan lingbao zhenling weiye tu*, the Celestial Primordial stands pre-eminent at 'the centre of the first rank in the Palace of the Three Primordials of the Heaven of Jade Clarity' and he is also its primary immortal Worthy.[177] Now, as the title of the *Shangqing dongtian sanwu jin'gang xuanlu yijing* begins with the honorific designation 'Shangqing', it is also clearly not a product of

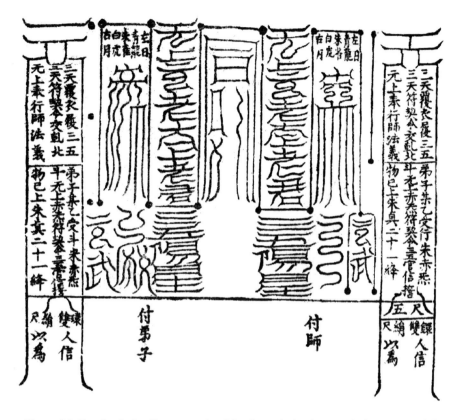

Figure 9.1 Bond of the Supreme, the Mystic and Ancient and the Most High.
Shangqing dongtian sanwu jingang xuanlu yijing, 9b.

the Zhengyi sect. It is accepted that during its formative period the Shangqing
sect absorbed elements of the Zhengyi. The 'Fu du sanwu zhangzou chuguan
yi' section of this scripture has an introductory section that begins with the
title, 'Lord Lao, the Most High of the Illimitable Great Way, the Mystic,
Primal and Inaugural *Qi*s, the Clear and Mystic Illimitable Perfected Upper
Three Heavens'.[178] 'Clear and Mystic' (*qingxuan*) is probably a contraction
of 'Mystic and Primal of Grand Clarity (*taiqing xuanyuan*)'. In Figure 9.1,
reproduced from the *Shangqing dongtian sanwu jin'gang xuanlu yijing*, the
phrase 'the Supreme Mystic and Ancient Lord Lao, the Most High (*wushang
xuanlao taishang laojun*)' that appears twice, once on either side of the
central register, is perhaps even earlier.[179]

Patience and caution are required when analysing these talismans and
registers, as mistakes are easy to make if our attention wanders. We are in
the predicament of being almost two millennia late on the scene looking at
material that has not been seen as valuable by scholars in the intervening time.
This obviously makes for a painstaking task. In fact, among the talismans

in the second chapter of the *Taishang Laojun hunyuan sanbu fu* that are designated as 'protecting the body' is one that states it was meant for 'Kings, Nobles and [those in positions whose stipend is at least] Two Thousand Bushels [of grain]', who were few and far between (see Figure 9.2).[180]

First, let us examine the case of registers. Registers were obtained by believers from their Master of the Law, for whom they had to prepare a 'token of belief (*faxin*)', which they respectfully presented as a gift. The purpose of obtaining a register was to gain the protection of the spirits invoked. It was also used to cast out evil, control ghosts or satisfy a wide range of wishes in life. Accordingly, the names of the various registers are very elaborate. There are some Daoist scriptures directly related to registers that record the names of the spirits, the affairs that they usually manage and their powers. Such Daoist scriptures do not themselves contain registers, but there are some examples that mention such-and-such a spirit that leads a certain number of functionaries down to earth to control ghosts, cast out evil, cure illness, preserve health and maintain social stability. These descriptions are almost identical with the text of the register. Each register gives a monotonous and tediously detailed record of all the spirits covered in the register, as well as the number of people they command. This number can be as few as two or as many as over a hundred. In the case of soldiers or generals they can stretch credibility by reaching up to a hundred thousand or hundreds of millions of people. Our goal, at this stage, is to divide spirits found within the registers into two groups depending on their periods.

The situation in the early period is comparatively simple and the range of activities corresponds to those of daily life in a rural society. The table of contents to the *Zhengyi fawen jing zhangguan pin* lists seventy-seven affairs over which the spirits had control. There are entries for spirits in charge of extricating offenders from legal cases when they admit their faults and are repentant, and those that resolve disputes with local magistrates. Other spirits protect the six domestic animals or expel thieves and robbers. Some record the Libationers who seek registers. There are entries for spirits that cure ague, and for those in charge of the ghosts of wells and kitchens, etc.[181] The titles of the spirit officials clearly refer to their roles: the Lord of the Green Dragon Spring,[182] the Lord of Relieving Adversity,[183] the Lord of the White Serpent in Heaven,[184] the Official who Protects the Foetus[185] and the Lord of the Plain Carriage and White Horse.[186] Their titles are really just explanations of their function: the Lord of the White Serpent in Heaven controls poisonous snakes, the Lord of the Plain Carriage and White Horse is concerned with ghosts and demons of tombs. These descriptions are neither complicated nor verbose.

Spirits like the 'Supreme' and 'Mystic and Ancient' are often found mixed in, as in the titles 'Supreme Old Man of the Nine Heavens' and the 'Mystic and Ancient Great General' which derive from them,[187] and the 'Most High' who 'regulates 400,000 heavenly soldiers and is in charge of containing the ghost who calls himself "The August Heavenly Emperor"'.[188]

Figure 9.2 Talisman that Protects the Body for Kings, Nobles and [those in positions whose stipend is at least] Two Thousand Bushels [of grain]. *Taishang Laojun hunyuan sanbu fu, zhong* 21a.

This raises the question of why in so many places in the previously cited *Taishang zhengyi mengwei falu* those seeking registers all say 'I (insert name) have always had the *qi* of the ascendant spirit of the August Emperor, the Most High, the Newly Emerged Lord Lao in my body and I cannot separate myself from it'.[189] The answer is that they do so in order to reinforce the efficacy of controlling ghosts. If one wanted to remove a ghost calling itself 'The August Heavenly Emperor', I suspect that the strength of the 'Newly Emerged Lord Lao' alone may not be sufficient – the power of the founding emperor of the Han dynasty had to be added to counter it. One special feature of Daoism is that it is all-inclusive; the worship of the 'Supreme' and 'Mystic and Ancient' was, in all likelihood, very early but the advent of the 'Newly Emerged Lord Lao' did not mean the abandonment of old memorials which would be preserved as before. The barbarian tribes Man and Yi

231

of ancient times were probably sexually promiscuous, but the aim of the teachings of the 'blending of the *qi*s of yellow and red' was to reform this behaviour with ritual and ideas of propriety, though the form of the old practices remained. The Newly Emerged Lord Lao could sometimes coexist with other Lords Lao (see Figure 9.3). This reflects a comparatively early development. We lack sufficient evidence to say with any certainty whether there was any influence from Luan Ba at this stage.

It is surprising, on close examination, that many of the spirits listed in two of the books that collect Law registers, the *Taishang zhengyi mengwei falu* and the *Taishang sanwu zhengyi mengwei lu*, are so different from those worshipped in the early period. The spirits in the Law registers of this phase naturally form an enlarged and exaggerated system. The number of soldiers commanded by these spirits frequently reaches a hundred thousand or several hundred thousand. The titles and names of the spirits often use those of Han dynasty government and military officials; for example, the Troops as Rapid as Tigers, Supervisor, Subordinate Clerk of a Department, General-in-chief, General of the Left and General of the Right. These titles are too numerous to list. But some of the titles are extremely specialised and will be unfamiliar to those used to reading the dynastic histories. For example, in the *Taishang sanwu zhengyi mengwei lu*, we find:

On the left, the 300,000 soldiers of the Five Regiments of the Supreme Eunuchs (*zhongguan*) who are in charge of containing greatly refractory ghosts.

On the right, the 300,000 soldiers of the Supreme City Gates who are in charge of containing impious ghosts.[190]

For more details we can refer to the *Taishang sanwu zhengyi mengwei yuelu jiaoyi*, which says:

Send out the 100,000 soldiers under the Colonel of the Five Regiments of Eunuchs. Send out the 400,000 soldiers under the Colonel of the City Gates.[191]

For the details of these two colonels we can refer to the fourth part of the treatise on the Hundred Officials of the *Xu Hanshu* in the section dealing with the Captain of the Central Region of the Northern Army. The *Taishang sanwu zhengyi mengwei lu* has the title 'Chief Mounted Inspectors who Examine Wickedness'.[192] This form of address has some similarity to the 'Inspector of Wickedness for Outside Inspection' in the first part of the treatise on the Hundred Officials of the *Xu Hanshu*,[193] and the *Zhengyi fawen jing zhangguan pin* has the 'Lord who Examines Wickedness . . . is in charge of Libationers who transgress the registers by drinking alcohol and eating meat, the commoners who are found lascivious and thieving.'[194]

The titles of these talismans and registers sometimes begin with the words 'Red Heaven', which of course has a very close relationship with the 'Great

Figure 9.3 Talisman of Lord Lao, the Most High and the Elder, the Most High. *Taishang zhengyi mengwei falu*, 13b.

Red Heaven' of the Three Heavens.[195] For example, over nine pages of entries in the *Taishang sanwu zhengyi mengwei lu* all begin with the phrase, 'The Chaos of the Three and the Five of the Red Heaven.'[196] To this they add the remaining title of each general. After this section, nine generals' titles begin with the phrase 'Controller of Destinies of the Central Yellow of the Three and the Five of the Red Heaven'.[197] 'Red Heaven' is embedded in two other phrases, as is the case in the *Taishang zhengyi mengwei falu* which lists the 'fifteen Spirit Officers who Get Rid of Hindrances to Union of the Red Heaven of the Upper Immortal Metropolis', but this is quite rare – there are only two examples.[198]

I have been referring to the *Taishang sanwu zhengyi mengwei lu* and the *Taishang zhengyi mengwei falu* as two collections that shed light on the use of talismans and registers in the Way of the Ghosts at the end of the Han dynasty. In this sense I have taken them as Han dynasty records but I should also point out several places where there is tampering or alteration as a result of later generations shaping them to suit new needs. The *Taishang sanwu zhengyi mengwei lu* has twenty-four items with a commentary under the title for each one. For example, below 'Taishang zhengyi tongzi yi jiangjun lu' it reads:

The *Qi*-levelling Libationer of the left who is stationed at the Yangping Parish is aligned with the astrological phase metal and is located in Jiulong County in Pengzhou; he responds to 'Barrens' (*xu*) among the twenty-eight lunar lodgings, 'Spring Begins' among the solar terms, and the first day of the first month.[199]

The *Qi*-leveller (*pingqi*), the Leader-in-General (*duling*) and Overseer-in-General (*dujian*) were all positions of the Masters of the Law in the twenty-four parishes. In the 'Zhuzhi mingmu' section of the *Shoulu cidi faxin yi*, the *Qi*-leveller and its affiliation to metal appear as they do in the *Taishang sanwu zhengyi mengwei lu*.[200] However, Pengzhou and the other place names mentioned in the commentaries to this text such as Hanzhou, Qiongzhou, Meizhou, Kuizhou and Langzhou were not current at the end of the Han but are of the Tang dynasty. In addition, Jintang County in Huaian garrison[201] was originally Jinshui County in Jianzhou, but it became Jintang when it was taken from Hanzhou in 967 during the Northern Song; and Xi County in Xingyuanfu is also a Song dynasty place name.[202] So in this part of the registers at least several details are late insertions. The *Taishang zhengyi mengwei falu* has the phrases, 'Mystic, Primal and Inaugural *qi*',[203] 'Supreme Mystic, Primal and Inaugural *qi*',[204] and 'Disciple of Lord Lao, the Most High, of the Illimitable Great Way of the Illimitable Three Heavens of the Mystic and Primal of Grand Clarity'.[205] These terms are comparatively early. Nevertheless, in the registers we repeatedly encounter believers who make entreaties that include the term, 'Master of the Law of the Three Caverns', when the 'Three Caverns' is a term that appears only after the Liu-Song dynasty.[206] These materials need to be treated with care – even if we are only grasping at straws we still need to pay attention to the details.

The term 'Central Yellow (*zhonghuang*)' in the title, 'Controller of Destinies of the Central Yellow of the Three and the Five of the Red Heaven' is worth investigation. Support for the notion that Central Yellow was an immortal from antiquity can be found in the *Shizi* which mentions 'Elder Central Yellow (*zhonghuang po*)'. The *Baopuzi* gives more variations including, 'Central Yellow', 'Master Central Yellow (*zhonghuang zi*)', 'Immortal Central Yellow (*zhonghuang xianren*)' and 'Mr Central Yellow (*zhonghuang xiansheng*)' and also refers to a text called the *Zhonghuang jing*.[207] Ge Hong's account of this text is brief, only listing its name.

Another line of investigation is to suppose that 'Central Yellow' had some connection with the popular Huang-Lao Way of the Han. At the beginning of the Eastern Han, Liu Ying, the King of Chu, 'in his later years became fond of the study of Huang-Lao' and made 'Buddhist fasts and sacrifices'.[208]

Huang-Lao appears originally to have been two distinct figures: the Yellow Emperor and Laozi, who, once taken as objects of worship, gradually became a single spirit.[209] Thus, the *Taishang zhengyi zhougui jing* says 'The Celestial Master said: "I climbed Mount Tai to pay respects to Lord Huang-Lao who taught me to slay ghosts";'[210] and the 'Si wuzang qi' section of the

Taishang sanwu zhengyi mengwei lu says, 'The yellow *qi* returns to the liver, and is ruled by Lord Huang-Lao'.[211] Furthermore, as mentioned above, Emperor Huan sacrificed to Huang-Lao at the Zhuolong Temple in 165. The biography of Huangfu Song in the *Hou Hanshu* says that Zhang Jue, who raised the Yellow Turban revolt, 'served the Way of Huang-Lao'. As Emperor Huan had sacrificed to Huang-Lao, he decided to prohibit all other sacrifices; thus, in 165 he issued the proclamation to 'destroy all the house sacrifices throughout the kingdoms and commanderies'.

Cao Cao did not necessarily serve Huang-Lao but when he was the Chancellor of Ji'nan he had 'prohibited and stopped licentious sacrifices'. Later, to the east of Shouzhang (in Dongpingguo in Yanzhou), he opposed the Yellow Turbans and Pei Songzhi's commentary to the 'Annals of Emperor Wu' in the *Sanguo zhi* cites the *Weishu* saying that the Yellow Turbans 'sent a letter to Taizu [Cao Cao] saying "Earlier, in Ji'nan, you destroyed the spirit altars. Your Way is at one with the Central Yellow Grand Monad (*zhonghuang taiyi*)."' So the Lord Huang-Lao to whom the Yellow Turbans sacrificed had either changed into – or originally was – the Central Yellow Grand Monad. The biography of Wei Shuqing in the *Shenxian zhuan* explains that Shuqing told his son it was not worth wasting words on Emperor Wu of the Western Han: 'Now with the Central Yellow Grand Monad we have settled the Heavenly Primordium; I will never return.' This is an instance of hagiographical material mentioning the Central Yellow Grand Monad.[212]

Wang Xuanhe's *Shangqing daolei shixiang* cites the *Dadong zhenjing* as saying that 'Senlang Metropolis has a hall for the Emperor Central Yellow Grand Monad (*zhonghuang taiyi shangdi*); the Primal and Inaugural Lad is inside.'[213] Neither the *Daozang* edition of the *Shangqing dadong zhenjing* nor the *Dadong yujing* has this passage. The former is based on an edition from about 1272 in which the term 'Grand Monad' appears more than once in all six chapters. However, the Grand Monad in this group of works is an internal spirit of the body, a usage different from that found in other Daoist scriptures. It does not have 'Central Yellow' although it does have the 'Lord Yellow *Qi* in the Womb (*baozhong huangqi jun*)' and the 'Lord Yellow *Qi* in the Foetus (*taizhong huangqi jun*)' but they are a different thing altogether.[214]

The *Dadong yujing*, a text of only two chapters, does not predate the Song either. It includes the phrase 'the travels of Zhen Wu',[215] and a note refers to 'King Chengming of the Filial Way'.[216] The spread of the Filial Way sect can be traced back to Xu Xun of the Eastern Jin but it only became widespread in Jiangxi during the Southern Song and Yuan periods when it was known as the Jingming sect.[217] For this reason it cannot be an early text. It mentions a 'Lord Yellow Silk in the Womb (*baozhong huangsu jun*)',[218] which the commentary glosses as 'Lord Yellow *Qi* in the Womb (*baozhong huangqi jun*)',[219] an identical formulation to that in the *Dadong zhenjing*.

However, in this work there are several places that do mention 'Central Yellow': in one place the commentary reads 'the horizontal line (*hengwen*) is the orthodox seal of Central Yellow',[220] and in another, 'the horizontal line, above, is the orthodox seal of Central Yellow'.[221] The text also refers to, 'Central Yellow expounding the precious scriptures'.[222] It also mentions the Central Lord Huang-Lao twice[223] and Grand Monad over a dozen times, but its use of these titles does not completely match their use in previous works. The letter the Yellow Turbans, who served the Huang-Lao Way, wrote to Cao Cao when they were at Shouzhang, stating that he had destroyed the spirit altars and the licentious sacrifices has been cited above. Since the style of this letter is identical to the writings of those who served the Central Yellow Grand Monad, we would not be too far off the mark if we suggested that those who served the Way of the Central Yellow Grand Monad in fact worshipped Huang-Lao.

The *Taishang sanwu zhengyi mengwei lu* says:

> The Controller of Destinies of the Central Yellow of the Three and Five of the Red Heaven surely give birth to the nine Generals-in-Chief, who rule the spleen and calm the spirit.[224]

The Central Yellow here seems to be employing the teachings of both Lord Huang-Lao and the Central Yellow Grand Monad. The phrase 'rule the spleen and calm the spirit' is like those found in medical theory of the time. Over the three pages from where this citation comes, there are more than nine entries alone that describe the Central Yellow having a role in ruling the spleen and calming, purifying or detaining the spirit.[225] In entries over the preceding few pages there are more than forty-five cases of generals who rule the kidneys, liver, heart and lungs where the Central Yellow does not appear.[226] Not a single instance such as this can be found in the contemporary *Taishang zhengyi mengwei falu*, that, I am convinced, was influenced by the *Taishang huangting neijing yujing*, the famous work of the Shangqing sect. Sections eight to fifteen and thirty-one to thirty-five of the *Daozang* edition of the *Huangting neijing yujing* are each dedicated to the function of the heart, lungs, liver, kidneys and spleen.[227] These have been copied across directly only omitting a number of specific terms. It appears that these several dozen entries were inserted at a later time.

Furthermore, if we regard Central Yellow as equivalent to Lord Huang-Lao or the Central Yellow Grand Monad, then we have difficulty explaining passages such as the following: 'The fifteen Controllers of Destiny of the Nine Courses of the Central Yellow Eunuch of the Wenchang Constellation, the Primal Fate of the Three and the Five of the Upper Three Heavens, rule the officials.'[228] And what of the meaning of 'the 120,000 Clerks of the Nine Courses of the Central Yellow Eunuch of the Upper Immortal Metropolis who settle the thoughts'[229] and five other entries that include the term 'the Central Yellow Eunuch (*zhongguan zhonghuang*)'? And even more so the following titles that include the term 'Eunuchs (*zhongguan*)'?

> The 7200 Eunuch Officers of the Upper Immortal Metropolis who ride on high carriages and direct affairs.

The 7200 Eunuch Officers of the Upper Immortal Metropolis who ride on uncovered carriages and bear the Red Talisman.

The 7200 Eunuch Officers of the Upper Immortal Metropolis who ride on uncovered carriages and examine and seize.

The 2,400,000 Eunuch Troops as Rapid as Tigers of the Upper Immortal Metropolis who capture cruel officials.

The 2,400,000 Eunuch Mounted Police of the Upper Immortal Metropolis who destroy enemies and examine wickedness.

The 2,400,000 Eunuch Supervisors of the Upper Immortal Metropolis who dismember the Three Officials.

The 2,400,000 Eunuch Supervisors of the Upper Immortal Metropolis who decapitate Metropolitan Officials.

The 2,400,000 Eunuch warriors of the Upper Immortal Metropolis who beat and stab the Heavenly Mounted Guards.[230]

Was not their power and influence truly of the ferocity of the eunuchs of the inner court at the end of the Han dynasty? Luan Ba's death came through submitting a critical memorial to the throne. In it he condemned the false accusations of Chen Fan and Dou Wu. In doing so he enraged the young Emperor Ling, only twelve years old and new to the throne. As dawn broke, Dou Wu and his younger brother Dou Shao, an infantry colonel, led the five regiments of the Northern Army troops, a force of several thousand people, into attack against the 'more than a thousand Troops as Rapid as Tigers, Feathered Forest, Stable Cavalrymen and the various captains with Sword and Lance' of Palace Regular Attendant Wang Fu and his group in front of the imperial palace. Wang Fu instructed his soldiers in the front row to yell out loudly and urge the others to surrender: 'the first to surrender will be rewarded!' The biography of Dou Wu in the *Hou Hanshu* states that, 'the regiments and the officials had long been in awe of, and submitted to, the eunuchs. Therefore Dou's soldiers gradually returned to Fu. In the period between dawn and the time for the morning meal most of the soldiers surrendered.' The eunuchs were so formidable!

The third part of the treatise on the Hundred Officials of the *Xu Hanshu* has some 'Central Yellow' materials related to eunuchs:

The Junior Attendants of the Yellow Gates; salary, 600 bushels. Original commentary: Eunuchs; no fixed quota. Their duty is to manage and serve as required, and receive the instructions of the Masters of Writing. When the Emperor is in the Inner Palace they serve as a conduit between the Inner and the Outer courts and manage all affairs for the Empress. If any of the Princesses or the Consort Dowager becomes sick they are sent to enquire after their health.

The Prefect of the Yellow Gates, one post; salary, 600 bushels. Original commentary: Eunuch; managed all the eunuchs in the department. There is one Assistant and one Attendant Assistant. Original commentary: Eunuchs; the Attendant Assistant managed all comings and goings.

The Supervisor of the Extra Retinue of the Palace Attendants of the Yellow Gates, one post; salary, 600 bushels. Original commentary: Eunuch; in charge of the Extra Retinue of the Palace Attendants within the Yellow Gate. Served as an Imperial Guard guarding gates and doors. When the Emperor went out he was his mounted escort riding by the side of his carriage.

The Palace Attendants of the Yellow Gates; salary, 100 bushels. Original commentary: Eunuchs; no fixed number. Later the salary was increased to 300 bushels. They served in the Imperial Palace.[231]

Earlier I referred to an 'Elder Central Yellow' in the *Shizi*. This actually comes from a citation from the *Shizi* in Li Shan's commentary to the *Wenxuan* (for the 'Xijing fu' by Zhang Heng of the Eastern Han), where it says: 'Elder Central Yellow said "with my left hand I grasp the *nao* ape of Taihang, and with my right I attack the striped tiger".'[232] In the *Wenxuan* there is also commentary on the 'Xijing fu' from Xue Zong of the Wu of the Three Kingdoms about which Liu Xie of the Liang (in the 'Zhixia' section of his *Wenxin diaolong*) was very critical: 'Xue Zong mistakenly names [Elder Central Yellow] as a Palace Doorman never having heard of the man who catches the striped tiger.'[233] The original text of Xue Zong's mistaken annotation is lost. The Palace Doorman was a eunuch. Elder Central Yellow was not a eunuch, he was a strongman like Xia Yu and Wu Huo of ancient times. Because of this, Liu Xie thought that Xue Zong's annotation was incorrect. This argument is sound, but considering that Xue Zong lived not long after Zhang Heng who was writing the *fu* around the year 98, and that Xue's *Erjing jie* was widely acclaimed in its day and contained many sharp remarks, how could he make such a resounding mistake?[234] Could it have been that by the end of the Han dynasty the term 'Central Yellow' had, in common parlance, long been a synonym for 'eunuch'? Suppose that Luan Ba really had helped Zhang Ling in the creation of talismans and registers using a large number of titles from the central government of the Han dynasty, including among them the imposing term 'Central Yellow Eunuch (*zhonghuang zhongguan*)' which had instilled fear in the people, and that they used them to destroy the various shrines dedicated to the superstitious belief in ghosts of the south-western Yi and Han peoples. If this were the case, the method employed would be, perhaps, not so different from the creation of the title 'the August Emperor, the Most High, the Newly Emerged Lord Lao' in terms of logical structure and motivation.

When we investigate the relationship between Luan Ba and Zhang Ling to determine whether they really were connected, then we would like to be able to back this up with material evidence or at least supportive written sources. This type of evidence, as we know, is difficult to find today but we can still seek out indirect corroborative evidence that can provide us with materials for reasonable conjecture. One example of this might be the 'Great Red (*dachi*) Heaven', one of the three heavens controlling the six heavens, promoted by the Covenantal Authority of Correct Unity. Because there are copious references to the 'Red Heaven' in the talismans and registers we have examined, it may bear some relation to Luan Ba. In the *Taishang sanwu zhengyi mengwei lu* the term 'Red Heaven' is used at the beginning of a title fourteen times in chapter one,[235] and fifty-four times in chapter two.[236] The *Taishang zhengyi mengwei falu* also has three examples in one location,[237] five examples in another,[238] and fifteen in a third.[239] Furthermore there is not a single example in either work of the Qingwei or Yuyu heavens being used at the head of a title of any of the various spirits.

The term 'the Heavenly Numinous Red Official' is also commonly used in the two works. In one location in the *Taishang sanwu zhengyi mengwei lu* there are ten examples,[240] while in another there are thirty-three.[241] In just four pages of text the *Taishang zhengyi mengwei falu* has thirty-two examples.[242] In these titles the word 'Red' has been specifically added. The *Mengwei falu*,[243] and the *Mengwei lu* both have the title 'Heavenly Numinous Official'.[244] It would not have required much effort to embed the character 'Red' between 'Numinous' and 'Official', and in doing so create a new respected spirit. But, why should we pay so much attention to the single character 'Red'?

The 'Xie changqi, 2' chapter of Tao Hongjing's *Zhen'gao* reads:

Luan Ba's Oral Instructions:

Walking through the mountains to all the numinous temples and shrines, hold a realised man in the mouth whose courtesy name is Red and Numinous Elder. He is attended to by two Jade Maidens, one called 'Flourishing Truth' (Hua Zheng), the other called 'Conserve Essence' (She Jing). The Elder wears a red silk robe, the two Jade Maidens clothed completely in yellow. Once they are held, then angrily shout: 'Ghosts and spirits in the temple, immediately send the hundred perversities to the Red and Numinous Elder for beheading!' The mass of spirits will withdraw a thousand *li*. This is the method of apprehending ghosts used by the Vanguard of the Three Heavens.[245]

Where it says 'hold a realised man in the mouth', this indicates that the person who carried out the method was visualising the spirit in his own body, and in such a way became the Red and Numinous Elder. But these 'oral instructions' were Luan Ba's, and Tao Hongjing called him the 'Vanguard of the Three Heavens', so we can confidently say that this Red and

Numinous Elder was a secret of his family. The term 'Red and Numinous' had already been used in the designation, 'Emperor Yan of the South's altar to Red and Numinous Zhu Rong' that appears in discussions between Wang Mang, Kong Guang and others over rectifying the mystic altars of the Five Emperors at the end of the Western Han.[246] Daoist works like the *Taishang dongshen sanhuang chuanshou yi* also have the title 'Red and Numinous Lord of the Grand Elixir of Grand Yang of the Most High Spiritual Brilliance, the True Numen of the Emperor of Humanity'.[247] This 'Lord of the Grand Elixir of Grand Yang' may be related to the 'Primal Yang Lord of Elixir-Extreme of the Red Heaven of the Three and the Five' found in the *Zhengyi xiuzhen lüeyi* in the register 'Taishang sanwu zhengyi mengwei tianling chiguan zhanxie lu'.[248] In the *Mengwei lu* that I previously cited, the 'Taishang sanwu zhengyi mengwei tianling chiguan zhanxie lu' is called the 'Taishang zhengyi zhanxie chilu'.[249] In the *Mengwei falu* it is referred to as the 'Taishang sanwu chiguan zhanxie lu'.[250] This is complicated and I will not try to come up with my own interpretation of it. I would, however, hazard that the 'Red and Numinous (*chiling*)' of the 'Red and Numinous Elder' is actually a shortened way of saying 'Red Heaven Primal and Numinous (*chitian yuanling*)', which we can find in the 'Red Heaven Primal and Numinous Register of Primal Yang' from the *Mengwei lu* (Figure 9.4).[251]

Suppose that Luan Ba likened himself to the Red and Numinous Elder. This particular epithet 'Elder' carried no implication of self-deprecation. The *Zhengyi fawen jing zhangguan pin* has 'the Elder of the Supreme Nine Heavens'.[252] The invocation in the *Taishang zhengyi zhougui jing* reads 'I invoke again the Lord of the Great Way the Most High, Lord Lao the Most High, the Elder the Most High, and the Three Masters: the Celestial Master, the Inheriting Master, and the Descendant Master.'[253] In other places this type of sentence is extremely common; the addition of the name 'Elder' is merely a variation of an established pattern (see Figure 9.3).

The passage from the *Zhen'gao* that mentions Luan Ba is also found in the *Zhengyi fawen xiuzhen zhiyao*.[254] The *Xiuzhen zhiyao*, in turn, was copied into chapters forty-five and forty-six of the *Yunji qiqian* but the text in the current *Daozang* edition of the *Xiuzhen zhiyao* is much shorter than that copied into the *Yunji qiqian*. There are several sections in the *Yunji qiqian* edition of the *Xiuzhen zhiyao* which are obviously Zhengyi, such as the 'Ming zhengyi lu',[255] the 'Chaozhen yi',[256] and the 'Santian zhengfa shi moshen'.[257] None of these is in the current *Daozang* edition of the *Xiuzhen zhiyao* so it is probably not complete. However, excerpts from a considerable number of Shangqing works like the *Zhen'gao*, the *Dengzhen yinjue*, the *Taidan yinshu*, and the *Taishang huangsu sishisi fangjing* can be found in both editions. The *Yunji qiqian* edition also mentions the *Daojiao lingyan ji*,[258] a work by Du Guangting from the end of the Tang and Five Dynasties period, so it is clear when this work must have been composed.

In form, at least, the *Zhiyao* follows the Zhengyi sect and Tao Hongjing was a giant in Shangqing. The Shangqing sect's attitude to the Zhengyi sect was always both reverent and contemptuous. Where there is no great con-

Figure 9.4 Red Heaven Primal and Numinous Register of Primal Yang. *Taishang sanwu zhengyi mengwei lu*, 1:13b.

flict in fundamental ideas, Shangqing texts had no objection to retaining traces of Zhengyi formulations such as calling Luan Ba the 'the Vanguard of the Three Heavens', which gives us something to work with. As the Way of the Five Pecks of Rice steadily developed into the Way of the Celestial Masters of the Wei-Jin period, that it was an enterprise of the Zhang family alone became the settled position, and gradually the traces of its early history were lost. However, in Tao Hongjing's *Zhenling weiye tu*, Luan Ba is placed close to the end of the list of those on right hand side in the fourth rank.[259] Yet Zhang Ling is the first person on the left hand side of the fourth rank.

The 'Daojiao xiangcheng cidi lu' section in chapter four of the *Yunji qiqian* (citing the *Yuntai zhizhong neilu*) has Zhang Ling 'as the sixth generation descendant of the Way'. Lord Lao, the Most High, is nominated as his 'Master of Transcendence' who conferred on him the title Celestial Master. It also states that 'Lord Little Lad of the Eastern Sea' was Zhang Ling's 'Master of Recommendation'.[260] The Little Lad of the Eastern Sea is an important Shangqing spirit.[261] This is an example of the old Shangqing

241

LIU TS'UN-YAN

habit of belittling the Zhengyi sect, yet they did not totally forget Luan Ba, for he became the tenth generation recipient of this same lineage.[262]

Translated by Benjamin Penny, with assistance from Anthony Garnaut, James Greenbaum, Wong Fung-xian and Nathan Woolley.

This translation is based on an edited and emended version of 'Zhang Tianshi shi bushi lishi renwu?' in Liu Cunren (Liu Ts'un-yan), *Daojiao shi tanyuan* (Beijing: Beijing daxue chubanshe, 2000), 67–136.

Notes

1 See, the biography of Liu Yan in the *Hou Hanshu* (Beijing: Zhonghua shuju, 1982), 75:2431–8; the biography of Zhang Lu in the *Sanguo zhi* (Beijing: Zhonghua shuju, 1982), 8:263–66; and the *Hanzhong zhi* in the *Huayang guozhi* (Chengdu: Bashu shushe, 1984), 2:103–73. Chen Shou, the author of the *Sanguo zhi*, died in 297, the seventh year of the *yuankang* reign period of Emperor Hui of the Western Jin. According to the biography of Li Shi in the *Jinshu*, Chang Qu, the author of the *Huayang guozhi*, persuaded Li Shi to surrender to Huan Wen (*Jinshu* (Beijing: Zhonghua shuju, 1982), 121:3048). Li Shi's surrender occurred in 347, in the third month of the second year of the *jianing* reign period of the Cheng-Han state, which corresponds to the third year of the *yonghe* reign period of the Emperor Mu of the Eastern Jin. Chang Qu was therefore active no more than fifty years after Chen Shou. His record is a little more detailed than that of Chen Shou and it predates Fan Ye's *Hou Hanshu* by many years. Fan Ye's *Hou Hanshu* is a compilation and abridgement of other versions of the *Hou Hanshu* which dates from the *yuanjia* reign period of the Liu-Song (424–453). Fan Ye died in the twenty-second year of that reign period (445), however the inspiration for his writing project was somewhat earlier – in his biography in the *Songshu* (Beijing: Zhonghua shuju, 1983), 69: 1820, he is credited with deciding to compile the *Hou Hanshu* after his demotion to Governor of Xuancheng at the end of the ninth year of the *yuanjia* reign period (432). Fan compiled and abridged the works of numerous writers; in addition to the *Dongguan Hanji* and the *Hou Hanji* there were probably another eight or nine works involved. The *Qijia Hou Hanshu* by Wang Wentai of the Qing includes works by Xie Cheng, Xue Ying, Sima Biao, Hua Qiao, Xie Chen, Yuan Shansong, Zhang Fan, and other writers whose names have been lost. During the Qing these works were also included in collections compiled by Huang Shi and Wang Renjun. The *Dongguan Hanji* is collected into the 'bieshi' section of the *Siku quanshu* as is the *Hou Hanshu buyi* by the Qing scholar Yao Zhiyin. The *Siku quanshu zongmu tiyao* makes some criticisms of the latter work but maintains that it still contains some useful material.
2 Hagiographies of Zhang Ling can be found in the *Shenxian zhuan* (Daozang Jinghua ed.), 4:73–6; *Sandong zhunang* (DZ 1139), 7:6a–7a; *Xianyuan bianzhu* (DZ 596), 2:13b; *Taiping guangji* (Beijing: Zhonghua shuju, 1994), 8:55–8; *Yunji qiqian* (DZ 1032), 109:19a; *Sandong qunxian lu* (DZ 1248), 2:7a and 14:9b; *Lishi zhenxian tidao tongjian* (DZ 296), 18:1a–24b and *Han tianshi shijia* (DZ 1463), 2:1b. Some of these materials are very fragmentary.
3 *Lishi zhenxian tidao tongjian*, 18:2a.
4 *Sandong qunxian lu*, 2:7a.

5 Chen Baoguang was also known as the Daoshi of the Jiangying Hermitage.
6 *Sandong zhunang*, 7:6a. The *Sandong zhunang* says that it was 'composed by Luhai yuke Wang Xuanhe of the Great Tang.' Two chapters in the book mention 'Nanhua.' The first is a citation of the 'Qiwu lun' from the *Nanhua*, that is the *Zhuangzi* (5:1a); the second cites the *Fuzhai weiyi* and says that, 'Zhuangzi was an immortal from Nanhua' (7:30b). However, at 5:2a there is also direct use of 'Dazong shi' from the *Zhuangzi*. Thus, I suspect that the writer was probably from the time of Xuanzong.
7 *Lishi zhenxian tidao tongjian*, 18:1a.
8 *Han tianshi shijia*, 1:1a. Chapters three and four include the accounts of the forty-third to the forty-ninth generations of Celestial Masters. It was published by the fiftieth Celestial Master, Zhang Guoxiang in 1607, the thirty-fifth year of the *wanli* reign period.
9 *Shijing* (Shisan jing zhushu edn, Beijing: Zhonghua shuju, 1979), 10:425.
10 *Shiji* (Beijing: Zhonghua shuju, 1985), 55:2048.
11 *Shiji*, 18:891.
12 Song Lian's preface says that Zhang Buyi had two sons, the elder called Dian and the second, Gao. In Dian's lineage there appears a 'Qianqiu, Duke of Yangling'. Such a person is known to have existed but whether he belongs in this lineage is difficult to say. In the section on the Marquis of Liu in the relevant Tables in the *Hanshu*, it says that in the fifth year of Emperor Wen (175 BCE), Buyi 'was sentenced for the killing of the Chu Chamberlain for the Capital, with the Grand Master of the Gates. By payment, this was reduced to four years corvee constructing city walls' (Bejing: Zhonghua shuju, 1983), 16:540. This can be used to supplement the omissions in the *Shiji* record, cited above. The grandson and the following two generations are missing. Then suddenly, when it reaches the sixth generation, we have 'in the fourth year of the *yuankang* reign period [of Emperor Xuan, 62 BCE] Liang's great-great-great-grandson Qianqui the Duke of Yangling who was a Grandee of the Eighth Order, had his patrimony restored by imperial edict', but that is all we are told. A Grandee of the Eighth Order was a noble rank in the military during Han times. In the second section of the 'Gaodi ji' of the *Hanshu*, it notes that once Gaozu had assumed the imperial throne he issued an edict which said 'All those holding or above the rank of Grandee of the Seventh Order and the Grandees of the Eighth Order are to be considered high nobles', (1.*xia*:54). The text says that Zhang Qianqiu was the sixth generation descendant of Zhang Liang. Chapter 56 of the *Hou Hanshu* has biographies of Zhang Hao and his son Zhang Gang. They were both historical figures and their names also feature in Song's preface where they appear in the lineage of Zhang Buyi's second son. However, the biography of Zhang Hao in the *Hou Hanshu* says that Zhang Hao's sixth generation ancestor was Zhang Liang (56:1815). Zhang Hao died, aged 83, in the first year of the *yangjia* reign period of Emperor Shun (132). He had been active during the reigns of Emperors An and Shun, some 160 or 170 years later than the fourth year of the *yuankang* reign period of Emperor Xuan of the Western Han. How could he and Qianqiu both be of the sixth generation? Zhang Gang was a young official of renown during the reign of Emperor Shun. During the first year of the *han'an* reign period (142) he was one of eight officials selected to tour the provinces and commanderies (56:1817). He was the only one who did not go. He halted the carriage he was travelling in at the Luoyang waystation and refused to move, saying 'When jackals and wolves are in authority, why should I investigate foxes?' and immediately presented a memorial implicating Liang Ji and Ji's younger brother, Liang Buyi, the Governor of Henan. This was shocking news in those days. We would calculate that he could have been a

contemporary of Zhang Ling but according to Song's preface he was Zhang Ling's grandfather. Zhang Gang's biography says that his son was called Chang (56:1821) and not Zhang Dashun, as Song's preface has it.

13 The thirteenth chapter of the *Hou Hanshu buzhu* by Hui Dong of the Qing under the entry for Zhang Hao cites He Zhuo: 'Studies of genealogies became confused in the Six Dynasties and traditions were taken on trust without investigation. As a result, Zhang Lu's descendants erroneously became part of the lineage of the Marquis of Liu. Ban [Gu] did not give credence to Feng Shang's claim that Zhang Tang and the Marquis of Liu had the same ancestor. How brilliant!' (*Hou Hanshu buzhu* (Congshu jicheng edn), vol. 6, p. 571). This is a reasonable conclusion. For what Feng Shang said, see the *zan* in the biography of Zhang Tang in the *Hanshu* (59:2657).

14 For the biographies of this Zhang family, see *Hou Hanshu*, 36:1241–44. As chance would have it, he has the same name as the figure who fabricated the spurious *Shangshu bailiang pian* during the time of Emperor Cheng of the Western Han.

15 According to Li Xian's commentary to Zhang Kai's biography in the *Hou Hanshu*, the Five Officials are the 'Grand Tutor, Grand Commandant, Minister Over the Masses, Minister of Works and General-in-chief.'

16 The 'Xiaoxianguo shijia' in the *Shiji* does not have the line 'not be required to have his name announced in an audience.'

17 The Japanese scholar Kamata Shigeo has spent a considerable amount of energy on this topic, although he has not pointed out in detail which part of which Daoist scripture has come from which part of which Buddhist scripture. See his *Dōzōnai bukkyō shisō shiryō shūsei* (Tokyo: Okura Shuppan, 1986). There is also some analysis of this kind in some of his other work.

18 Lü Simian, *Qinhan shi* (Shanghai: Kaiming shudian, 1947), vol. 2, p. 830.

19 For example, Tang Changru suspected that the Zhang Xiu killed by Zhang Lu was not the same person as the 'Zhang Xiu, the sorcerer of Ba Commandery' who rebelled in the first year of the *zhongping* reign period of Emperor Ling. See Tang Changru, 'Weijin qijian beifang tianshi dao de chuanbo' in *Weijin nanbeichao shilun shiyi* (Beijing: Zhonghua shuju, 1983), p. 222, footnote 1.

20 Lü Simian, *Qinhan shi*, vol. 2, p. 830.

21 This statement appears as the last sentence under the eleventh month of the fifth year of the *zhongping* reign period of the 'Annals of Emperor Ling' but in which month it occurred cannot be stated for certain.

22 For Liu Yan's proposal see his biography in the *Hou Hanshu*, 75:2431.

23 It says, 'Zhang Xiu was for the Way of Great Peace, Zhang Jue propagated the Way of the Five Pecks of Rice.' If we swap the two names around then it is correct.

24 *Hou Hanshu*, 8:349. The title 'Liu Ai's *Ji*' is an abbreviation of *Han Ling Xian erdi ji*, as it is recorded in the second chapter of the bibliographical treatise of the *Suishu*, where its author is given as the Palace Attendant Liu Fang, a mistake for Liu Ai. Liu Ai had been a Palace Attendant at the court of Emperor Xian and many of his statements and actions are recorded in citations from different books in Pei Songzhi's commentary to the *Sanguo zhi*. Liu Ai's *Ji* can be reckoned as a primary source for the daily life of Emperors Ling and Xian.

25 See the fifth section of the treatise on kingdoms and commanderies in the *Hou Hanshu* (the twenty-third chapter of the treatises) compiled by Sima Biao of the Jin supplemented by Liu Zhao of the Liang.

26 When I wrote my article 'Luan Ba and Zhang Tianshi' (in Li Fengmao and Zhu Ronggui eds, *Yishi, miaohui yu shequ – Daojiao, minjian xinyang yu minjian*

wenhua, Taipei: Zhongyang yanjiu yuan zhongguo wenzhe yanjiu suo, 1995), I
was inclined to agree with Tang Changru's opinion that the two Zhang Xius
were not the same person (p. 23, note 12).
27 *Sanguo zhi*, 8:263.
28 *Lishi* (Siku quanshu edn), vol. 681, 11:575–76.
29 Wang Xianqian, *Hou Hanshu jijie* (Taipei: Yiwen yinshu guan, photographic
reproduction of Wang's Changsha edn), 75:2a (p. 869). Discrepancies in the
chapter numbering of the *Hou Hanshu* derive from the different treatment editors have accorded the treatises that were taken from the *Xu Hanshu* and added
by Liu Zhao.
30 *Sanguo zhi*, 8:263.
31 *Hou Hanshu*, 75:2432.
32 *Huayang guozhi*, 2:107.
33 *Huayang guozhi*, 10*xia*:809.
34 See also *Sanguo zhi*, 39:983–4 and 43:1049–50.
35 *Hou Hanshu*, 75:2432, 9:375–6, *Sanguo zhi*, 31:865–70.
36 Lü Simian, *Qinhan shi*, vol. 2, p. 830.
37 Nine sentences have been left out here.
38 *Sanguo zhi*, 8:364.
39 *Huayang guozhi*, 10*xia*:809.
40 *Hou Hanshu*, 75:2432.
41 Liu Yan's biography in *Hou Hanshu* gives different characters for the courtesy
name Gongqi, 31:2435.
42 *Huayang guozhi*, 2:114.
43 *Sanguo zhi*, 8:263.
44 *Hou Hanshu*, 75:2435.
45 *Sanguo zhi*, 8:263.
46 *Huayang guozhi*, 2:114.
47 *Huayang guozhi*, 9:661.
48 *Jinshu*, 120:3023.
49 *Huayang guozhi*, 8:609.
50 *Sanguo zhi*, 31:867.
51 For similar examples, see Pei Songzhi's commentary to Hua Tuo's biography
from the *Sanguo zhi* (29:805) where he cites Cao Pi's *Dianlun* to the effect that,
'Gan Shi of Ganling was proficient at circulating *qi*, though old he appeared
young;' Li Xian's commentary to the biography of Gan Shi from the *Hou
Hanshu* citing Cao Zhi's *Biandao lun*; *Zhen'gao* (DZ 1016, 13:14a) on Sun
Hanhua; and Lao Nüsheng in the *Jinsuo liuzhu yin* (DZ 1015, 6:17a).
52 For a broad outline of the later *sanshi*, see *Dongxuan lingbao sanshi minghui
xingzhuang juguan fangsuowen* (DZ 445) compiled by Zhang Wanfu of the Tang.
53 *Shangqing huangshu guoduyi* (DZ 1294), 22a.
54 *Yuanchen zhangjiao licheng li* (DZ 1288), *shang*:18a.
55 *Dengzhen yinjue* (DZ 421), *xia*:8a.
56 *Hou Hanshu*, 86:2842–3.
57 *Huayang guozhi*, 4:349. The 'Annals of Emperor Ling' from the *Hou Hanshu*
says that this occurred during the fifth year of the *xiping* reign period (176),
however the record is not very detailed, just saying, 'in Yizhou Commandery
the Yi rebelled; the Grand Administrator, Li Yong, punished and pacified them.'
The 'Biographies of the Southern Man and the South-Western Yi' record this
event in the section on the south-western Yi and largely agrees with the *Huayang
guozhi*.
58 See *Hou Hanshu*, 75:2432–5 and *Sanguo zhi*, 31:868–870.

59 Meng Wentong, 'Daojiaoshi suotan,' *Zhongguo zhexue* 4 (1980), p. 309, however he does not mention where this citation can be found in the *Jinshu*. See, also, the record for *yongjia* 3 (309) in the reign of Emperor Huai in *Jinshu* 5:119.

60 *Hou Hanshu*, 72:2333.

61 *Huayang guozhi*, 2:118.

62 *Sanguo zhi*, 8:264.

63 *Sanguo zhi*, 1:46, under the ninth month of the twentieth year of the *jian'an* reign period.

64 There are not many records of the activities of the Yi kings in historical sources. Among those that can be consulted is the 'Fanzhang Zhang Chan deng timing' in Hong Kuo's *Lixu* (Siku quanshu edn), chapter 16, which aside from listing the Han government officials also has many other titles such as 'Duke of the Yi,' 'Commander of the Yi,' 'Lord of the Yi' and the 'Yi people' as well as names such as 'Xie Jie, the White Tiger King of the Yi' and 'Zi Wei, the White Tiger King of the Yi.' 'Fan' indicates Fan County in Shu Commandery. The biography of Liu Chan (Houzhu) from the *Sanguo zhi* records that in the tenth year of the *yanxi* reign period (which was the eighth year of the *zhengshi* reign period of King Qi of Wei, 247), 'in Liangzhou the King of the Hu, White Tiger Wen, along with Zhi Wudai and others, led the people to surrender. The General of the Guards, Jiang Wei, welcomed and pacified them. He moved them to Fan County' (33:898).

65 He ruled from Nanzheng. The 'Annals of Emperor Wu' in the *Sanguo zhi* says that, 'when the Duke's (Cao Cao's) army entered Nanzheng, they took all the precious jewels in Lu's treasury' (1:45). This was because Zhang Lu had sealed up the treasury before he fled into Ba. The biography of Liu Yan from the *Hou Hanshu* says: 'When Cao entered Nanzheng, he was very pleased' (75:2437).

66 *Hou Hanshu*, 75:2436. Zhang Lu's biography from the *Sanguo zhi* (8:263) reads, 'who guards the people' instead of 'who guards the Yi people.' Fan Ye seems to have been more accurate.

67 This inscription can be found in the 3rd chapter of Hong Kuo's *Lixu*. See also, my article 'Luan Ba yu Zhang Tianshi,' p. 27.

68 See Rao Zongyi, *Laozi xiang'er zhu jiaozheng* (Shanghai: Shanghai guji chubanshe, 1991), pp. 159–160.

69 *Zhengyi fawen tianshi jiaojie kejing* (DZ 789), 12a. The translation is based on that of Stephen R. Bokenkamp, *Early Daoist Scriptures* (Berkeley: University of California Press, 1997), p. 165.

70 *Zhengyi fawen tianshi jiaojie kejing*, 10a–b.

71 This is the commonly employed shorthand – the full name is *Dongxuan lingbao zhenling weiye tu* (DZ 73). Zhang Daoling is merely referred to as the 'Realised Man of Orthodox Unity, Master of the Law of the Three Heavens' and is the first person on the left hand side of the fourth rank (12a).

72 *Shangqing huangshu guoduyi*, 5b. The branch 'yin' is at two o'clock, the branch 'shen' is at eight o'clock.

73 *Shangqing huangshu guoduyi*, 13a–b.

74 *Shangqing huangshu guoduyi*, 2a.

75 *Shangqing huangshu guoduyi*, 13b.

76 *Shangqing huangshu guoduyi*, 13b–14a.

77 *Shangqing huangshu guoduyi*, 1a.

78 *Shangqing huangshu guoduyi*, 3a, 8a.

79 See the *Liushi jiazi benming yuanchen li* (DZ 1289) and the *Yuanchen zhangjiao licheng li* (DZ 1288). Current popular beliefs about the cycle of sixty Heavenly Stems and Earthly Branches can be found in almanacs like the ones on sale in

Hong Kong. They have the names of the sixty spirits in them but only a few preserve their original forms.

80 *Zhengyi fawen shilu zhaoyi* (DZ 1210), 2a. These terms are left untranslated in this section to reduce possible confusion.

81 *Zhengyi fawen shilu zhaoyi*, 2a–3b.

82 *Huayang guozhi*, 2:114.

83 *Taishang zhengyi fawen jing* (DZ 1204), 4b.

84 *Dengzhen yinjue* (DZ 193), 2:8b.

85 Such as, 'Shangqing Jade Emperor' (3b) and 'Primal and Inaugural Lingbao' (10a, 11a).

86 Namely, 'Mystic and Primal of Grand Clarity' (2:8b), and the Celestial Master, Female Master and Descendant Master (2:8a).

87 For the rubbings see *Wenwu* 6 (1965), p. 20; in *Laozi xiang'er zhu jiaozheng*, p. 126, Rao Zongyi discusses the section, 'do not harm the ascendant *qi*' and also has some discussion relating to *xuanyuan*.

88 See, 'Changsha chutu Nanchao Xu Fu mai di juan,' *Hunan kaoguxue jikan* 1 (1982); Wang Yucheng, 'Xu Fu di juan zhong Tianshi Dao shiliao kaoji,' *Kaogu* 6 (1993), pp. 571–575.

89 *Laozi xiang'er zhu jiaozheng*, p. 17. The translation is based on that of Bokenkamp, *Early Daoist Scriptures*, p. 96.

90 *Laozi xiang'er zhu jiaozheng*, p. 19, *Early Daoist Scriptures*, p. 99.

91 *Laozi xiang'er zhu jiaozheng*, p. 18, *Early Daoist Scriptures*, p. 98.

92 *Laozi xiang'er zhu jiaozheng*, p. 16, *Early Daoist Scriptures*, p. 96.

93 *Laozi xiang'er zhu jiaozheng*, p. 8, *Early Daoist Scriptures*, p. 82.

94 *Laozi xiang'er zhu jiaozheng*, p. 17, *Early Daoist Scriptures*, p. 96.

95 *Laozi xiang'er zhu jiaozheng*, p. 9, *Early Daoist Scriptures*, p. 84.

96 Wang Ming, *Taiping jing hejiao* (Beijing: Zhonghua shuju, 1960), p. 272 (*Taiping jing*, DZ 1101, 69:11a).

97 *Taiping jing hejiao*, p. 707 (*Taiping jingchao*, 9:82).

98 This is referred to in the 'Nansui' chapter of *Lunheng* cited above. It allocates *wang, xiang, tai, mo, si, qiu, fei* and *xiu* to the eight periodic changes of the year. Their progression follows the *Shuogua* of the *Yijing* – which came to refer to the positions of the 'Eight Trigrams of King Wen' – going clockwise. However, this begins with the trigram *gen* in the north-east. *Gen* represents 'Beginning of Spring,' it is the 'ascendant'. Following it is the trigram *zhen* which represents 'Vernal Equinox', it is the 'adjutant.' These changes are regular and although different from the account in the *Shuogua*, which begins with the trigram *zhen*, the order within the cycle itself is the same. Early on, such discussions relied on the cycles of the five phases, for instance in the 'Dixing' chapter of the *Huainanzi* it says, 'Wood is strong, water is old, fire is born, metal is captive and earth is dead,' or in the 'Xuanshu' section of Yang Xiong's *Taixuan* which says, 'Among the five phases, the one who has authority is the ascendant.' The 'Wuxing' chapter of the *Bohu tong* also uses similar language. From the Eastern Han on these correlations become even more complex and changed their relationships with the eight trigrams. See the 'bagua xiuwang' section of chapter two of the *Wuxing dayi* by Xiao Ji of the Sui.

99 *Taiping jing hejiao*, pp. 630–31 (*Taiping jing*, 116:2a); the equivalent passage in *Taiping jingchao* (7:33b), replaces 'subtle *qi*' with 'dead and captive *qi* (*si qiu qi*)'.

100 See *Taiping jing hejiao*, pp. 17 (*Taiping jingchao* 2:6a), and 274 (*Taiping jing*, 69:14a).

101 See *Taiping jing hejiao*, pp. 100 (*Taiping jing*, 43:2b), 178 and 217 (*Taiping jingchao*, 3:15b–16a and 4:10a).

102 There was a drought in 85. For the text of the memorial, see *Hou Hanshu*, 46:1551.

103 *Hou Hanshu*, 3:152.

104 *Bohu tung suzheng* (Beijing: Zhonghua shuju, 1994), 8:362. See also, Tjan Tjoe Som, *Po Hu T'ung: The Comprehensive Discussions in the White Tiger Hall* (Leiden: E.J. Brill, 1952), vol. 2, p. 550.

105 *Hanshu*, 21a:984–5.

106 For example, the first part of the 'Tangong' chapter of the *Liji* says that Yu the Great of the Xia honoured black, the Yin people honoured white, and the Zhou people honoured red. The commentary of Kong Yingda of the Tang cites the *Yuanming bao*, an apocryphon to the *Chunqiu*, and the *Jiyao jia*, an apocryphon to the *Yuejing*, to the same effect. This understanding can be seen in Xing Bing's Northern Song commentary to the *Lunyu* passage: 'Zizhang asked, "Can we know what will happen in ten generations' time?"' (Shisan jing zhushu edn), 2:2463.

107 The *Qianzuo du*, with Zheng's annotations, can be found in the *Yayu tang congshu* and the *Hanxue tang congshu*. For Hui Dong's comments, see *Hou Hanshu buzhu*, vol. 1, p. 54.

108 See also, He Yan's commentary to the *Lunyu*, compiled during the Wei of the Three Kingdoms, citing Ma Rong of the Eastern Han (Shisan jing zhushu edn), 2:2463.

109 For the first year of Duke Yin of Lu the *Gongyang* reads, 'the first month is the ruler', which is glossed as 'this is the Grand Unified Calendar' (Shisan jing zhushu edn), 1:2196. However, in the third and fourth years of Duke Yin it reads 'Spring. The second month is the ruler' (2:2203–4) while the seventh year reads 'Spring. The third month is the ruler' (3:2208). He Xiu of the Eastern Han in his *Jiegu* annotated the line 'Third year. Spring. The second month is the ruler', with 'The second and third months were both rulers. The second month was Yin's first month while the third month was Xia's first month'. This is also in accordance with the progression of *jianzi*, *jianchou* and *jianyin*.

110 The *Gongyang* explains the Three Calendars very clearly. Liu Xin loved the *Zuozhuan* but his father, Liu Xiang, studied the *Guliang*. In the biography of Liu Xiang in the *Hanshu* it says that Liu Xin had 'raised several difficulties for [Liu] Xiang on the *Zuozhuan* and Xiang was unable to find fault with his arguments.' However Xin's explanation of the Three Calendars relied on the *Zuozhuan* and the *Gongyang* being interdependent. The biography of Liu Xiang records that in the time of Emperor Cheng he presented an admonitory memorial which stated, 'The ruler must correspond with the Three Calendars.' Thus, on this point, the three commentaries to the *Chunqiu* agree.

111 *Zhengyi fawen tianshi jiaojie kejing*, 16b.

112 The actual year of Zhang Lu's death is not recorded in the official histories. *Zhen'gao* 4 says that, 'Lord Bao Ming [ie Mao Zhong] said, "Master Xu can now abandon his form and transform in profundity."' The original commentary reads, 'Zhang the Inherited Master was the general of Zhennan, he died in the twenty-first year of the *jian'an* reign period [216].' This may be the only record.

113 *Zhengyi fawen tianshi jiaojie kejing*, 14a–b; the translation is based on Bokenkamp, *Early Daoist Scriptures*, pp. 170–171.

114 See the 'Annals of Emperor Huan' in the *Hou Hanshu*, under 'Spring' in the first month of the eighth year of the *yanxi* reign period.

115 *Taishang zhengyi mengwei falu* (DZ 1209), 6b.

116 *Shangqing huangshu guoduyi*, 7b.

117 *Zhengyi fawen falu buyi* (DZ 1242), 20a.

118 *Santian neijie jing* (DZ 1205), 1:5b–6a.

119 *Sandong zhunang*, 7:6b.
120 Wang Bao's *Dongxiao fu* and *Shengzhu dexianchen song* can be found in *Wenxuan* (Beijing: Zhonghua shuju, 1990), 17:244–46 and 47:658–60. For his biography, see *Hanshu* 64*xia*:2821–2830. This Wang Bao, courtesy name Ziyuan, lived in the time of Emperor Xuan of the Han (r.73–48 BCE). Hagiographies of the immortal Wang Bao, courtesy name Zideng, who came from Xiangping in Fanyang, can be found in *Xianyuan bianzhu*, 2:13a; *Sandong qunxian lu*, 9:14b, 13:14b, 14:1a; *Lishi zhenxian tidao tongjian*, 14:8b; *Maoshan zhi*, 10:3b and *Qingwei xianpu*, 3b. The *Zhen'gao* (1:2b) refers to him as, 'King of the Xiaoyou Heaven of Pure Vacuity Wang Zideng.' His most complete biography can be found in the *Lishi zhenxian tidao tongjian* which generally follows the *Wangshi shenxian zhuan* of Du Guangting of the Five Dynasties, a work which is no longer extant. See also, Yan Yiping's *Daojiao yanjiu ziliao* (Taipei: Yiwen yingshu guan, 1974), vol. 1, pp. 9–13 which is taken from the *Lishi zhenxian tidao tongjian*. The *Sandong zhunang*, alone, mentions Wang Ziyuan. However, there was another Wang Bao historically whose courtesy name was also Ziyuan active during the Liang and Northern Zhou dynasties, see *Zhoushu* (Beijing: Zhonghua shuju, 1983), 41:729–33.
121 *Santian neijie jing*, 1:5b.
122 The periods of the 'Dadao jialing jie' and the *Xu Fu diquan* have already been discussed. For the *Nüqing lüling* see the *Nüqing guilü* (DZ 563), a treatise on controlling ghosts. The second chapter of this work begins, 'By order of the Most High Regulations of the Supreme Three Heavens of the Mystic and Primal of Grand Clarity' (2:1a); and chapter six lists the ghost masters of the five directions as Liu Yuanda, Zhang Yuanbo, Zhao Gongming, Zhong Shiji and Shi Wenye (6:2a–b). These five names turn up repeatedly in later Chinese mythology. In the last chapter of the Yuan dynasty *Wuwang fazhou pinghua* (which exists in a *zhizhi* period (1321–1323) edition) these names have been transformed into Shi Yuanhua, Zhao Gongming, Yao Wenliang, Zhong Shicai and Liu Gongyuan. Only Zhao Gongming's name has not changed.
123 *Santian neijie jing*, 1:5b.
124 *Sandong zhunang*, 7:6b.
125 *Wushang biyao*, 84:10b. A small amount of this chapter is preserved in the Dunhuang ms. S.5751, however it is not connected with this passage.
126 *Zhengyi fawen tianshi jiaojie kejing*, 20a–b.
127 *Zhengyi fawen tianshi jiaojie kejing*, 18a; the translation is based on Bokenkamp, *Early Daoist Scriptures*, p. 180.
128 *Zhengyi fawen tianshi jiaojie kejing*, 16b. The date was originally rendered as the seventh day of the first month of the second year of the *zhengyuan* reign period of Gaogui xianggong of the Wei.
129 *Taishang zhengyi mengwei falu*, 6a.
130 *Sandong zhunang*, 7:6a–b.
131 *Dongzhen huangshu* (DZ 1343), 1b–2a.
132 *Dongzhen huangshu*, 7b.
133 *Dongzhen huangshu*, 12b–13a.
134 Dong Zuobing, *Zhongguo nianli zongpu* (Hong Kong: Hong Kong University Press, 1960) vol. 2, p. 18.
135 *Santian neijie jing*, 1:7b; this translation, and those below, are based on those of Bokenkamp in *Early Daoist Scriptures*.
136 *Santian neijie jing*, 1:2a.
137 *Santian neijie jing*, 1:2b.
138 *Santian neijie jing*, 1:9a. See note 19 in Bokenkamp, *Early Daoist Scriptures*, pp. 228–29. For this event see also the imperial edict of the first day, *jimao* in

the cycle, of the fourth month of the second year of the *yongchu* reign period (421) in the 'Annals of Emperor Wu, 2' in the *Songshu*.

139 *Zhengyi fawen tianshi jiaojie kejing*, 20b.
140 *Zhengyi fawen tianshi jiaojie kejing*, 19b–20a.
141 *Santian neijie jing*, 1:5b; the translation is based on Bokenkamp, *Early Daoist Scriptures*, p. 215. The 'six heavens' are what people usually regard as the heaven of the ordinary world. The *Yunji qiqian*, 8:22b, names the six heavens as the Chixu heaven, the Taixuandu heaven, the Qinghao heaven, the Taixuan heaven, the Taixuancang heaven and the Taiqing heaven.
142 *Santian neijie jing*, 1:5b–6a; the translation is based on Bokenkamp, *Early Daoist Scriptures*, pp. 215–16.
143 *Santian neijie jing*, 1:6a; the translation is partly based on Bokenkamp, *Early Daoist Scriptures*, p. 216.
144 Cited at the beginning of section four of this article.
145 See, 'Yanshixian Nancai zhuangxiang Han Feizhimu fajue baogao,' *Wenwu* 9 (1992), 37–42; Wang Yucheng, 'Wenwu suojian Zhongguo gudai daofu shulun,' *Daojia wenhua yanjiu* 9 (Shanghai: Guji chubanshe, 1996), 267–301; Wang Yucheng, 'Donghan daojiao diyi shike Fei Zhi bei yanjiu,' *Daojiao xue tansuo* 10 (Tainan chenggong daxue lishixi daojiao yanjiu shi, 1997), 14–28.
146 See the citation from the *Hanguan* in the commentary of Liu Zhao of the Liang to the third part of the treatise on the hundred officials from the *Xu Hanshu* under the entry for the Prefect of the Lateral Courts. After the line: 'Expectant Appointee: five persons,' the *Hanguan mulu* says: 'Women presented from the kingdoms and commanderies who were yet to be viewed by the Emperor awaited their orders in the Lateral Courts, the officials were therefore known as Expectant Appointees' (Hui Dong, *Hou Hanshu buzhu* (Congshu jicheng edn), vol. 12, 24:1296).
147 The second part of the treatise on the kingdoms and commanderies from the *Xu Hanshu* reads, 'Emperor Gao established it but Emperor Huan, in the second year of the *jianhe* reign period [148], changed it to Ganling.'
148 *Hou Hanshu*, 6:272.
149 *Wushang biyao*, 9:7a.
150 *Yuanshi wulao chishu yupian zhenwen tianshu jing* (DZ 22), 3:3a.
151 In the paragraph cited here from the *Daozang* edition the character *ling* is mistakenly printed as *tai*, but is correct elsewhere.
152 *Yuanshi wulao chishu yupian zhenwen tianshu jing*, 3:2a.
153 See the treatise on the Feng and Shan sacrifices in the *Shiji* and the first part of the treatise on the state sacrifices in the *Hanshu*. In the latter, 'taiyi' is rendered using a different character for *tai*.
154 *Hou Hanshu*, 78:2535.
155 *Hou Hanshu*, 57:1841.
156 *Hou Hanshu*, 11:479–80.
157 For Liu Zhang, see material related to Qi Daohuiwang Fei in the Gao Wuwang biographies in the *Hanshu* (38:1987–2003) and the first section of the third part of the 'Wangzi Hou biao' (15:427–482). The Marquis of Zhu Xu was enfeoffed as King Jing of Chengyang in the second year of Emperor Wen.
158 *Hou Hanshu*, 76:2469.
159 See the biographies of Huangfu Song and Zhang Rang in the *Hou Hanshu* 71:2299–306 and 78:2534–537, respectively.
160 *Sanguo zhi*, 1:4.
161 See the entry for Zhonghuang Taiyi in Shen Zengzhi, *Hairilou zhacong* (Beijing: Zhonghuan shuju, 1962), 6:234–5.
162 *Hou Hanshu*, 57:1841.

163 Apart from the biography of Luan Ba, see also the fourth part of the treatise on the five phases from the *Xu Hanshu*. The entry regarding the earthquake in the capital occurs in the ninth month of the first year of the *jiankang* reign period (*Hou Hanshu, treatises,* 16:3330–331).

164 *Lishi zhenxian tidao tongjian,* 18:4b–5a.

165 Emperor Chong had not been on the throne a year when he died. Emperor Zhi who followed did not last a year and a half before Liang Ji poisoned him. See the annals of Emperors Shun, Chong and Zhi in the *Hou Hanshu*.

166 *Hou Hanshu,* 57:1841.

167 See the fourth part of the treatise on the commanderies and kingdoms from the *Xu Hanshu* in the *Hou Hanshu, treatises,* 22:3482–843 and Liu's biography in the *Sanguo zhi,* 39:980–82.

168 *Xianyuan bianzhu,* 2:4a, *Yunji qiqian,* 85:11a–b (under the entry *bingjie*), and 109:21a–22a, and *Sandong qunxian lu,* 3:15a.

169 *Lishi zhenxian tidao tongjian,* 15:3a.

170 *Lishi zhenxian tidao tongjian,* 15:5a.

171 See the entry 'Shenxian zhuan' in the *Siku quanshu zongmu,* 146; the entry for the '*Shenxian zhuan* in ten chapters' in Yu Jiaxi, *Siku tiyao bianzheng* (Taipei: Yiwen yinshuguan, photolithographic edn), 19:1212–1213.

172 Cited in *Zhen'gao,* 14:18b.

173 *Yunji qiqian,* 85:12a.

174 *Hou Hanshu,* 57:1839.

175 *Hou Hanshu,* 67:2202.

176 *Huayang guozhi,* 2:114.

177 *Dongxuan lingbao zhenling weiye tu,* 1a.

178 *Shangqing dongtian sanwu jin'gang xuanlu yijing,* 20b.

179 *Shangqing dongtian sanwu jin'gang xuanlu yijing,* 9a–10b.

180 *Taishang laojun hunyuan sanbu fu, zhong*:21a.

181 *Zhengyi fawen jing zhangguan pin* (DZ 1218), *contents,* 1a–2b.

182 *Zhengyi fawen jing zhangguan pin,* 1:1b.

183 *Zhengyi fawen jing zhangguan pin,* 1:10b.

184 *Zhengyi fawen jing zhangguan pin,* 2:8a.

185 *Zhengyi fawen jing zhangguan pin,* 2:14a.

186 *Zhengyi fawen jing zhangguan pin,* 3:3a.

187 *Zhengyi fawen jing zhangguan pin,* 2:19a.

188 *Zhengyi fawen jing zhangguan pin,* 2:18a.

189 *Taishang zhengyi mengwei falu,* 4a, 6a, 8b, 11b, 17a, etc.

190 *Taishang sanwu zhengyi mengwei lu,* 5:15b. The two lines cited here occur in the fifteenth register: 'Taishang zhengyi jiutian bingfu lu.' This collection has six chapters altogether, with a total of twenty-four registers. The names of these registers are not vital for this paper so I have omitted them to avoid over-elaboration.

191 *Taishang sanwu zhengyi mengwei yuelu jiaoyi,* 7b.

192 *Taishang sanwu zhengyi mengwei lu,* 1:2a, 3b, 5a, 6b, etc.

193 *Hou Hanshu, treatises,* 24:2564.

194 *Zhengyi fawen jing zhangguan pin,* 1:16a.

195 The three heavens are the Qingwei heaven, Yuyu heaven and the Dachi – or Great Red – heaven. The third section of this paper cited the *Zhengyi fawen shilu zhaoyi* in this regard. Meng Anpai's *Daojiao yishu,* 7, on 'hunyuan' cites the *Taizhen ke* to the effect that 'the Daluo [heaven] produces the Mystic, Primal and Inaugural *qi*s which transform into the Heavens of the Three Clarities. The first is called the Qingwei Heaven, the territory of Jade Clarity, which comes into being through the Inaugural *qi*; the second is called the Yuyu Heaven, the

territory of Upper Clarity, which comes into being through the Primal *qi*; the third is called the Dachi Heaven, the territory of Grand Clarity, which comes into being through the Mystic *qi*' (7:5b). See also, *Yunji qiqian*, 3:4b–5a which, in addition, refers to the three Lords: Heavenly Jewel, Numinous Jewel and Spirit Jewel.

196 *Taishang sanwu zhengyi mengwei lu*, 2:9a–13b.
197 In the *Taishang sanwu zhengyi mengwei lu* there are nine entries in three pages (2:13b–14b).
198 *Taishang zhengyi mengwei falu*, 25a.
199 *Taishang sanwu zhengyi mengwei lu*, 1:1b.
200 *Shoulu cidi faxin yi* (DZ 1244), 14a.
201 *Taishang sanwu zhengyi mengwei lu*, 4:1b.
202 For the two place names mentioned, see the fifth section of the geographical treatise of the *Songshi* (Beijing: Zhonghua shuju, 1977), 89:2220–221. *Taishang sanwu zhengyi mengwei lu*, 6:3b.
203 *Taishang zhengyi mengwei falu*, 28a.
204 *Taishang zhengyi mengwei falu*, 26b.
205 *Taishang zhengyi mengwei falu*, 29b.
206 *Taishang zhengyi mengwei falu*, 11b, 21b, 29b, 34a–b, 38b.
207 See *Baopuzi* (DZ 1185), 4:13b, 11:18a, 17:20a, 18:2a, 19:4a and 20:7b.
208 *Hou Hanshu*, 42:1428.
209 See Wang Shumin's 'Huanglao kao' in his *Zhuangxue guankui* (Taipei: Yiwen yinshuguan, 1978), pp. 159–75.
210 *Taishang zhengyi zhougui jing*, 2b.
211 *Taishang sanwu zhengyi mengwei lu*, 6:15a.
212 'Zhonghuang Taiyi' is sometimes written with different characters.
213 *Shangqing daolei shixiang*, 1:5b.
214 *Shangqing dadong zhenjing*, 5:20b.
215 *Dadong yujing*, xia:27a.
216 *Dadong yujing*, shang:23a.
217 See my article 'Xu Xun and Lan Gong' in *Hefengtang wenji* (Shanghai: Shanghai guji chubanshe, 1991), vol. 2, pp. 714–52.
218 *Dadong yujing*, xia:15a.
219 *Dadong yujing*, xia:17a.
220 *Dadong yujing*, xia:7b.
221 *Dadong yujing*, shang:18b.
222 *Dadong yujing*, xia:26a.
223 *Dadong yujing*, xia:15a, 17a.
224 *Taishang sanwu zhengyi mengwei lu*, 2:13b.
225 *Taishang sanwu zhengyi mengwei lu*, 2:13b–14b.
226 *Taishang sanwu zhengyi mengwei lu*, 2:9a–13b.
227 See Wang Ming's 'Huangting jing kao' in his *Daojia he daojiao sixiang yanjiu* (Chongqing: Zhongguo shehui kexue chubanshe, 1984), 324–71.
228 *Taishang sanwu zhengyi mengwei lu*, 2:9a.
229 *Taishang sanwu zhengyi mengwei lu*, 2:15b.
230 *Taishang sanwu zhengyi mengwei lu*, 2:16a–b.
231 *Hou Hanshu*, treatises, 26:3594.
232 *Wenxuan*, 2:21a. This commentary is to the line, 'They send out the warriors of Central Yellow, the peer of Xia Yu and Wu Huo.' In his commentary to the line 'I shall seize the striped tiger and challenge the elephant,' from Zhang Heng's 'Sixuan fu,' Li also cites this passage (15:2b). These translations are based on those of David R. Knechtges, *Wen Xuan or Selections of Refined Literature* (Princeton: Princeton University Press, 1982–1996), vol. 1, 220–21 and vol. 3, 108–09.

233 *Wenxin diaolong jiaozhu* (Yang Mingzhao ed., Shanghai: Gudian wenxue chubanshe, 1958), 41:264.
234 See the biography of Xue Zong in the *Sanguo zhi*, 53:1250–57.
235 *Taishang sanwu zhengyi mengwei lu*, 1:8a–9a.
236 *Taishang sanwu zhengyi mengwei lu*, 2:9a–14b.
237 *Taishang zhengyi mengwei falu*, 3a.
238 *Taishang zhengyi mengwei falu*, 5a–b.
239 *Taishang zhengyi mengwei falu*, 40a–41a.
240 *Taishang sanwu zhengyi mengwei lu*, 2:19a–b.
241 *Taishang sanwu zhengyi mengwei lu*, 6:2a–8b.
242 *Taishang zhengyi mengwei falu*, 9a–10b.
243 *Taishang zhengyi mengwei falu*, 21a–b
244 *Taishang sanwu zhengyi mengwei lu*, 2:19a, 6:27a.
245 *Zhen'gao*, 10:23b.
246 See the discussions of the eighty-nine scholars (including Wang Mang, Kong Guang, Ma Gong and Liu Xin) in the *Hanshu*, 25*xia*:1268.
247 *Taishang dongshen sanhuang chuanshou yi* (DZ 1284), 7b.
248 *Zhengyi xiuzhen lüeyi* (DZ 1239), 8a.
249 *Taishang sanwu zhengyi mengwei lu*, 6:6a.
250 *Taishang zhengyi mengwei falu*, 8b.
251 *Taishang sanwu zhengyi mengwei lu*, 1:13b.
252 *Zhengyi fawen jing*, 2:19b.
253 *Taishang zhengyi zhougui jing*, 6a.
254 *Zhengyi fawen xiuzhen zhiyao* (DZ 1270), 5a–b.
255 *Yunji qiqian*, 45:2a–5a.
256 *Yunji qiqian*, 45:7b.
257 *Yunji qiqian*, 46:7a.
258 *Yunji qiqian*, 45:18a.
259 *Dongxuan lingbao zhenling weiye tu*, 16b.
260 *Yunji qiqian*, 4:12b.
261 For the Little Lad Lord of the Eastern Sea see the *Shangqing dadong zhenjing*, 1:5a and also the invocations that begin the first chapter of the *Dadong yujing*, *shang*:1b–2a as well as *xia*:15b–16a.
262 *Yunji qiqian*, 4:13a.

CHARACTER GLOSSARY

Anu 阿奴
Anyang 安陽
Asheshi Wangnü Ashuda Pusa Jing
  阿闍世王女阿術達菩薩經
Ba 巴
Baduan Jin Fa 八段錦法
Bagua Xiuwang 八卦休王
Baihu Wen 白虎文
Baijun Sijiang 敗軍死將
Baimai 百脈
Baixue 白雪
Baiyuan 白元
Bajing 八景
Bajun Taishou Fanmin 巴郡太守樊敏
Ban Gu 班固
Bandun Manyi 板楯蠻夷
Bao Ming 保命
Baohuang 抱黃
Baopuzi 抱朴子
Baopuzi Neipian 抱朴子內篇
Beidi 北帝
Beidou 北斗
Beiwang 北望
Benming Fu 本命符
Benwen 本文
Bian 變
Biandao Lun 辯道論
Bianwen 變文
Biaozou 表奏
Biduowei 髀多衛
Biejie 別解
Bieshi 別史
Bingjie 兵解
Bingwu 丙午
Bo 伯
Bohu Tong 白虎通
Bu 部
Bugang 步罡

Buyi 不疑
Buzheng Daoshi 不正道士
Can 參
Cang 藏
Cao 曹
Cao Bolu 曹伯魯
Cao Cao 曹操
Cao Pi 曹丕
Cao Zhi 曹植
Cemian Tu 側面圖
Cha 察
Chan 禪
Chang Qu 常璩
Chang'an 長安
Changsheng Yuli 長生玉歷
Chaozhen Yi 朝真儀
Chen Baoguang 陳葆光
Chen Chong 陳寵
Chen Fan 陳蕃
Chen Ping 陳平
Chen Rui 陳瑞
Chen Shou 陳壽
Chen Shujing 陳叔敬
Chen Tiao 陳調
Chen Zhixu 陳致虛
Cheng 城
Cheng Taochui 成桃椎
Chengdu 成都
Chengfu 承負
Chengming 成明
Chengyang 城陽
Chi (Command) 敕
Chi (Fool) 癡
Chichi 池池
Chimei 螭魅
Chiqi 赤氣
Chishi Wall 赤石牆
Chixu 赤虛

254

Chizi 赤子
Chizi Zhi Fu 赤子之府
Chong 虫
Chong Fu 重復/複
Chou 籌
Chu (Drive Away) 除
Chu (Revealed) 出
Chu Sanzang Jiji 出三藏記集
Chuci 楚辭
Chukuang 觸壙
Chunqiu 春秋
Chunyang 純陽
Chushen 出神
Ciyin 次胤
Cong 賨
Cun (Gauge) 忖
Cun (Maintain, Preserve) 存
Cunsi 存思
Cunxiang 存想
Cuo 酇
Da Daojun 大道君
Da Ling Ji Shi Zhi Qi 大陵積尸之氣
Da Ming Daozang Jing 大明道藏經
Dachi 大赤
Dadao Jialing Jie 大道家令戒
Dadong Yujing 大洞玉經
Dadong Zhenjing 大洞真經
Dafan Tianwang 大梵天王
Dai 代
Daluo 大羅
Dan 丹
Dangqu 宕渠
Dangshen 黨參
Danlu 丹爐
Danshi 丹室
Dantian 丹田
Dao 倒
Dao Zhi Fu 道之父
Daoan 道安
Daochang 道場
Daoci 道慈
Daofa 倒法
Daojiao Lingyan Ji 道家靈驗記
Daojiao Xiangcheng Cidi Lu 道家相承次第錄
Daojun 道君
Daolang 道朗
Daoxue Zhuan 道學傳
Daoyin 導引
Daoyin Tu 導引圖
Dazhao 大召
De Taiqing Daoren Pin 得太清道人品
Deng (Amended Character) 等

Deng (Consort Dowager) 鄧
Deng Yougong 鄧有功
Dengzhen Yinjue 登真隱訣
Dianlüe 典略
Dianlun 典論
Dili 地吏
Dingling 丁零
Dixia 地下
Dixia Ji Teqing 地下擊特卿
Dixing 地形
Diyi Zunjun 帝一尊君
Diyu 地獄
Dong Qin 東秦
Dong Zhuo 董卓
Dongdi 東邸
Dongfang 洞房
Dongguan Hanji 東觀漢記
Donghai 東海
Donghai Xiaotong Jun 東海小童君
Donghan Shukan Wu 東漢書刊誤
Dongpingguo 東平國
Dongwang Fu 東王父
Dongxiao Fu 洞簫賦
Dongxuan Yuanshi Wulao Chishu Yupian Jing 洞玄元始五老赤書玉篇經
Dongyuan Shenzhou Jing 洞淵神咒經
Dongzhen Huangshu 洞真黃書
Dongzhen Taiji Beidi Ziwei Shenzhou Miaojing 洞真太極北帝紫微神咒妙經
Dou Shao 竇紹
Dou Wu 竇武
Du 度
Du Daojian 杜道堅
Du Gen 杜根
Du Guangting 杜光庭
Du Huo 杜濩
Du Qiao 杜喬
Duan Chengshi 段成式
Dujian 都監
Duling 都領
Duren Jing 度人經
E 惡
Erjing Jie 二京解
Erqian Shi 二千石
Ershisi Shengtu 二十四生圖
Fa 罰
Fajie 法戒
Fajing 法經
Faju 法句
Falu 發爐
Fan (District) 繁

Fan (Sanskrit) 梵
Fan (Violate) 犯
Fan Chong 樊崇
Fan Li 范蠡
Fan Ye 范嘩
Fan Ying 樊英
Fangfa 方法
Fangmatan 放馬灘
Fangshu Zhuan 方術傳
Fangxiang 方相
Fantai 反胎
Fanyang 范陽
Faxin 法信
Fayuan Zhulin 法苑珠林
Fei 廢
Fei Changfang 費長房
Fei Zhi Bei 肥致碑
Feng Shang 馮商
Feng Xian 馮羨
Feng Xu 封諝
Fengdu 酆都
Fengfa Yao 奉法要
Fengsu Tongyi 風俗通易
Fu 符
Fu Du Sanwu Zhangzou Chu Guanyi
 付度三五章奏出官儀
Fu Xi 伏羲
Fuchu Zhi Yao 復除之藥
Fukui Kōjun 福井康順
Fushu 符書
Fuzhai Weiyi 敷齋威儀
Fuzi 符字
Gan Shi 甘始
Ganling 甘陵
Gansu 甘肅
Gao Daokuan 高道寬
Gaodi Ji 高帝紀
Gaojiu 誥咎
Gaoping 高平
Gaozu Gongchen Houzhe Nianbiao
 高祖功臣侯者年表
Ge Chaofu 葛巢甫
Ge Hong 葛洪
Ge Xuan 葛玄
Gen 艮
Geng Yan 耿弇
Geshi Dao 葛氏道
Geshi 葛氏
Gong 宮
Gongqi 公祺 (Alternate Form, 公旗)
Gongsun Qiang 公孫彊
Gongyang 公羊
Gongzi 公子

Gu 蠱
Guan (Contemplate) 觀
Guan (Irrigate) 灌
Guan Ba 管霸
Guanghan 廣漢
Guanxi 關西
Guanzi 管子
Gui (Ghost, Demon, Name Of A
 Constellation) 鬼
Gui (Return) 歸
Guidao 鬼道
Guiyang 桂陽
Guizhu 鬼注
Guizu 鬼卒
Guliang 谷梁
Guming Chishi Mountains 鵠鳴赤石山
Guming Mountains 鵠鳴山
Guo Pu 郭璞
Guo Si 郭汜
Guo Xian 郭憲
Guo Zun 郭遵
Guxu 孤虛
Han 漢
Han Lingxian Erdi Ji 漢靈獻二帝記
Han Tianshi Shijia 漢天師世家
Han Yu 韓愈
Hanzhong 漢中
Hanzhong Zhi 漢中志
Hanzhou 漢州
Hao Suo 郝索
Haoli 蒿里
He 和
He Xiu 何休
He Yan 何晏
He Zhuo 何焯
Hebei 河北
Heisha Fu 黑煞符
Hengwen Dizibin 橫文帝子賓
Hong Kuo 洪適
Hongnong Shan 弘農山
Hongshui 汞水
Hou 侯
Hou Hanji 後漢記
Hou Hanshu 後漢書
Hou Hanshu Buyi 後漢書補逸
Hu 胡
Hu Jiu 胡九
Hu Qi Ming 呼其名
Hua 畫
Hua Qiao 華嶠
Hua Zheng 華正
Huagai 華蓋
Huaian 懷安

Huaifeng 徊風
Huainanzi 淮南子
Huan (Emperor) 桓帝
Huan Wen 桓温
Huang Chang 黃長
Huang Shi 黃奭
Huangchang Zi 黃裳子
Huangdi 黃帝
Huangfu Song 皇甫嵩
Huanghou 皇后
Huanghu 恍惚
Huangjing 黃精
Huang-Lao 黃老
Huangshen Yuezhang 黃神越章
Huangshigong 黃石公
Huangtian Shangdi 皇天上帝
Huangting 黃庭
Huangting Jing 黃庭經
Huasheng Shen 化生身
Huayang Guozhi 華陽國志
Huayin 華陰
Huguo Jiaohai Pin 護國醮海品
Hui Dong 惠棟
Hui Yuan 慧遠
Huiju Bidao 迴車畢道
Huizi 迴紫
Hun 魂
Hundun 混沌
Hunyuan 混元
Huo 域
Ji (Clan) 姬
Ji (District) 冀
Ji (Examine) 稽
Ji (Records, Annals) 紀
Ji (Records, Registers) 籍
Ji (Stem) 己
Ji Linzi 計林子
Ji Xianlin 季羨林
Jia (Family) 加
Jia (Section) 乙
Jia Long 賈龍
Jiang Wei 姜維
Jianggong 絳宮
Jiangnan 江南
Jiangyin 江陰
Jiangzhou 江州
Jianhe 建和
Jianling 奸令
Jianzhou 簡州
Jiawu 甲午
Jie (Binding) 詰
Jie (Disperse, Release) 解
Jie (Substituted Character) 借

Jiechu 解除
Jiegu 解沽
Jiejie 結節
Jielü 戒律
Jieshi 解適
Jietu 解土
Jiezhe 解讁
Jiji Ru Lüling 急急如律令
Jiming 雞鳴
Ji'nan 濟南
Jindan Zai Zi Xing 金丹在子形
Jindan Zhi Dao 金丹之道
Jing (Essence) 精
Jing (King, Luminous Spirits) 景
Jing Fang 京房
Jingang 金剛
Jingjun Yuanyang 景君元陽
Jingming 净明
Jingshen 精神
Jingyan 精延
Jingying 静應
Jingzhou 荆州
Jinjing 金精
Jinli 金醴
Jinlou 金樓
Jinmen 金門
Jinque 金闕
Jinren 金人
Jinshi (Recent Generation) 近世
Jinshi (Golden Chamber) 金室
Jinshu 晉書
Jinshui 金水
Jintang Xian 金堂縣
Jinye 金液
Jinye Jing 金液經
Jiu 咎
Jiudan 九丹
Jiudan Jing 九丹經
Jiude Zhi Guan 九德之冠
Jiujiang 九江
Jiulong Xian 九隴縣
Jiutian Zhi Qi 九天之氣
Jiuyi 九一
Jiyao Jia 稽耀嘉
Jizhuan 記傳
Junguo Zhi 郡國志
Juqu 沮渠
Kamata Shigeo 鎌田茂雄
Kamitsuka Yoshiko 神塚淑子
Kang Senghui 康僧會
Kao 考
Kobayashi Masayoshi 小林正美
Kong Guang 孔光

Kong Qiu (Zhongni) 孔丘 (仲尼)
Kong Yingda 孔穎達
Kou Qianzhi 寇謙之
Kou Zongshi 寇宗奭
Kouchi 口敕
Kui 揆
Kuizhou 夔州
Kun 坤
Kunlun 昆侖
Kuxian 苦縣
Lai Junchen 來俊臣
Lang Yi 郎顗
Lang Zong 郎宗
Langzhou 閬州
Lanlan 藍藍
Lao Nüsheng 老女生
Laojun 老君
Laozi Bianhua Jing 老子變化經
Laozi Huahu Jing 老子化胡經
Laozi Huahu Jing Xuange 老子化胡經 玄歌
Laozi Ming 老子銘
Laozi Xiang'er Zhu 老子想爾注
Laozi Zhongjing 老子中經
Laozi 老子
Le 樂
Li (Baneful Demon) 厲
Li (Clan) 李
Li (Passing Through) 歷
Li Gu 李固
Li Jiong 李駉
Li Jue 李傕
Li Sanzheng Ji 禮三正記
Li Shi 李勢
Li Te 李特
Li Xian 李賢
Li Xueqin 李學勤
Li Yifu 李義府
Li Yong 李顒
Liandu 鍊度
Liang 梁
Liang Buyi 梁不疑
Liang Ji 梁冀
Liangzhou 涼州
Lianshui 連水
Lianxing 練形
Lianzhi 鍊質
Liao 獠
Liezi 列子
Ligui 厲鬼
Liji 禮記
Lijia Dao 李家道
Lin Yuan 林轅

Ling (Command) 令
Ling (Emperor, Numinous) 靈
Lingbao 靈寶
Lingbao Jingmu 靈寶經目
Lingbao Wufu 靈寶五符
Lingbao Wufu Xu 靈寶五符序
Lingling 零陵
Lingtu 靈圖
Linlü Mountains 林廬山
Linqiong 臨邛
Linxian 林縣
Liquan 醴泉
Lishi 隸釋
Lishi Zhenxian Tidao Tongjian 歷世真 仙體道通鑒
Liu 留
Liu Ai 劉艾
Liu Ba 劉巴
Liu Ban (Eastern Han) 劉班
Liu Ban (Northern Song) 劉攽
Liu Boping 劉伯平
Liu Fang 劉芳
Liu Gongyuan 劉公遠
Liu Mangdang 劉芒蕩
Liu Mao 劉瑁
Liu Penzi 劉盆子
Liu Qin 留秦
Liu Tao 劉陶
Liu Ts'un-yan 柳存仁
Liu Wenshu 劉溫舒
Liu Xi 劉熙
Liu Xiang 劉向
Liu Xie 劉勰
Liu Xin 劉歆
Liu Xiuren 劉休仁
Liu Yan 劉焉
Liu Yi 劉顗
Liu Ying 劉英
Liu Yiqing 劉義慶
Liu Yu 劉裕
Liu Yuanda 劉元達
Liu Zhang 劉璋
Liu Zhao 劉昭
Liuding 六丁
Liudu Jijing 六度集經
Liufu 六腑
Liuhou Shijia 留侯世家
Liujia 六甲
Liujia Liushi Zhenhui Jue 六甲六十真 諱訣
Liutai 留胎
Liutian 六天
Liutian Guqi 六天故氣

258

Liuyi 六夷
Lizang 歷藏
Lizhi Muli 立制牡厲
Longhu Shan 龍虎山
Longyu Hetu 龍魚河圖
Lu (Emoluments) 祿
Lu (Record) 錄
Lu (Register) 籙
Lu Qinli 逯欽立
Lu Xiansheng Daomen Kelüe 陸先生道門科略
Lu Xiujing 陸修靜
Luan Ba 欒巴
Luhai yuke 陸海 客
Lunyu 論語
Luo Yao 駱曜
Luocheng 雒城
Luodong 雒東
Luosha 羅殺
Luoyang 洛陽
Lü 慮
Lü Chan 呂產
Lü Dongbin 呂洞賓
Lü Lu 呂祿
Lü Simian 呂思勉
Lüxing Bu Douxiu 履行步斗宿
Ma Danyang 馬丹陽
Ma Gong 馬宮
Ma Rong 馬融
Ma Shu 馬樞
Ma Teng 馬騰
Ma Xiang 馬相
Ma Yuanyi 馬元義
Mai Di Juan 賣地券
Mao Zhong 茅衷
Master Shangyang 上陽子
Matsūra Takeshi 松浦崇
Mawangdui 馬王堆
Meizhou 眉州
Meng 盟
Meng Wentong 蒙文通
Meng Xi 孟喜
Mian 兔
Mianzhu 綿竹
Mie 滅
Ming (Chirp) 鳴
Ming (Destiny) 命
Ming (Emperor) 明
Ming Sengshao 明僧紹
Ming Zhengyi Lu 明正一籙
Mingjing 明景
Mingmen 命門
Mingqi 明器

Mingtang 明堂
Miwu Jijiu Zhang Pu Tizi 米巫祭酒張普題字
Mixian 密縣
Moshi 末世
Mouzi 牟子
Mouzi Lihuo Lun 牟子理惑論
Mowang 魔王
Mo 沒
Mu 穆
Mu Changzhao 牧常晁
Mufu 墓父
Muli 牡蠣
Muqiu 墓丘
Muquan 墓券
Muzhu 墓注
Najia 納甲
Nandou 南斗
Nanhua 南華
Nanji Laoren 南極老人
Nanji 南極
Nansui 難歲
Nanzheng 南鄭
Nanzhong Zhi 南中志
Nanzong 南宗
Nao 猱
Nei 內
Neidan 內丹
Neiguan 內觀
Neiguan Jing 內觀經
Neihuang 內黃
Neijing 內境
Neipian 內篇
Neiye 內業
Nihuan Jing 泥洹經
Niwan Jun 泥丸君
Nuo 儺
Nüqing 女青
Nüqing Guilü 女青鬼律
Nüqing Lüling 女青律令
Ōfuchi Ninji 大淵忍爾
Pei 沛
Pei Songzhi 裴松之
Pei You 裴優
Peitai 培胎
Penglai Shan 蓬萊山
Pengzhou 彭州
Penxing Jing 本行經
Pingqi 平氣
Pingyang 平陽
Pizi 皮子
Po 魄
Pu Hu 朴胡

259

Pulu 譜錄
Qi (Pneuma) 氣 (Alternate Form 炁)
Qi (Dervish) 僛
Qi Rendao Zai 豈仁道哉
Qiang 羌
Qianqiu 千秋
Qianwei 犍為
Qianzuo Du 乾鑿度
Qie Jian 郄儉
Qijia Hou Hanshu 七家後漢書
Qin 親
Qinghao 清皓
Qingwei 清微
Qingxuan 清玄
Qingyang 青陽
Qingyue 清約
Qingzhou 青州
Qinhan Shi 秦漢史
Qiongzhou 邛州
Qipo 七魄
Qitou 魁頭
Qiu 囚
Qiyun 氣韻
Quting 渠停
Quxie Yuan 驅邪院
Ri 日
Richen 日辰
Rouzi 肉子
Ru Lüling 如律令
Runze 潤澤
Sanbao Lun 三報論
Sanchong 三虫
Sandai 三代
Sandong 三洞
Sandong Jingshu Mulu 三洞經書目錄
Sandong Qunxian Lu 三洞羣仙錄
Sandong Zhunang 三洞珠囊
Sanfa Song 三法頌
Sanguang 三光
Sanguang Fu 三光符
Sanguo Yanyi 三國演義
Sanguo Zhi 三國志
Sanlicun 三里村
Sanlüe 三略
Sanqi 三氣
Sanqing Tian 三清天
Sanshi (Three Cadavers) 三尸
Sanshi (Three Teachers) 三師
Sanshi (Three Generations) 三世
Santai 三台
Santian 三天

Santian Neijie Jing 三天内解經
Santian Zhengfa Shi Moshen 三天正法視魔神
Santong Li 三統曆
Sanwei Xuwu Bijing 三微虛無秘經
Sanyuan 三元
Sanzheng 三正
Sengyou 僧祐
Senlang 森郎
Shaanxi 陝西
Shan 山
Shan Shu 善書
Shangdang 上黨
Shangdi 上帝
Shangqing 上清
Shangqing Daolei Shixiang 上清道類事相
Shangqing Dongtian Sanwu Jingang Xuanlu Yijing 上清洞天三五金鋼玄篆儀經
Shangqing Huangshu Guoduyi 上清黃書過度儀
Shangqing Lingbao Dafa 上清靈寶大法
Shangshang Taiyi 上上太一
Shangshang Zhongji Jun 上上中極君
Shangshu Bailiang Pian 尚書百兩篇
Shanhai Jing 山海經
Shanxi 山西
Shanzhe Chenshi Ji Chang Ezhe Wu Jing Zi Shou Qi Yang 善者陳氏吉昌惡者五精自受其殃
She Jing 攝精
Shen (Body, Person) 身
Shen (Branch) 申
Shen (Inspect) 審
Shen (Spirit) 神
Shenfu 神符
Sheng 生
Shengjian 聖監
Shengzhu Dexianchen Song 聖主得賢臣頌
Shenshen 神身
Shenshui 神水
Shenxian Zhuan 神仙傳
Shenyao 神藥
Shi (Generation) 世
Shi (Substitute Character) 適
Shi (Inaugural) 始
Shi (Master) 師
Shi (Time) 時
Shi Wenye 史文業
Shi Yuanhua 史元華

Shier Lei 十二類
Shifu 師父
Shiji 史記
Shijie 尸解
Shijing 詩經
Shilu 十籙
Shilu Zhaoyi 十籙召儀
Shiming 釋名
Shimu 師母
Shiqing 始青
Shiyuan Tongzi 始元童子
Shizhe 使者
Shizhu 尸注
Shizi 尸子
Shou Xuanyi 守玄一
Shou Zhenyi 守真一
Shoulu Cidi Faxin Yi 受籙次第法信儀
Shouyi 守一
Shouzhang 壽張
Shu (Writings) 書
Shu (State) 蜀
Shuihudi 睡虎地
Shuogua 說卦
Shuowen 說文
Si (Death) 死
Si (Thought) 思
Si Qiu Qi 死囚氣
Si Sanqi 思三氣
Si Wangqi 思王氣
Si Wuzang Qi 思五藏炁
Si Yigong 思一宮
Sifen Lü 四分律
Sihai 四海
Siji 死籍
Sikong Gong 司空公
Siku Quanshu 四庫全書
Sili Xiaowei 司隸校尉
Siling 四靈
Silu 司錄
Sima Biao 司馬彪
Sima Chengzhen 司馬承禎
Siming 司命
Siming Shi 司命史
Sinian 思念
Sishen 私神
Situ Gong 司徒公
Siyi Gong 思一宮
Song 宋
Song Lian 宋濂
Songshu 宋書
Sou 叟
Su 俗
Su Gu 蘇固
Suan 筭
Sudāna 須大拏
Sufu 宿福
Sui 遂
Suiyue Chongfu Shi 歲月重復適
Sun Chuo 孫綽
Sun Hanhua 孫寒華
Sunü 素女
Susi 俗祀
Suzhe Zuihun 宿謫罪魂
Suzuki Hiromi 鈴木裕美
Tai 台
Taicang 太倉
Taichu 太初
Taidan Yinshu 太丹隱書
Taihang 泰行
Taihe Jun 太和君
Taiji Tu 太極圖
Taiping Dao 太平道
Taiping Guangji 太平廣記
Taiping Jing 太平經
Taiping Jingchao 太平經鈔
Taiping Qingling Shu 太平清領書
Taiqing 太清
Taiqing (Alternate Form) 泰清
Taiqing Jing 太清經
Taiqing Xuanyuan 太清玄元
Taishang 太上
Taishang Chu Sanshi Jiuchong Baosheng Jing 太上除三尸九蟲保生經
Taishang Dongshen Sanhuang Chuanshou Yi 太上洞神三皇傳授儀
Taishang Dongxuan Lingbao Sanyuan Pinjie Gongde Qingchong Jing 太上洞玄靈寶三元品戒功德輕重經
Taishang Huangsu Sishisi Fangjing 太上黃素四十四方經
Taishang Huangting Neijing Yujing 太上黃庭內景玉經
Taishang Laojun 太上老君
Taishang Laojun Hunyuan Sanbu Fu 太上老君混元三部符
Taishang Lingbao Laozi Huahu Miaojing 太上靈寶老子化胡妙經
Taishang Qishiwuguan Tongzilu 太上七十五官童子籙
Taishang Sanmeng Fushou Yi 太上三盟付授儀
Taishang Sanwu Chiguan Zhanxie Lu 太上三五赤官斬邪籙

Taishang Sanwu Zhengyi Mengwei Lu 太上三五正一盟威籙

Taishang Sanwu Zhengyi Mengwei Tianling Chiguan Zhanxie Lu 太上三五正一盟威天靈赤官斬邪籙

Taishang Xinchu 太上新出

Taishang Xinchu Laojun 太上新出老君

Taishang Zhengyi Mengwei Falu 太上正一盟威法籙

Taishang Zhengyi Tongzi Yi Jiangjun Lu Pin Diyi 太上正一童子一將軍籙品第一

Taishang Zhengyi Zhanxie Chilu 太上正一斬邪赤籙

Taishang Zhengyi Zhougui Jing 太上正一咒鬼經

Taishi 太始

Taisu 太素

Taiwei 太微

Taiwei Zhenjun 太微真君

Taixian 胎仙

Taixuan 太玄

Taixuan (Alternate Form) 泰玄

Taixuancang 泰玄倉

Taixuandu 泰玄都

Taiyang 太陽

Taiyi 太一 (Alternate Form 泰一)

Taiyi Shengshui 太一生水

Taiyin 太陰

Taiyin Xuanguang Yunü 太陰玄光玉女

Taiyuan 太淵

Tai 胎

Tan 探

Tang Changru 唐長孺

Tang Yongtong 湯用彤

Tangong 檀弓

Tao Hongjing 陶弘景

Taohai 桃孩

Taokang 桃康

Te 特

Tian 天

Tiandi 天帝

Tiangang Fu 天罡符

Tianguang 天光

Tianshi Dao 天師道

Tianshi Jiao 天師教

Tiansun 天孫

Tiantai Shan 天台山

Tianwen 天文

Tianyi Shengshui 天一生水

Tianzhu Shan 天柱山

Tianzun 天尊

Tingwei 廷尉

Tingzhang 亭長

Tiyao 提要

Tong 通

Tongbo Guan 桐柏觀

Tongbo Shan 桐柏山

Tongli 通理

Tongshen 通神

Tongshi 同時

Tongyang 通陽

Tongyin 通陰

Tongzi 童子

Tu 圖

Tui 推

Tujiu 土咎

Tuxiang 圖象

Tuzheng Xi Waixie 吐正吸外邪

Wai 外

Waidan 外丹

Wang 王

Wang Bao (Zideng) 王褒 (子登)

Wang Bao (Ziyuan) 王褒 (子淵)

Wang Chang 王長

Wang Chong 王充

Wang Fou 王浮

Wang Fu 王甫

Wang Huan 王渙

Wang Jian 王翦

Wang Jie 王玠

Wang Jingwen 王景文

Wang Jingzong 王景宗

Wang Jun 王濬

Wang Liqi 王利器

Wang Mang 王莽

Wang Ping 王平

Wang Renjun 王仁俊

Wang Sheng 王盛

Wang Weicheng 王維誠

Wang Wentai 汪文台

Wang Xizhi 王羲之

Wang Xuanhe 王懸河

Wang Yin 王英

Wang Zhi 王稚

Wang Ziqiao Bei 王子喬碑

Wanglai 往來

Wangzi Jin 王子晉

Wei 尾

Wei Qi 衛琪

Wei Sheng Ren Chu Yang Wei Si Ren Jie Shi 為生人除殃為死人解適

Wei Shuqing 衛叔卿

Weichu 未出

Weijing 微經
Weilü 尾閭
Weishu 緯書
Weiyang 微陽
Weiyi 威儀
Weiyin 微陰
Wenchang 文昌
Wencheng 文成
Wengui 溫鬼
Wenming 文明
Wenxin Diaolong 文心雕龍
Wenxuan 文選
Wenyan 文言
Wo Xi Ceng Wen 我昔曾聞
Wu (Empress) 武
Wu (I) 吾
Wu (Loathing) 惡
Wu (Non-Being) 無
Wu (Shaman) 巫
Wu (Stem) 戊
Wu Bu Zhi Qi Ming 吾不知其名
Wu Huo 烏獲
Wu Kang 呉伉
Wu Rongzeng 呉榮曾
Wu Yizong 武懿宗
Wu Zhe Tongyuan 吾輒同願
Wugu 巫蠱
Wuji Taishang Yuanjun 無極太上元君
Wuqi 五氣
Wushang 無上
Wushang Biyao 無上秘要
Wushi 巫師
Wutou Huaijun 無頭壞軍
Wuwan 烏丸
Wuxing Dayi 五行大義
Wuxing Wuming 無形無名
Wuxing 五行
Wuying 無英
Wuzang 五藏
Wuzhi Ji 伍之籍
Xi Chao 郗超
Xi Hui 郗回
Xi Jian (Dianlun) 郗儉
Xi Jian (Xi Hui's Father) 郗鑒
Xi Wu 犀武
Xi Yin (Fanghui) 郗愔 (方回)
Xia Fu 夏馥
Xia Lan 遐覽
Xia Yu 夏育
Xiang (Adjutant) 相
Xiang (Image) 象
Xiang (Mark on the Body) 相

Xiang Kai 襄楷
Xiang'er 想爾
Xiangping 襄平
Xiangzhou 相州
Xianxian Shinü Zongzan 先賢上女總贊
Xiao He 蕭何
Xiao Ji 蕭吉
Xiaodao Lun 笑道論
Xiaoshen 小神
Xiaoxianguo Shijia 蕭相國世家
Xici Commentary 繫辭傅
Xie (Perverse) 邪
Xie (Valley) 斜
Xie Changqi 協昌期
Xie Chen 謝沈
Xie Cheng 謝承
Xie Jie 謝節
Xijing Fu 西京賦
Xin 心
Xinchu Laojun 新出老君
Xing 性
Xing Bing 邢昺
Xingjin 行禁
Xingming 性命
Xingqi 行氣
Xingshi 行尸
Xingshi Zougu 行尸走骨
Xingyuanfu 興元府
Xiongnu 匈奴
Xiongxie Zhi Qi 凶邪之氣
Xiping 熹平
Xiu (Extended) 休
Xiu (Lodging) 宿
Xiwang Mu 西王母
Xixian 西縣
Xu (All) 徐
Xu (Constellation) 虛
Xu (Master) 許
Xu (The Disciple Of The Three
    Heavens) 徐
Xu Feng 徐奉
Xu Fu Diquan 徐副地券
Xu Hanshu 續漢書
Xu Heshui Qing 須河水清
Xu Mi 許謐
Xu Xuanzhi 徐玄之
Xu Xun 許遜
Xu Zhu 徐翥
Xuan 玄
Xuan Yuan 軒轅
Xuancheng 宣城
Xuanlao 玄老

Xuanzhu 玄珠
Xue Ying 薛瑩
Xunzi 荀子
Xutuoluo 须陀羅
Yan Ji 顏幾
Yan Pengzu 嚴彭祖
Yan Pu 閻圃
Yan Zhitui 顏氏推
Yang Feng 楊奉
Yang Xiong 楊雄
Yangjia 陽嘉
Yangling 陽陵
Yangmen 陽門
Yan'gong 言功
Yangping 陽平
Yangping Pass 陽平關
Yangping Zhi 陽平治
Yanshi 偃師
Yanshi Jiaxun 顏氏家訓
Yanyu 偃玉
Yanzhou 兗州
Yao (Demonaical) 妖
Yao (Medicine) 藥
Yao Jingxin 樂淨信
Yao Wenliang 姚文亮
Yao Zhiyin 姚之駰
Yaojiu 藥酒
Yaowu 妖巫
Ye 葉
Yelian Zhi Shui 冶鍊之水
Yellow Emperor 黃帝
Yeshen 野神
Yi (One) 一
Yi (People) 夷
Yicheng 宜城
Yichu 已出
Yijing (Book Of Changes) 易經
Yijing (Translator) 義淨
Yili 儀禮
Yima 意馬
Yin (Branch) 寅
Yin (Print) 印
Yindao 陰道
Ying Shao 應劭
Ying'er 嬰兒
Yingmeng 應夢
Yinsi 淫祀
Yiqie Chi 一切持
Yizhou 益州
Yongchang 永昌
You 有
You Ren Zhi Xing Wu Ren Zhi Qing
  有人之形無人之情

You Zhi Yiwei Li Wu Zhi Yiwei
  Yong 有之以為利無之以為用
Youguan 幽關
Youming Lu 幽明錄
Youshi 幽室
Youxuan Zhenren 右玄真人
Youyang Zazu 酉陽雜俎
Yu 禹
Yu Huan 魚豢
Yu The Great 大禹
Yuan 元
Yuan Can 袁粲
Yuan Shansong 袁山松
Yuan Yue 袁約
Yuanbao 元胞
Yuanchen Zhangjiao Lichengli 元辰章
  醮立成曆
Yuanfu 元夫
Yuanguang Taiyi Jun 元光太一君
Yuanjing 元精
Yuanming Bao 元命苞
Yuanmu 元母
Yuanqi 元氣
Yuanshi Shangdi 元始上帝
Yuanshi Tianzun 元始天尊
Yuanshi Wulao Chishu Yupian
  Zhenwen Tianshu Jing 元始五老赤書
  玉篇真文天書經
Yubao 育胞
Yuchi 玉池
Yudao Lun 喻道論
Yue 約
Yuejing 樂經
Yuejun Ziguang 月君子光
Yuesang 樂喪
Yuji Jiangjun 游擊將軍
Yujiang 玉漿
Yujue 玉訣
Yunji Qiqian 雲笈七籤
Yunmeng 雲夢
Yuntai Zhizhong Neilu 雲台治中内錄
Yunü 玉女
Yuqing 玉清
Yushi Mingyan 喻世明言
Yuye 玉液
Yuying 玉英
Yuyu 禹餘
Yuzhang 豫章
Zaju 雜劇
Zang 葬
Zansong 讚頌
Zazhu Jiejing 雜著捷徑
Zhai (Dwelling) 宅

Zhai (Purification) 齋
Zhang 章
Zhang Ba 張霸
Zhang Buyi 張不疑
Zhang Daoling 張道陵
Zhang Dashun 張大順
Zhang Dian 張典
Zhang Fan 張璠
Zhang Gang 張綱
Zhang Gao 張高
Zhang Guoxiang 張國祥
Zhang Hao 張皓
Zhang Heng 張衡
Zhang Jue 張角
Zhang Kai 張楷
Zhang Liang (Zifang) 張良 (子房)
Zhang Ling 張陵
Zhang Pu 張普
Zhang Rang 張讓
Zhang Shangying 張商英
Zhang Shao 張劭
Zhang Shujing 張叔敬
Zhang Tang 張湯
Zhang Tianshi 張天師
Zhang Tianshi Ershisi Zhitu 張天師二
   十四治圖
Zhang Tianshi Qishi Zhao Sheng 張天
   師七試趙升
Zhang Wanfu 張萬福
Zhang Xiu 張修
Zhang Yuanbo 張元伯
Zhang Yuqing 張宇清
Zhang Zhengchang 張正常
Zhang Zhong 張仲
Zhangguan Pin 章官品
Zhao Bu 趙部
Zhao Daoyi 趙道一
Zhao Gongming 趙公明
Zhao Guang 趙廣
Zhao Mengfu 趙孟頫
Zhao Sheng 趙升
Zhao Song 趙嵩
Zhaohun 招魂
Zhe 讁
Zhen 震
Zhen Wu 真武
Zhen'gao 真誥
Zheng (Orthodox) 正
Zheng (State) 鄭
Zheng Xuan 鄭玄
Zhengjiao 正教
Zhengtong Daozang 正統道藏
Zhengyi 正一

Zhengyi Fawen Falu Buyi 正一法文法
   錄部儀
Zhengyi Fawen Jing 正一法文經
Zhengyi Fawen Jing Zhangguan Pin 正
   一法文經章官品
Zhengyi Fawen Shilu Zhaoyi 正一法文
   十籙召儀
Zhengyi Fawen Tianshi Jiaojie Kejing
   正一法文天師教戒科經
Zhengyi Fawen Xiuzhen Zhiyao 正一
   法文修真旨要
Zhengyi Mengwei Lu 正一盟威籙
Zhengyi Xiuzhen Lüeyi 正一修真略儀
Zhenhong 真汞
Zhenling Weiye Tu 真靈位業圖
Zhenmu Wen 鎮墓文
Zhenmu Wu 鎮墓物
Zhennan 鎮南
Zhenqian 真鉛
Zhenshou 真受
Zhenwen 真文
Zhenwu Zhi Shi 真吾之師
Zhenxing 真形
Zhi (Fungi) 芝
Zhi (Substitute Character) 牴
Zhi Qian 支謙
Zhi Wudai 治無戴
Zhicao 芝草
Zhigui Shizhu 魃
Zhihui Dingzhi Tongwei Jing 智慧定志
   通微經
Zhiren 至人
Zhixia 指瑕
Zhong Hui 鍾會
Zhong Shicai 鍾士才
Zhong Shiji 鍾士季
Zhongdan 中丹
Zhongdou 中斗
Zhongguan 中官
Zhonghuang 中黃
Zhonghuang Zhenren 中黃真人
Zhonghuang Jing 中黃經
Zhonghuang Po 中黃伯
Zhonghuang Taiyi Shangdi 中黃太一上
   帝
Zhonghuang Taiyi 中黃太乙 (Alterna-
   tive Form 中黃太一)
Zhonghuang Xianren 中黃仙人
Zhonghuang Xiansheng 中黃先生
Zhonghuang Zi 中黃子
Zhongji Beichen 中極北辰
Zhongji Huanglao 中極黃老
Zhongmin 種民

Zhongshan 中山
Zhongshu 眾術
Zhongzhong Yuji 塚中游擊
Zhongzhu 冢注
Zhongzi 種子
Zhou Ju 周舉
Zhou Lizhen 周利貞
Zhou Xu 周栩
Zhouhou Beiji Fang 肘後備急方
Zhouli 周禮
Zhouliu 周流
Zhouyi Cantong Qi 周易參同契
Zhu (Invocator) 祝
Zhu (To Rule) 主
Zhu Fonian 竺佛念
Zhu Xu 朱虛
Zhuang 莊
Zhuangshan 莊山
Zhuangzi 莊子

Zhuanwen 篆文
Zhulian 注連
Zhumu Yushi 主墓獄史
Zhuo Mao 卓茂
Zhuolong 濯龍
Zhuzhi Mingmu 諸治名目
Zi Wei 資偉
Zidan 子丹
Zifang 紫房
Zifang Gong 紫房宮
Zigong 紫宮
Ziye 滋液
Ziyou 子游
Ziyuan 子淵
Zizhang 子張
Zuo Ci 左慈
Zuo Guan 左悺
Zuoxuan Zhenren 左玄真人
Zuozhuan 左傳

BIBLIOGRAPHY

DZ refers to works in the *Zhentong Daozang*, with the text number as recorded in
K. M. Schipper, *Concordance du Tao-Tsang* (Paris: École Française d'Extrême-
Orient, 1975).
T refers to works in the *Taishō shinshu daizōkyō*.

PRE-MODERN WORKS

Baopuzi neipian jiaoshi, Wang Ming (ed.), revised and enlarged edn, Beijing: Zhonghua
shuju, 1985.
Baopuzi shenxian jinzhuo jing, DZ 917.
Baopuzi neipian, DZ 1185.
Bawei zhaolong miaojing, DZ 361.
Bohu tung suzheng, Beijing: Zhonghua shuju, 1994.
Boyun xianren lingcao ge, DZ 932.
Chisongzi zhangli, DZ 615.
Chongxu zhide zhenjing, DZ 668.
Chu sanzang jiji, T 2145.
Dadong jinhua yujing, DZ 254.
Danfang xuzhi, DZ 900.
Daofa zongzhi tu yanyi, DZ 1277.
Dengzhen yinjue, DZ 421.
Dongxuan lingbao ershisi sheng tujing, DZ 1407.
Dongxuan lingbao sandong fengdao kejie yingshi, DZ 1125.
Dongxuan lingbao sanshi minghui xingzhuang juguan fangsuowen, DZ 445.
Dongxuan lingbao zhenling weiye tu, DZ 167.
Dongyuan shenzhou jing, DZ 335.
Dongzhen taiji beidi ziwei shenzhou miaojing, DZ 49.
Fayuan zhulin, T 2122.
Fengsu tongyi jiaozhu, Wang Liqi (ed.), Beijing: Zhonghua shuju, 1981.
Fo benxing jijing, T 190.
Foshuo taizi ruiying benqi jing, T 185.
Gaoshang dadong wenchang silu ziyang baolu, DZ 1214.
Genben shuo yiqie youbu binaiye posengshi, T 1450.
Gongyang, Shisan jing zhushu edn.
Gushen pian, DZ 252.
Han tianshi shijia, DZ 1463.
Hanshu, Beijing: Zhonghua shuju, 1983.
Hongming ji, T 2102.

267

Hou Hanshu buzhu, Hui Dong (ed.), Congshu jicheng edn.

Hou Hanshu jijie, Wang Xianqian (ed.), Taipei: Yiwen yinshu guan, photographic reproduction of Wang's Changsha edn.

Hou Hanshu, Beijing: Zhonghua shuju, 1982.

Huainanzi honglie jijie, Liu Wendian (ed.), Taipei: Taiwan shangwu yinshuguan, 1978.

Huangdi bashiyi nanjing zuantu jujie, DZ 1024.

Huangdi jiuding shendan jingjue, DZ 885.

Huangdi neijing lingshu, Congshu jicheng edn.

Huangting dunjia yuanshen jing, DZ 873.

Huangting neijing wuzang liufu buxie tu, DZ 432.

Huanzhen ji, DZ 1074.

Huayang guozhi, Chengdu: Bashu shushe, 1984.

Jinshu, Beijing: Zhonghua shuju, 1974, reprinted 1982.

Jinsuo liuzhu yin, DZ 1015.

Jinyi huandan yinzheng tu, DZ 151.

Laojun zhongjing, DZ 1168.

Laozi xiang'er zhu jiaozheng, Rao Zongyi (ed.), Shanghai: Shanghai guji chubanshe, 1991.

Lidai sanbao ji, T 2034.

Liji, Shisan jing zhushu edn.

Lingbao wufu xu, DZ 388.

Lishi zhenxian tidao tongjian, DZ 296.

Lishi, Siku quanshu edn.

Liudu jijing, T 152.

Liushi jiazi benming yuanchen li, DZ 1289.

Lixu, Siku quanshu edn.

Lu xiansheng daomen kelüe, DZ 1127.

Lunheng jiaoshi, Beijing: Zhonghua shuju, 1990.

Lunyu, Shisan jing zhushu edn.

Lüzu zhi, DZ 1484.

Nüqing guilü, DZ 790.

Pusa benyuan jing, T 153.

Sanbao lun, T 2120.

Sancai dingwei tu, DZ 155.

Sandong qunxian lu, DZ 1248.

Sandong zhunang, DZ 1139.

Sanguo zhi, Beijing: Zhonghua shuju, 1982.

Santian neijie jing, DZ 1205.

Shangcheng xiuzhen sanyao, DZ 267.

Shangqing changsheng baojian tu, DZ 429.

Shangqing dadong zhenjing, DZ 6.

Shangqing dantian sanqi yuhuang liuchen feigang siming dalu, DZ 675.

Shangqing dongtian sawu jingang xuanlu yijing, DZ 1390.

Shangqing housheng daojun lieji, DZ 442.

Shangqing huangshu guoduyi, DZ 1294.

Shangqing jinque dijun wudou sanyi tujue, DZ 765.

Shangqing jiudan shanghua taijing zhongji jing, DZ 1382.

Shangqing lingbao dafa, DZ 1221.

Shangqing qusu jueci lu, DZ 1392.

Shangqing shi dichen Tongbo zhenren zhen tuzan, DZ 612.

Shangqing tianxin zhengfa, DZ 566.

Shangyang zi jindan dayao tu, DZ 1068.

Shanhai jing jianshu, Chengdu: Bashu shushe, 1985.

Shenxian zhuan, Daozang jinghua edn.

Shiji, Beijing: Zhonghua shuju, 1959, reprinted 1985.

Shijing, Shisan jing zhushu edn, Beijing: Zhonghua shuju, 1979.

Shoulu cidi faxin yi, DZ 1244.

Shuowen jiezi duanzhu, annotated by Duan Yucai, Chengdu: Chengdu guji shudian, 1981.

Sifen lü, T 1428.

Siqi shesheng tu, DZ 766.

Songshi, Beijing: Zhonghua shuju, 1977, reprinted 1983.

Soushen ji, Beijing: Zhonghua shuju, 1979.

Suishu, Beijing: Zhonghua shuju, 1991.

Suwen rushi yunqi lun'ao, DZ 1022.

Taiping guangji, Beijing: Zhonghua shuju, 1994.

Taiping jing hejiao, Wang Ming (ed.), Beijing: Zhonghua shuju, 1960.

Taiping jing, DZ 1101.

Taiping yulan, Shanghai: Zhonghua shuju, 1960.

Taiqing jing tianshi koujue, DZ 883.

Taishang beiji fumo shenzhou shagui lu, DZ 1215.

Taishang chu sanshi jiuchong baosheng jing, DZ 871.

Taishang dongshen sanhuang zhuan shouyi, DZ 1284.

Taishang dongxuan lingbao sanyuan pinjie gongde qingchong jing, DZ 456.

Taishang dongxuan lingbao wuliang duren shangpin jingfa, DZ 93.

Taishang dongxuan lingbao zhihui dingzhi tongwei jing, DZ 325.

Taishang Laojun da cunsi tu zhujue, DZ 875.

Taishang Laojun hunyuan sanbu fu, DZ 673.

Taishang lingbao dongxuan miedu wulian shengshi miaojing (Dunhuang ms. P. 2865).

Taishang lingbao wufu xu, DZ 388.

Taishang lingbao zhicao pin, DZ 1406.

Taishang tongling bashi shengwen zhenxing tu, DZ 767.

Taishang tongxuan lingyin jing, DZ 859.

Taishang wuji zongzhen Wenchang dadong xianjing, DZ 5.

Taishang zhengyi fawen jing, DZ 1204.

Taishang zhengyi jie wuyin zhouzu bilu, DZ 1217.

Taishang zhengyi mengwei falu, DZ 1209.

Taishang zhuguo jiumin zongzhen biyao, DZ 1227.

Taizi Xudanu jing, T 171.

Tujing yanyi bencao, DZ 769.

Wenxin diaolong jiaozhu, Yang Mingzhao edn, Shanghai: Gudian wenxue chubanshe, 1958.

Wenxuan, Beijing: Zhonghua shuju, 1990.

Wushang biyao, DZ 1138.

Wushang huanglu dazhai licheng yi, DZ 508.

Wushang xuanyuan santian yutang dafa, DZ 220.

Wuwang fazhou pinghua (*zhizhi* period edn).

Xianyuan bianzhu, DZ 596.

Xiuzhen liyan chaotu, DZ 152.

Xiuzhen shishu, DZ 263.

Xiuzhen taiji hunyuan tu, DZ 149.

Xu taishi zhenjun tuzhuan, DZ 440.

Xuanlan renniao shan jingtu, DZ 434.

Xuanlu lüwen, DZ 188.

Xuanyuan shizi tu, DZ 163.

Xuanzong zhizhi wanfa tonggui, DZ 1066.
Yanshi jiaxun, Wang Liqi (ed.), Beijing: Zhonghua shuju, 1993.
Youyang zazu, Taipei: Taiwan xuesheng shuju, 1975.
Yuanchen zhangjiao licheng li, DZ 1288.
Yuanshi wulao chishu yupian zhenwen tianshu jing, DZ 22.
Yudao lun, T 2120.
Yunji qiqian, DZ 1032.
Yuqing wuji zongzhen Wenchang dadong xianjing zhu, DZ 103.
Yuyang qihou qinji, DZ 1275.
Zhen'gao, DZ 1016.
Zhengyi fawen falu buyi, DZ 1242.
Zhengyi fawen shilu zhaoyi, DZ 1210.
Zhengyi fawen tianshi jiaojie kejing, DZ 789.
Zhengyi fawen xiuzhen zhiyao, DZ 1270.
Zhengyi xiuzhen lüeyi, DZ 1239.
Zhoushu, Beijing: Zhonghua shuju, 1983.
Zhouyi tu, DZ 157.
Zhuanji baiyuan jing, T 200.
Ziran jiutian shengshen zhangjing, DZ 318.
Zongjing mulu, T 2146.
Zuozhuan, Shisan jing zhushu edn, Taipei, 1985.

MODERN WORKS

Akizuki Kan'ei, 'Rikuchō dōkyō ni okeru ōhōsetsu no hatten – kyōri tenkai tsuiseki no itsu shiron', *Hirosaki daigaku jimbun shakai*, 33, *Shigakuhen*, 55.
—— 'Sangen shisō no keisei ni tsuite – dōkyō no ōhō shisō', *Tōhōgaku*, 22 (1961).
Allan, Sarah, *The Shape of the Turtle: Myth, Art, and Cosmos in Early China*, Albany, NY: State University of New York Press, 1991.
—— and Williams, Crispin (eds), *The Guodian Laozi: Proceedings of the International Conference, Dartmouth College, May 1998*, Berkeley, CA: Institute of East Asian Studies, 2000.
Anderson, Poul, 'Talking to the Gods: Visionary Divination in Early Taoism (The Sanhuang Tradition)', *Taoist Resources*, 5 (1994), 1–24.
Barrett, T. H., 'Introduction', in Henri Maspero (trans. Frank A. Kierman Jr), *Taoism and Chinese Religion*, Amherst, MA: University of Massachusetts Press, 1981, pp. vii–xxiii.
—— 'The Origin of the Term *pien-wen*: An Alternative Hypothesis', *Journal of the Royal Asiatic Society* (third series), 2, 2 (July 1992), 241–6.
—— 'The Emergence of the Taoist Papacy in the T'ang Dynasty', *Asia Major* (third series), 7, 1 (1994), 89–106.
Baxter, William H., 'Situating the Date of the Lao-tzu: The Probable Date of the *Tao-te-ching*', in Livia Kohn and Michael LaFargue (eds), *Lao-tzu and the Tao-te-ching*, Albany, NY: State University of New York Press, 1998, pp. 231–53.
Beal, Samuel, *Texts from the Buddhist Canon, Commonly Known as the Dhammapada, with Accompanying Narratives*, London: Trübner and Co., 1902.
Besançon, Alain, *The Forbidden Image: An Intellectual History of Iconoclasm* (trans. Jane Marie Todd), Chicago, IL: University of Chicago Press, 2000.
Blacker, Carmen, *The Catalpa Bow: A Study of Shamanistic Practices in Japan*, London: Allen & Unwin, 1975.
Bodde, Derk, *Festivals in Classical China*, Princeton, NJ: Princeton University Press, 1975.

Bokenkamp, Stephen R., 'Sources of the Ling-pao Scriptures', in M. Strickmann (ed.), *Tantric and Taoist Studies in Honour of R. A. Stein*, Brussels: Institut Belge des Hautes Études Chinoises, 1983, vol. 2, pp. 434–86.

—— 'Ko Hung', in William H. Nienhauser Jr (ed. and comp.), *The Indiana Companion to Traditional Chinese Literature*, Bloomington, IN: Indiana University Press, 1986.

—— 'The Purification Ritual of the Luminous Perfected', in Donald S. Lopez Jr (ed.), *Religions of China in Practice*, Princeton, NJ: Princeton University Press, 1996, pp. 268–77.

—— 'The Yao Boduo Stele as Evidence for the 'Dao-Buddhism' of the Early *Lingbao* Scriptures', *Cahiers d'Extrême-Asie*, 9 (1996–7), 54–67.

—— with a Contribution by Peter Nickerson, *Early Daoist Scriptures*, Berkeley, CA: University of California Press, 1997.

—— 'Lu Xiujing, Buddhism and the First Daoist Canon', in Scott Pearce, Audrey Spiro and Patricia Ebrey (eds), *Culture and Power in the Reconstitution of the Chinese Realm, 200–600*, Cambridge, MA: Harvard University Press, 2001, pp. 181–99.

—— 'The Silkworm and the Bodhi Tree: The Lingbao Attempt to Replace Buddhism in China and Our Attempt to Place Lingbao Daoism', in John Lagerwey (ed.), *Religion and Chinese Society*, Hong Kong: Chinese University Press, 2004, vol. 1, 'Ancient and Medieval China', pp. 317–39.

Boltz, Judith, 'Opening the Gates of Purgatory: A Twelfth-century Taoist Meditation Technique for the Salvation of Lost Souls', in Michel Strickmann (ed.), *Tantric and Taoist Studies in Honour of R. A. Stein*, Brussels: Institut Belge des Hautes Études Chinoises, 1983, vol. 2, pp. 488–510.

—— 'Not by Seal of Office Alone: New Weapons in Battles with the Supernatural', in P. Ebrey and P. Gregory (eds), *Religion and Society in T'ang and Sung China*, Honolulu, HI: University of Hawaii Press, 1993, pp. 241–305.

Bumbacher, Stephan Peter, *The Fragments of the Daoxue zhuan*, Frankfurt am Main: Peter Lang, 2000.

Cedzich, Ursula-Angelika, 'Das Ritual der Himmelsmeister im Spiegel früherer Quellen: Übersetzung und Untersuchung des liturgischen Materials im dritten *chüan* des *Teng-chen yin-chüeh*', PhD dissertation, Julius-Maximilians-Universität, Würzburg, 1987.

—— 'Ghosts and Demons, Law and Order: Grave Quelling Texts and Early Taoist Liturgy', *Taoist Resources* 4, 2 (Dec. 1993), 23–35.

—— 'Corpse Deliverance, Substitute Bodies, Name Change, and Feigned Death: Aspects of Metamorphosis and Immortality in Early Medieval China', *Journal of Chinese Religions*, 29 (2001), 1–68.

Chavannes, Édouard, *Cinq centes countes et apologues*, Paris: Ernest Leroux, 1910–34.

—— *Le T'ai Chan: essai de monographie d'un culte chinois*, Annales du Musée Guimet, vol. 21, Paris: Ernest Leroux, 1910.

—— 'Le jet des dragons', *Mémoires concernant l'Asie Orientale*, 3 (1919), 53–220.

Chaves, Jonathan, 'The Legacy of Ts'ang Chieh: The Written Word as Magic', *Oriental Art*, 23 (1977), 200–215.

Chen Guofu, *Daozang yuanliu kao*, Beijing: Zhonghua shuju, 1963, reprinted 1985.

Ch'en, Kenneth K. S., *Buddhism in China: A Historical Survey*, Princeton, NJ: Princeton University Press, 1964.

Christin, Anne-Marie, *L'image écrite ou la déraison graphique*, Paris: Flammarion, 1995.

Cone, Margaret and Gombrich, R., *The Perfect Generosity of Prince Vessantara*, Oxford: Clarendon Press, 1977.

Creel, Herrlee G., *The Origins of Statecraft in China*, Chicago, IL: University of Chicago Press, 1970.

Darnton, Robert, *The Great Cat Massacre and Other Episodes in French Cultural History*, New York: Vintage Books, 1985.

Das Gupta, Kabita, *Viśvantarāvadāna, Eine Buddhistische Legende: Edition eines Textes auf Sanskrit und auf Tibetisch, Eingeleitet und Übersetzt*, Berlin: Freie Universität Berlin, 1977.

Delahaye, Hubert, 'Les Antécédents Magiques des Statues Chinoises', *Revue d'esthétique*, nouvelle série, 5 (1983), 45–53.

Demiéville, P., 'Preface', in Liu Ts'un-yan, *Selected Papers from the Hall of Harmonious Wind*, Leiden: E. J. Brill, 1976, vii–viii.

Derrida, Jacques, *Of Grammatology* (trans. Gayatri Chakravorty Spivak), Baltimore, MD: Johns Hopkins University Press, 1976.

Despeux, Catherine, *Immortelles de la Chine ancienne: Taoïsme et alchimie feminine*, Puiseaux: Pardès, 1990.

— *Taoïsme et corps humain: Le Xiuzhen tu*, Paris: Guy Trédaniel, 1994.

Ding Ruomu, 'Daojiao yu zhongguo hua lüelun', *Daojia wenhua yanjiu*, 9 (1996), 347–73.

Dong Zuobing, *Zhongguo nianli zongpu*, Hong Kong: Hong Kong University Press, 1960.

Drège, Jean-Pierre, 'Du texte à l'image: les manuscrits illustrés', in *Images de Dunhuang: dessins et peintures sur papier des fonds Pelliot et Stein*, Paris: École Française d'Extrême-Orient, 1999.

Drexler, Monika, 'On Talismans of the Later Han Dynasty', Paper presented at the Second International Academic Conference on Daoist Culture, Huanglong gong, Lefu Mountains, Guangdong, China, 27–31 December 1998.

Dudbridge, Glen, *The Hsi-yu Chi: A Study of Antecedents to the Sixteenth-century Chinese Novel*, Cambridge: Cambridge University Press, 1970.

Ebrey, Patricia Buckley, *The Aristocratic Families of Early Imperial China: A Case Study of the Po-ling Ts'ui Family*, Cambridge: Cambridge University Press, 1978.

— 'Introduction', in Rubie S. Watson and Patricia Buckley Ebrey (eds), *Marriage and Inequality in Chinese Society*, Berkeley, CA: University of California Press, 1991, pp. 11–14.

Eliade, Mircéa, *Images et symboles: essai sur le symbolisme magico-religieux*, Paris: Gallimard, 1952.

Erkes, Eduard, 'The God of Death in Ancient China', *T'oung Pao*, 35 (1940), 185–210.

Fairbank, John K., *China Perceived*, New York: Vintage Books, 1974.

Fang Guangchang, *Fojiao dazangjing shi*, Beijing: Zhongguo shehui kexue chubanshe, 1991.

Faure, Bernard, 'The Concept of One-practice Samādhi in Early Ch'an', in Peter N. Gregory (ed.), *Traditions of Meditation in Chinese Buddhism*, Honolulu, HI: University of Hawaii Press, 1986, 99–128.

Feng, H. Y. and Shryock, J. K., 'The Black Magic in China Known as Ku', *Journal of the American Oriental Society*, 55 (1935), 1–30.

Forte, Antonino, *The Hostage An Shigao and His Offspring*, Kyoto: ISEAS, 1995.

Fox, Robin Lane, *Pagans and Christians*, New York: Knopf, 1987.

Freedberg, David, *The Power of Images: Studies in the History and Theory of Response*, Chicago, IL: University of Chicago Press, 1989.

Fu Juyou and Chen Songchang, *Mawangdui Han mu wenwu*, Changsha: Hunan chubanshe, 1992.

Fukui Kōjun, 'Kashidō no kenkyū', *Tōyō shisō kenkyū*, 5 (1953), 45–86.

— 'Kashidō to Bukkyō', *Indogaku Bukkyōgaku kenkyū*, 4 (1953), 51–3.

Gombrich, Ernst H., *Aby Warburg: An Intellectual Biography*, London: Warburg Institute, 1970.

—— *Symbolic Images: Studies in the Art of the Renaissance 2*, Oxford: Phaidon Press, 1972.
Granet, Marcel, *Danses et légendes de la Chine ancienne*, Paris: F. Aloan, 1926.
Grey, Leslie, *A Concordance of Buddhist Birth Stories*, Oxford: Pāli Text Society, 1990.
Guo Moruo, 'You Wang Xie muzhi de chutu lundao 'Lanting xü' de zhenwei', *Wenwu*, 6 (1965).
Gyss-Vermande, Caroline, 'Les Messagers Divins et Leurs Iconographie', *Arts Asiatiques*, 46 (1991), 96–110.
Haloun, Gustav, 'The Liang-chou rebellion, 184–221 AD', *Asia Major*, second series, 1, 1 (1949), 119–32.
Harada Masami, 'Bokenbun ni mirareru meikai no kami to sono saishi', *Tōhō shūkyō*, 29 (1967), 17–35.
—— 'Minzoku shiryō to shite no boken', *Philosophia*, 45 (1963), 1–26.
Harper, Donald, 'The *Wu Shih Erh Ping Fang*: Translation and Prolegomena', PhD dissertation, Department of Oriental Languages, University of California, Berkeley, 1982.
—— 'A Chinese Demonography of the Third Century BC', *Harvard Journal of Asiatic Studies*, 45, 2 (1985), 459–98.
—— 'Resurrection in Warring States Popular Religion', *Taoist Resources*, 5, 2 (1994).
—— 'Spellbinding', in Donald S. Lopez Jr (ed.), *Religions of China in Practice*, Princeton, NJ: Princeton University Press, 1996.
—— *Early Chinese Medical Literature: The Mawangdui Medical Manuscripts*, London: Kegan Paul, 1997.
—— 'The Nature of Taiyi in the Guodian Manuscript *Taiyi sheng shui* – Abstract Cosmic Principle or Supreme Cosmic Deity?', *Chūgoku shutsudo shiryō kenkyū*, 5 (2001), 1–23.
Hawkes, David, *The Songs of the South*, Harmondsworth: Penguin, 1985.
Hayashi Minao, *Kandai no kamigami*, Kyoto: Rinsen shoten, 1989.
Hendrischke, Barbara, 'The Concept of Inherited Evil in the *Taiping jing*', *East Asian History*, 2 (1991), 1–30.
Holzman, Donald, 'The Wang Ziqiao Stele', *Rocznik Orientalistyczny*, 47, 2 (1991), 77–83.
Honda Wataru, *Hōbokushi, Chūgoku koten bungaku taikei*, vol. 8, Tokyo: Heibonsha, 1969.
Hucker, Charles O., *A Dictionary of Official Titles in Imperial China*, Stanford, CA: Stanford University Press, 1985.
Huntington, Richard and Metcalf, Peter, *Celebrations of Death: The Anthropology of Mortuary Ritual*, Cambridge: Cambridge University Press, 1979.
Ikeda On, 'Chūgoku rekidai boken ryakkō', *Tōyō bunka kenkyūjo kiyō*, 86 (1981), 193–278.
Jampa Losang Panglung, 'Preliminary Remarks on the *Uddānas* in the *Vinaya* of the *Mūlasarvāstivādin*', in Michael Aris and Aung San Suu Kyi (eds), *Tibetan Studies in Honour of Hugh Richardson*, Oxford: St. John's College, 1979.
—— *Die Erzählstoffe des Mūlasarvāstivāda-vinaya Analisiert auf Grund der Tibetischen Übersetzung*, Tokyo: Reiyukai Library, 1981.
Ji Xianlin, 'Zai tan futu yu fo', *Zhonghua foxue xuebao*, 5 (1992), 19–30.
Jiang Shaoyuan, *Le voyage dans la Chine ancienne, considéré principalement sous son aspect magique et religieux* (trans. Kiang Chao-yuan and Fan Ren), Shanghai: Commission mixte des oeuvres franco-chinoises, Office de publication, 1937.
Juhl, Susan, 'Cultural Exchange in Northern Liang', in S. Clausen, R. Storrs and A. Wedell-Wedellsborg (eds), *Cultural Encounters: China, Japan and the West*, Aarhus: Aarhus University Press, 1995, pp. 55–82.

Kalinowski, Marc, *Cosmologie et divination dans la Chine ancienne: Le Compendium des Cinq Agents (Wuxing dayi, VIe siècle)*, Paris: École Française d'Extrême-Orient, 1991.

Kamata Shigeo, *Dōzōnai bukkyō shisō shiryō shūsei*, Tokyo: Okura Shuppan, 1986.

Kamitsuka Yoshiko, 'Reihōgyō to shoki kōnan bukkyō – inga ōhō shisō o chūshin ni', *Tōhō shūkyō*, 91 (1998), 1–21.

—— 'Taihei kyō no shōfu to taihei no riron ni tsuite', in *Rikuchō dōkyō shisō no kenkyū*, Tokyo: Sobunsha, 1999.

Katō Chie, 'Rōshi chūkyō to naitan shisō no genryū', *Tōhō shūkyō*, 87 (1996), 21–38.

—— 'Tai no shisō', in Noguchi Tetsurō (ed.), *Dōkyō no seimeikan to shintairon*, Tokyo: Yūzankaku shuppansha, 2000, pp. 100–19.

Katsumura Tetsuya, 'Ganshi kakun kishinhen to enkonshi o megutte', *Tōyōshi kenkyū*, 26, 3 (1967).

Keightley, David N., 'The Religious Commitment: Shang Theology and the Genesis of Chinese Political Culture', *History of Religions*, 17, 3/4 (1978), 211–25.

—— 'Dead but not Gone: The Role of Mortuary Practices in the Formation of Neolithic and Early Bronze Age Chinese Culture, c.8000 to 1000 BC', Paper prepared for the Conference on Ritual and the Social Significance of Death in Chinese Society, Oracle, Arizona, 2–7 January 1985.

—— 'Early Civilization in China: Reflections on How It Became Chinese', in Paul S. Ropp (ed.), *The Heritage of China*, Berkeley, CA: University of California Press, 1990, pp. 15–54.

Kleeman, Terry F., 'Land Contracts and Related Documents', in *Makio Ryōkai Hakase shōju kinen ronshū, Chūgoku no shūkyō: shisō to kagaku*, Tokyo: Kokusho kankōkai, 1984, pp. 1–34.

—— 'Licentious Cults and Bloody Victuals: Sacrifice, Reciprocity, and Violence in Traditional China', *Asia Major*, 7, 1 (1994), 185–211.

—— *Great Perfection: Religion and Ethnicity in a Chinese Millennial Kingdom*, Honolulu, HI: University of Hawaii Press, 1998.

Kobayashi Masayoshi, *Rikuchō Dōkyōshi no kenkyū*, Tokyo: Sōbunsha, 1990.

Kohn, Livia, 'Taoist Insight Meditation: the Tang Practice of Neiguan', in Kohn (ed.), *Taoist Meditation and Longevity Techniques*, Ann Arbor, MI: University of Michigan, 1989.

Kominami Ichirō, 'Gan Shisui "enkonshi" o megutte', *Tōhōgaku*, 65 (1983).

Kyoko Tokuno, 'The Evaluation of Indigenous Scriptures in Chinese Buddhist Bibliographic Catalogues', in Robert E. Buswell Jr (ed.), *Chinese Buddhist Apocrypha*, Honolulu, HI: University of Hawaii Press, 1990, pp. 31–74.

Lagerwey, John, *Wu-shang pi-yao: Somme taoïste du VIe siècle*, Paris: École Française d'Extrême-Orient, 1981.

—— *Taoist Ritual in Chinese Society and History*, New York: Macmillan, 1987.

—— 'Deux écrits taoïstes anciens', *Cahiers d'Extrême-Asie*, 14 (2004).

Lai Chi-tim, 'The Opposition of Celestial-Master Taoism to Popular Cults during the Six Dynasties', *Asia Major*, 11 (1998), 1–20.

Lau, D. C. (trans.), *Mencius*, Harmondsworth: Penguin, 1970.

Ledderose, Lothar, 'Some Taoist Elements in the Calligraphy of the Six Dynasties', *T'oung Pao*, 70 (1984), 246–78.

Lee Cheuk Yin and Chan Man Sing (eds), *Daoyuan binfen lu [A Daoist Florilegium]*, Hong Kong: Shangwu yinshu guan, 2002.

Legeza, Laszlo, *Tao Magic: The Secret Language of Diagrams and Calligraphy*, London: Thames and Hudson, 1975.

Legge, James (trans.), *The Ch'un Ts'ew, with the Tso Chuen*, Chinese Classics, vol. 5. Hong Kong: Hong Kong University Press, 1960.

—— *Li Chi: Book of Rites*, New Hyde Park, NY: University Books, 1967.

Lévi, Jean, 'The Body: The Daoists' Coat of Arms', in Michel Feher *et al.* (eds), *Fragments for a History of the Human Body*, New York: Zone, 1989, pp. 105–26.

Lévi, Sylvain, 'L'Apramāda-varga. Etude sur les recensions des Dharmapadas', *Journal Asiatique*, 20 (Sept./Oct. 1912), 203–94.

Lévi-Strauss, Claude, *Tristes Tropiques* (trans. John and Doreen Weightman), New York: Penguin, 1984.

Lewis, Mark Edward, *Sanctioned Violence in Early China*, Albany, NY: State University of New York Press, 1990.

—— *Writing and Authority in Early China*, Albany, NY: State University of New York Press, 1999.

Li Fengmao, 'Dongxian zhuan zhi zhucheng ji neirong', *Zhongguo gudian xiaoshuo yanjiu zhuanji*, 1 (1979), 77–98.

—— and Zhu Ronggui (eds), *Yishi, miaohui yu shequ – Daojiao, minjian xinyang yu minjian wenhua*, Taipei: Zhongyang yanjiu yuan zhongguo wenzhe yanjiu suo, 1995.

Li Xueqin, 'Fangmatan jianzhong de zhiguai gushi', *Wenwu*, 4 (1990), 43–7.

Li Yuanguo, 'Lun daojiao fulu de fenlei', *Zongjiao xue yanjiu*, 2 (1997), 39–47.

Little, S., *Taoism and the Arts of China*, Chicago, IL and Berkeley, CA: Art Institute of Chicago and University of California Press, 2000.

Liu Cunren (Liu Ts'un-yan), *Daojiaoshi tanyuan*.

—— *Zhongguo wenxue shi fafan*, Suzhou: Wenyi shuju, 1935.

—— *Qingchun*, Hong Kong: Xingdao ribao, 1968.

—— 'Daozang keben zhi si ge riqi', in Sakai Tadao sensei koki shukuga kinen no kai (ed.), *Rekishi ni okeru minshū to bunka. Sakai Tadao sensei koki shukuga kinen ronshū*, Tokyo: Kokusho Kankōkai, 1982, reprinted in *Hefeng tang wenji*, Shanghai: Shanghai guji chubanshe, 1991, vol. 2, pp. 942–73.

—— 'Lun Daozangben Gu Huan zhu Laozi zhi xingzhi', in *Hefeng tang wenji*, Shanghai: Shanghai guji chubanshe, 1991, vol. 1, pp. 204–22.

—— 'Daozangben sansheng zhu Daode jing huijian', in *Hefeng tang wenji*, Shanghai: Shanghai guji chubanshe, 1991, vol. 1, pp. 223–471.

—— 'Daozangben sansheng zhu Daode jing zhi deshi', in *Hefeng tang wenji*, Shanghai: Shanghai guji chubanshe, 1991, vol. 1, 472–94.

—— 'Xu Xun and Lan Gong', in *Hefeng tang wenji*, Shanghai: Shanghai guji chubanshe, 1991.

—— 'Yiqian babainianlai de daojiao', in *Hefeng tang wenji*, Shanghai: Shanghai guji chubanshe, 1991, vol. 2, pp. 649–71.

—— 'Zhang tianshi de qinümen', in *Hefeng tang wenji*, Shanghai: Shanghai guji chubanshe, 1991, vol. 2, pp. 672–6.

—— *Dadu*, Tianjin: Baihua wenyi chubanshe, 1996.

—— 'Daojiao she shenma?', in *Hefeng tang xinwenji*, Taipei: Xinwenfeng chuban gongsi, 1997, vol. 1, pp. 231–40.

—— '*Xiang'er zhu* yu Daojiao', in *Hefeng tang xinwenji*, Taipei: Xinwenfeng chuban gongsi, 1997, vol. 1, pp. 281–337.

—— *Daojia yu daoshu*, Shanghai: Shanghai guji chubanshe, 1999.

—— 'Han Zhang tianshi shi bushi lishi renwu?', in *Daojiaoshi tanyuan*, Beijing: Beijing daxue chubanshe, 2000, pp. 67–136.

Liu Ts'un-yan, *Buddhist and Taoist Influences on Chinese Novels*, Wiesbaden: Kommissionsverlag Otto Harrassowitz, 1962.

—— 'The Compilation and Historical Value of the *Tao-tsang*', in Donald D. Leslie, Colin Mackerras and Wang Gungwu (eds), *Essays on the Sources for Chinese History*, Canberra: Australian National University Press, 1973, pp. 104–19.

—— 'On the Art of Ruling a Big Country: Views of Three Chinese Emperors', the 34th George Ernest Morrison Lecture in Ethnology, 1974, most conveniently consulted in *East Asian History*, 11 (June 1996), 75–90.

—— 'Traces of Zoroastrian and Manichaean Activities in Pre-T'ang China', in *Selected Papers from the Hall of Harmonious Wind*, Leiden: E. J. Brill, 1976, pp. 3–55.

—— 'The Taoists' Knowledge of Tuberculosis in the Twelfth Century', in *Selected Papers from the Hall of Harmonious Wind*, Leiden: E. J. Brill, 1976, pp. 59–75.

—— 'The Penetration of Taoism into the Ming Neo-Confucian Elite', *Selected Papers from the Hall of Harmonious Wind*, Leiden: E. J. Brill, 1976, pp. 76–148.

—— 'Lin Chao-en: the Master of the Three Teachings', *Selected Papers from the Hall of Harmonious Wind*, Leiden: E. J. Brill, 1976, pp. 149–74.

—— 'Lu Hsi-hsing: A Confucian Scholar, Taoist Priest and Buddhist Devotee of the Sixteenth Century', *Selected Papers from the Hall of Harmonious Wind*, Leiden: E. J. Brill, 1976, pp. 175–202.

—— 'Lu Hsi-Hsing and His Commentaries on the Ts'an T'ung Ch'i', *Selected Papers from the Hall of Harmonious Wind*, Leiden: E. J. Brill, 1976, pp. 203–31.

—— 'Yüan Huang and His Four Admonitions', *Selected Papers from the Hall of Harmonious Wind*, Leiden: E. J. Brill, 1976, pp. 232–56.

—— 'The Essence of Taoism: Its Philosophical, Historical and Religious Aspects', in *New Excursions from the Hall of Harmonious Wind*, Leiden: E. J. Brill, 1984, 117–44.

—— 'Wang Yang-ming and Taoism', *New Excursions from the Hall of Harmonious Wind*, Leiden: E. J. Brill, 1984, pp. 147–67.

—— 'Shao Yüan-chieh and T'ao Chung-wen', in *New Excursions from the Hall of Harmonious Wind*, Leiden: E. J. Brill, 1984, pp. 168–83.

— 'Wu Shou-yang: The Return to the Pure Essence', *New Excursions from the Hall of Harmonious Wind*, Leiden: E. J. Brill, 1984, pp. 184–208.

—— 'My Childhood and My Dreams', in *New Excursions from the Hall of Harmonious Wind*, Leiden: E. J. Brill, 1984, pp. 357–77.

Liu Zhaorui, '*Taiping jing* yu kaogu faxian de Han zhenmuwen', *Shijie zongjiao yanjiu*, 4 (1992), 111–19.

—— 'Zaoqi daojiao yongyin kaoshu', *Daojiao xue tansuo*, 8 (1994), 58–83.

Lu Qinli, *Xian Qin, Han, Wei, Jin, Nanbeichao shi*, Beijing: Zhonghua shuju, 1983.

Lu Renlong, 'Zhao Mengfu yu daojiao: jianlun song mo yuan chu daojiao fazhan de yixie tezhi', *Shijie zongjiao yanjiu*, 3 (1991), 24–34.

Lü Simian, *Qinhan shi*, Shanghai: Kaiming shudian, 1947.

Lu Yaodong, *Cong Pingcheng dao Luoyang*, Taipei: Lianjing chuban shiye gongsi, 1979.

Maeda Shigeki, '*Rōshi chūkyō* oboegaki', in Sakade Yoshinobu, *Chūgoku kodai yōsei shisō no sōgōteki kenkyū*, Tokyo: Hirakawa shuppansha, 1988, pp. 474–502.

—— '"Tonkōhon" to "Dōkyōhon" no sa-i nitsuite – ko "Reichōkei" o chūshin toshite', *Tōhō Shūkyō*, 84 (1994).

Maspero, Henri, 'Methods of "Nourishing the Vital Principle" in the Ancient Taoist Religion' (trans. Frank Kierman), in *Taoism and Chinese Religion*, Amherst, MA: University of Massachusetts Press, 1981.

Mather, Richard, 'K'ou Ch'ien-chih and the Taoist Theocracy at the Northern Wei Court, 425–45', in Holmes Welch and Anna Seidel (eds), *Facets of Taoism*, New Haven, CT: Yale University Press, 1979, pp. 103–22.

Mathieu, Rémi, *Étude sur la mythologie et l'ethnologie de la Chine ancienne: traduction annotée du 'Shanhai jin'*, Paris: Collège de France, Institut des hautes études chinoises, 1983.

Matsūra Takeshi, *Hokugi shi sakuin*, Fukuoka: Tōka shoten, 1986.

Mauss, Marcel, *The Gift: Forms and Functions of Exchange in Archaic Societies* (trans. I. Gunnison), London: Cohen & West, 1970.

Meng Wentong, 'Daojiaoshi suotan', *Zhongguo zhexue*, 4 (1980).

Mollier, Christine, *Une apocalypse taoïste du Ve siècle. Le Livre des incantations divines des grottres abyssales*, Paris: Collège de France, Institut des Hautes Études Chinoises, 1990.

—— 'La méthode de l'Empereur du Nord du mont Fengdu: une tradition exorciste du taoisme medieval', *T'oung Pao*, 8 (1997), 331–85.

Mugitani Kunio, '*Kōtei naikei kyō* shiron', *Tōyō bunka*, 62 (1981), 29–59.

—— '*Daidō shinkyō sanjūkyū shō* o megutte', in Yoshikawa Tadao (ed.), *Chūgoku ko dōkyōshi kenkyū*, Kyoto: Dōhōsha, 1992, pp. 55–87.

Munakata Kiyohiko, *Sacred Mountains in Chinese Art*, Urbana and Chicago, IL: Krannert Art Museum/University of Illinois Press, 1991.

Nakajima Ryūzō, 'Dōkyō ni okeru innensetsu uke-ireru no itsu sokumen', in *Araki Kyōju taikyō Chūgoku tetsugakushi kenkyū ronshū*, Fukuoka: Ashi shobō, 1981.

—— 'Chūgoku ni okeru bukkyō uke-ireru no zentei', in *Rikuchō shisō no kenkyū: shitaifu to bukkyō shisō*, Kyoto: Heirakuji shoten, 1985.

—— (ed.), *Shutsu sanzō ki shū jokan sakuin*, Kyoto: Hōyū shoten, 1991.

Needham, Joseph, *Science and Civilisation in China. Vol. 5, Chemistry and Chemical Technology. Part 2, Spagyrical Discovery and Invention: Magisteries of Gold and Immortality*, Cambridge: Cambridge University Press, 1974.

Ngo Van Xuyet, *Divination, magie et politique dans la Chine ancienne*, Paris: Presses Universitaires de France, 1976.

Nickerson, Peter, 'Shamans, Demons, Diviners and Taoists: Conflict and Assimilation in Medieval Chinese Ritual Practice (*c*.AD 100–1000)', *Taoist Resources*, 5 (1994), 41–66.

—— 'Abridged Codes of Master Lu for the Daoist Community', in Donald S. Lopez Jr (ed.), *Religions of China in Practice*, Princeton, NJ: Princeton University Press, 1996, pp. 347–59.

—— 'Taoism, Death, and Bureaucracy', PhD dissertation, Department of History, University of California, Berkeley, 1996.

—— 'Great Petition for Sepulchral Plaints', in Stephen R. Bokenkamp, with a contribution by Peter Nickerson, *Early Daoist Scriptures*, Berkeley, CA: University of California Press, 1997.

—— 'Opening the Way: Exorcism, Travel, and Soteriology in Early Daoist Mortuary Practice and Its Antecedents', in Livia Kohn and Harold D. Roth (eds), *Daoist Identity: History, Lineage, and Ritual*, Honolulu, HI: University of Hawaii Press, 2002.

Noguchi Tetsurō, Sakade Yoshinobu, Fukui Fumimasa and Yamada Toshiaki (eds), *Dōkyō jiten*, Tokyo: Hirakawa shuppansha, 1994.

Norman, K. R., 'Dhammapada 97: A Misunderstood Paradox', in K. R. Norman, *Collected Papers*, Oxford: The Pāli Text Society, 1991, vol. 2, pp. 187–93; originally in *Indologica Taurinensia*, 7 (1979), 325–31.

Ōfuchi Ninji, 'Taihei kyō no shisō ni tsuite', *Tōhō Gakuhō*, 28, 4 (1941).

—— 'On Ku Ling-pao Ching', *Acta Asiatica*, 27 (1974).

—— *Tonkō Dōkyō: Mokuroku hen*, Tokyo: Fukutake shoten, 1978.

—— *Shoki no Dōkyō*, Tokyo: Sōbunsha, 1991.

Ohnuma, Reiko, 'Dehadāna: The "Gift of the Body" in Indian Buddhist Narrative Literature', PhD dissertation, University of Michigan, 1997.

Pelliot, Paul, 'L'origine du nom de "Chine" ', *T'oung pao*, 13 (1912), 727–42.

Pregadio, Fabrizio, 'The Representation of Time in the *Zhouyi cantong qi*', *Cahiers d'Extrême-Asie*, 8 (1995), 155–73.

—— 'Elixirs and Alchemy', in Livia Kohn (ed.), *Daoism Handbook*, Leiden: E. J. Brill, 2000, pp. 165–95.

—— 'The Early History of the *Zhouyi cantong qi*', *Journal of Chinese Religions*, 30 (2002), 149–76.

—— *Great Clarity: Daoism and Alchemy in Medieval China*, Stanford, CA: Stanford University Press, 2005.

Puett, Michael, *To Become a God: Cosmology, Sacrifice, and Self-divinization in Early China*, Cambridge, MA: Harvard University Asia Center, 2002.

Pulleyblank, E. G., *Middle Chinese: A Study in Historical Phonology*, Vancouver: University of British Columbia Press, 1983.

Reiter, Florian, 'The Visible Divinity: The Sacred Icon in Religious Taoism', *Nachrichten der Gesellschaft für Natur- und Völkerkunde Ostasiens*, 144 (1988), 51–70.

Ren Jiyu (ed.), *Zhongguo fojiao shi*, Beijing: Zhongguo shehui kexue yuan chubanshe, 1985.

Rickett, W. Allen, *Guanzi: Political, Economic and Philosophical Essays from Early China*, Princeton, NJ: Princeton University Press, 1998.

Robinet, Isabelle, 'Randonnées extatiques des taoïstes dans les astres', *Monumenta Serica*, 32 (1976), 159–273.

—— 'Metamorphosis and Deliverance from the Corpse in Taoism', *History of Religions*, 19 (1979), 37–70.

—— *La révélation du Shangqing dans l'histoire du taoïsme*, Paris: École Française d'Extrême-Orient, 1984.

—— 'Original Contributions of Neidan to Taoism and Chinese Thought', in Livia Kohn (ed.), *Taoist Meditation and Longevity Techniques*, Ann Arbor, MI: University of Michigan, 1989, pp. 297–330.

—— *Taoist Meditation: The Mao-shan Tradition of Great Purity* (trans. Julian F. Pas and Norman Girardot), Albany, NY: State University of New York Press, 1993.

—— *Taoism: Growth of a Religion* (trans. Phyllis Brooks), Stanford, CA: Stanford University Press, 1997.

Roth, Harold D., *Original Tao*, New York: Columbia University Press, 1999.

Sailey, Jay, *The Master Who Embraces Simplicity*, San Francisco, CA: Chinese Materials Center, 1978.

Sakade Yoshinobu, 'Zui-Tō jidai ni okeru fukutan to naikan to naitan', in *Chūgoku kodai yōsei shisō no sōgōteki kenkyū*, Tokyo: Hirakawa shuppansha, 1988, pp. 566–99.

Saussy, Haun, 'The Prestige of Writing: Letter, Picture, Image, Ideography', *Sino-Platonic Papers*, 75 (1997), 4–5.

Schafer, Edward H., *Pacing the Void: T'ang Approaches to the Stars*, Berkeley, CA: University of California Press, 1977.

—— 'A T'ang Taoist Mirror', *Early China*, 4 (1978–9), 56–9.

Schipper, Kristofer, 'Démonologie chinoise', in *Génies, anges et démons*, Paris: Éditions du Seuil, 1971, pp. 405–29.

—— 'Gogaku shinkei zu no shinkō', in Yoshioka Yoshitoyo and Michel Soymié (eds), *Dōkyō kenkyū*, 2, Tokyo: Shorinsha, 1967.

—— 'Le Calendrier de Jade: Note sur le *Laozi zhongjing*', *Nachrichten der Deutsche Gesellschaft für Natür- und Völkerkunde Ostasiens*, 125 (1979), 75–80.

—— 'Taoist Ritual and Local Cults of the T'ang Dynasty', in *Tantric and Taoist Studies in Honour of R. A. Stein* (ed. Michel Strickmann), Brussels: Institut Belge des Hautes Etudes Chinoises, 1985, vol. 3, pp. 812–34.

—— 'Vernacular and Classical Ritual in Taoism', *Journal of Asian Studies*, 45, 1 (1985), 21–57.

—— *The Taoist Body* (trans. Karen C. Duval), Berkeley, CA: University of California Press, 1993.

—— 'Purity and Strangers: Shifting Boundaries in Medieval China', *T'oung Pao*, 80 (1994), 61–81.

—— 'The Inner World of the *Laozi zhongjing*', in Huang Chun-chieh and Erik Zürcher (eds), *Time and Space in Chinese Culture*, Leiden: E. J. Brill, 1995, pp. 114–31.

—— and Verellen, Franciscus (eds), *The Taoist Canon: A Historical Companion to the Daozang*, Chicago, IL: University of Chicago Press, 2004.

—— 'The True Form – Reflections on the Liturgical Basis of Taoist Art', *Sanjiao Wenxian*, 4 (2005).

Schopen, Gregory, 'Filial Piety and the Monk in the Practice of Indian Buddhism – A Question of 'Sinicization' viewed from the Other Side', in *Bones, Stones, and Buddhist Monks: Collected Papers on the Archaeology, Epigraphy, and Texts of Monastic Buddhism in India*, Honolulu, HI: University of Hawaii Press, 1997, pp. 56–71; originally published in *T'oung Pao*, 70 (1984), 110–26.

Seidel, Anna, *La divinisation de Lao tseu dans le Taoïsme des Han*, Paris: École Française d'Extrême-Orient, 1969.

—— 'Imperial Treasures and Taoist Sacraments: Taoist Roots in the Apocrypha', in Michel Strickmann (ed.), *Tantric and Taoist Studies in Honour of Rolf A. Stein*, Brussels: Institut Belge des Hautes Études Chinoises, 1981–5.

—— 'Le sūtra merveilleux du Ling-pao Suprême, traitant de Lao Tseu qui convertit les barbares (Le manuscrit S. 2081)', in M. Soymié (ed.), *Contribution aux Études de Touen-houang*, Paris: École française d'Êxtrême-Orient, 1984, vol. 3, pp. 305–52.

—— 'Geleitbrief an die Unterwelt: Jenseitsvorstellungen in den Graburkunden der Späteren Han Zeit', in Gert Naundorf, Karl-Heinz Pohl and Hans-Hermann Schmidt (eds), *Religion und Philosophie in Ostasien: Festschrift für Hans Steininger zum 65. Geburtstag*, Würzburg: Königshausen und Neumann, 1985, pp. 161–84.

—— 'Post-mortem Immortality, or: The Taoist Resurrection of the Body', in S. Shaked, D. Shulman and G. G. Stroumsa (eds), *Gilgul: Essays on Transformation, Revolution and Permanence in the History of Religions dedicated to R. J. Zwi Werblowsky*, Leiden: E. J. Brill, 1987, pp. 223–37.

—— 'Traces of Han Religion in Funeral Texts Found in Tombs', in Akizuki Kan'ei (ed.), *Dōkyō to shūkyō bunka*, Tokyo: Hirakawa shuppansha, 1987, pp. 21–57.

—— 'Chronicle of Taoist Studies in the West, 1950–1990', *Cahiers d'Extrême-Asie*, 5 (1989–90), 223–347.

Shen Zengzhi, *Hairilou zhacong*, Beijing: Zhonghuan shuju, 1962.

Shi Dongchu, *Zhongguo fojiao jindaishi*, Taibei: Zhongguo Fojiao wenhua guan, 1974.

Stein, R. A., 'Remarques sur les mouvements du taoïsme politico-religieux au IIe siècle ap. J.C.', *T'oung Pao*, 50 (1963), 1–78.

—— 'Religious Taoism and Popular Religion from the Second to the Seventh Centuries', in Holmes Welch and Anna Seidel (eds), *Facets of Taoism*, New Haven, CT: Yale University Press, 1979, pp. 53–81.

Strickmann, Michel, 'The Mao Shan Revelations: Taoism and the Aristocracy', *T'oung Pao*, 63 (1977), 1–64.

—— 'On the Alchemy of T'ao Hung-ching', in Holmes Welch and Anna K. Seidel (eds), *Facets of Taoism: Essays in Chinese Religion*, New Haven, CT: Yale University Press, 1979, pp. 123–92.

—— 'The Seal of the Law: A Ritual Implement and the Origins of Printing', *Asia Major* (third series), 6, 2 (1993), 1–84.

—— *Chinese Magical Medicine* (ed. Bernard Faure), Stanford, CA: Stanford University Press, 2002.

Stuart, G. A., *Chinese Materia Medica: Vegetable Kingdom*, Taipei: Southern Materials Center, 1976; reprint of the 1911 edn printed at the American Presbyterian Mission Press, Shanghai.

Suzuki Hiromi, 'Koyaku, kyūyaku seiten no warichū ni tsuite', *Indogaku Bukkyōgaku kenkyū*, 78 (March 1991), 90–2; 79 (Dec. 1991), 43–5; 82 (March 1993), 17–19; 84 (Dec. 1993), 39–41. Title changed in the last article to 'Kanyaku seiten . . .'.

Tan Shibao, *Han-Tang foshi tanzhen*, Guangzhou: Zhongshan daxue chubanshe, 1991.

Tang Changru, 'Weijin qijian beifang tianshi dao de chuanbo', in *Weijin nanbeichao shilun shiyi*, Beijing: Zhonghua Shuju, 1983.

Tang Yongtong, 'Du taiping jingshu suojian', *Guoxue jikan*, 5, 1 (1935).

Teiser, Stephen, '"Having Once Died and Returned to Life": Representations of Hell in Medieval China', *Harvard Journal of Asiatic Studies*, 48 (1988), 433–64.

Teng Ssu-yü, *Family Instructions for the Yen Clan by Yen Chih-t'ui*, Leiden: E. J. Brill, 1968.

Thompson, Laurence G., 'On the Prehistory of Hell in China', *Journal of Chinese Religions*, 17 (1989), 27–41.

Thompson, P. M., *The Shen Tzu Fragments*, Oxford: Oxford University Press, 1979.

Tjan Tjoe Som, *Po Hu T'ung: The Comprehensive Discussions in the White Tiger Hall*, Leiden: E. J. Brill, 1952.

Tsukamoto Zenryū, *A History of Early Chinese Buddhism, from Its Introduction to the Death of Hui-yüan* (trans. Leon Hurvitz), Tokyo: Kodansha, 1985.

Twitchett, Denis and Loewe, Michael (eds), *Cambridge History of China, Vol. 1*, Cambridge: Cambridge University Press, 1986.

Unschuld, Paul U., *Medicine in China: A History of Ideas*, Berkeley, CA: University of California Press, 1985.

—— *Medicine in China: A History of Pharmaceutics*, Berkeley, CA: University of California Press, 1986.

Utsunomiya Kiyoyoshi, 'Ganshi kakun kishinhen oboegaki', in *Chūgoku kodai chūseishi kenkyū*, Tokyo: Sobunsha, 1977.

Verellen, Franciscus, '"Evidential Miracles in Support of Taoism": The Inversion of a Buddhist Apologetic Tradition in Late T'ang China', *T'oung Pao*, 78 (1992), 256–7.

—— 'The Beyond Within: Grotto-heavens (*dongtian*) in Taoist Ritual and Cosmology', *Cahiers d'Extrême-Asie*, 8 (1995), 265–90.

von Falkenhausen, Lothar, 'Sources of Taoism: Reflections on Archaeological Indicators of Religious Change in Eastern Zhou China', *Taoist Resources*, 5, 2 (1994), 1–12.

Wang Gungwu, de Crespigny, Rafe and de Rachewiltz, Igor (eds), *Sino-Asiatica*, Canberra: Faculty of Asian Studies, Australian National University, 2002.

Wang Ming, '*Huangting jing* kao', in *Daojia he daojiao sixiang yanjiu*, Beijing: Zhongguo shehui kexue chubanshe, 1984, pp. 324–71.

Wang Shumin, 'Huanglao kao', in his *Zhuangxue guankui*, Taipei: Yiwen yinshuguan, 1978.

Wang Weicheng, '*Sishizhangjing*: Daoan jinglu quezai yuanyin', in Zhang Mantao (ed.), *Xiandai fojiao xueshu congkan*, Taipei: Dasheng wenhua chubanshe, 1978, vol. 11, pp. 35–41.

Wang Yucheng, 'Donghan Dao fu shili', *Kaogu xuebao*, 1 (1991), 45–56.

—— 'Luoyang yangguang nian zhushu taoguan kaoshi', *Zhongyuan wenwu*, 1 (1993).

—— 'Xu Fu di juan zhong Tianshi dao shiliao kaoji', *Kaogu*, 6 (1993), 571–5.

—— 'Nanliwang taoshu yu xiangguan zongjiao wenti yanjiu', *Kaogu yu wenwu*, 2 (1996), 61–9.

—— 'Wenwu suojian Zhongguo gudai daofu shulun', *Daojia wenhua yanjiu*, 9 (1996), 267–301.

—— 'Donghan daojiao diyi shike Fei Zhi bei yanjiu', *Daojiao xue tansuo* 10, Tainan chenggong daxue lishixi daojiao yanjiu shi, 1997, pp. 14–28.

Wang Zhongmin, *Dunhuang guji xulu*, Beijing: Zhonghua, 1979.

Ware, James, *Alchemy, Medicine and Religion in the China of AD 320: The Nei P'ien of Ko Hung (Pao-p'u tzu)*, Cambridge, MA: MIT Press, 1966.

Watson, Burton (trans.), *Hsün-tzu: Basic Writings*, New York: Columbia University Press, 1963.

Willemen, Charles, 'The Prefaces to the Chinese Dharmapadas *Fa-chü ching* and *Ch'u-yao ching*', *T'oung Pao*, 59 (1973), 203–19.

Wu Hung, 'From Temple to Tomb: Ancient Chinese Art and Religion in Transition', *Early China*, 13 (1988), 78–115.

Wu Rongzeng, 'Zhenmuwen zhong suo jiandao de Donghan daowu guanxi', *Wenwu*, 3 (1981), 56–63.

Yamazaki Hiroshi, 'Rikuchō Zuitō jidai ōhō shinkō', *Shirin*, 40, 6 (1957).

Yan Yiping, *Daojiao yanjiu ziliao*, Taipei: Yiwen yingshu guan, 1974.

Yasui Kōzan and Nakamura Shōhachi (eds), *Isho shūsei*, Tokyo: Meitoku shuppansha, 1981.

Yoshikawa Tadao, 'Gan Shisui ron', in *Rikuchō seishishi kenkyū*, Kyoto: Dohosha, 1984.

—— 'Rikuchō Zuitō ni okeru shūkyō no fūkei', *Chūgoku shigaku*, 2 (1992).

—— 'Chūgoku rikuchō jidai ni okeru shūkyō no mondai', *Shisō*, 4 (1994).

Yoshioka Yoshitoyo, *Dōkyō to Bukkyō*, Tokyo: Kokusho kankōkai, 1976.

Yu Jiaxi, *Siku tiyao bianzheng*, Taipei: Yiwen yinshuguan, photolithographic edn.

Zhan Shizhuang, *Daojiao wenxue shi*, Shanghai: Shanghai wenyi, 1992.

Zhu Jiang, 'Jiangsu Gaoyu Shaojiaguo Handai yizhi de qingli', *Kaogu*, 10 (1960).

Zürcher, Erik, *The Buddhist Conquest of China*, Leiden: E. J. Brill, 1959.

—— 'Buddhist Influence on Early Taoism: A Survey of Scriptural Evidence', *T'oung Pao*, 66 (1980), 84–147.

INDEX

Lightning Source UK Ltd.
Milton Keynes UK
UKOW030606040512

192001UK00002B/49/P